of migrants? Can Europe's predominantly secular societies absorb and integrate millions of Muslim migrants while maintaining the best attributes of their own societies, including those that have become liberal cultural norms?

Professor Farer is unblinking in describing the difficulties. He does not evade any hard questions. Asserting that 'My highest priority is the survival of liberal democracy, an outcome by no means assured,' his thoughtful answers are based on that priority.

Tom Farer's important book is essential reading for those who share that priority."

Aryeh Neier, President Emeritus of the Open Society (Soros) Foundations, and Founding Director of Human Rights Watch

"Tom Farer has produced . . . the best possible statement of the liberal nationalist approach to migration and integration. It is, as it claims, 'liberalism without tears, conservatism without hate.' Farer argues that liberal democrats can meet the challenge of 21st-century mass migration, but only if they can rediscover the courage of their convictions while shedding policy dogmatism. The stakes could not be higher."

Tom Pegram, Associate Professor of Global Governance, University College London

"A timelier and better case for a liberal nationalism than Tom Farer's account cannot be imagined."

Monica Serrano, Professor of International Relations, El Colegio de Mexico

MIGRATION AND INTEGRATION

Migration and Integration clarifies and proposes answers for all of the politically toxic questions associated with large-scale migration from the Global South to the Western liberal democracies. Driven by the conviction that the alt-right is using the issues of migration and integration effectively to batter the defenses of liberal democracy, Professor Tom Farer argues that despite its strength, the moral case for open borders should be rejected and that while broadly tolerant of different lifestyles, the state should enforce core liberal values. Examining closely the policies and practices of various European states, Farer draws on their experience, contrasts it with that of the United States, and provides a detailed strategy for addressing the issues of who should be allowed to enter, how migrant families should be integrated, and how cultural conflicts should be resolved. This remarkable elaboration of a liberal position on migration and integration to which moderate conservatives could adhere combines powerful analysis with passionate advocacy.

TOM FARER is University Professor at the University of Denver where he served for fourteen years as Dean of the Josef Korbel School of International Studies. Among his many titles, he was the first US citizen elected president of the Inter-American Commission on Human Rights and he has consulted for Amnesty International and Human Rights Watch. He is also the author of *Confronting Global Terrorism and American Neo-Conservatism* (2008).

Migration and Integration

THE CASE FOR LIBERALISM WITH BORDERS

TOM FARER
University of Denver

CAMBRIDGE
UNIVERSITY PRESS

CAMBRIDGE
UNIVERSITY PRESS

University Printing House, Cambridge CB2 8BS, United Kingdom

One Liberty Plaza, 20th Floor, New York, NY 10006, USA

477 Williamstown Road, Port Melbourne, VIC 3207, Australia

314–321, 3rd Floor, Plot 3, Splendor Forum, Jasola District Centre, New Delhi – 110025, India

79 Anson Road, #06–04/06, Singapore 079906

Cambridge University Press is part of the University of Cambridge.

It furthers the University's mission by disseminating knowledge in the pursuit of
education, learning, and research at the highest international levels of excellence.

www.cambridge.org
Information on this title: www.cambridge.org/9781108485715
DOI: 10.1017/9781108757997

First published 2020

Printed and bound in Great Britain by Clays Ltd, Elcograf S.p.A.

A catalogue record for this publication is available from the British Library.

ISBN 978-1-108-48571-5 Hardback
ISBN 978-1-108-70750-3 Paperback

For our beloved grandchildren Linus and Luc

and

*In memory of my dear friend Sir Nigel Rodley,
happy warrior in the defense of human rights*

The philosophy of global egalitarianism remains a file in the archives of utopianism.
– Samuel Moyn, *Not Enough: Human Rights in an Unequal World*

Contents

Contents

Figures

Figures

Acknowledgments

It didn't take a village to help me with all the details of finalizing the manuscript, rechecking the footnotes, completing the marketing questionnaire, and organizing the metadata a contemporary publisher rightly desires, but it sure helped to have the assistance of a group of graduate students as talented and assiduous as they are gracious. One, Vahaken Mouradian, who will someday be the EU's Foreign Minister if merit prevails, worked with me for more than a year until he graduated and went off to spend time at a think tank in DC. Then came the team of four, stars of my fall classes in human rights and US foreign policy, Mike Knutzen, Zorana Knezevic, Franklin Hughes, and Joshua Coakley. Mike, who before coming to the Josef Korbel School Master's Program, had soldiered in a very bleak part of Afghanistan, served as team captain. Like Vahaken, they all began as assistants and evolved into friends. The same is true of Peter Kerins, a previous assistant, who helped me in early stages of this enterprise.

My friend Chris Brown, a professor on the faculty of the university library, has been helping me since I arrived at the school a barely believably long twenty-three years ago. A man of encyclopedic knowledge and luminous skill in navigating the cyber world, he enabled me to remain a functioning scholar even when my main task was serving as a dean who, unlike a university president who lives in a mansion and begs, lived in a modest home, also begged donors, and, in addition, begged my faculty to appreciate the skill all long-tenured deans share: Blaming the heavens or the Provost for having to say "no."

I am indebted to Professors Alison Brysk and Tom Pegram for inviting me, respectively, to UC Santa Barbara and University College London where, in the process of explaining one or another of the hypotheses which drive this book, I was the beneficiary of very thoughtful (and not always uncritical) comments leading me to think again and at least explain my positions more clearly. Speaking of constructive criticism, I must thank the anonymous peer reviewers for reading my first draft so closely. Their suggestions were exceedingly valuable, even or perhaps particularly the ones that had a bit of an edge.

I also want to thank my colleague and old friend Ved Nanda, for giving me the opportunity to present certain of my ideas at the University of Denver Law School's annual Sutton and McDougall Colloquium and express appreciation to another old friend, Bert Lockwood of the University of Cincinnati law school, for airing certain of my preliminary views in the distinguished journal he founded and continues to edit, *Human Rights Quarterly*.

From the time of the first draft to the point at which I submitted the final one, I enjoyed the support and advice of John Berger, then a senior editor at Cambridge University Press. I am very much in his debt and hope to work with him again. I want in addition to thank Danielle Menz, John's editorial assistant, who also helped me to reach the production phase. In that phase I enjoyed the assistance of Saritha Srinivasan, Birgitte Necessary, and Stephanie Sakson. Now I look forward to working with Paris West and Laura Blake as the book goes to market. I am also indebted to the free-lance editor Jeff Alexander, a congenial guide to refining very substantially my original, barely remembered draft.

Being surrounded by congenial and productive colleagues is a boon to any scholar. I owe a particular thanks to Martin Rhodes, a distinguished authority on European politics who took the time to review the draft chapters on the Nordic States, the United Kingdom, and France and to reassure me that I had captured without gross distortion the part of their reality most relevant to my subject. Other scholars to whom I am indebted for their comments are Jose Alvarez, Simon Chesterman, Claudio Grossman, Michael Ignatieff, Aryeh Neier, Tom Pegram, and Monica Serrano.

Although I have said this in the Acknowledgment section of previous books, I cannot finish this one without naming my best friend, the love of my life, my wife Mika, who expresses concretely in her everyday existence the values about which I principally theorize.

Introduction

Challenges to Liberalism with Borders

Hope is the desperate brother of despair. The following is a news report from a front line of our global migration crisis:

> [O]n the tenth day of [Djipy Diop's] journey to the Canary Islands, everyone's prayers mingled together, voices rising jagged and hoarse, calling on the Great, the Merciful, to save them. Water poured over the sides as the wind knocked them from wave crest to trough and back up again.... They ran out of food. Then they ran out of water. Some dipped their cups into the sea. Others jumped overboard, hallucinating land.... Others babbled, terrified, unseeing.... Diop saw men suffocate to death under others. "If you screamed no one would help you.... It was every man for himself, God for all." When Diop finally reached Tenerife, he spent a month in a [Spanish] detention center before being sent back to Senegal.[1]

He and tens of thousands like him had once made an adequate living fishing in small wooden boats off the Senegalese coast. Year by year his struggles grew. The mangrove forests along the coast where certain species had gone immemorially to spawn had shrunk. The warming of the seas pushed some fish stock farther out in search of colder water. Accessible stocks also dwindled as industrial-scale fishing boats from other nations invaded Senegal's coastal waters.

When he got back to Senegal, Diop told the journalist Laura Dean, he felt "a little crazy," and suffered nightmares. "The dead would come back to me at night. My parents would wake up at three and four in the morning because I was hitting the walls and doors in the dark.... I no longer dream of the dead." In spite of the trauma of his attempt, Dean reports, Diop still thinks about leaving.[2]

There is no reason to believe that 2015, a year in which Germany alone admitted over one million strangers, will prove to have been the high-water mark of migration from the Global South into the wealthy and comparatively well-ordered countries of the North. Potentially tens of millions more, many not yet born, will attempt to follow, pushed by the economic, social, and political pathologies of the lands of their birth and pulled by visions of affluence and security. They will go North toward hope.

The prospective arrival of tens of millions of Diops fills many, though by no means all, of the West's legacy inhabitants with, well, if "fear" is too strong a word, then let us say "anxiety" inspired by economic, cultural, and security concerns. For that part of the indigenous population viscerally aroused under the best of circumstances by the appearance of racially or ethnically disparate people, fear can mix with rage. The ranks of the enraged should shrink if the concerns which generate anxiety prove largely baseless. But what constitutes "proof" is often a contentious issue. The fact that Confederate flags are flown in parts of the United States one hundred and fifty years after the Civil War confirms, if confirmation were needed, that great hosts of people cling fiercely to their premises and prejudices.

Do those who read Diop's tale and tens of thousands like it without some empathic anguish have hearts of stone? Not necessarily. They may, like a couple I know, shake with pity for a beaten, starved dog they meet at the local shelter. They may even take it home, nurse it back to health, make it part of their family, while disparaging most forms of social support as giveaways to the unworthy. Or they may sympathize with humans too, unthreatening individual humans toward whom they feel a bond, an obligation, a sensation of identity – there but for the grace of God go I or my son: the veteran crippled by the Afghan war; the scarred fireman who came too close to the flames; the newly unemployed neighbor made obsolete by the workings of the marketplace; yes, and even the living remains of a once-large Syrian family introduced to the neighborhood by a sympathetic minister of a nearby church.

Compassion is not rare, just limited, the limits varying in part with the scope of our respective moral imaginations and in part with our sense of threat to our identity, our security, our status, our quotidian comforts. It is not unusual for people to take impoverished dogs home, but how many invite the cripple with the sign saying "VERY HUNGRY" to dine at their table or offer beds for the night to the exhausted mother and child who have fled the abattoir of Honduras, survived the long road through Mexico, and endured the nocturnal desert crossing to arrive in the United States?

Critical thinking, I tell my students, begins at home. None of us starts with a blank slate. In writing about migration I have tried to bring to the surface of my mind all those half-buried assumptions, preferences, and convictions about cause and effect which are the baggage of our intellectual journeys. In an effort to take each reader with me on this trip, I have tried to reveal mine, so that if, in the end, we arrive at different places, at least we will be clear about why we parted.

A MATTER OF PERSPECTIVE

You have a right to know at the outset, in the idiom of this identity-obsessed moment, where I am coming from. Which is the political camp I normally call home even if not all of the other residents, a fairly diverse lot, always recognize me as one of them? I approach the mass migration phenomenon from the standpoint of a twenty-first-century liberal who believes (1) that every human being should enjoy the rights enumerated in the Universal Declaration,[3] (2) that public policy should seek to equalize opportunity, and (3) that really gross inequalities of wealth, even where not the result of predation, corruption, or market failure, are a threat to the long-term survival of liberal democracy.

A premise of the liberal imagination is that the ultimate meaning of life is not susceptible to common apprehension. Liberalism does not dictate a grand design to which all rational persons must conform their lives. Instead, all we have are competing convictions about the nature of the design, some more widely and zealously shared than others, or the conviction that there is no primordial design, only designs constituted by the various narratives respectively shared by one or another cluster of believers. If there is no design for life on which all people can in theory agree, whether guided by right reason or by revelation, then, given the human need for political community, we face two alternatives. One is perpetual struggle among groups of believers, each seeking to impose its preferred design on society. The other, the liberal alternative, is agreement within some limits to organize the political community on the basis of mutual acceptance of divergent beliefs about what conduct should be applauded and what conduct condemned.

Liberalism, however, is more than a mere pragmatic formula for coexistence. If that were all it is, how could it match the emotional power of the Abrahamic and pagan faiths, with their operatic narratives? How could it compete with the ecstatic totalitarian political creeds, with their heroic races and classes, which engulfed the twentieth century in so much gore? Liberalism has its own dramatic story, a tale of Promethean individuals smashing through inherited constraints in pursuit of personal freedom *and a more just world.*

Understood this way, liberalism is a life-shaping view with a distinct history and established practices, rituals and symbols. It can thus be thought of as a culture and a faith, albeit one without deities. Hence there is an irreducible tension within liberalism. On the one hand, as I have proposed, it is a formula, the only possible formula (other than empire) for peaceful coexistence of diverse belief systems within a single political community. On the other, it is itself a belief system, at least a conviction about what constitutes a fulfilling life – continuous critical inquiry into the nature of things and the coincident shaping and revising of a life plan – and about the character of a good society. So in practice there is a tension between the commitment to tolerance of diverse beliefs – often the property of distinct ethnic or religious groups – and the conviction that neither public nor private power should be exercised to prevent the individual from being an entrepreneur of the self, *albeit one who respects the equal right of others to fashion a dignified life*[*] *and accepts the civic duties and communal obligations which permit a relatively free society to endure.*

My conception of liberalism draws from two of its primal sources: John Locke's emphasis on the rights of individuals in the face of state power and the French Revolution's call for not only "liberty" but also "equality and fraternity."[4] As recent progressive critics of both liberalism and the discourse of human rights have implicitly argued in calling for greater emphasis on equality and mutual support,[5] the former source can lead down the Ayn Randian road to the oligarchy of billionaires soaring in their minds above the great mass of the less successful and regarding all redistributive measures as theft.[†] The liberalism coloring my world view draws substantially on the one limned by the great twentieth-century political theorist John Rawls. Rawls hypothesized that individuals, if unaware of the positions they would occupy in society, would rationally choose to live in one where every person enjoys a broad, well-protected freedom of choice in shaping her or his life and where inequalities could be justified only if they improved the condition of the worst off (the so-called difference principle). My vision of liberalism draws as well on the Nobel Laureate Amartya Sen's restatement of human rights as in essence a right of each individual to develop his or her capabilities.[6] Governments have a duty to try and create the conditions essential for such development to occur.

One's political identity may influence analysis; it undoubtedly influences conclusions and recommendations. It does not, however, preclude productive conversation with observers viewing the issues from a different ideological perspective. For instance, while a traditional nationalist by definition feels no duty to citizens of other countries, she might nevertheless favor large-scale migration if convinced, for example, that it would stimulate the economy, facilitate social support for aging legacy citizens, and enhance national security. Or consider another example: conservative but rational nationalists might reflexively support the settled majority's right to impose its inherited culture on minorities, and yet still decide, after empirical inquiry and mature reflection, that the most efficient way to defend conservative values is to tolerate certain minority cultural practices at odds with their own.

In short, conservatives and liberals, though proceeding by different paths, might conceivably reach the same policy conclusions – from time to time. But the liberal's path will be trickier to negotiate because she does not enjoy the conservatives' single-mindedness. Unlike them she does feel some measure of cosmopolitan sympathy.

---

[*] "[E]verybody . . . should have a variety of decisions to make in shaping a life. And for a person of a liberal disposition these choices belong, in the end, to the person whose life it is." Kwami Anthony Appiah, *The Ethics of Identity* (Princeton: Princeton University Press, 2005), xii.

[†] As I note in Chapter 6 on France, the call for "liberty and equality" also can be twisted to illiberal ends.

But Western liberals may conclude (or automatically assume) that the national state into which they are born is, as a practical matter, the main instrument for defending and enhancing liberal values. In fact, many do. So, contrary to the common conservative critique, the term "liberal nationalism" is not an oxymoron.[7]

Moreover, as I noted above, while liberalism is a recipe for tolerance, it is also a faith and like most faiths ardent in defense of its ethical turf against bearers of antagonistic value systems. "Isms" often politically allied with liberalism and seen at least by conservatives as subsets or outgrowths of liberal culture – I am thinking principally of feminism – are likely to feel equal or even greater antipathy to the non-liberal cultural practices which dominate many societies in the Global South and are still very much alive within the native population of rich democracies. Liberal schizophrenia may thus produce more points of policy convergence with conservative nationalism on migration-related policy recommendations than one might initially assume. That remains to be shown.‡

One observation and one hypothesis drive this book's policy analysis and recommendations. The observation is that the liberal center in Western European politics is eroding at a dangerous pace. For me, that center extends from German Chancellor Angela Merkel to the Scandinavian Social Democrats. It includes all those who respect the cosmopolitan discourse of human rights, who experience some measure of sympathy for, some sense of obligation to, desperate people beyond their national borders. It includes the political parties and leaders who built the EU and the welfare state and take seriously the duties of government arising from ratification of the principal UN human rights covenants and the European Convention on Human Rights. For all the considerable differences among the parties and elites embraced by this conception of the center, they are united in opposing the illiberal democracy trumpeted by Prime Minister Viktor Orban of Hungary and caricatured by President Vladimir Putin of Russia.

My associated hypothesis is that the single largest source of electoral erosion is the center's failure to deal effectively and openly with the issues associated with the post–World War II settlement in Western Europe of people from the Global South. The center's response to migration and settlement has come to represent for growing segments of the electorate a failure of candor, consultation, competence, and will on the part of socially liberal elites. The resulting anger and distrust are not entirely misdirected.

‡ Within the United States, liberalism's internal tension insinuates itself into problems of both domestic and foreign policy. In the realm of foreign policy liberalism as a faith complicates Sino-American cooperation even in areas where interests clearly coincide. And it has been known to lubricate or, it might be more accurate to say, it has "put lipstick on the pig" of costly crusades against illiberal governments such as Saddam Hussein's in Iraq. In the domestic realm, liberalism as a faith contributes to the polarization of politics by resisting (with varying success) the political claims of communities of faith generally labeled "fundamentalist," communities which then form what would otherwise be anomalous cross-class alliances with a tiny elite of economic royalists.

As a group the long-dominant centrist parties have not entered into a frank dialogue with their respective electorates to the end of developing a broad consensus about numbers of annual entrants, conditions of entry and permanent settlement, and distribution of costs and gains from migration. Political leaders have also failed to bring into balance the number of new entrants with the state's capacity to feed, house, and prepare them for economic integration. Where leaders have promised limits on new entrants, they have generally failed to enforce them without even a public confession and explanation of their failure. In defending the center, the liberal intelligentsia has tended to indict indiscriminately as racist or xenophobic all criticism of migration outcomes, thereby undermining its credibility as definer of respectable opinion. In fairness I should also note the liberal political establishment's insufficient communication with migrant communities. It has often displayed a deaf ear or sheer indifference to their immediate concerns with, for example, hate speech, unemployment, discrimination, and police harassment.

Political leaders and the officials who execute their directives, having assumed the role of stewards of the public good, are obliged to see beyond the individual case. They may be required to act on behalf of the present majority or of something more abstract: the survival of the state or of a certain form of government. Having accepted that obligation they may try not to know very much about individual cases because it is those cases that can rend the heart, torture the conscience.

Authors, by contrast, have choices. They can write about the long horrible chain of causation that uproots one intimately described family from its ancestral home and drives it to an excruciating death under the waters of the Mediterranean Sea. Or they can assume the role of grand strategist, setting out political and social goals and proposing in light of the available metrics what they take to be the most efficient or least inhumane means for achieving them. Or they can oscillate uneasily between those options, writing sometimes as if human beings were interchangeable units best handled in one way or another for the enhancement of the national interest or the species' betterment. They can defend an idea of the good society and, at other times, however occasional, take note of people with names, people with the same fragile body and hopes and dreams as the author's, people struggling to navigate through a very badly organized world with limited reserves of compassion.

Suppose a migration policy adviser had no psychological defenses against intimate pictures of the individuals behind the units living within his mind. Suppose at the moment he awakened every day that he visualized Lingo, a thirty-five-year-old geography teacher from Eritrea climbing aboard a rescue ship leased by Doctors Without Borders and saying to the first man who greets him, "'I must thank you.' . . . When we saw you, we automatically changed from animals into humans.'"[8] Then, midday, he met in his mind the three children rescued from another ship whose mother had died during their odyssey, who asked the nurse who tended to them after their rescue whether she could be their mother.[9] And at night as he tried to digest dinner, he saw a man named Sunday from Nigeria, trapped for months in a desolate refugee camp in the heel of Italy, after struggling for a year in Libya under terrible conditions, who walks kilometers every day in search of work, usually in vain, and says to a journalist: "I've come to zero in this place."[10] That adviser might have to find another profession.

My parents, the children of Jewish immigrants, had no ideology. Theirs was unconsciously the novelist's view of life. They saw fellow humans, not units. They felt the injustice of the world one person at a time. You may recall the old saw: "Where you stand is where you sit." When I was a member of the Inter-American Commission on Human Rights, I felt what my parents felt, saw what they saw. But before that time, when I worked in the Pentagon and wrote a memorandum for the Secretary of Defense, I saw the "big picture."

Most of my life, like any person who writes about policy, I have oscillated between these viewpoints. If you are not necessarily a liberal, if you are just any comfortable middle-class person who does not have a heart of stone, you end up saying, "Yes, something must be done, people are not interchangeable units." But to preserve liberal democracy in one of the few parts of today's world where it still flourishes, it may be necessary to see the larger picture. It may be necessary for governments not to suspend but to restrain the humanitarian impulse; to open the door, but not too widely; to be generous, yet not too generous; to appeal to the electorate's better angels, while acknowledging its attachment to the idea of a community less broad than the world, a bounded space.

Given my fear for the future of liberal democracy, I have written this book with one question foremost in my mind: What grand strategy for managing migration and integrating migrant families into the economic and social order is most likely to enable the defenders of liberal democracy to defeat the authoritarian right with the least possible compromise of human rights norms? The chapters that follow record the dialectic of my thought and the evolution of my answer.

I began by visualizing the principal migration-related questions Western governments need to address. The first is: Does a sovereign state, absent limitations assumed by ratifying relevant treaties, have an absolute ethical and legal discretion to determine who other than a national has a right to enter and, where permission to enter has been granted, to determine how long a person can remain and on what terms? If the state's discretion is not absolute, by what legal or moral norms is it qualified? Assuming we are convinced that a broad discretion should be imputed to states, we should then consider the legal and ethical norms that arguably constrain their choice of means for excluding persons seeking to enter or for removing undocumented persons.

Among persons seeking to enter or remain without valid documentation, refugees have long been thought to enjoy privileged status. The number of persons satisfying the definition of a refugee has multiplied dramatically in recent years. Meanwhile the moral distinction between persons fleeing from persecution for their race, ethnicity, religion, or political opinions and persons fleeing simply for their lives in the face of civil war, criminal gangs, and religious fanatics or in the wake of natural disasters has become increasingly hard to maintain. Does it not then follow that governments determined to limit annual migration to the number they can integrate without miniaturizing their electoral support or unsustainably straining public resources will need to modify their obligations under the 1951 Refugee Convention and its 1967 Protocol?

Questions about the morality of limiting and conditioning entry are linked to questions about the means states may employ to integrate those who are admitted and their descendants into a country's economy and social order, starting with the question of how integration should be defined. In particular, should one end of integration be adoption of the native majority's social norms and practices even where they conflict with those which migrants bring with them from their country of birth? If that is a proper end of integration, does it follow that the state has the right to make as a condition of entry and settlement a migrant's readiness to accept or at least tolerate cheerfully even those of the native majority's norms and practices which conflict with his or hers inherited ones?

Finally, there are questions stemming from the increasingly common perception – promoted by Donald Trump, Viktor Orban, and other entrepreneurs of xenophobic populism – that there is a connection between migration from poor countries, particularly those with Muslim majorities, and the threat of mass-casualty terrorism. And assuming there might be a connection, however tenuous, what measures, particularly internal measures, could Western states adopt to minimize the risk, and do potentially effective measures conflict with the values and traditions of a liberal state?

For the most part I will use the term "migrants" in reference to all persons from the Global South seeking to enter rich liberal capitalist states or, having already entered, who remain without a valid visa. I will use this term regardless of their motives and hence their status under international law. If they seek to settle because of a well-founded fear of persecution in their home countries, they qualify for the special rights international law accords to persons seeking asylum.[5] Because of those special rights, most of the persons in recent migration flows claim to be fleeing

[5] An "asylum seeker" is a person who has arrived at the border of a state or gained entry by whatever means and has applied for asylum under the 1951 Refugee Convention. The application rests on the ground that he or she has a well-founded fear of persecution on account of race, religion, nationality, political belief, or membership in a social group if they return to their country of origin. Technically a refugee is a person whose application for asylum has been successful, but in lay discourse the term is often applied to anyone who appears to have fled their country of origin either because of the stipulated fear of persecution or to avoid being caught in the crossfire of an armed conflict. The term is often applied as well to persons uprooted by a natural disaster which has put their lives at risk. Some national courts have stretched the concept still wider to embrace individuals fleeing fearsomely abusive spouses or families. Once a person has come within the jurisdiction of a state, the principle of "non-refoulement" precludes a state from expelling the person to a country, whether or not the country of origin, where he or she is at risk of torture or execution. While this principle is

persecution or at the very least a civil conflict marked by indiscriminate killing of civilians or threats of deadly violence from criminal gangs.

Although from the perspective of international law (and the migrant), motive is crucial, it is in many respects irrelevant to the political, social, economic, and administrative problems the mass entry of people from distinctive cultures pose to the host nation. It is because those problems are my main concern that I will generally use the term "migrant" indiscriminately to cover both persons who do and those who do not meet the criteria for asylum.

WHY FOCUS ON EUROPE?

This book is intended as much for readers in the United States as for those in the United Kingdom and Continental Europe. Why then, you may ask, do I spend so many pages discussing immigration and its effects on various wealthy European countries? In the United States immigration is a current propelling right-wing populism within the long-established political order's channels. In Europe immigration is an immense wave tearing at the very foundations of the centrist political order and the liberal values and policies that order has embodied. What Europe is experiencing now may well augur challenges the United States will experience in the not-too-distant future.

The challenge is larger and more immediate in Europe for a number of reasons. One is that, unlike Americans, many Europeans have seen themselves as citizens of countries made by successive generations of essentially the same people. Americans, perforce, have seen the country as one made by successive waves of new people bonded to their predecessors by adherence to constitutional values and a shareable historical narrative, shareable in its currently evolved form because it emphasizes the nationalist bonding of immigrant streams and their collaboration in building the world's most powerful state.

Another reason is the laissez-faire form of capitalism which in the United States organizes the economy and dominates the political culture, a culture which imputes poverty to lack of effort rather than structural inequities. The emphasis on individual effort and the relative freedom of private-sector actors to manage their enterprises, including the terms on which they employ people, together with the weakness of the trade-union movement, helps make American labor markets more flexible than European ones. In addition, the United States economy generates demands for un- and semi-skilled labor considerably greater than Western European counterparts. The propensity for home ownership and suburban sprawl long encouraged by various public policies is one source of that demand. Vast suburbs now spreading out into exurbs with their prized lawns, shrubs, trees,

embodied in the 1951 Refugee Convention and its 1967 Protocol, it has arguably evolved into a principle of customary law and thus is binding on all countries.

and flowers generate work for groundskeepers. Sprawl and weak public transport systems foster car dealerships and maintenance and repair shops. Shifts in economic activity from one section of the country to another and the growing population of retirees fleeing northern climes generate work in the construction industry. A more dynamic economy than Europe's, deeper capital markets, and looser regulation facilitate opening of new businesses and a concomitant requirement for new commercial structures, which adds to the demand not only for new construction but also for more cleaners and maintenance workers.

Also generating demand for low-skilled labor is the country's huge agricultural sector. You don't need a high school degree to pick berries or pack meat, just as you don't need an advanced degree to vacuum carpets or sponge aging bodies. We are talking about hard, not generally pleasant work, but that won't deter newcomers from taking it on, because they discover quickly the thinness of the welfare state. In America you can go hungry and lie down at night without a roof over your head. The state offers no guarantees against destitution. "Work or suffer (if you are not lucky enough to inherit)" could be the national motto. Actually, you can work and suffer, since the market much more than the state governs wages and benefits and there are relatively few impediments to persons down-pricing themselves into the workforce.

A third distinction between the United States and Western Europe is the difference in composition of the immigrant flow, which is largely a function of geography. In the United States, immigration has been primarily from Latin America.[**] Latin Americans overwhelmingly identify as Christian and they are migrating to a country where the great majority also identifies as Christian. Whereas Western Europe is essentially a secular place where religion is tolerated, the United States is a decidedly religious country where atheists are tolerated.[11] Moreover, aspects of Latin culture – music, dance, literature, food, and drink – have for decades integrated into the North American one. There is no difference in dress. Women, native and migrant alike, are conspicuously in the workforce and societal life. Moreover, many Latins arrive in the United States with at least some smattering of English and many Americans have at least a smattering of Spanish or some syntactically similar Romance language. Each picks up the other's language with relative ease, at least if we compare the effort required of an Arab speaker to acquire German. In short, within the Western Hemisphere, conspicuous cultural clash has not marked south-to-north migration.

In Western Europe, immigrants from the south have been and remain predominantly Muslim. Whether due to religion or tradition, many differ at least initially from legacy Europeans in their dietary restrictions, holidays, and day of rest. In many families, at least when they arrive, women have relatively limited contact with the wider society. Cultural differences are simply more conspicuous than they have

---

[**] However, an Asian component now grows rapidly.

been in the American case. Add the relative inflexibility of Western Europe's labor markets, slower growth, a welfare state under increasing strain, and a less entrepreneurial environment, and you have potentially greater difficulties of economic as well as social integration.

Even though immigration is not quite as toxic an issue in the United States as it is in Europe, it already roils the waters of party politics and political discourse, embittering partisan differences and blocking the compromises essential to democratic governance. What if the composition of US immigration begins to look more like Europe's?

That is a not implausible scenario. With the exception of the little countries of Central America's northern triangle and the collapsing one of Venezuela, pressure on US borders from Latin America has declined noticeably. In the case of Mexico, hitherto its main source, migration figures in the last couple of years are negative: more people have been returning to Mexico than are migrating north.[12] Meanwhile, as I will describe below, a demographic wave is building in the Middle East, sub-Saharan Africa, and West Asia (Afghanistan, Pakistan, and Bangladesh). The populist movements in Western Europe will raise increasing barriers to migration, not halting it altogether, but possibly deflecting a portion of the tide toward North America. So, there should be lessons for Americans in the way the rich countries of Europe address the issues large-scale migration presents.

DOES THE PAST ILLUMINATE THE PRESENT?

The appearance in Western Europe of migrants from the Global South is hardly a novel phenomenon. In countries such as Germany, France, Great Britain, Belgium, Sweden, and the Netherlands, their number has been growing since the 1950s, in most cases initially encouraged by governments experiencing post-war labor shortage in their suddenly robust economies. Rapid economic growth also drew people from the poor periphery of European empires like the United Kingdom's Caribbean Islands. The violence attendant on decolonization exemplified by the Wars of Independence in the Dutch East Indies and Algeria propelled to the metropoles tens of thousands of colonists and also local people who had served on what turned out to be the wrong side, the side of their metropolitan masters.

A second migration front opened when the former Soviet Union's Eastern European satellites were absorbed into the EU and their citizens were allowed to move freely within the Union. These migrants were distinguishable more in language than culture from the legacy population, however. Thus, Europe's history of integrating migrant groups provides a certain measure of accumulated experience by which to judge both the substantive basis of the anxieties roiling contemporary political discourse in migrant-receiving countries and the public policies adopted to mitigate them.

But history's ability to guide us has limits. Over the last several decades at least seven facets of the migration phenomenon have altered dramatically. One is the explosive entry into transnational political life of evangelical terrorist groups self-identifying with Islam and declaring implacable war against the West. A second is the slow growth verging in some cases on stagnation of European economies, the dwindling economic prospects of its middle and upper working classes,[13] and the transition in most countries from a manufacturing to a primarily service economy,[14] all combined with stunning levels of youth unemployment[15] in a number of countries, particularly Italy and Spain, related in part to rigid labor markets.[16]

A third is the swelling demography of Africa, the Middle East, and South and Southwest Asia, collectively leaping beyond the numbers projected only two decades ago and marked by a huge youth bulge. A fourth is the failure of most states in the areas of the Global South where population is swelling to develop political and social norms and institutions conducive to broad-based economic expansion or any sense among the citizenry of participation in governance. The paradoxical fifth is the expansion, partially the result of accelerated urbanization, of a class in the relevant countries with sufficient income to finance migration at least for one family member.[17] A sixth is the exponentially reduced cost of traveling and communicating transnationally. A seventh is the progressive deepening of trans-national criminal networks adept at moving human traffic clandestinely from one point on the globe to another.[18]

In *Expulsions*, her penetrating analysis of global political economy, the brilliant sociologist Saskia Sassen has proposed an eighth facet, or perhaps it is another way of describing and understanding several of the previous seven.[19] What she sees is a process in which huge agglomerations of both private and public finance are operating to expel smallholders from agricultural lands and reduce the living standards and life chances of farmers, workers, and small business people. The deterioration in the condition of tens of millions of people and the reduction in the plausible avenues for enhancing their conditions includes in her eyes the progressive shrinkage of government revenues in most countries (particularly taking inflation into account). This has resulted in the privatization and consequent marketization of once public services, such as health care and education, partially a result of the success of concentrated wealth in shaping politics and producing a reinforcing ideological discourse.

Conservatives like Douglas Murray, associate editor of the *Spectator*,[20] add yet another element, namely, what they see as the European elite's loss of nationalist élan and the arguably related leap to prominence of the cosmopolitan discourse of humanitarianism and human rights. The European establishment, they assert, has lost cultural self-confidence. Feeling implicated by historical association with the Holocaust and dismayed by intra-mural slaughter between 1914 and 1945, they have been driven to revalue their countries' now-demolished imperial projects. The educated classes, according to these right-wing intellectuals, feel morally compromised and have retreated to a tepid cosmopolitanism which inhibits the vigorous defense of borders from the incursions of previously subordinate peoples.[21] It also inhibits insistence on their adopting norms such as gender equality achieved in the West after long and bitter struggle, a struggle, of course, against conservative intransigence.

The post–World War II stream of migrants from the Global South and the prospect of its intensifying in the coming decades has raised for the elites and electorates of the rich liberal democratic countries an overlapping set of bitterly contentious issues which have widened political polarization in the United States and threaten the social contract at the heart of Western Europe's eight-decade-long era of peace and prosperity. Migration-related issues have aggravated other sources of stress on the European political elites who have built and maintained the Continent's welfare states and who have subordinated nationalist discourse to one of liberal internationalism with its themes of progressively freer trade, institutionalized cooperation among European countries, and compassionate response to misery in the Global South. That stress is evidenced by the rise of populist parties attributing social ills and felt anxieties to a hostile "other" including in this case immigrants, whether fleeing from persecution, violence, and destitution or toward opportunity.

There is a rich literature on various aspects of the post–World War II migration from poor countries to rich ones populated predominantly by persons who think of themselves as "white" and Judeo-Christian in their cultural roots irrespective of their level of religious observance. But I have yet to find one book which aspires to illuminates the full range of the overlapping ethical, legal, political, social, economic, and administrative issues implicated in that migration. My goal is to fill the gap with a book of moderate dimension examining a range of acute problems political leaders and their electorates need to address.

Within that range, a peculiarly thorny problem is the widely perceived cultural clash between the native majority and minority communities formed by migrants from countries in the Global South where the predominant norms and practices are in important ways illiberal. For the most part those are countries with Muslim majorities, and to a dangerous extent both migrants and host country electorates assume, not always accurately, that the migrants' norms and practices are embedded in their faith. But illiberal cultures are by no means limited to Islamic-majority states. You can, for instance, encounter some of the ugliest expressions of homophobia in African countries like Uganda[22] where Christianity is dominant. As for sectarian bigotry, another severe expression of illiberalism, it finds massive numbers of practitioners in Hindu-majority India and Buddhist-majority Burma. Nor, as any consumer of social media or talk radio is reminded each day, has old-fashioned bigotry, both racial and sexual, disappeared from the West. Nevertheless, Europeans tend to perceive cultural clash in terms of the relationship between the largely secular long-settled majority and the growing minority of persons who self-identify as Muslims.

For a tangle of reasons, the psychological relationship between Europe's secular societies and their Islamic immigrant communities is prickly. One reason is the fact that cultural practices in Muslim-majority countries (as in most countries outside the West) are predominantly patriarchal. A second is the long history of international conflict between Christian and Muslim communities. A third is the spread within the global Islamic community of fundamentalist views that discourage cooperation with people of other faiths or, for that matter, with Muslims from other branches of the faith. This strain of Islamic belief is blind to the possibility of reinterpreting traditional canons in light of changes in knowledge and society and hostile to the very idea of "theology" understood as the rational development of faith in light of human experience and new knowledge.[††]

Fourth is the deep political-military involvement of Western nations, led by the United States, in the internal and external politics of the Middle East and West Asia. These interventions have identified the West with radically unjust and deeply dysfunctional governments, particularly in the Middle East and North Africa, the major sources of Islamic migration to the Continent. Then there is the dismal quality of educational institutions, particularly below the university level, in most Muslim-majority countries[23] which, in conjunction with authoritarian government and fundamentalist beliefs, discourages critical reflection on inherited norms and identities. Sixth is the Qur'an's unusually detailed prescriptions for everyday conduct. Seventh is Islam's integration of faith and governance, church and state; there is no Islamic counterpart to the early Christian precept to render unto Caesar what is Caesar's. Thus, for Muslims, the movement from a country suffused with Islam to ones in which Islam is just a minority passion can be shocking. And then, ominously shadowing all the others, is the appearance in Western migrant communities of a violent politicized Islamic identity: jihadist. In short, the past may not cast much light on the future.

[††] Of course, the anti-modernist move to literal interpretations of the faith and hostility to liberalism and scientific thought finds parallels in contemporary Protestantism.

PART I

Entry and Integration

1

The Looming Wave

"The most striking thing about the current migration crisis," a *New York Times* reporter wrote in the fall of 2015, "is how much bigger it could still get."[1] Less than twenty years ago, the conventional wisdom among demographers – extrapolating from, among other factors, falling birth rates in poorer countries associated with urbanization, income growth, increased education for women, and sharply reduced infant mortality – was that the world's population would peak in 2050 at nine billion.[2] Now, according to UN reports, it is expected to hit almost ten billion by mid-century and surpass eleven billion by 2100.[3] Some pessimists, pointing to grossly erroneous underestimates in the past, see a considerable likelihood of the global population rising right over the eleven billion peak and ascending toward one, two, even three billion more human beings,[4] absent nuclear war or a global plague combining the virulence of Ebola with the contagiousness of the common cold.

The largest slice of that growth will occur in Africa. On this point there is widespread consensus. Experts estimate that a population which has already grown 50 percent in the last fifteen years will by 2050 double from the present 1.25 billion to approximately 2.5 billion and continue to surge toward 4 billion by the century's end.[5] Of that 2.5 billion, 2.2 billion will reside south of the Sahara. To convey a sense of what that means for individual countries, Nigeria's population alone is projected to leap from today's roughly 180 million to 500 million by mid-century and then proceed at a more leisurely rate to a mere 700 million by 2100.[6] At that point Nigeria should have at least 250 million more people than the United States, even though the latter is expected to grow, almost entirely through immigration, from today's 320 million to approximately 450 million[7] (see Figure 1.1).

During the same period population in the risibly misnamed Democratic Republic of the Congo should expand from the current 75 million (an increase of 55 million since 1970) to 194 million even in the face of endemic disease, civil conflict, and egregious misgovernment.[8] Meanwhile most of the other now rich

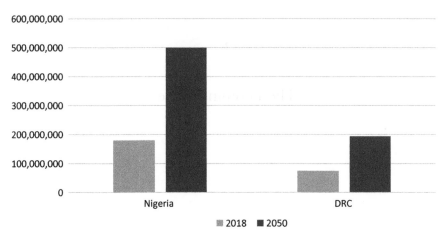

FIGURE 1.1. Projected population growth: Nigeria and DRC

countries will shrink, absent large-scale immigration. Japan is a particularly
extreme case. With a birth rate of 1.1 children per woman (well under the replacement rate of 2.1), it is projected to diminish from today's approximately 125 million
(with one-third over the age of sixty-five) to under a 100 million, possibly as low as
93 million by the middle of the century. In terms of the percentage over sixty-five
and the rate of decline, Italy, Spain, and Germany without continuing migration
would tag not very far behind.[9]

By comparison to Africa, Asia's population, now four times the size of Africa's, is
projected to increase only 11 percent over the next 85 years, to 4.9 billion from
today's 4.4.[10] However, that is Asia as a whole. While China's numbers have almost
peaked and seem certain to begin contracting as the full effect of its one-child policy
(now slightly loosened) is realized and India's population is markedly slowing,[11]
Pakistan's increasingly violent and dysfunctional society should grow from today's
190 million or so to 306 by 2050.[12] Swelling numbers are also predicted for Afghanistan and Bangladesh: in the former's case, from today's roughly 25 million to
62 million in 2050; in Bangladesh from the current 162 million to 202 million in
2050[13] (see Figure 1.2).

Demographic pressure in the Middle East also presents a daunting challenge
despite the recent decline in its fertility rate, which is still hardly in hailing distance
of developed world numbers. The problem lies in the area's explosive growth during
the preceding half-century when, in this singular respect, it led the rest of humanity.
As a consequence of this preceding growth, the number of women of child-bearing
age is high. So population is projected to almost double by 2050,[14] an arresting
number until, perhaps, it is considered next to the four-fold increase from 1950 to

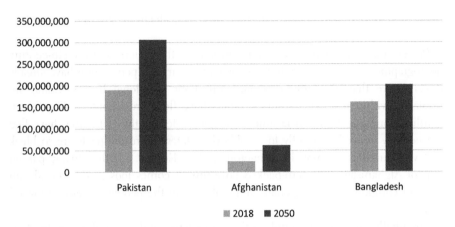

FIGURE 1.2. Projected population growth: Pakistan, Afghanistan, and Bangladesh

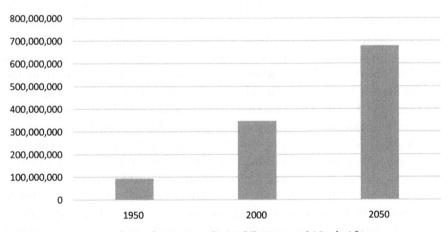

FIGURE 1.3. Projected population growth: Middle East and North Africa

2000 (from about 93 to something between 347 and 380 million inhabitants).[15] The demographers' current projection for 2050 is 678 million tightly packed persons[16] (see Figure 1.3).

Of course, the prospective degree of pressure on Europe's borders is not a function of numbers alone. As a general rule, human beings do not casually leave their supportive family and social networks and legacy culture even when they can travel without great risk. They need to be driven by mortal danger, virulent persecution, or severely limited economic and social prospects and pulled by visions of safety, abundance, and opportunity now projected electronically into the furthest reaches of the Global South.

Powerful push factors are at work in virtually all the regions of twentieth-century demographic eruptions. Anarchic violence, civil war, and persecution have already driven more than 60 million people from their traditional homes. Some are displaced within national territories; others have fled across borders. The Syrian conflict alone has displaced 12 million people, at least a third of whom have fled the country altogether, mostly to neighboring states where prospects are so bleak that vast numbers attempt the dangerous exit to Europe.[17] If the already palsied grip of Afghanistan's Western-backed government comes loose, one can add an Afghani component, fleeing chaos and violence, to the peoples streaming toward Europe.

Potentially dwarfing the numbers fleeing violence and persecution are the tens of millions of young people seeking entry into the labor markets of developing countries, which seem incapable of providing stable employment, much less offering any opportunities to prosper. In the Middle East and North Africa, young people between the ages of fifteen and twenty-four constitute about 20 percent of the population but approximately 50 percent of the unemployed, and the figures for those who have just left that age group are hardly better.[18] Unemployment coupled with low wages and meager economic opportunities translate into blighted lives. Marriage and family formation for men in the twenty-five- to twenty-nine-year-old range is a historic rite of passage. Today 50 percent of Middle Eastern men in that range are unmarried.[19] And a demographic multitude looms. Sixty percent of the population in the Middle East and North Africa is now under the age of twenty-five, with those yet to enter the workforce even more numerous than the fifteen-to-twenty-four-year-old cohort.[20] For many young job searchers, formal educational qualifications appear irrelevant: according to the World Bank, 30 percent of the unemployed in the Middle East and North Africa are university graduates, the victims of low-quality education and a lack of relevant job skills, as well as insufficient private sector capital investment and persistent misgovernment.[21]

Conditions in sub-Saharan Africa, where many governments are hardly more than vertically integrated criminal conspiracies for the extraction of wealth from tortured societies, are grimmer still following more than a decade of nominal high growth. An economic adviser to Kenya's foreign minister states flatly that "two-thirds of the youth in most African countries are not gainfully employed. In addition to those unemployed, a large number of young Africans are only partially employed. Yet others ... work long hours under difficult conditions but earn very little."[22] One study shows 70 percent of Africa's youth living on less than US$2 per day, the internationally defined poverty threshold.[23] According to the International Labor Organization, up to 82 percent of African workers fall in the category of the "working poor."[24]

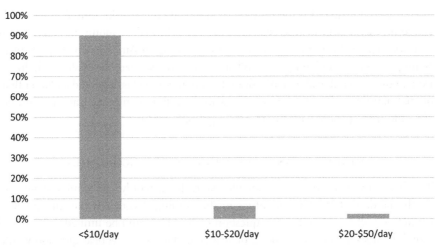

FIGURE 1.4. African income distribution

In this region, too, even a university degree is not a consistent avenue to stable poverty-escaping employment. Writing in the May 2013 issue of the magazine *Africa Renewal*, Kingsley Ighobor quotes a jobless university graduate in Lagos, Nigeria, describing the conditions of many fellow graduates: "They clean floors in hotels, sell recharge [mobile phone calling] cards – some even work in factories as labourers."[25] In Asia, factory work has been a principal labor absorption mechanism for countries rising to middle-income status.[26] In sub-Saharan Africa, where manufacturing over the last twenty years has fallen from 16 to 11 percent of GDP,[27] there is little of it to go around. According to data marshaled by EIU Canback, a consultancy and sister company of *The Economist* magazine, 90 percent of Africans still earn less than $10 per day, the middle-class threshold figure used by international financial institutions. In the course of a decade-long commodity export boom, the number of Africans earning $10–$20 per day rose from 4.4 to 6.2 percent, while those earning $20–$50 per day (the "upper middle class") rose from 1.4 to 2.3 percent[28] (see Figure 1.4). Still, there has been growth along with its outward signs of high-rise buildings, malls, car-congested streets, and high-end coffee shops through whose windows those university grads polishing hotel floors can peer.

It should hardly be a surprise that a survey of inhabitants of Nigeria found that 40 percent would move to Europe if they could.[29] Increasingly, they can, in part because the sub-Saharan-African diaspora sends at least $20 billion a year home to kith and kin,[30] along with the implicit promise of a friendly face and a bed for the night for those who survive the trek. The actual figure could be four times that since experts reckon that about 75 percent of remittances flow through informal channels.[31] Moreover, in part to evade government predation, many Africans who own or work for small businesses choose to operate outside the formal, measurable economy. According to one recent study, the informal economy in sub-Saharan countries ranges from 20–25 percent of GDP in South Africa to 50–65 percent in Benin, Tanzania, and Nigeria.[32] Whatever its precise size, its existence helps to explain the material evidence of a discretionary-income class a good deal larger than official statistics indicate. More people with discretionary income translates, ironically, into more people with the means to get out of Africa.

MIGRATION AND WESTERN EUROPE'S ECONOMIES

The facts above constitute an inexorable reality that can only lead to intense pressure on the borders of Western countries in the coming decades. If the migrant flow cannot be halted, interest in the question of "right" should be limited to legal and moral theorists at play in the fields of academe. The only practical question would then be: How should governments cope with the successive waves of people seeking entry?

Let us put aside for the moment questions about immigration-related conflicts that arise over identity and the pace of cultural change. Instead, looking only at the European economies, let's see how well prepared these countries are to handle a massive influx of people from poor countries. There are grounds for unease. Economic growth is sluggish and youth unemployment is already high.

Consider the data for a few representative countries. Take France, for example. Its per capita economic growth for the decade beginning 1970 was 32.6 percent. For the entire decade beginning year 2000 it was 4.1 percent. Germany in the 1970s increased GDP per capita by just over 31 percent. The total for the last decade was 4.2 percent. In the United Kingdom GDP/capita growth fell from 24.5 percent in the 1970s to 9.1 percent for the decade beginning 2000.[33]

Turning to unemployment statistics: as a percent of the total labor force for France it has been high for decades: 9.1 percent in 1991 and 10.3 percent in 2014.[34] Unemployment for youth defined as persons between the ages of fifteen and twenty-four was 17 percent in 1991 and had risen to 25.1 percent in 2014.[35] However, it is believed to be much higher for Muslim youth, upward of 40 percent.[36] In the United Kingdom youth unemployment was just over 20 percent in 1980 when overall unemployment was 8.5 percent.[37] In 2014 youth unemployment was only slightly improved at 16.9 percent. That was low compared with Sweden and Italy, two Continental countries also with large immigrant populations. Their youth unemployment figures for 2014 were, respectively, 22.9 (Sweden) and 42.7 percent (Italy).[38]

While most economic studies support the conclusion that immigration contributes at least modestly to a nation's gross national product,[39] there is some difference of opinion about its effect on poorly skilled members of the indigenous working class.[40] And there is little doubt that at least in some countries, certainly in parts of the United Kingdom, it has led to increased competition for public goods, particularly housing.[41] In terms of the effect of large-scale migration on public finance, up to now most studies indicate a positive impact for the obvious reason that persons of working age tend to predominate among migrants.[42] Thus, if employed, they contribute to government through taxes and social payments while requiring relatively modest amounts of medical assistance and other forms of social support. However, if family reunification is given priority, adult migrants will be followed by aging parents. Even assuming they are not past working age, except where they have special skills, they will have difficulty finding employment. Therefore, they will make relatively small if any contributions to the social support system. Moreover, because of their age, they will for the most past require rapidly increasing quantities of medical assistance. A study in the United States showed that medical costs in the last two years of the average person's life are greater than the totality of medical costs they generated in all of the preceding years starting with birth.[43]

CAN THE TIDE BE CONTROLLED?

Some observers write about migration from the Global South to rich countries in Europe as if it were almost a force of nature, something essentially uncontrollable, at best lightly managed. For support, they can cite, among other things, the gross disparity between the migration-reducing commitments of political aspirants, responding to public opinion polls demonstrating the majority's hostility to extant levels of immigration, and their post-election achievements.

Take the British case, for instance. The Conservative Party Manifesto for the 2010 General Election stated: "We will take steps to take net migration back to the levels of the 1990s – tens of thousands a year, not hundreds of thousands."[44] In a speech the following year, the Conservative Prime Minister, David Cameron, reaffirmed his party's position, declaring that he would hit the target, "'no ifs, no buts'" and adding, "'that's a promise we made to the British people and it's a promise we are keeping.'"[45] The net migration figure for the twelve months leading up to the 2015 General Election in which Cameron would again lead his party was more than 300,000.[46]

Why is it so difficult to translate political commitment into exclusionary practice?[47] The primary obstacle is that these countries are pluralistic, liberal, and capitalist democracies. In such systems, power is divided and policy moves one way and then another, usually in very small increments. Governments mediate and channel the incessant competition of interest groups.[48] Focused and intense goal-seeking by those groups often trump diffuse majoritarian preferences, particularly when it comes to blocking action. Moreover, independent courts monitor and restrain the executive's application to individual cases of broad legislative directives or executive decrees. The executive branch itself has internal restraints including shrinking discretionary income[49] and relentless increases in the costs of security and social support.[50]

Being liberal, both the generality of officials and the surrounding society tend to regard with unease the direct application of coercive state power against individuals, a liberal reflex – hence for many people an incident of national as well as personal identity – reinforced over the past half-century by a dense international network of human rights treaties, human rights–monitoring NGOs, and a related discourse. Being capitalist, each of these countries has a built-in constituency sympathetic to open borders. Why would the owners and managers of capital disdain a larger pool of labor and a greater number of consumers?[51] Immigration, moreover, is the one issue bridging the ideational gap between corporate oligarchs emotionally at peace with social hierarchies and leftist elites committed as a matter of principle to the view that, where practicable, arbitrary inequality in life chances should be reduced.

From its beginning in the age of the American Revolution, that principle has had a cosmopolitan character. Remember the words of the Declaration of Independence: "We hold these truths to be self-evident: That all men [i.e., not simply all white inhabitants of the British Empire] are created equal." The international human rights movement, which declares the condition of human rights in a country to be an appropriate matter of concern for everyone, reinforces, along with the echo of nineteenth-century socialist internationalism,[52] the cosmopolitan bent of the left.

It is no wonder then that the *Wall Street Journal's* right-wing editorial page[53] as well as that sturdy voice of transatlantic centrist opinion, *The Economist* magazine,[54] and *The Nation*,[55] the print vehicle of the liberal left in the United States, should form a virtual united front in support of a latitudinarian approach to immigration. Not that they advocate wholly open borders; the issue arises in more subtle forms having to do with both the limits on legal migration, including asylum, and, often more importantly, the enforcement of limits now on the books.

With ever-increasing muscle a third electoral constituency tugs against restraints on aspiring immigrants from the Global South, namely, their predecessors, who have been arriving since the end of World War II. The economist Paul Collier, a former senior official of the World Bank and currently a professor at Oxford, envisions a gradual loosening of ties between individual members of diasporas and their countries of origin at a rate corresponding to the rate of assimilation.[56] He assumes that as ties loosen, the diaspora constituency for additional migration will shrink. Perhaps in so predicting he is relying unconvincingly on the assimilation into US society of Germans, Italians, and other immigrants from Europe who reached the United States in the nineteenth or early twentieth centuries.

One does not see the massed ranks of European-origin Americans converging from their diverse points on the left–right political spectrum to demand or quietly to facilitate more immigration from their countries of origin. To the extent they still think of themselves as "hyphenated Americans" – as German-American or Italian-American or whatever – the American identity seems paramount, the

European one merely a sweet, lightly weighted set of inherited cultural practices, like the composition of Christmas dinner and bibulous festivity on some saint's name day.

Obviously the same cannot be said without qualification of more recent arrivals like Cubans and Mexicans even into the second and third generations. The large amounts they send back to relatives in their countries of origin[57] evidence their identification with the peoples they left behind coincident, to be sure, with a pronounced embrace of traditional American cultural practices and perspectives from baseball to Christianity.

The ascendancy of the US identity for European-Americans is no doubt related in part simply to the passage of multiple generations. The prestige of identifying with the world's greatest economic and military power must also play a role. But there are at least two other factors helping to explain the ascendancy of the American identity. One is the disappearance over the course of about two generations of social and economic discrimination against the ethnic groups that arrived in the successive waves of European migration.[58] The other is their rise into the middle and upper classes over the past century,[59] with individual members coming to occupy many of the highest positions in the land. Their successes have signified the triumph of assimilation in the long national epoch before the discourse of diversity and multiculturalism gained traction. For example, the grandson of a German immigrant now serves as president of the United States.

The same factors driving assimilation in the United States have also operated in Western European countries with respect to certain classes of migrants from other European countries. The president of France from 2007 to 2012, Nicholas Sarkozy, had a Hungarian father (from the aristocratic class) and Jewish antecedents through his mother. Its recent Socialist Party prime minister, Manual Valls, was born in Spain, as was the present mayor of Paris, Anne Delgado.

Later I will return to the whole question of what assimilation could and should mean today. At this point I merely note that North America and every country in Western Europe now houses diasporas from countries containing masses of people with strong incentives to join their ethnic peers. These diasporas constitute formidable obstacles to enforcing severe limits on new migration, especially when combined with capitalist interests, limited enforcement resources, legal restraints, liberal NGOs, and an overall liberal ethos among the educated classes that staff NGOs, courts, and most national bureaucracies.

I am nevertheless convinced that the flow can be significantly restrained and channeled. In this book's final chapter, I will elaborate the means that seem necessary. Not all of them are consistent with the ethos of human rights.

Until very recently, the adoption of a regime grating across the human rights sensibility would have been unthinkable, at least for someone who believes, however abstractly, in the moral equality of all human beings. Now, when xenophobic populist demagogues are banging on the gates of power and in some countries have already broken through them, such a regime has become thinkable beyond the purlieus of the right. That is why the question of the legitimate discretion of a state or the people already inside it to decide – for whatever reason, prejudice, or whim – who and how many may enter and on what conditions is not a philosophical plaything, unless you believe (as I do not) that moral reasoning is useless in the face of nativist passion. To that question I now turn.

Sovereignty, Nationalism, and Human Rights

THE ENDURING STRENGTH OF NATIONAL IDENTITY

There is to be sure a substantial minority within Western electorates deaf to moral arguments supporting even a qualified right to cross borders in search of safety or opportunity. Its members are deaf because all such arguments presume at least a latent sense of obligation to all people with endangered or stunted life chances. At the very least they presume some feeling of a common humanity. But this sense is missing from right-wing nationalists, for they subscribe to the set of convictions that ferociously expressed themselves in the bloody Balkan war of the 1990s. In that conflict, Croatians and Serbians, though intermarried in large numbers and essentially indistinguishable to outsiders in looks and language,[1] slaughtered each other. The impetus for their animosity was national identities that had been constructed by political adventurers and rabid intellectuals out of carefully selected or willfully reshaped fragments of a largely common history.[2]

Although liberating in its initial formulation, the idea that the world was organized into "peoples," each with a fixed and unique identity[3] that was expressed in their respective beliefs and practices, deteriorated in the course of the nineteenth century into claims of a Darwinian struggle for group survival. Blood-and-soil nationalism reached its nadir in the twentieth century with fascist regimes like Mussolini's in Italy, which purported to reclaim the grandeur of ancient Rome as it dropped mustard gas on the defenders of Ethiopian space.[4] In the twisted mind of fascism's most barbarous figure, Adolf Hitler, the insidious idea that needed to be extinguished was the idea of a common humanity and that a state could be held to external legal standards expressing humanity's common interests. This, according to Hitler, was an illusion purveyed by Jews as part of a conspiracy to weaken and ultimately dominate the strong.[5]

Attacks on mosques, refugee centers, and refugees in Western Europe and the United States remind us that a feral nationalism is not restricted to the Balkans.

Its embers still smolder around the edges of the populist parties fueled in part by Europe's economic stagnation, ostentatious growth in inequality, and the deteriorating conditions in provincial cities and towns, but driven in equal or larger measure by the rising tide of immigration from the Global South.[6] The parties themselves are not uniform. Some reveal their connection to their fascist predecessors in their deep visceral hostility not only to immigration but to tolerance and the cosmopolitan spirit in all its quotidian expressions.[7] Some right-wing activists, however, position themselves as the true defenders of liberal values, particularly freedom of speech, undermined by craven cosmopolitan elites indulging in the name of multiculturalism the practices of migrants from the Global South.[8]

All of them, however, decry the recession of a cozy familial nation. The Swedish Democrats are typical. In a conversation with James Taub, the thoroughly liberal investigative journalist and columnist, Paula Bieler, a Swedish Democrat activist, described herself as a "nationalist" who fears that an increasingly multicultural Sweden is in danger of losing its identity, which she defined as "the feeling that you live in a society that is also your home." Bieler, Traub writes, "objects not to immigrants themselves, but to the official state ideology of integration, which asks Swedes as well as newcomers to integrate into a world that celebrates diversity, and thus casts Sweden as a gorgeous mosaic." Apparently reflecting her views, Traub then asks: "Are native Swedes to think of their own extraordinarily stable thousand-year-old culture as simply one among many national identities?"[9]

This concern is not limited to people with a naturally conservative bent. In an interview following the New Year's Eve sexual assaults in Cologne by young men identified as being for the most part immigrants from North Africa, Alice Schwarzer, a leading German feminist, said:

> In recent decades, millions of people have come to us from cultural groups within which women have no rights. They do not have a voice of their own and they are totally dependent on their fathers, brothers or husbands. That applies to North Africa and that applies to large parts of the Middle East. It isn't always linked to Islam. But since the end of the 1970s, at the beginning of the revolution in Iran under Khomeini, we have experienced a politicization of Islam. From the beginning it had a primary adversary: The emancipation of women. With more men now coming to us from this cultural sphere ... this is a problem. We cannot simply ignore it.[10]*

However uneasy they may be about immigration from Islamic or, more generally, patriarchal societies, the majority of Europeans, at least West Europeans, arguably like the great majority of Americans,[11] are not blood-and-soil nationalists. They imagine themselves as defenders of what they take to be core Western values and

---

* She does not speculate whether a large group of young male migrants from Christian-majority countries might have behaved much the same in the darkened precincts of a lightly policed perhaps bibulous throng.

are, therefore, implicitly committed to a discourse of universal rights. In that discourse rights restrain absolutist conceptions of sovereignty.

Thus everyone who believes however casually that all people are entitled to the means for creating a dignified life should be open to arguments supporting at least a conditional opportunity to enter for persons fleeing persecution or war or a dead-end existence.[12] One of the issues I will ultimately address is the character of those conditions. More particularly I want to examine the claim that the defense of liberal values requires limiting entry to those who already respect those values and concede the authority of the admitting state to inculcate those values in their children. Should liberal governments feel correspondingly free to reject prospective migrants who, for example, believe homosexual relations should be criminalized or that marital rape is an oxymoron?

The terms and conditions for initial entry constitute only one of the divisive issues raised by global migration. A second is whether a person entering as either an economic migrant or a refugee should immediately become entitled to the full measure of social protection and the economic opportunities available to long-settled residents. A third is whether granting entry to one person entails an obligation subsequently to admit members of his or her family and to a prospective spouse and grandparents, what migration skeptics often refer to as "chain migration." There is, in addition, the question of whether the receiving state should use its power and resources to incentivize integration of the migrants and their families, and, if so, to what extent.

For instance, a government might require that, in order to move from the status of provisionally admitted to that of permanently settled, migrants would have to demonstrate fluency in the native language. It could condition citizenship on evidence of participation in civic life: joining parent–teacher associations, book clubs, conversation groups, volunteer firefighters, and so on. It could establish compulsory early-childhood programs in which children of migrant background would be mixed with those of indigenous families. Or, conversely, should the state accommodate a migrant's inherited culture through exceptions to laws of general application and assist migrant communities in maintaining their culture? Should a Sikh motorcyclist, for instance, be compelled to wear a helmet, a requirement at odds with the religious requirement to wear a turban? Finally, shadowing all of these questions is the issue of what measures states should take to reduce the risk of mass-casualty terrorism, a problem made increasingly urgent by the growing incidence of barbaric violence in the name of one or another jihadi party.

The most formidable obstacle that advocates of a generous opportunity to enter must overcome is what I take to be the average legacy Westerner's self-conscious identity as the citizen of a particular state. As Paul Collier notes in his book *Exodus,*

> While nationalism does not necessarily imply restrictions on immigration, it is clearly the case that without a sense of nationalism there would be no basis for

restrictions. If the people living in a territory do not share any greater sense of common identity with each other than with foreigners, then it would be bizarre collectively to agree to limit the entry of foreigners: There would be no "us" and "them." So without nationalism it is difficult to make an ethical case for immigration restrictions.[13]

In Western Europe, unlike the United States, traditional displays of nationalist ardor are rare. People of different nationalities no longer seem able to imagine each other as prospective enemies, and by the millions they work and retire in each other's countries as casually as if they were simply moving from the north to the south in their own. And yet, when the debt crisis bloomed, those same Germans who throng the beaches of Greece, basking in its sun and chatting amiably with its bilingual waiters, discovered a host of non-Germanic vices in their erstwhile hosts and said "no" to bailouts, however much misery that might entail for the average Greek.

The Germans had as much fellow feeling for the Greeks in their moment of need as the French seemed to have for Germans, their co-authors of the European Union project, when they began struggling to cope with a wave of impoverished asylum claimants. By contrast, New Yorkers and Californians, sharing as they do a single national identity, do not clamor against the transfer through federal taxation of a portion of their income to states like Mississippi, whose politics they despise, a sentiment amply reciprocated.[†] Globalization has not entirely hollowed out the citizen's identity with fellow citizens of a given nation-state.

That identity is the product of a shared political history, a self-congratulatory narrative of heroism and sacrifice inculcated through all of the society's means of cultural reproduction. Nationalist narratives don't require recognized borders; the Kurds, for instance, have the narrative without the concomitant borders, but their struggle to acquire them underscores the felt anomaly of a people without an independent homeland.

Nationalism is based on more than just feel-good, ego-swelling tales of martial sacrifice and triumph. It is also the personal security of Copenhagen's well-policed streets and Denmark's cushioning welfare state or the US passport which enables Americans to travel without fear, knowing that if a Cairene pickpocket takes our wallet in a crowded bazaar or if we are arrested for a punch-up in a Liverpool pub, there will always be a consular official to call. And finally, and I think perhaps most importantly, there is the belief – and to some slight extent the reality – that as a citizen one is contributing to the community's continuous history.

For persons in Europe and North America with a commitment to liberal values of individual freedom and formal equality, that history is a narrative of struggle, against defenders of racial and class privilege, patriarchy, and intolerance of all deviations

---

[†] Admittedly, the phenomenon may be attributable more to widespread ignorance about the allocation of federal funds than to fellow feeling.

from traditional views of sexuality and gender. To anyone who watched in 2016 the US Republican Party's primary election debates, Donald Trump's rallies, or experienced the aftermath of his victory and the renewal of right-wing populism in Europe, it is evident that the struggle continues.

Liberal values require constant protection. So, defenders of those values have reason to reject the claim of a right to cross borders, particularly if that right allows newcomers to participate in political processes and institutions. Because if there is a largely unqualified right to enter, persons coming from societies where liberal values have not prevailed might bring with them the dominant values of those societies and thus serve as reinforcements for liberalism's enemies. Hence the irony of Western conservatives hostile to liberal values opposing immigration from countries where social values similar to their own predominate. Liberals, by contrast, are at worst ambivalent.

A further irony, at least from a liberal cosmopolitan perspective, is the role of the UN Charter, an iconic document among liberal cosmopolitans, in consolidating or at least in reflecting the strict division of the world into sovereign states. Nationalism alone could ignore or threaten borders because the "nation" as defined by the histories constructed by intellectuals and their political partners could and often did spread across frontiers. Hence it could spur wars to change borders in order to unite the ethnic nation, as Hitler claimed to be doing in his assaults on Czechoslovakia and Poland.[14] In light of that experience, the Charter drafters outlawed the use of force for any purpose, implicitly including wars of "national unification."[15] The Charter is first and foremost a defender of existing states from any threat to their "territorial integrity and political independence."[16]

IS THERE A MORAL CASE FOR OPEN BORDERS?

As opponents of any right to migration have argued, what meaning can the political independence and territorial integrity of states have if citizens of other countries can wander across their borders and settle on their territory? The International Covenant on Civil and Political Rights,[17] the widely ratified statement of core human rights, omits a right to enter, reinforcing the Charter's guarantee of state sovereignty.[18] Nevertheless, in the view of a number of thoughtful liberal political theorists, such a right should be seen to exist if not strictly speaking as a matter of law then at least as an emanation of the totality of liberal values reflected in the various human rights treaties including the Covenant.[19]

FROM WHAT SPECIFIC RIGHTS MIGHT THIS EMANATION FLOW?

How about the freedom of association? What could be more basic than my right to invite someone to share dinner in my home or to share my home permanently with an invalid parent or my sister and her family or the woman I want to marry or a new friend I met on the internet? In 1948, when the UN General Assembly adopted the Universal Declaration on Human rights, and even in 1967 when the International Covenant on Civil and Political Rights was adopted, friends and family and prospective partners of persons in the member states would rarely have lived in another state. In the globally connected world of 2019, and with the already enormous migration of people from the lands of their birth, many citizens of every state are likely to have human connections, both intimate and professional, that cross national boundaries. So to say that the state has a largely unconstrained right to close its borders (except to the extent it has explicitly waived that right in an international agreement) is to concede to the state the authority sharply to diminish my associational rights and, incidentally, to create great disparities among citizens in the enjoyment of that right: those citizens whose intimate connections are entirely local will enjoy the right fully, while those whose connections are transnational will be vulnerable to whatever limits the state chooses to impose.

Individuals are not islands. Most people hunger for some measure of companionship and feel profound ties to their families. So where a state limits the entry of loved ones currently residing in other countries, it coincidentally limits the freedom of the concerned citizens.[‡]

A right to enter can in certain circumstances be associated with the right to life. As persuasively interpreted by the Supreme Court of India, this right has application far beyond protection from summary execution by tyrants. In a case brought on behalf of impoverished street-dwellers rousted out of their shanties by a municipal government bent on some urban renewal project, the Court held that the demolition of their meager habitat and consequent separation from the place where they had eked out a living threatened their lives. So, it required the government to provide alternate shelter for long-term inhabitants of the redevelopment area, shelter so located as to allow them some hope of continuing the activities which supported their subsistence.[20]

It is true that migrants from the Global South rarely come from the ranks of the destitute. Movement requires funds to pay smugglers and to purchase the bare necessities of life on the long trek north. Not only do they lack any financial margin; in addition, the truly destitute often are too weak and sick to move and too close to the edge to risk any deviation from their life-supporting regime even if it is no more than scavenging on the mountains of urban garbage. Moreover, they lack access to the sources of information and the wider human networks which persons above the poverty line, even if just above, are these days likely to possess. While stunning numbers of poorer people in Africa now possess cell phones,[21] the poorest in their tens of millions possess little more than the rags on their backs.

[‡]　Since the associational and equal-treatment rights belong to a national, derivative benefits flow only to those migrants who have some sentimental or vocational link to a resident of the country they wish to enter.

In general, then, migrants aspiring to enter the Global North other than those fleeing persecution or civil war cannot normally invoke the right to life. But there are exceptions, exceptions certain to increase. Traditional sources of income like fishing, small-scale cultivation, or herding can suddenly disappear as a result of dramatic climatic shifts or natural disasters like earthquakes and typhoons. Therefore, people may flee north when destitution is only approaching. As the seas and the thermometer rise and pollution and overfishing increase along with the intensity and frequency of killer storms, so will the number of migrants able to invoke the right to life.

THE DEEP NORMATIVE PREMISES BEHIND SPECIFIC RIGHTS

A right to enter need not rest only on specific rights. It may rest, perhaps even more securely, on the principles that inform the various legal enumerations. One of these principles, arguably, is that the state cannot legitimately use violence against individuals whose actions do not threaten the rights of others. A person approaching a border who wants to find work or rejoin his family does not meet that test. If he is determined, only violence will stop him: clubs, water cannon, stun guns, antipersonnel mines, tear gas, rubber bullets, real bullets.

A norm immunizing the individual from violence for crossing a border without malicious intent is not spun out of the sentimental imaginings of scholars and divines. Its emotional force is implied by the relative restraint most Western governments have used in dealing with migrants. Consider the protests that erupted in Spain several years ago over reports that border guards in the North African enclave of Ceuta had fired rubber bullets at Africans struggling to swim around the barriers erected to keep them out.[22] More than a dozen drowned in the attempt.

Equally suggestive is Spain's erratic use of razor wire on top of the fences around its Moroccan enclaves. Having employed it in 2005, a socialist government removed the wire two years later in response to reports that the wire had inflicted gory wounds on a number of wall crossers. In 2013 a conservative party government put the wire back up despite Spanish Catholic bishops calling the wire inhumane. The present socialist government's interior minister has promised, albeit somewhat ambiguously,[§] to take it down again.[23]

It is telling that despite their determination to halt the flow of migrants through their territories, most governments in Central and Eastern Europe have not used live ammunition to control migrant surges. The French authorities, not widely known for their pacifism, hesitated for years to clear through main force the encampments around Calais of the migrants seeking to access the United Kingdom through the

---

[§] Implementing a pledge made during the last general election campaign, he has tasked a commission with finding the "least bloody possible means" of preserving border security. BBC World News (online), June 14, 2018.

Channel Tunnel. In September 2014, ordinary citizens of Rome were "shocked" when police in riot gear used water cannon to disperse migrants who were camping out in front of a building from which they had just been evicted.[24]

Also telling in this regard has been the reluctance of European governments to deport by main force persons whose asylum claims have been rejected. Rather than shackling obdurate lingerers and hauling them by plane or boat to whatever country would accept them, at least one European government has tried to induce compliance with orders to leave by offering not only free passage home but also a modest emolument.[25] An effort by the UK government to encourage self-deportation by cutting off support payments was stymied by a judicial decision finding the termination of support an unacceptable employment of destitution as an instrument for enforcing immigration law.[26]

It seems reasonable to assume that authorities in democratic states hesitate to use violence against participants in large-scale and blatant violations of the law (which do not threaten public security) in part because they fear triggering popular hostility to their actions. When a series of migrant drownings occurred in the wake of an EU decision to reduce naval search-and-rescue patrols in the Mediterranean, there was editorial outrage in the respectable organs of opinion.[27] If evidence of mere indifference to the possible deaths of migrants can generate outrage, active employment of the violence needed to drive away migrants would seem to be an a fortiori case – for now and not for the United States under the administration of Donald Trump.

Of course, opposition to the use of violence to deter and prevent undocumented migration is not universal, in France or anywhere else. Germany has seen repeated attacks on persons believed to be migrants, as well as the torching and vandalizing of migrant residences.[28] This shows that a violent subculture can thrive even in a country where human rights norms are embedded in the national constitution[29] and supported by government practices and the great body of public opinion.[30] The possible shifting of opinion throughout Europe, the discernible growth of right populism and even in some cases an apparent renewal of fascist movements is a subject requiring more discussion. My only point here is that, in spite of these worrying trends, there remains a deep-seated unease about the use of violence against non-threatening border crossers.

Libertarian purists ought to make a similar argument but in more straightforward terms. For them the use of force is not the issue. Even if governments defended their borders by filling the air around them with a repellant smell or a substance inducing extreme lethargy, they would still be violating human rights because, in the libertarian view, every human has the right to do anything which does not threaten anyone else's identical right. From the libertarian perspective, harm occurring incidentally from large numbers of persons exercising their rights simultaneously – harm, for instance, in the form of sudden elevation in the cost of housing or a wage-deflating oversupply of unskilled labor – is irrelevant. The state has no right to make distributional decisions. Only free markets should make them.[31] The premise is that individuals will act rationally to optimize their conditions. If mass migration makes a place less attractive, people will adjust by moving elsewhere and new migrants will adjust their choice of destination. To be sure, this is not an argument with broad appeal.

A second moral conviction which animates and shapes the concrete legal articulations of human rights, particularly the Covenant on Economic, Social and Cultural rights, is that no one should be denied the opportunity to lead a dignified life for reasons beyond their control or through the application of irrelevant criteria. By "dignified" I mean a life with some opportunity for improvement and a measure of choice. Consider a person struggling from day to day in some southern country's informal economy, a person like Mohamed Bouazizi, the street vendor whose self-immolation in 2011, in front of the governor's office in the Tunisian city of Ben Arous, ignited the Arab Spring. When that person moves from his or her country of birth into a comparatively well-governed, capital-rich country in Europe or North America, he or she enters a new universe of opportunity. Where inequality springs from differences in how hard one works, most liberals will see it as justified. Where, by contrast, it is the result of sheer chance – being born in Louisville, for instance, rather than Lagos – justification is rather more difficult.[32]

If one of the defining features of a liberal world view is some sense of an individual and collective obligation to help people escape extreme poverty and powerlessness, then actions affirmatively restricting the capacity of people to escape poverty and predatory governments would seem morally dubious. Barring entry of non-threatening migrants is precisely such an affirmative action. It is a means of enforcing what the political scientist Joseph Carens calls a geographical caste system, which he defines as "the modern equivalent to feudal privilege which was an inherited status that greatly enhanced one's life chances."[33] Similarly, in her brilliant exploration of the conceptual analogy between birthright citizenship and inherited property, the scholar Ayalet Sachar writes:

> [Birthright citizenship] provides a state-sponsored apparatus for handing down from generation to generation the invaluable security and opportunity that attach to membership in a stable, affluent, and rule-of-law society. It also allows members of well-off polities an enclave in which to preserve their accumulated wealth and power through time.... For those granted a head start simply because they were born into a flourishing political community, it may be difficult to appreciate the extent to which others are disadvantaged due to the lottery of birthright.... Citizenship laws assigning political membership by birthright play a crucial role in the distribution of basic social conditions and life opportunities on a global scale.[34]

That is one way of perceiving the great disparities between rich and poor nations. But it is not the only one. Even a person who feels some degree of sympathy for the stunted life chances of a majority of people living in poor countries may question whether the naked fact of disparity implies a moral obligation of rich countries to open their doors. The countries of the Global North are rich, she might say, because successive generations built governments which facilitated and protected private initiative, built infrastructure, established great systems of education, and enforced the rule of law. If other peoples build the right sort of governments, they would have better life chances.

But suppose conditions in poor countries do not stem solely from failures attributable to their inhabitants? Suppose they are at least in part the result of the actions of today's rich countries. The slave trade decimated parts of Africa. European armies crushed long-established political orders. By various means, European officials in Africa and Asia turned millions of small farmers into landless laborers.[35] Rather than being able to develop organically, many of today's poor countries are the creations of Western states which drew borders serving their own administrative and political interests irrespective of the ways those boundaries compromised the evolution of political orders reflecting cultural affinities and constituting geographically rational units of administrative control.

Imperialism is just a word until you look behind it to find the stuff of real life. When you do, the picture is not pretty. Take one case, India, still home despite recent economic growth to hundreds of millions of immensely poor people. Compare it with Germany or the United States in terms of industrial development. To protect their nascent industries in the nineteenth century, both of the latter two erected high tariffs. For centuries before the industrial revolution, India was a leading producer and exporter of cotton goods woven by hand.[36] Had it been an independent state, then following the mechanization of textile production beginning in Great Britain, it would have erected its own barriers to allow Indian businessmen time to manage the transition from hand weaving to factory production. But being a colony, it was unable to prevent British-made goods from flooding its huge internal market and thereby preempting textile-led development. Incidentally, the flood drowned tens of thousands of suddenly penniless weavers. They starved to death.

If, as I think it is reasonable to conclude, more than a few of today's rich states contributed to what one writer called the "development of underdevelopment"[37] in many of today's relatively poor ones, then a generous welcome to migrants could seem justified morally by the broad principle of restorative justice, the principle which underlies contract and tort law. An essential feature of a capitalist economy, it should appeal to conservatives no less than liberals.

The principle does not dictate that the door be wide open to immigration. It would not prevent states from vetting for threats to public health and safety or from limiting entry to numbers which could be digested without threatening the very qualities of government, economy, and society which attract migrants. What it does weigh against, however, is a door open barely a crack and the mean treatment of those few allowed to squeeze through. So, for instance, the case can be made that the United States, having contributed over the years to the awful poverty and insecurity of Honduras, El Salvador, and Guatemala by providing political and military aid to governments, military establishments, and oligarchs ruthless in their defense of the grotesquely unequal distribution of wealth and power in those states, has a special obligation to families currently fleeing the social violence which engulfs them today.

In making the case for a right to exclude, Christopher Heath Wellman concedes a transnational obligation to help all people toward an existence with some measure of freedom to shape and actualize a life plan. But, he argues, open borders are not required to satisfy it.[38] It could be done, he proposes, through dramatic increases in foreign assistance programs of one kind or another. What he does not go on to explain is how increased levels of assistance, however large, could escape the predations of the many deeply corrupt governments of the Global South, which routinely steal from their citizens, investing what they do not consume back into northern safe havens like the London property market.

THE MORAL CASE AGAINST A PRESUMPTIVE RIGHT TO ENTER

I have described the moral case for a presumptive right to enter. What is the moral argument against? Why shouldn't we begin with the presumption that, rather than being constrained by deep moral values, sovereign states should and indeed do have a broad right to defend their borders, if necessary with proportional force, against private individuals seeking without prior authorization to cross those borders or to remain after short-term permission has lapsed?

For starters, one can argue that in light of the political and ideological climate in which the seminal human rights texts were adopted, as well as the absence from those texts of an explicit right to enter a country other than one's own, any fair-minded interpretation of those texts must conclude that the absence was a deliberate omission. The very fact that the Covenant includes the right of a person to enter *her own country*[39] excludes any claim that the failure to include a general right of entry was inadvertent.

Given the tenor of the times, its inclusion at that point would have been inconceivable. After all, the World War II, among the great slaughters in recorded history, had been fought by the victors in defense of the sanctity of borders. Against any claim of their inviolate character Hitler had invoked the rights of cultural nations divided by historical contingencies to unite. (That, of course, was the least fanciful and toxic of his visions.)

The United Nations Charter adopted in the war's immediate aftermath did not merely deny the primacy of communal reintegration at the expense of recognized states. It resolved the ambivalence which had threatened the peaceful intercourse of sovereigns ever since the seventeenth-century treaties ending the European continent's sanguinary religious wars established the authority of sovereigns to govern matters of religious faith within their domains. Equality of right to govern matters of faith developed into equality of right to govern all internal matters. Each sovereign could govern at will without legitimate remonstrance from any other sovereign unless the latter's material interests, such as the protection of its nationals when passing through or residing in another sovereign's territory, were prejudiced.

This equal right would endure, however, only as long as the sovereign did. Respect for internal self-governance did not include a prohibition against one sovereign deciding to extinguish another. Therefore, sovereignty was conditional until the Charter prohibited threats or acts against the political independence and territorial integrity of another state.[40] The Charter thus appeared to make sovereignty the basis of a peaceful international order. To claim after its adoption that a state did not enjoy a largely unfettered right to deny entry would have been very odd. Imagine a powerful and populous state we will call A sharing a long border with a weak, thinly populated, and culturally distinct one we will call B. The Charter prohibits the former from occupying the latter through main force. But insofar as political independence is concerned, if citizens of A can at will cross the border into B and settle there and if, in fact, a sizable number do so while sustaining subjective ties of loyalty to A, the Charter's promise to B of political independence and territorial integrity would seem to be hollow.

Beginning in the 1960s, however, the decolonization movement – an amalgam of a new collective self-consciousness uniting hitherto fragmented subaltern populations and a new not unrelated change in metropole perceptions of the cost–benefit ratios of colonial rule – demanded a one-time exception to the territorial-integrity principle. It did not attack the principle as such. Instead, it insisted that the principle be construed not to include territories of culturally distinct populations acquired by force during Europe's imperial expansion. But by insisting on the right to self-determination within the colonial boundaries and denying it to ethnic minorities within those boundaries, decolonization's champions reinforced the sanctification of borders and the concomitant vision of a global political order in which each state is a high-walled castle whose masters legitimately control its gate.

Still, the impact of decolonization campaigns on perceptions of sovereignty is not unambiguous. After all, in their bid for independence, the champions of decolonization drew on the emergent canons of human rights law, including the right to participate in self-governance; they drew, in other words, on a vision of human equality which made each state's treatment of the people under its authority a matter of legitimate concern to other states.[41]

As I will discuss later, however, the ideology of human rights has more than one sharp edge. Because it rests on the idea of the moral equality of all human beings and imputes non-negotiable rights to every human being by virtue of being born, it undermines grandiose notions of sovereignty. But at the same time, in its legal formulations it expresses duties owed *by states* to persons within their jurisdiction. In other words, the process of normalization and institutionalization of human rights implicitly recognizes the individual state as the principal actor in world affairs albeit one with strict duties along with a wide ambit of discretion in fulfilling them.

Recent developments in the area of human rights, in particular the Responsibility to Protect (R2P) doctrine,[42] have not necessarily undermined the perceived importance of the state understood as a particular people living within a determinate territory and enjoying international legal protection from actions threatening its territorial integrity or political independence. After all, R2P looks to the individual state as the main vehicle for preventing the commission of grave crimes against its inhabitants and recognizes a power in the Security Council to authorize third parties to intervene only where all else fails. As Christopher Wellman argues in his contribution to *Debating the Ethics of Integration,* "a state has an obligation to protect the human rights of its inhabitants. If it performs this obligation in a satisfactory way, it has a right not to be interfered with, i.e. it enjoys moral dominion over its internal affairs."[43]

Interpretations of law shift as political interests and societal values change in response to a multitude of factors including new technologies like those which over the past three decades have radically reduced the material barriers to the global movement of goods, services, capital, and people. Without the revolution in the ease and cost of movement and of communication, the gathering migration tsunami would, I think, more closely resemble a strong but plainly manageable current. Without the revolution and the resulting denationalization of manufacturing and transnationalization of the service and financial sectors, the capitalist elements of the migration-supporting coalition would be weaker.

Another result of the revolution is exposure of Western populations to real-time images of slaughter and misery in the poorer and less well-governed parts of the world. This intimate revelation of the terrible lives other people endure by virtue of being born within the wrong borders strengthened advocates of a Good Samaritan exception to the rule of non-intervention in the affairs of sovereign states. At a minimum, it strengthened the sentiment "to do something." Given the dubious results of sporadic interventions from Somalia through Libya to Iraq and Afghanistan, *the only "something" pretty much guaranteed to improve the life chances of determinate human beings living in bad places is to allow them to move to good ones.*

Do the changes I have described enable an argument that a presumptive right to enter is emerging in customary international law? Most international lawyers and governments would say "no." State practice, a principal evidence of customary law,[44] is not encouraging. The leading African states seem to tolerate mass movement across their borders without inquiring very closely or at least systematically into whether people are fleeing persecution, civil conflicts, generalized violence, great poverty, or tyranny.[45] In the face of the Syrian bloodbath, Jordan, Lebanon, and Turkey initially opened the gates to fleeing Syrians as if virtually all satisfied the legal criterion for refugee status.

Their relaxed views on that status[46] mirrored until very recently those of the most accommodating European states like Germany and Sweden, which in 2015 decided to assume that all Syrian nationals were refugees[47] and thus expanded the definition of refugee from someone with a well-founded fear of persecution to anyone reasonably presumed to fear becoming collateral damage in a country's civil wars. [**] Meanwhile other countries notoriously deny an obligation to accept any migrants, whether or not they have plausible claims to asylum, and assert a right to discriminate among asylum claimants on the basis of their religious identity.[48]

Certainly nothing in recent US practice under a liberal president, much less political discourse during and since the 2016 presidential electoral season, evidences implicit acceptance of an emergent right to enter. The multiplying ranks and increasingly high-tech gear of the border patrol, the deployment of troops along the southern border, and the employment of a chemical weapon to drive back asylum-seekers hardly attest to relaxed views about unauthorized entry. While the Obama administration conceded that the breakdown of social order in the northern triangle countries of Central America was responsible for the human tide moving through Mexico toward the Rio Grande,[49] the close detention of migrants and the stated intent to deport large numbers of them back to Honduras, El Salvador, and Guatemala demonstrated continued rejection of a right to enter.[50]

Actually, you do not need the aid of international law to defend a broad right to exclude migrants. You can find solid ground for it, paradoxically, in the very liberal values invoked by advocates of open borders.

One of those values is freedom of association, if not standing alone then in conjunction with the right to self-determination and the right to participate in government. The founding of a sovereign state[51] can be seen both as an exercise in self-determination and as an expression of the shared desire of persons settled within a determinate territory to associate for mutual security and the generation of other public goods essential to individual autonomy and dignity. Arguably the corollary of associational freedom is the freedom *not* to associate.

According to the two human rights covenants, self-determination is a right belonging to "peoples," a term neither defines. "Peoples" is essentially a synonym for what nineteenth- and early twentieth-century enthusiasts for self-determination called "nations." So, what is a nation? Ernest Gellner, a brilliant analyst of the nationalist phenomenon, proposed two possibilities:

[**] The more elastic the criteria for refugee status, the more difficult it is to distinguish fairly among migrants from ungoverned, misgoverned, violent, and miserably poor states.

1. "Two men are of the same nation if and only if they share the same culture, where culture in turn means a system of ideas and signs and associations and ways of behaving and communicating."

2. "Two men are of the same nation if and only if they recognize each other as belonging to the same nation.... A mere category of person (say, occupants of a given territory, or speakers of a given language, for example) becomes a nation if and when the members of the category firmly recognize certain mutual rights and duties to each other in virtue of their shared membership of it."[52]

The nation, the political scientist and historian Benedict Anderson has written, "is imagined as *limited because* even the largest of them ... has finite, if elastic, boundaries, beyond which lie other nations."[53] An earlier writer, the Frenchman Ernest Renan, spoke of nations as people sharing memories of "endeavors, sacrifice, and devotion." More importantly for present purposes he wrote that the members of the nation reinforce themselves in a "daily plebiscite" of a common will to live together.[54]

However imagined – Renan wrote sardonically that the members of the nation believe that they have many things in common although they cannot remember what they are – the participants in Renan's metaphorical plebiscite believe themselves members of a community: "regardless of the actual inequality and exploitation that may prevail in each, the nation is always conceived as a deep, horizontal comradeship" which aspires to freedom and the "gage and emblem of this freedom is the sovereign state."[55]

From these several efforts to capture the essence of nationalism one can see the elements of the moral argument for a right to limit entry. For better or worse people imagine themselves as forming an enduring political association with boundaries within which members share a history, a sense of comradeship in a historical voyage, and a host of everyday practices and understandings. From that association they derive an identity, not their only identity but one of such power that, when necessary, they risk their lives for it. In states that have a long history of cultural homogeneity and, until recently, little immigration, the association is more than metaphorically familial in its affect. That imagined blood connection is not possible in states formed by successive waves of immigration. Their nationalism is civic in character; the comradeship is one of belonging to a historically defined association, and new arrivals are entitled and, in a view at least once widely held, are obligated to share vicariously in that history recalled as a successful struggle for independence.

Article 25 of the International Covenant on Civil and Political Rights declares the right of citizens "to take part in the conduct of public affairs, directly or through freely chosen representatives." Taking part in public affairs through freely chosen representatives would be gaseous rhetoric if it were not construed to mean that majorities can decide issues of great moment. Who can enter the country and on what conditions has long been such an issue.

To be sure, majorities cannot override any of the other rights enumerated in the Covenant, but as I noted earlier, there is no explicit right to enter. In addition to invoking the absence of a legal right to enter and insisting that the right to participate in government implies electoral control of migration, advocates of a largely unfettered state discretion to decide who and how many may enter could argue that the coherent management of public affairs is impossible without a fairly stable body politic. Issues need to be defined, proposals for their resolution tested, potential representatives identified and assessed. How can this be accomplished if millions of people unfamiliar with the society's problems and personalities, its resources and institutions and historical experiences, persons who may not even be able to read or speak its principal language, can pour into the body politic in an unending stream?

An answer is the explicit restriction of the right to vote, unlike most others in the Covenant, to "citizens." Indeed, with the exception of local elections no Western society extends the vote to persons very shortly after they enter. They require a period of settlement and in many cases a demonstration by applicants for citizenship that they have some knowledge at least of the country's constitutional arrangements.[56]

While a period of settlement is an uncontroversial condition for admission to the electorate, the length of that period and the level of knowledge the extant majority can reasonably require of candidates for admission is not clear. Lengthy delay and a standard of political sophistication higher than that demanded traditionally of voters in a particular country would certainly violate the spirit of the Covenant, because the power to participate in the electoral process is one of the most important means for persons to defend their rights, particularly persons constituting an identifiable minority. Hence it could be argued that the pressure to grant political rights to persons not long after their admission to a country for settlement prejudices the linked rights of association, self-determination, and participation in self-government.

Even if admission to the electorate is delayed, new arrivals bearing different values than the legacy electorate can impede the implementation of long-term social projects by quietly refusing to comply with authoritative norms. Suppose, for example, that after a long period of contestation and discourse, there had emerged within a democratic electorate agreement in principle to eliminate racial, ethnic, religious, and gender barriers to real equality of opportunity. As a result, anti-discrimination laws had been adopted, bureaucracies established to enforce them, and, coincidentally, the ethos of informal discrimination had begun to dissolve. Then there arrived in the country masses of people from a culture in which favoring your extended family, your clan, and your co-religionists is the predominant norm. Not only might they passively resist enforcement of the equal-opportunity norms, they might reinforce the dwindling minority of legacy inhabitants unreconciled to the new normative dispensation.

Thus, recognizing a broad discretion in a liberal government to limit the pace and number of persons entering enables it to honor associational freedom. For that freedom includes associating with the end of formulating and progressively implementing complicated social projects. It is allied to the freedom of individuals to develop and implement and continuously revise personal life plans, a freedom stemming from the totality of enumerated individual rights.

The issue of entry weighs with particular severity on persons drawn to the more libertarian side of liberalism, which emphasizes the freedom of individuals to do anything which does not intrude (other than incidentally) on the exercise of like freedoms by others. For libertarians, there is an unassuageable tension between an assumed freedom of movement and the linked rights just discussed. That tension eases for communitarians, persons like the theorist Michael Walzer, who argues in effect that individual rights have to be understood and enforced in ways compatible with the survival of enduring political and cultural communities.[57]

Communitarians do not visualize any long-settled and stable political order as analogous to a contract permanently open to participation by any number of additional signatories. Instead, they see the political order as the outcome of negotiation and struggle over time and in a particular place toward a "common standpoint of morality," a moral settlement.[58] Individuals have rights, but they also have duties to reconcile their private interests with the collective interest in preserving the essential rules and practices, the institutions of the settlement. And each settlement is the product of a unique set of collective experiences, a unique history.

Borders set the framework within which that settlement evolved. The legacy participants in the settlement have a right, indeed, an obligation to defend it and its borders against all threats. And where the moral settlement not only sustains civic peace but is as well the source of individual freedom and the relatively equal application of the law, it can be defended in the name of liberalism. So, if migration of a certain size or composition is reasonably calculated to undermine the settlement, then on this view the liberal democratic society is entitled to limit and condition it.

LIMITS ON THE DISCRETION TO EXCLUDE

Suppose we conclude on the basis of the arguments discussed above that governments enjoy a broad right to exclude. Does it follow that they can exclude on the basis of whatever criteria they choose? No, it does not. To conclude otherwise would be to reject the belief in the moral equality of human beings, which supports the entire edifice of human rights and expresses the core conviction of the Christian faith.

Apportioning goods, including opportunity, on the basis of criteria which have nothing to do with the protection of national security, public order, public health, or morals or the rights of others, apportioning them on the basis of criteria which simply express visceral dislike or contempt for whole classes of people, cannot be reconciled with the belief in moral equality.

The Covenant implicitly underscores this irreconcilability. Article 4, for instance, while authorizing governments to suspend certain rights in times of public emergency, limits government policy to measures which "do not involve discrimination solely on the ground of race, color, sex, language, religion or social origin." Beyond those negative restraints on state action, the Covenant lays out positive standards governments must satisfy when limiting personal rights. For example, in declaring liberty of movement for all persons legally residing in a sovereign state, including the right to leave the national territory, the Covenant requires states to justify any limitation on free movement as "necessary to protect national security, public order (*ordre public*), public health or morals, or the rights and freedoms of others." Since the Covenant authorizes states to limit free movement (and other rights subject to suspension when there is a national emergency) where necessary to achieve those stated purposes, purposes which constitute the central obligations a state owes to persons settled within its borders, I think it follows that even if one came to believe in a moral right to cross borders in pursuit of a better life, that right would appear similarly limited.

The essence of the matter, it seems to me is this: when persons who imagine themselves as supporters of the idea of human rights debate public policies concerning migrants, they must conduct the debate in terms of not only the effect of those policies on persons seeking to enter, but also the effect on the rights and interests, *individual and collective*, of persons already settled within the country, the persons whose security and well-being the state is obligated to protect. Imagine a case where no single member of a prospectively huge group of migrants arriving at the border in a given year poses a threat to public health, public morality, public order, or national security. It does not follow that the group as a whole is unthreatening to those interests.

The threat in my scenario is not willful. It is, rather, implicit in the sheer size of the group where its numbers exceed the capacity of a society to absorb it without jeopardizing the very qualities which make the country appear to be a haven in a harsh world. Jeopardy may stem in part from the fears and prejudices of a large fraction of the electorate. Supporters of migration whether moved by humanitarian or instrumental concerns should work to ease the fears and shame or convert the prejudiced. Liberalism's historic task is, in Robert Putnam's words, "to redraw more inclusive lines of social identity."[59] But until liberals succeed, fear and prejudice sufficient to threaten the survival of liberal democratic leadership are as much a contextual given as insufficiency of space and resources.

THE SPECIAL CASE OF REFUGEES

However strong the moral case for a wide measure of state discretion in deciding whether and on what conditions to admit the generality of migrants, the case shrinks in the face of refugees. David Collier and Alexander Betts argue in their illuminating book *Refuge*[60] that in principle and increasingly in the practice of states the category should include not only those fleeing persecution (the International Refugee Convention definition) but equally those fleeing threats to their lives stemming from internal conflicts or the predation of private groups.[††] Their condition activates the universally felt obligation to rescue, an obligation the emotional power of which leaps over cultural rifts.

Collier and Betts invoke that hypothetical case popular among moral philosophers: the anonymous drowning child you observe while strolling home from the office. The cost to you, a strong swimmer, of saving her would be the dry cleaner's charge for your suit. The cost to her if you keep walking is her life. The person fleeing persecution or deadly violence who has arrived at the door of your nation is the child drowning in the pond. The ethic of rescue says you cannot send her home.

As the authors acknowledge, in the more precise analogy you are merely one among a number of potential rescuers. Their presence does not, however, relieve you of the obligation to rescue if no one else acts. Their delinquency will not excuse yours.

How far does the analogy extend? In terms of efficiency, the strongest swimmer or the one closest to the drowning child or best clothed for swimming should perform the rescue. Ideally, all the neighborhood adults will have met and anticipated this scenario and have agreed on who should take the lead. In any event, let's assume the child is saved, but she is shivering in the cold air and, it turns out, famished. Is the Samaritan who pulled her from the water now obliged to swathe her in his coat and bring her home for dinner? And if her parents cannot be found or are dead, does the obligation to rescue lead in this instance to an obligation to adopt?

If the child will die without further assistance, clearly you do not satisfy the duty to rescue merely by pulling her from the water. Either you or someone else must provide the food, shelter, and medical care needed to sustain her life or the initial rescue is futile. In addition, she will need protection from human traffickers and other predators that may be lurking.

For decades, the specialized agency called the UN High Commissioner for Refugees, a title that includes the person of the High Commissioner and a very large staff, has tried to be that someone else. Establishing itself with government approval often in countries adjacent to the one from which refugees have fled, it

---

[††] The Trump administration in the person of former Attorney General Jeff Sessions has rejected this broad reading of national obligations under international refugee law.

finances the construction and operation of camps providing food, shelter, and medical care. Successive High Commissioners have interpreted their mandate to require keeping the refugees alive, protected from human predators, and in reasonable good health pending either repatriation, if the source of their fears disappears, or, if the conditions for repatriation do not occur, then permanent settlement either in the country where the camp is located or in a third one.

At any given time, hundreds of thousands survive in these humanitarian-relief camps, but few if any thrive. How could they? These are people ripped from their homes, ripped from the dense social networks of their previous life, from the diurnal rhythms of work and play, and cast down in desolate landscapes in haven countries, dependent on others for their daily bread, which is at best meager because the camps are grossly underfunded by the generality of UN member states with the capacity to donate.[61] Humanitarian relief is nowhere near enough, Betts and Collier argue. It may suffice to satisfy the primordial duty to rescue, a duty only ethical monsters would deny. But it certainly does not satisfy either the humanitarian impulse codified in the refugee treaty regime or the national interests of the states that are most proximate to the main contemporary generators of refugees (Syria, Afghanistan, Myanmar, Eritrea, and Somalia prominent among them). Neither do the camps in their present form serve well the interests of the rich states, primarily the European ones, which in recent years have become the final destinations for refugees who find life in the proximate havens unbearable.

For both ethical and prudential reasons (prudence from the perspective of countries impacted by the refugee wave), the authors argue, the loosely related community of states should aspire to restore refugee families to a condition of normality, or as close to that as possible, a condition where parents can work, their children can go to school, and where a noise outside the window of their dwellings can be attributed to the last of the evening's revelers rather than the secret police. The present system is grotesquely inefficient while managing at the same time to be inhumane. Both qualities are captured in a few striking facts.

Syria's murderous civil wars have displaced about twelve million people. Roughly four million of the displaced sought refuge outside the country. At first, almost all fled to the neighboring states of Jordan, Lebanon, and Turkey. These states opened their borders in the face of political and economic stress, and despite the fact that none of them has ratified the Refugee Convention and therefore has no legal obligation to serve as a haven. Consistent with its long-established practice, in each country the UNHCR initiated humanitarian relief by setting up camps for the displaced. It used the resources at hand under its single-year funding cycle while urgently imploring rich states for additional funds.

These arid camps offer little more than the bare essentials of survival and were avoided by the great majority of the displaced. Instead, close to 85 percent, according to Betts and Collier,[62] favored cities, where most sank toward destitution as they exhausted whatever capital they had brought from Syria. Largely denied the opportunity to compete for legal employment by governments fearing backlash from their citizens, most families survived by piling into a decrepit room or two and working for pitiful wages in the informal economy. The great majority preferred this marginal existence to the camps in spite of the fact that only those in camps could receive subsistence grants from the UNHCR or be among the relative few for whom the UNHCR found places in rich countries.

As the Syrian wars raged on, a series of developments spurred hundreds of thousands of those refugees to set out for Europe. One was the fading hope of achieving stable lives either through a peace which would allow the displaced to repatriate or through real integration into the economy and society of the proximate havens. A second was an increase in refugees stemming in large measure from Russia's intervention in the war, marked by pulverizing aerial assaults on areas of the country still held by rebel forces. A third was a growing realization that Europe's external borders were virtually unguarded and that once on European territory the risk of expulsion was minimal. Finally, a large-scale organization of people-smuggling operations centered in Libya and Turkey got underway.

The terrible austerity and loss of hope together with the potential for refuge in the rich countries of Western Europe and the omnipresence of facilitators overcame the natural reluctance of people to break decisively with a familiar culture and set out for a world in which they would be a conspicuous minority. Those who had the resources to pay the people-movers began spilling in ever larger numbers over the wall of inertia onto what for Syrians in particular had become the main route north, from Turkey to the Greek islands and then on through the Greek mainland to those rich nations that had by 2014 thrown open their doors, however transiently.

The resulting mass of asylum-seekers merging with the mass of persons simply in search of a better life washed first over Greece and Italy. Leaving fragments behind in impoverished campsites or random urban spaces, the larger body flooded north primarily toward Germany and Sweden, although subsidiary streams flowed to Austria, Belgium, France, and Norway.

The 2008 financial crisis and resulting explosion of unemployment had cracked the economic pillar sustaining the West European secular-liberal political establishments consisting of the parties and officials of the center-right to left, which had governed Western Europe since World War II. After years of growing public concern about immigration particularly from the Global South and the proven emptiness of promises to limit it, the great migration wave of 2014–2015 also weakened public confidence in the political process as a vehicle for translating popular feelings into effective policies, as well as governmental competence to deliver fundamental public goods. To many, it seemed governments had lost control of their borders and their ability to preserve public order and safety.

Nightly, citizens were treated to pictures on television of tens of thousands of strangers seeming to pour over Europe's southern borders and then march north. Coinciding in 2014 with anxiety occasioned by the perceived migrant flood was the onset of terrorist attacks after a nearly decade-long lull. The 2015 assaults on women during festive Christmas gatherings in Cologne and other German cities only aggravated the sense of governmental failure at the national level. Failure was equally evident in Brussels, home of the EU core institutions. The banal rhetoric and lame responses of EU officials confirmed for many the absence not only of competence and will to act, but even of a strategy for action to any degree commensurate with the perceived challenge to the order of things. What followed, then, was Brexit, that furious body blow to the European project, and on the Continent a giant step forward for xenophobic parties and politicians.

For me the single most arresting number in the Betts–Collier book was the $135-to-$1 ratio (no doubt a very rough-and-ready calculation)[‡‡] of daily spending on an asylum claimant who reached a rich country in Europe versus spending by the UNHCR of European relief funds on a refugee in the Middle East.[63] What they argue not unpersuasively is that if the billions spent to process, shelter, feed, teach, and otherwise attempt to settle asylum claimants in Germany or Sweden or other European countries had been spent to provide the semblance of a normal life for the displaced millions in Lebanon, Jordan, and Turkey, the overwhelming majority of them would have remained in place.

Exploring in all its complex political, intellectual, economic, and institutional detail the failure by national political leaders and senior EU officials to anticipate the surge, its consequences, and the strategic options available for avoiding it would require another book. What one can say with confidence is that it would not have taken prescience on the order of Nostradamus to envision the surge. Nor would it require the strategic vision of Clausewitz to imagine ways of incentivizing the displaced of Syria to remain close to the borders of their national home, where they would be in a familiar cultural setting and, incidentally, not have to risk their lives on a thousand-mile trek into the unknown. That said, the immediate question is what lessons can be learned from the intellectual, political, and strategic failure of Europe's political establishment, and how can those lessons help European and other wealthy countries manage the pressure on their borders, which for reasons I sketched in Chapter 1 are bound to grow. In the final chapter of this book I will suggest an answer.

[‡‡] The ratio, even if accurate, may be misleading about the real costs of converting refugee camps into the functioning communities Betts and Collier propose and I elaborate in Chapter 8.

3

Integration and Cultural Difference

The Liberal's Dilemma

Since World War II, millions of people have made the journey to the wealthy and liberal societies of Europe and North America. Many of these family units have been settled for two, three, or even four generations. There are members of these families who have achieved great success, rising in the worlds of business, politics, academia, the arts, the media – in all realms of life.[1] While they may retain certain sentimental ties to their countries of origin and possibly practice or at least identify with a minority faith, they have achieved what the academic analysts call economic and social integration: they are comfortable in their country of settlement, have adopted its core values and stylistic vernacular, and are optimistic about their future.

In every group, however, some members have been successful only in relation to the misery and danger which drove their migration. Moreover, people can be fed and housed, even comfortably, and still be alienated. They may have achieved a fair measure of economic success without acquiring a strong identity with and loyalty to and acceptance of the social practices and constitutional values of the country to which they or their parents or grandparents migrated. And even in cases where migrants from the south have accepted those practices and values, they may feel badly treated, their legitimate needs disregarded, their identity an obstacle to realizing their aspirations. One liberal camp proposes "multiculturalism" as a paradigm for addressing their discontents.

WHAT IS MULTICULTURALISM?

Within the past decade the heads of state of the European Union's most powerful countries – Germany, France, and the United Kingdom (pre-Brexit) – have announced the failure of multiculturalism and its consequent death as a guide to government post-migration policy even as the number of inhabitants from or with roots in culturally dissimilar countries has multiplied.[2] What in their different ways Angela Merkel, Francois Hollande, and David Cameron appeared to be signaling is

49

a shared belief that large fragments of multigenerational migrant communities have failed to adopt in sufficient measure the beliefs, commitments, and practices of the legacy population, in particular its supposed commitment to socially liberal values. All three have spoken in the context of escalating concern about the lived reality of terrorist attacks carried out in the name of Islam.

A natural place to begin a discussion of multiculturalism is with a definition simply of culture. "Culture," according to Ernest Gellner, "means a system of ideas and signs and association and ways of behaving and communicating."[3] Bhikhu Parekh, multiculturalism's most prominent British defender, refers to it as a "way of life with a normative authority that is thought to be binding on a community . . . It is an intergenerational community which provides a lived structure of values, beliefs and obligations."[4] David Miller proposes that "a culture exists when a group of people share a distinctive conception about how life ought to be lived, and embody that conception in shared practices."[5] Along the same lines Paul Kelly urges seeing cultures as "richly textured practices that provide the context for practical deliberation in a common form of life. They provide the language, symbols and rules within which we navigate."[6]

Multiculturalism is a large umbrella under which a fairly wide range of normative ideas find shelter. For all their differences, multicultural theorists have at least three things in common. One is hostility to any policy of state-driven assimilation of cultural minorities. They also share a fierce rejection of the claim that the liberal state has a laissez-faire policy toward culture in the sense that the state neither helps nor hinders the efforts of cultural groups to reproduce themselves indefinitely. Finally, they are inclined to dismiss the claim that a laissez-faire policy (cultural survival of the fittest) is the only policy consistent with the liberal state's constitutive values.

Historically, multiculturalists argue, the liberal state, epitomized by France, has sought to construct a powerful national identity out of the various cultural communities in place at the time of its inception. Viewed from one angle, liberty, equality, and fraternity are bright ideals. But in order to construct the fraternity of shared national citizenship, France, to take one example, had to flatten more parochial identities, such as the strong, historically evolved local cultures found in Brittany, the Basque country, Corsica, and Languedoc. Because fraternity was the foundation of liberty and equality, parochialisms had to go. And go they gradually did, helped along by the army of schoolteachers, serving an ethos of secular-democratic nation-building, who marched into every village and town to shape the minds of the young.[7]

In France, the project's results were peculiarly evident, seen in the dwindling over the nineteenth century of the many entrenched, distinct, regional cultures that existed at the time of the Revolution. France succeeded in part because from the time of Louis XIV, it had a relatively strong centralized state which the revolutionary authorities and then Napoleon made much stronger and more intrusive. But the nation-building project was also successful in the United States, even though its central government in the nineteenth and early twentieth centuries was relatively weak and education was a distinctly local enterprise.

What the American experience demonstrates is that it is misleading to claim that as long as the government does not press assimilation on minorities, a laissez-faire policy toward cultures can be deemed neutral on the question of which cultures survive. Once a particular culture has become dominant in public and private institutions, once fluency in its language and its style are important – if not decisive – criteria for political, economic, and social success, new arrivals from different cultural zones will feel tremendous pressure at least to appear to assimilate. The state can choose to ease those pressures, for instance, by requiring civil servants and judicial officials to be multilingual, by relaxing or diversifying style codes, by passing and vigorously enforcing anti-discrimination laws, and by guaranteeing representation of new communities in political decision-making processes. But if the state does nothing more and nothing differently than it did when the society was monocultural, it is by the nature of things reinforcing the legacy culture.

To a degree, I should admit, the term "legacy culture" is a bit misleading to the extent culture means more than a shared language. It misleads by implying the existence of something fixed and sharply defined when, to a degree varying by time and place, cultures are fluid and their norms and practices internally contested. As the Yale-based political theorist Seyla Benhabib has written, "I do not believe in the purity of cultures, or even in the possibility of identifying them as meaningful discrete wholes ... [because they] are internally riven by conflicting narratives ... [and] are constituted by contested practices [and] complex dialogues with other cultures."[8] When they are in continuous contact, she adds, cultures mix and over time form hybrids. However, with all their internal conflicts and fluid character, cultures can become a source of common identity and fierce demands for recognition by somewhat heterogeneous groups if they are perceived by others as a homogenous mass and as such disrespected.

THE CORE OF THE LIBERAL'S DILEMMA

While an array of Western leaders were heralding the death of multiculturalism as an approach to incorporating migrants from the Global South, a considerable number of prominent academics were hailing its emergence as a moral paradigm for the day-to-day expression and long-term survival of liberal values in de facto multicultural societies.[9] An admittedly contentious way of framing the issues embedded in the debate about multiculturalism is in terms of the limits of liberal tolerance. It provokes strong advocates of multiculturalism because they construe it as an implicit allocation of norm-setting authority to a presumptive legacy majority: Western governments channeling that majority will decide which of the norms and practices migrants bring with them from their home countries they will allow and which they will suppress. Moreover, the word "tolerance" sounds in some ears as condescension, a sort of noble self-restraint concerning the exercise of legitimate power to suppress practices and values deemed morbid. Toleration is not "respect" for other cultures.

One way of viewing the contemporary cultural condition of Western Europe is as follows. Partially as a result of successive waves of post–World War II migration from the Global South and partially as a result of the survival of illiberal norms within segments of the native European populations, Western European countries now house two cultures with sharply contrasting conceptions of how a good life is to be lived. One is secular-liberal-individualistic-egalitarian. By "egalitarian" I refer to the conviction that all people – regardless of race, ethnicity, gender, class, caste, or religious faith – should be treated with respect, enjoy freedom of conscience, be able to compete on fair terms for social goods and to be rewarded on the basis of meritocratic criteria, and in general be free to shape their lives through a process of continuous choice. The other is variously called "illiberal," "traditional," or "fundamentalist." It idealizes and organizes family life along patriarchal lines with women in a subordinate and constrained position insofar as decisional powers and relations with the larger society are concerned.

Typifying the latter mind-set is the Egyptian Muslim Brotherhood's criticism of a proposed UN Declaration condemning violence against women. The declaration included a statement of a woman's right to choose her marriage partner, to work, to travel, to use contraception without her husband's permission, and to take her husband to court for marital rape.[10] In a ten-point memorandum, the Brotherhood stated: "This declaration, if ratified, would lead to complete disintegration of society, and would certainly be the final step in the intellectual and cultural invasion of Muslim countries."[11] Of course a not wholly dissimilar mind-set exists within important elements of rich countries. For instance, Southern Baptists in the United States, the country's largest Protestant denomination, have endorsed a doctrine they call "complementarianism," which espouses male leadership in the home and in the church and states that a wife "is to submit herself graciously to the servant leadership of her husband."[12]

The traditionalist culture, in addition to being paternalistic, incorporates the premise that identity is inherited and permanent rather than individually constructed and fluid. Also, one's moral convictions are not a matter of choice but rather are defined by inherited canons. Virtue consists of unquestioning adherence to inherited moral norms. Internal challenge to received beliefs is punishable heresy. Attempted departure from the belief system and the community of faith is punishable apostasy. And external criticism, satire, or insult is punishable blasphemy.

Illiberal minorities present public policy challenges to a secular liberal state in a host of areas: free speech; sexual and reproductive freedom (in particular, contraception, abortion, sodomy, and extramarital intimacy); educational standards; the regulation of marriage; gender equality with respect to divorce, control of family property, and protection from physical coercion; and treatment of children.

Aside from free speech and worship issues, which I will discuss later, the primary cultural conflict arises over issues of gender. Patriarchal immigrant cultures – and in Europe these are most frequently Muslim – demand the separation of boys and girls at school and the avoidance of encounters between Muslim women and men outside the family. In addition, they demand separate swimming facilities for girls and women, insist that women cover their heads, their bodies, and, in a relatively small number of cases, even their faces. Men are given privileged status in regulating family life. All of these practices ultimately relate to views about women (and correspondingly about the rights and appetites of men), which are now anathema to a majority of the citizens of Western liberal democracies. Their roots may rest in ancient, pre-Islamic traditions which to varying degrees have insinuated themselves into Islamic law as the religion penetrated new territories.

The precise character of the practices that rub harshly against liberal norms vary between and within national even subnational groups, and among adherents of different schools of interpretation of Islamic law (sharia). To a degree, they doubtless also vary with social class and education. Just as many American and European Catholics ignore Church teaching on contraception, sexual relations outside marriage, and abortion,[13] survey data show that Muslims in Europe vary across a wide spectrum in the intensity of their faith and in their adherence to traditional views and practices.[14]

Over time, practice and belief could well change in response to the steady pressure exerted on traditionalist norms among all faith-observant groups by a pervasive and increasingly globalized postmodern consumerist culture emphasizing self-expression and gender equality. After all, it is not so long ago that wives in a typical European and American working- or middle-class family were expected to devote themselves to cooking, cleaning, and rearing children. For the most part women in the West did not even have the vote until the twentieth century and until deep into the century police forces largely ignored the battery and rape of wives by their husbands. One should further note in connection with the question of the rigidity of cultural beliefs and practices in the contemporary world the extraordinarily rapid change in attitudes toward gay and interracial marriage. In a mere two decades the large majority of Americans have moved from opposition to support of the former.[15] Meanwhile hostility to the latter has dwindled. In 2010, only 24 percent of Americans told Pew Research Center pollsters that interracial marriage was good for society. By 2017 the number had risen to 39 percent,[16] a change mirrored in the growing number of interracial couples appearing in television advertisements for popular products and services.

Rapid change in cultural norms is by no means a rich-country phenomenon now that we are in an era of global communications. A *New York Times* journalist, Dionne Searcey, reported recently on "a quiet revolution" playing out in Niger, "a place where women have less education, lower living standards and less equality with men than just about anywhere else in the world."[7] According to the Islamic judge who presides over a street-side religious court in Maradi, Niger's third largest city, divorces initiated by women have doubled over the past three years. "'These young women don't want to suffer anymore,'" judge Alkali Laouali Ismael told Ms. Searcey. "'There is a solution to their problems, and they know they can find it here.'" Women appearing before the judge do not have to claim gross abuse; frustrated expectations about love, respect, and financial support are sufficient. Searcey interviews the founder of a women's center in Maradi who has been counseling wives for nearly two decades. "'Ten years ago,'" she informs the journalist, "'women didn't know their rights. They thought they were just stuck in a marriage, be it good or bad.'"[18]

Niger is not exceptional. In Senegal's capital, Dakar, the Association of Female Lawyers says female clients seeking divorce have tripled in just the past four years. "In Nigeria," Searcey, writes, "a . . . movie called 'Wives on Strike,' about a group of women who band together against a bad husband and father, was so popular it spawned a sequel and a television series."[19]

Unfortunately, the arc of rapid cultural change does not invariably bend toward liberalism. "Nautch" is a sophisticated form of dance and music developed over centuries in South and West Asia and performed by the so-called dancing girls of Lahore, the post–Indian partition location of its principal training center. Once the most talented Nautch artists danced at the courts of maharajahs both in what today is northern India and Pakistan and had a status loosely analogous to the geisha in Japan. Some acquired patrons among the rich and became wealthy themselves. Suddenly, in the late 1970s, the extremely conservative form of Islam centered in Saudi Arabia washed over Pakistan transforming a respected profession and art form into something deemed degraded. Increasingly harassed by police and religious militants, the profession became a barely tolerated vice bordering on prostitution, its performers transformed from geishas into the equivalent of nude dancers in sleazy American bars.[20]

MINORITY RIGHTS AS HUMAN RIGHTS

What legal protection do international human rights norms offer to minority communities in general and to illiberal minorities in particular? Article 18 of the Covenant on Civil and Political Rights requires states "to have respect for the liberty of parents ... to ensure the religious and moral education of their children in conformity with their own convictions."[21] However, it makes that liberty subject to "such limitations ... as are necessary to protect public safety, order, health, or morals or the fundamental rights and freedoms of others." That limitation can cover a lot of ground. It could, for instance, be construed to give governments discretion to require private schools established by Islamic and Christian fundamentalists or ultra-orthodox Jews to teach (1) the necessity of respect for members of other faiths and for agnostics and atheists, (2) the equality of men and women and their equal right to shape their individual lives and the life of their family, (3) the value of free speech including speech critical of religious beliefs, and (4) the right of every person to change his or her religious identity.

Article 19 guarantees the right to freedom of expression, "which shall include freedom to seek, receive, and impart information and ideas of all kinds, regardless of frontiers, either orally, in writing or in print ... through any media." But it contains the same qualifying language as the previous article, language which could reasonably be invoked to deny visas to foreign imams who in the government's judgment reinforce the jihadi narrative by claiming that the Islamic world is under siege by the West and that violent jihad is an exercise in communal self-defense. Restrictions on the expression of militant views, whether by imams or simply bloggers on the internet, might also be grounded on Article 20's requirement that "any advocacy of national, racial or religious hatred that constitutes incitement to discrimination, hostility or violence shall be prohibited by law."[22]

Such ambiguities in the legal norms affecting fundamentalist-minority values and practices can also be seen in Article 23, which declares the family to be "the natural and fundamental group unit of society and entitled to protection by society and the state." An emphasis on the family unit rather than the individual is promising from the fundamentalist perspective. However, it turns out that the family being protected is not necessarily the fundamentalist's idea of a proper family model, for the Article also provides that "States Parties ... shall take appropriate steps to ensure equality of rights and responsibilities of spouses as to marriage, during marriage and at its dissolution." In addition, it declares: "No marriage shall be entered into without the free and full consent of the intending spouses." So much for arranged marriages, particularly of the very young.

TOLERANCE WITH LIMITS OR MUTUAL RESPECT?

On both principled and prudential grounds, strong multiculturalists like Chandran Kukathas urge liberals to reject the "what-should-be-tolerated" framing of the policy issue. Instead, he asks them to think of cultures enjoying an equal right to reproduce themselves. He concedes that that way of thinking probably would lead to an archipelago of cultural identities and social practices within the liberal nation-state. All parts of the archipelago would be committed to mutual toleration and acceptance of the institutional framework established by the constitution only to the extent it is compatible with the autonomy of cultural communities.[23]

Multiculturalists differ in the lengths to which they would push the idea of communal cultural autonomy. Kukathas would deny the liberal state the right to override community practices and beliefs which offend liberal sensibilities such as the patriarchal organization of the family, isolation of women, arranged marriages, perhaps child marriages, and gendered differences in education.[24] Presumably, if an Aztec minority were to suddenly appear, he would draw the line at human sacrifice. What he does insist on, however, is a state-protected right of exit from the community.

The Canadian multiculturalist Will Kymlicka's formula is cultural autonomy for migrant communities up to the point where their practices violate basic human rights.[25] It leaves us with a serious line-drawing problem. Which human rights are basic? Can the government in the name of equal protection punish Sunni fundamentalist owners of restaurants who refuse to serve Shia Muslims, Christians, Jews, and others who do not share their beliefs? Can it enforce rape law against a fundamentalist who did not have the consent of his wife for sexual intercourse? Can it insist in the name of protecting fundamental rights that all children attend public preschools where they will be taught liberal values embedded in the constitution?

Michael Walzer, often characterized as a communitarian more than a liberal, enters the debate from a slightly different angle. What every successful society needs, he argues, is a "common standpoint of morality" but one defined in primarily political not cultural terms.[26] The common standpoint is a consensus about a just organization of society, which means it defines the terms on which groups compete for social and economic goods – income, wealth, access to education, celebrity – and identifies the things they should share equally like impartial application of the law, equal access to public services, equal opportunity to work in the state bureaucracy, and protection from destitution. The consensus, in his words, "represents the gradual shaping of a common life – at least, a common political life." "Religious differences and cultural pluralism," he adds, "are entirely compatible with this kind of commonality; indeed, they are likely to make for social conflict and civil war without it."[27]

This addition may be a bit glib. Suppose a religious culture demands that its devotees treat the members of other cultures as enemies, refuse to collaborate with them in any common project, and categorically favor co-religionists in every sphere of life? Kukathas would apparently insist on respect for it, as long as devotees did not urge or execute violations of the civil and personal rights of members of other cultures.

What Walzer seems to be arguing is that both a common moral standpoint and respect for cultural diversity are essential for the survival of liberal democratic states. How persuasive is his position? Do even the legacy majorities in Europe and North American democracies have a common moral standpoint?

Consider the United States. Can its electorate be said to enjoy a "common moral standpoint"? Where is the point of commonality between those who believe that abortion is largely a matter of choice for a woman and those who label it murder, that physically intimate same-sex relationships are sinful and those who believe that sexual relationships between consenting adults are entirely a matter of choice, or that the state should protect all members of the society from destitution and those who believe that in most cases destitution is the result of personal failings and therefore its consequences should not be mitigated? I am hardly alone in arguing, as I did in my last book,[28] that what we face today is not a clash between civilizations, but a clash of values and beliefs *within* each of what the late political theorist Samuel Huntington called civilizational "zones."[29]

Could it nevertheless be argued despite those polar differences in value that there exists a "common moral standpoint" among the settled inhabitants of the United States? My reply is "maybe, if common implies a healthy majority." But first we need to consider what we mean by a "common moral standpoint." Walzer writes of "the gradual shaping of a common life – at least, a common *political* life."[30] Thus, a common moral viewpoint for him may only be a consensus about the justness of a society's constitutional arrangements, about, that is, the procedures by which it produces public policies rather than the policies themselves. And arguably there is commonality in a second sense. Opinion polling suggests that a very broad swathe of the American electorate believes that all citizens should have equal opportunities to improve the conditions of their lives.[31]

This common standpoint of morality, however, has been achieved only through struggle, including the vicious Civil War. Even that bloody conflict failed to achieve a universal consensus, as evidence of enduring racial animus among significant numbers of white people continues to accumulate.[32] There are, in fact, many indications, in addition to the effort to suppress voting by minority constituencies, that the common moral standpoint may belong to a majority rather than a consensus and that it may be brittle.

Consider, for instance, the percentage of the population that refused to recognize the legitimacy of the Obama presidency. A 2009 poll indicated that only 47 percent of potential voters in states of the old Confederacy believed that President Obama was born a US citizen.[33] Twenty-five percent of respondents to a nationwide Harris Poll in 2010 took the position that he probably was not born in the United States.[34] Also relevant, I think, are views about torture. A 2010 Pew Research Center Poll[35] explored levels of support for torture to gain important information from suspected terrorists. Respondents were given the alternatives of "often," "sometimes," "rarely," and "never." Fifteen percent said "often" and 34 percent said "sometimes." In short, about 50 percent were prepared to torture more than "rarely."

Nevertheless, the common vision seems to endure insofar as it refers to the conviction of a large majority that recourse to private violence for any purpose including the advancement of personal moral convictions is indefensible.[36] If the great majority of Americans believe that moral values can be enforced only through constitutional means and endorse the basic constitutional restraints on governmental power – an independent court system, the impartial enforcement of the law, separation and overlapping of institutional power at the national level, and enforcement of the Bill of Rights – then we could reasonably conclude that a common moral perspective endures.

But Walzer may have had something more in mind. I think he would argue that respect for the political settlement, including enforcement of the Bill of Rights, depends on consensus at a deep psychological level about the day-to-day equal application of the law and equality of opportunity to compete for wealth, power, and celebrity While most Americans reject caste and disapprove of explicit race-based discrimination, a considerable segment of the white electorate appears indifferent to the gross disparities between white and black in wealth, rates of incarceration, quality of schools, and hostile interactions with the police.[37]

Whether the common moral perspective, such as it is, can survive the strains of the present moment remains to be seen. An ominous portent is recent polling data indicating that a growing number of Americans are beginning literally to hate each other because of their respective political party identity, an identity that is increasingly equated with the possession of alien and contemptable values.[38] Observing the venomous discourse of contemporary American politics, it is hard to contest the philosopher Alasdair McIntyre's claim that "Modern politics [in the West] is civil war carried out by other means."[39]

At a minimum, it seems fair to say that constitutional arrangements protecting human rights are more likely to survive new incidents of jihadi terrorism if they reflect a broad even if not comprehensive moral consensus about the substance and premises of human rights. In order to defend such consensus as exists in the West, won't liberals instinctively tilt against a proposal that the states of the West, the original heartland of human rights, tolerate violations of human rights by members of illiberal minority communities? To concede within areas of national jurisdiction that women be treated unequally and children cruelly and that heresy, apostasy, and blasphemy be severely punished, whether by official or unofficial means, could reasonably be construed as evidencing a lack of faith in the very idea that human rights are universal. And if they are not universal, then how can they be said to be human? Can a faith so flaccid inspire effective defense of civil and political rights?

THE LIBERAL CASE AGAINST GOVERNMENT-FOSTERED ASSIMILATION

In theory, conservative thinkers might be attracted to multiculturalism because, theoretically, they are the defenders of tradition and nurse a suspicion of all innovative social projects. It was conservatives, after all, who showed little enthusiasm for using national power to overthrow the American South's peculiar tradition of race-based feudalism. Yet it is in the name of liberalism that scholars like Parekh, Kymlicka, and Kukathas urge restraint in pressing liberal values on migrants or migrant-background families with illiberal values and practices.

I see two arguments for toleration by social liberals for illiberal practices embedded in certain minority cultures. One is the claim that toleration is the best recipe for social peace and that liberal polities cannot indefinitely survive furious cultural wars.

As Michael Walzer notes in his extended essay on *Politics and Passion*,[40] individuals begin life in a community of fate, not choice, namely, the family and the religious or racial or ethnic fragment of society with which it is identified. While individuals may ultimately seek a more cosmopolitan identity, initially they acquire the identity into which they are born, acquire it in the double sense of how they are perceived by the wider society and how they perceive themselves. Where the wider society treats the group with contempt, it necessarily injures the self-respect of individual members, diminishes their sense of life's possibilities, and encourages them to adopt in conjunction with other group members a defensive crouch. To avoid those consequences, the argument goes, the secular majority should at a minimum grant to every community, including ones illiberal in some of their beliefs and practices, public expressions of respect and the maximum opportunity for self-realization and reproduction consistent with the imperatives of maintaining a basically liberal state.

The second reason for respecting or at a minimum tolerating a range of illiberal practices is the role of culture, any culture, in making the world meaningful to those born into it. The newly born enter a world of overwhelming sensation, a roaring, buzzing confusion of impressions. How can people make coherent, conscious choices about the life they want to lead if life seems incoherent? A dense, tightly integrated culture, according to this argument, provides young members with a strong sense of who they are. It imparts meaning and direction to their lives by locating them in a moral order. Thus, the argument continues, it tends to give the individual the kind of confident, integrated personality which is a precondition for engaging effectively with life and exploring one's potential.

This positive effect is lost where cultures are unable to control the socialization of the young and are compelled by liberal governments to jettison key cultural elements such as authoritative patriarchy with its numerous corollaries. The result is exponential increase in anomie and alienation, in intellectual confusion and loss of self-respect, in persons poorly equipped to be entrepreneurs of the self. Those raised in conditions of cultural confusion resulting from the collision between their inherited cultural identity and the one identified by the majority as desirable become susceptible to new prophets and dangerous cults, a result still more likely where cultural tension coincides with a family's move often under traumatic circumstances to an alien environment.

Therefore, the argument concludes, a government that watches with positive indifference the erosion of traditional cultures or actively seeks to detach young people from their legacy identity in order to strengthen their identity with the cultural majority and the state should not be deemed liberal. Such intrusiveness threatens the confident sense of self it is the purpose of liberalism and human rights to protect and enhance, however little that self may value liberalism and human rights.[41]

While not implausible as an explanation of multiple reports and signs of alienation among second- and third-generation immigrant youth in Europe, neither is it compelling. In a world with a globalized media and a profit-driven consumerist culture penetrating even remote villages in Africa, traditional dense cultures are, in the image proposed by the great French anthropologist Levi-Strauss, like blocks of ice melting under an equatorial sun. The remarkable shift in American public opinion on gay marriage, from 57 percent opposed to 62 percent in favor, over the course of a single decade, is suggestive in this respect as are the developments in West Africa I mentioned earlier.[42]

A world in which *American Idol* is duplicated in Kabul[43] is, for better or worse, a cultural buffet. If even oppressive authoritarian regimes like the Saudi Arabian seemingly cannot halt the erosion of tradition, one can doubt whether accommodating Western governments could sustain traditional cultures indefinitely even if they wished to. That doubt, however, may fail to take sufficient account of fundamentalism's appeal particularly in an era of tumultuous change, dashed expectations, and pervasive insecurity. When people feel the social, moral, and intellectual ground shifting violently under their feet, many reach to embrace visions of a remembered or imagined order, a new version of an old dispensation. In the United States, the churches of formerly mainstream Protestantism, which adapted its canons to reconcile with modernity, are largely empty; those of Pentecostals and Evangelicals are full.[44]

LIBERAL VERSUS LIBERAL: THE DEBATE PERSONIFIED

Each European country with high levels of immigration has experienced at least one defining moment that brought to light the often long-simmering cultural tensions growing within its borders. For Great Britain it was the Rushdie affair.

In 1989 Iranian Ayatollah Khomeini issued a fatwa calling on Muslims to kill the writer Salman Rushdie, a lapsed Muslim and a British citizen, for an allegedly blasphemous rendering of the prophet Muhammad and Islam more generally in his novel *The Satanic Verses*. The fatwa included a call to murder all involved in its publication who were aware of its contents.

Khomeini's denunciation and call to action incited violent demonstrations in the Muslim world and drove Rushdie into hiding, where he remained for nine years protected round-the-clock by guards assigned by the British police. He survived, but not everyone associated with the book was as fortunate. A translator of the book into Japanese was stabbed to death.

The fatwa, along with the book's actual content as it was construed by various Islamic consumers, galvanized segments of Britain's Muslim population. In the northern cities of Bolton and Bradford, Muslims gathered to burn the offending book, a scene which secular liberals found disquietingly reminiscent of Nazi burning of books by Jewish and other hated writers. According to the author Melanie Phillips,

> There was a positive feeding frenzy of incitement. Sayed Abdul Quddus, the Secretary of the Bradford Council of Mosques, claimed that Rushdie had "tortured Islam" and deserved to pay the penalty by "hanging." [He added] that "I would willingly sacrifice my own life and that of my children to carry out the Ayatollah's wishes should the opportunity arise."[45]

The fact that the Bradford Council of Mosques, an organization fostered by the city government, had organized the book burning helped sharpen the perceived multi-cultural dimension of the affair. Seven years earlier the City Council had announced that every section of that "multiracial, multicultural city [had] an equal right to maintain its own identity, culture, language, religion and customs."[46]

Although the furious reaction in the Muslim community occurred in the context of anti-Muslim racist attacks, including stabbings and fire bombings of Muslim-owned establishments and prayer sites, much of the press and the political and intellectual establishment pictured the book burnings and other expressions of Muslim anger as a profoundly menacing attack on core British and indeed Western values. To them, it was the opening of nothing less than a culture war. Typical of this viewpoint was the novelist Martin Amis's statement that "the west confronts an irrationalist, ... theocratic/ideocratic system which is essentially and unappeasably opposed to its existence."[47]

Looking back reflectively some years later on the Rushdie affair, Bhikhu Parekh, the British intellectual most identified with the defense of multiculturalism, now a Labour member of the House of Lords, proposed a rather different understanding of the matter. He begins by recalling statements supportive of the fatwa made following its issuance by leaders of several British Muslim organizations. While he does not mitigate Khomeini's injunction to kill the author, he uses the affair to raise questions about free-expression absolutism and to illustrate the consequences of a failure to dialogue with a minority community about issues very important to it.

Rushdie, an Indian migrant, may have intended various characters' scurrilous references to Islam, Muhammad, and his wives merely as metaphorical vehicles for exploring the migrant experience, Parekh suggests. Nevertheless, he argues, they are subject to misinterpretation as willful and contemptuous lampoons of the prophet and his faith. Casual or unimaginative readers, he continues, could easily impute those views to the author himself. And that in fact is what happened, although Rushdie painted the characters in unflattering terms.

Should Rushdie be deemed at fault for that interpretation and the convulsions that followed? Parekh seems to think so. "[An author [who fantasizes] the history of momentous historical movements ... might end up treating recognizable men and women as ... manipulable [sic] material [and thus be] not just disrespectful and irreverent but supercilious and dismissive, a shade crude and even perhaps exhibitionist, scoring cheap points off half-real characters. If he seeks to explore religion, he runs the further risk of violating its integrity, even vulgarizing it, and outraging conventional norms of good taste. Religion is the realm of the sacred and the holy par excellence and arouses strong feelings of piety and reverence, which can be easily offended if subjected to the indelicate play of an undisciplined fantasy."[48] Putting the relevant passages in a dream sequence "does not diminish their offensiveness in the eyes of those who believe that such things should not be said at all, whether by a sane or a demented person and knowingly or in a dream."[49]

Having declared his own view of Rushdie's work, Parekh turns to that of the British Muslim communities. They found the work to be a "totally inaccurate account of Islam and [to] spread 'utter lies' about it" and therefore they "had a right to stand up for the honour of their faith and the integrity of their cultural heritage." The book was "'abusive,' 'insulting,' 'scurrilous,' 'vilificatory' in its treatment of men and women whom they considered holy and of whose sacred memories they were custodians. It discussed their religion in a most 'obscene', 'indecent,' 'filthy' and 'abominably foul' language, violated all norms of civilized discussion, and was guilty of . . . an insult to Muhammed, for Muslims an unforgiveable capital crime."[50] They did not object to a critique of the religion. What they objected to was "Rushdie's tone, attitude and language."

In addition, Muslim leaders declared that "the book had demeaned and degraded them in their own and especially others' eyes. It reinforced many of the traditional stereotypes . . . [and] it presented [Muslims] as barbarians following a fraudulent religion created by a cunning manipulator and devoid of a sound system of morality."[51]

Initially, according to Parekh's account,

> Muslim leaders were content to demand that the book should carry a note disclaiming its historical credentials and that the author should apologize. Later they asked that the book . . . be banned and existing copies removed from public libraries. If it could not be banned, they wanted it issued after removing the offending passages. They also demanded that in order to prevent the occurrence of such provocative books in the future, the existing UK anti-blasphemy law which protects Christianity should be extended to other religions, especially Islam.[52]

It was after government officials ignored the protests of community representatives that Bradford Muslims held their book-burning ceremony. That act did attract a powerful response from the media and the intellectual community, but not the one the community desired. On the contrary, it generated a torrent of denunciation.

Khomeini's fatwa produced a spiral of increasingly furious rhetoric on both sides. Even so liberal an intellectual as Roy Jenkins, an eminent political figure and author of a Race Relations Act designed to protect minorities from discrimination, worried publicly about the consequences of allowing a large Muslim community to form in the United Kingdom. The fatwa and the general response in the United Kingdom fed Muslim rage and a newfound sense of empowerment which damaged inter-communal relations and strengthened the hand of the most intolerant and rigidly orthodox members of the Muslim community.

"The Rushdie affair," Parekh concludes, "would most probably have been resolved peacefully if the *unproblematic* Muslim demand that the book should carry a note disavowing its historicity had been met, or if Rushdie had taken the kind of conciliatory approach he took a year later," after he required a twenty-four-hour armed guard, had to move furtively every few days from one residence to another, and saw publishers and translators attacked in various parts of the world and in one case killed.[53]

Instead of at least trying to understand the depth of the hurt experienced by British Muslims, Parekh writes, "conservative and liberal British writers argued that Muslims were opposed to free speech, whereas the latter were only asking why free speech should include untrue and deeply offensive remarks about religions and religious communities," why serious criticism of religious beliefs and practices could not be distinguished from "mocking, ridiculing and lampooning religious beliefs, practices and prophets."[54]

> If British Muslims had dissociated themselves from Khomeini's *fatwa* and shown some appreciation of the British commitment to free speech, they would have allayed some of the prevailing fears and perhaps encouraged a section of liberal opinion to view their demands with sympathy. Similarly, if the prominent spokes-men of British society had shown some understanding of the reasons for Muslim anger and distress and some sympathy for their cause and then gone on to show why on balance they considered the ban on *The Satanic Verses* unwise, they would have diffused the Muslim sense of isolation and even perhaps won over some of them to their point of view.[55]

Unfortunately, he continues, while "dialogue is the only morally acceptable way of settling controversial issues," in practice it is not always possible, in part because the majority is deaf to claims against practices the majority takes for granted or regards as untrue beyond reasonable dispute. When dialogue is not initially possible, then the minority may legitimately engage in vigorous protest with the end of conveying its feelings and making the indisputable disputable. Protest would be less necessary if we could find "new institutional forums where representatives of the various com-munities can meet regularly to explore contentious issues, acquire a better under-standing of each other's ways of thinking and living, and hopefully arrive at a consensus on what issues are at stake and what arguments and considerations are relevant to their resolution which can then be fed into a wider public debate."[56]

Before entering the House of Lords, Parekh had chaired the quasi-official Com-mission on the Future of Multi-Ethnic Britain. In 2000 its very respectable mem-bership had issued a report, generally assumed to have been authored in large part by Parekh; the report strongly supported public adoption of a multicultural perspective on living in what as a matter of fact had become a culturally and ethnically diverse society. The Report was one of the many straws in the wind on both sides of the Atlantic Ocean appearing to herald a loss of hegemonic status for the cultural norms, practices, and historical narratives of the long-settled white majority in Western societies.

No doubt it was the sight of those straws together with personal preference that led the Canadian advocate of multiculturalism Will Kymlicka to claim a few years ago that the war is over and multiculturalists have won.[57] Not long thereafter, Brian Barry, an Oxford don and political theorist with an appetite for battle, demonstrated in his caustic polemic *Culture and Equality* that, despite Kymlicka's claim to the contrary, peace had not broken out.[58] With evident glee, Barry tore into what he saw as the misbegotten and dangerous premises and policy implications of the main theorists of multiculturalism, in particular Parekh and also Chandran Kukathas, another important scholar with South Asian roots.

"[T]he driving force behind much multicultural theory," Barry claims, are "cultural relativism and an overculturalized conception of human beings."[59] By the latter he means the view that the particular cultural context which people inherit at birth shapes and is integral to their sense of who they are (in other words their "identity") and the moral character of their beliefs and actions. Both of these features of multiculturalism are "philosophically unsound ... and [imply or undergird] policy recommendations which are, on balance, more likely to do harm than good, especially to the most vulnerable members of those minority cultures that are intended to be [their] primary beneficiaries."[60] Kwame Anthony Appiah, another distinguished political theorist, makes much the same point when he writes that "it is far from clear that we can always honor ... [cultural] preservationist claims while respecting the autonomy of future individuals." Invoking the case of migrant-background traditionalists from India and Pakistan wishing to impose arranged marriages on their daughters, he argues that the "ethical principles of equal dignity that underlie liberal thinking" seem to militate against toleration of this traditional social arrangement. Consistent with their convictions liberals must "care about the autonomy of these young women."[61]

Central to the "liberal egalitarianism" which Barry champions are two claims which he sees stemming from the Enlightenment and which he believes most multiculturalists reject. The first is that "there are universal criteria for judging societies and polities which can be arrived at by a process of general reasoning and are valid for all societies regardless of the actual beliefs and norms of the people who live in them." The second is that citizens ought to be seen as "related to the state in an identical manner, enjoying equal status and possessing identical rights and obligations." This contrasts with "premodern polities which were embedded in and composed of such communities as castes, clans, tribes and ethnic groups."[62] These two claims rest, however, on the bedrock I have previously described in clarifying my own perspective, namely, the view of the moral equality of human beings and their consequent right to be treated with dignity and fairness and to enjoy a broad autonomy to shape their lives according to their respective conceptions of what constitutes a fulfilling life.

From Barry's perspective, multiculturalism provides a rationale for allowing dominant members of illiberal minorities to limit the autonomy of weaker members, primarily women and children, but also those members who question the group's legacy norms and structures, namely, "heretics." The rationale is "tolerance of difference" or "equal respect." For Barry, respect is owed to individuals not to groups.

At the same time, however, Barry locates himself in the middle of what he sees as a continuum of views about what liberal governments should do when confronted with illiberal minorities in their midst. Some liberals, he notes, urge employing state power against illiberal practices of voluntary associations such as religious groups. Those liberals would, for instance, apply anti-discrimination laws to religious organizations which deny women access to privileged positions such as the priesthood in the Catholic Church.

The state, in Barry's view, should not interfere in the practices of voluntary organizations precisely because they are expressions of the right of free association and members are at liberty to leave the organization if they object to its practices. Where the state can and should intervene is where the organization's members engage with the general public by selling goods and services but discriminate among purchasers on the basis of prejudices native to their faith. A recent example would be the Colorado baker who, allegedly because of his religious opposition to gay marriage, refused to concoct and sell a wedding cake to a gay couple.[63] In addition, members of the organization are subject to the state's laws protecting the life, liberty, and physical integrity of all persons within its jurisdiction. So, of course, members cannot threaten heretics or apostates with physical violence or authorize husbands to force themselves sexually on unwilling wives. Nor can they subject children to cruel initiation rites and punishments.

In light of Barry's views about the limits of state intervention, how great, really, is the gap between the principles and policies he advocates and those of intellectual adversaries like Parekh and Kukathas, who also locate themselves within the liberal camp? Perhaps a helpful preliminary question is whether their claim to be in the camp is persuasive.

I think the correct answer is "yes." After all, as I already noted, Parekh and Kukathas both employ the liberal values of equal respect, equal opportunity, tolerance of diversity, and individual choice, to defend multiculturalists. Second, both invoke human rights to set limits to the autonomy of illiberal groups. Kukathas emphasizes protection of the right to exit the illiberal community. Presumably, he would not allow community leaders to enforce their values through gross physical coercion, although I am not clear on his stance toward a husband's claimed sexual prerogatives or right to enforce his will in the family through beating its other members. Perhaps he believes the option of exit will largely constrain such practices. It will not, however, protect boys from ritual scarring or girls from the removal of the clitoris and labia.

Parekh, if I read him correctly, would support state intervention to protect baseline rights of adults and children. But he regards state action as a last resort after the resources of dialogue between the state representing majority sentiment and representatives of the minority have been exhausted. For Parekh, the principal of equal respect requires dialogue before diktat.[64] The majority, in his view, should attempt persuasion before it resorts to force, and in its efforts to persuade it should reference deep values of the minority which could be construed against the practice the majority deems intolerable.

To illustrate the desirable method of intercultural dialogue, Parekh cites as an analogy the way in which supporters of abortion could dialogue with hardline Catholic opponents. Rather than debating whether personhood begins with conception, a pro-choice advocate could note that Catholic theology justifies killing in the context of "just wars." So why not consider the possibility of "just abortions"?[65] Then the argument would shift to the conditions of justness.

While the pro-life interlocutor may in the end reject the analogy and refuse to accept any conditions as justifying abortion, at least by shifting into an idiom familiar to the pro-life advocate, the champion of choice has signaled an understanding of where her opponent is "coming from" and has implied respect for that place. So while the advocates may in the end continue to disagree, they may now be able to do so in tones of mutual respect. At a minimum, therefore, the majority should explain why the disputed practice in its current form cannot be reconciled with the values and interests of the state and be open to exploring modifications of the practice which could achieve reconciliation.

The abortion-debate example also illustrates another of Parekh's point of emphasis, which happens to be compatible with Barry's, namely, that even within a culture, in this case Western culture, there can be passionate differences about norms. Many conservative members of Western societies, he notes, do not share the value of equality, just as not all Asians would rate social harmony and order above individual autonomy. Moreover, norms can change, since culture is not frozen. Today, with cultural interaction being unavoidable, the consequent mingling of cultures stimulates cultural evolution, possibly resulting among other things in mutual adaptation through compromise or newly evolved understandings.[66] This is much less likely to occur, however, if the culture with superior secular power displays contempt for the norms and practices of the other. Contempt will drive the weaker community into a fierce protectionist stance.

So where, exactly, do Barry and mainstream multiculturalists like Kukathas and Parekh part company? Not, as Barry seems to think, on the question of whether cultures in their entirety can be invidiously compared. Parekh, as I read him, is not a pure cultural relativist. He writes: "[D]ifferent cultures represent different systems of meaning and visions of the good life. *[This does not mean] that cultures cannot be compared and judged, that they are equally rich and deserve equal respect, that each of them is good for its members, or that all cultural differences deserve to be valued."*[67] That said, he urges his readers to recognize that all cultures have some intrinsic value since all respond to human needs in ways shaped by the particular human and physical ecology in which each evolved.[68] Cultures which do not emphasize individual autonomy may respond effectively to other human needs, such as a sense of having a secure and dignified place in the arms of a harmonious, well-ordered community with the affect of an extended patriarchal family.[69]

Where Barry most clearly distinguishes his brand of liberalism is in his view of culture. The multiculturalists, in his view, fail to appreciate culture's fluidity. In part because of that failure, they impute to culture a more central and fixed role in individual identity than it actually possesses. What he means, I think, is that multiculturalists mistakenly see culture as it impacts individuals in excessively organic terms, as if each norm or practice is like a loose thread in a sweater which, if pulled, could possibly unravel the entire garment. If this were so, then in the case of conservative Muslims, a ban on the full-face covering would threaten their core identity. In reality, Barry seems to be saying, *a thick identity is only loosely connected to the many practices associated with it* which may have evolved and been responsive to conditions in a different place and time. It follows that people whose observance of legacy practices varies widely – one goes to mosque every day and is abstemious, the other rarely attends and drinks alcohol copiously – may nevertheless identify as Muslims with equal fervor.

Nothing Parekh has written tells me he would disagree. He would, however, argue (in a jiu-jitsu–like intellectual move) that the very strength of the minority identity makes manifestations of respect for it by the majority essential for social peace. Whatever their level of commitment to particular practices, members of the minority will feel individually assaulted when the majority imperiously outlaws any of them rather than searching for compromise through mutually respectful dialogue.

To be sure, that is not all there is to Parekh's position. Social harmony is only one strand of his argument. As a liberal he is more concerned with individual well-being and autonomy than with social policy. Parekh worries as Barry apparently does not about the psychologically disintegrating effect of rapid erosion of a group's norms and practices and the trauma of being forced to choose between non-compliance with the majority's cultural norms and full access to the main society's opportunity structure. If they feel that they do not enjoy equal opportunities and if they feel that the group with which they identify if only by dint of the circumstances of their birth is deemed substandard by the nation's arbiters of respect, members of the minority will have diminished chances to live the flourishing lives liberalism is intended to nourish.

Barry's response to Parekh's claims would, I assume, take the following form. First, he would argue that Parekh exaggerates the consequences of the majority's refusal to countenance one or another of a minority's inherited practices as distinguished from the core norms and narrative of its faith. Second, among the practices a liberal society will not happily tolerate are precisely those, like female genital mutilation or a male's control of family property and possession of unconsented sexual access to his wife, which deprive half the minority of freedom and a fulfilling life. Finally, he would argue that whatever their effect, core norms and practices of the culturally liberal majority like freedom of speech cannot, consistent with commitment to the liberal faith, be sacrificed to the cause of avoiding insult to minority sensibilities.

Writing on the other side of the Atlantic, the Yale-based scholar Benhabib makes much the same point but in a softer tone:

> It matters a great deal whether we defend culturalist demands because we want to *preserve* minority cultures within the liberal-democratic state or because we want to *expand* the circle of democratic inclusion. Unlike the multiculturalist, the demo-cratic theorist accepts that the political incorporation of new groups into established societies will result more likely in the hybridization of cultural legacies on both sides. Modern individuals may choose to continue to subvert their cultural trad-itions; equally, immigrants may be incorporated into the majority culture through processes of *boundary crossing, boundary blurring, or boundary shifting* between dominant and minority cultures. [But] *if one must choose, I value the expansion of democratic inclusion and equality over the preservation of cultural distinctiveness.*[70]

It is particularly in the area of speech that the difference in perspective between Parekh's multiculturalism and Barry's "egalitarian liberalism" leads indisputably to differences in recommended policies. Salman Rushdie's controversial book is, in Barry's view, exemplary of the type of case where liberals must take a stand against appeals for censorship of expression that offends cultural minorities. For Barry and like-minded liberals, the state must protect expression, however offensive, except where it advocates violence.

For Parekh, by contrast, the Rushdie affair leads him to the concept of "group libel," that is, to willfully disparaging remarks about racial, religious, and ethnic groups reinforced by what today on university campuses are labeled "micro-aggres-sions," or "disparaging and offensive remarks, each individually perhaps good-humored and tolerable but all collectively contributing to the dehumanization or demonization of the relevant groups."[71] In the generality of cases, Parekh argues, "organized disapproval by enlightened public opinion, social or economic sanctions against [guilty] individuals and organizations . . . and a declarative and non-punitive law" would be sufficient means for preventing or sanctioning group libel. However, where these measures "do not seem enough and the situation requires urgent action," the "blunt" instrument of punitive action by the state may be required. While "free speech is one of the highest values . . . it is not . . . inviolable" and the traditional defense of it is unsatisfactory:

Its champions tend to consider the question largely from the standpoint of men of ideas, and assume that what is good for them is necessarily good for society as a whole. This is not only philosophically suspect but unlikely to carry conviction in a democratic society whose members might legitimately ask why they should put up with "iconoclastic attacks" by "exhibitionist" intellectuals taking "perverse pride" in knocking established values, as a Catholic Bishop put it at the height of the Rushdie controversy.[72]

Free speech, he concludes,

is not the only great value and needs to be balanced against such others as avoidance of needless hurt, social harmony, humane culture, protection of the weak, truthfulness in the public realm, and self-respect and dignity of individuals and groups. There is no "true" way of reconciling them; it all depends on the history, traditions, political circumstances, and so on of a society. In a country with a long history of inter-ethnic violence, or in which some groups are systematically humiliated or in which religion means a great deal to its members, free speech would be rightly subject to greater constraints than elsewhere.[73]

Given all of the proposed factors to weigh against criticism of a group's beliefs, icons, and practices, particularly if criticism assumes imaginative literary form, including satire, the constraints Parekh's proposed tests would impose on the scholar – much less the creative writer – are onerous. Parekh says that multiculturalism is a perspective not an ideology.[74] After reading Parekh's discussion of the Rushdie affair it is easy to understand why a more traditional liberal like Barry sees an imposing chasm between his perspective on the good society and that of the multiculturalist. But does this conflict in feeling and sentiment and worldview preclude some common ground in the concrete realm of public policy for diverse communities in liberal democratic states? It is to that question which I now turn.

RECONCILING CULTURAL DIVERSITY WITH THE NORMS OF THE LIBERAL DEMOCRATIC STATE

How should European democracies respond to the cultural self-defense claims of traditionalists within the migrant minority community? On the one hand, liberals cannot consistent with their identity countenance violent enforcement of cultural norms or tolerate discrimination on the basis of race, ethnicity, or piety in the provision of goods and services to the general public. They are necessarily committed as well to the protection of children from cruel practices. On the other hand, following the distinction drawn by Brian Barry, they could (although not all of us necessarily would) concede the freedom of illiberal persons to perpetuate their illiberal beliefs and practices whether through indoctrination within the domain of the family or through educational and other private associations and institutions they form to that end.

Certain minority-community claims are entirely compatible with liberal values. Some, above all the demand for equal treatment by the public authorities and equal opportunity to compete for all the good things on offer in society, are intrinsic to the liberal project. Claims for what sounds like special treatment can be more problematic, are indeed certain to be more problematic when they are made on behalf of recent waves of migrants arriving at a time of slowing growth and increasing unemployment and differing in color and/or religion and cultural style from the bulk of the native population.*

Even so fervent a liberal opponent of multiculturalism as Brian Barry is inclined to give a *laissez passer* to the Sikh motorcycle enthusiast who wants to ride with only a turban on his head. In this he is at one with what is normally an institutional champion of uniformity, namely, the United States Army, which recently agreed that a Sikh graduate of the US Military Academy at West Point can wear a small turban as long as it can fit under his helmet when he needs to wear one.[75]

One way of addressing claims for exemption from norms of general applicability is through recourse to the Covenant criteria for limiting the rights it enumerates. The state can limit the exercise of most rights† when their exercise dangerously inhibits the state from protecting national security, public order, public health, fundamental moral norms, and human rights themselves. Applying the criteria requires some sort of balancing test since it will always be possible to argue that an exemption (or other category of claim for special treatment) has some impact, however remote, on national security, public order, public health and morals, or the rights of others. The balance is between, on the one hand, the threat the minority claim poses for the public interest or individual rights and, on the other, the importance to the

---

* Kymlicka insists on distinguishing the claims of minorities from those of what he calls "captive nations" like First Peoples in Canada, Native Americans in the United States, and the French-speaking population of Quebec. Unlike migrants, these are not people who have chosen to enter countries where their inherited cultural norms are alien. Having settled earlier than the persons who constitute the present cultural majority, they have had minority status thrust upon them. Their claims, therefore, are more akin to positions adopted in negotiations between two states reconsidering the terms of their federation. Within Canada, for instance, Quebec can be seen as an entity similar to a nation, a nation captured by the fortunes of eighteenth-century colonial wars, not as the place of a minority who chose to live in a country dominated by Anglo-Scottish culture. While French-speakers are a minority in Canada as a whole, in the Province of Quebec, where they form a large plurality if not an absolute majority of the population, they have won the right to insist that new migrants attend schools teaching primarily in the French language and that no commercial signage be in English only. Looked at historically, then, the Provincial majority's "privileges" do not even fall into the category of successful minority claims; rather, they are the outcome of negotiations between two nations and a condition of continued coexistence of those nations within a single state. Aside from language, moreover, relative to most differences between majorities and minorities the difference between the French minority and the English-speaking majority culture is a nuance. Both cultures are liberal.
† With a very few exceptions, notably the rights to life, humane treatment, due process, and non-discrimination.

minority's cultural identity of the interest it is trying to protect. In the above case, it appears that the turban is for Sikhs an important feature of their cultural heritage.

To be frank, for purposes of lighting the way to consistent good faith judgments, the word "important" is a very low-watt bulb. And a condition precedent to its use is deciding whose view should prevail: high-profile figures with a credible claim to speak for the minority or outside experts on the minority's culture? Moreover, if you decide that the minority's view should be decisive, you have to resolve the previously discussed question of to whom in the minority you turn in order to discover its view.

There is no single obvious answer to that set of questions. We can ask no more of officials, legislators, and courts than that they recognize the questions and try to answer them in good faith knowing that the answers will not always be consistent, because the answer in any given case will be shaped by some unpredictable mix of empiricism, reason, intuition, and personal inclination. However, certain procedural rules, consistently employed, could provide a measure of coherence to answers in particular cases.

The essential procedures are twofold. In trying to assess the salience of the relevant practice for members of the minority, official rule-makers and appliers should consult as many minority voices as is feasible along with scholars who have closely studied the minority and may therefore provide, among other things, help in identifying a diversity of voices within the minority where they exist. On the issue of salience, the burden of persuasion should lie with the community seeking an exception. Conversely, on the question of whether recognizing an exemption to a rule of general application would significantly compromise the public interest or individual rights, the burden should rest on the champions of uniformity.

This symmetrical division of burdens should enhance the appearance as well as the reality of fairness. Where officials, judges, or legislators conclude that a practice is salient but a threat to individual rights or the public interest, before overriding the practice they should see if a compromise protective of the public interest or individual rights can be negotiated. When the Sikh graduate of West Point proposed wearing an unusually small turban which could fit under his helmet, the US military decided this was tolerable. Some Somali migrants in the United States have agreed to accept as an alternative to the removal of the clitoris and labia a small cut performed by a doctor which draws blood but is no more traumatic and indeed probably less so than male circumcision.[76]

While there will doubtless be cases where reasonable people can disagree about the proper balance, others will remind us, as Dr. Johnson is once supposed to have observed, that the fact of twilight does not obscure the difference between day and night. The case of the Sikh Harley-enthusiast falls in the day and night category. To be sure, in the event of an accident, a turban-wearing Sikh motorcyclist is somewhat more likely than a helmet-wearer to leave a part of his brain smeared on the pavement. Should he nevertheless survive, the cost of the Sikh's long-term care may be greater than if he had worn a helmet. Nevertheless, the number of cases in relation to the entire population likely to satisfy the conditions needed to produce the marginal cost is certain to be trivial. Moreover, it is doubtful that an advocate of uniformity could persuasively challenge the exemption for Sikhs on the grounds that it would threaten public health by provoking widespread non-compliance with the helmet ordinance by non-Sikh riders with a passion for soft caps or a head altogether naked. Some arguments don't pass the laugh test.

More in the twilight realm is a hypothetical request for exemption from a law requiring all parents to enroll their children in public preschool programs intended primarily to facilitate economic and social integration of migrant-community children and to enhance their life chances. Muslim parents who adhere to Wahhabi doctrine, a fundamentalist variety of Islam emanating originally from the interior of the Arabian Peninsula, might object sincerely on the grounds both that their religious beliefs prohibit non-essential interaction with non-Muslims and that the preschool curriculum and social mixing will have the long-term effect of encouraging their children to deviate from Wahhabist convictions and practices, thus becoming apostates.

Dedicated multiculturalists like Kukathas would presumably urge exemption not only on general multicultural grounds but also on grounds that Article 18 of the Covenant can be read to guarantee parents the right to educate their children as they see fit. Applying my balancing test, I would reject the exemption on the grounds that social and economic integration are related and have proven difficult to achieve with certain groups, and that the failure of integration represents a serious threat to national security and public order. In addition, given the demonstrable effect of family income and culture on educational outcomes, preschool programs are the only practical way of mitigating the growing tendency of socioeconomic hierarchies to reproduce themselves.[77] So I would argue that the Covenant language should not be construed in a way which allows parents to reduce sharply the life chances of their children. Furthermore, the Covenant needs to be read in light of the subsequent Convention on the Rights of the Child which in its general tenor and its particulars thrusts against the view that the child is little more than a bottle into which parents can without restraint pour their preferences.

For an additional reason, one appealing only to advocates for human rights, I would also balance against exemptions from a law that made schooling compulsory for boys and girls until the late teens or at least the completion of secondary education. Kukathas ought to agree, because he supports the right to exit a cultural community. Destitution is the destiny of the minimally educated person in today's world, especially those who leave a tightly bound ethnic or religious community. Allowing parents to truncate their children's education practically empties the right to exit of practical meaning.

The national security and public order interests of the liberal state arguably justify forbidding private schools altogether in favor of state schools integrating students from different classes and cultures. Still, up to this point no liberal democratic state has prohibited private schools. The moral and legal authority of the liberal state to use compulsory education as a means of pushing migrant children to assimilate culturally whether by banning private schools or imposing on them a curriculum largely indistinguishable from that of the public schools and insisting that it be delivered exclusively in the majority's language is controversial. An almost century-old decision of the United States Supreme Court casts some light on this issue, although its age and the distinctiveness of the political culture of the United States raises some question about its contemporary relevance for Europe. In *Meyer v. Nebraska*,[78] the Court declared unconstitutional a law adopted by the state of Nebraska in the wake of World War I which forbid any teaching in a foreign language in private as well as public schools. World War I–related antipathy to the state's German migrants plainly inspired the law.

While the facts of the case make its outcome seem irrelevant to the question of whether the state, in pursuit of the rapid integration of migrants, may forbid private schooling, the majority opinion could be construed to point in that direction. Writing for the majority, the very conservative and notoriously anti-Semitic Justice McReynolds declared:

> That the state may do much, go very far, indeed, in order to improve the quality of its citizens, physically, mentally and morally, is clear; but the individual has certain fundamental rights which must be respected. The protection of the Constitution extends to all, to those who speak other languages as well as to those born with English on the tongue. Perhaps it would be highly advantageous if all had ready understanding of our ordinary speech, but this cannot be coerced by methods which conflict with the Constitution – a desirable end cannot be promoted by prohibited means.[79]

But Justice McReynolds went on to acknowledge that wartime circumstances might justify a different outcome. Nebraska had not demonstrated sufficient need "in time of peace and domestic tranquility" to justify the "infringement of rights long freely enjoyed."

One could hardly describe the present moment in the West as a "time of peace and domestic tranquility." Moreover, Oliver Wendell Holmes, still one of the most widely admired Supreme Court Justices, dissented on the grounds that in areas of Nebraska with sizable German immigrant communities, children might hear only a foreign language spoken at home, so in demanding instruction in English, the state was pursuing a reasonable objective by means that were not clearly arbitrary.[80] While I do not yet see any movement in this direction, new and still more deadly acts of terror in Western streets will open paths hitherto blocked. Integration through compulsory public schooling is one of the least morbid directions in which trauma-tized Western publics might move. If governments were to move in that direction, they could still evince respect for minority cultures by making minority language training available within the public-school curriculum.

For the moment, the widely operative compromise, its details varying from place to place, has governments setting minimum curriculum requirements for private schools. If committed multiculturalists set the limits of government curriculum review, presumably the standards would be designed to ensure nothing more than literacy and numeracy sufficient to permit graduates a chance of economic survival. Whether they would uniformly insist that literacy be in the national as well as the immigrant family's original language is unclear to me. What they would not require, presumably, is course content challenging tenets of the migrant community's canons of belief about religion, history, the family, gender relations, ethics, honor, and civic obligations.

Would European multiculturalists follow the precedent set by some American states and allow Muslim or, for that matter, Christian private schools to present evolution as merely a theory in competition with the theory of intelligent design? Would they allow them to go further and teach Genesis as a factual account of the origins of the human species? Allowing it would seem consistent with the archipelago paradigm for intercultural relations. After all, for millions of people biblical narratives are not metaphors or parables; they are literal truth. Allowing Genesis to be taught as such would not threaten public morals, order, or health other than possibly limiting the number of potential scientists. Would it violate human rights? Only if one concluded that a stunted scientific education *unreasonably* limits the life chances of minority children. Since many Christians from fundamentalist denominations which read the Bible literally have prospered in politics, business, and religious entrepreneurship, the "stunting" argument would not seem to carry much weight.

Where the curricula of minority-run private schools *should* become a matter of public concern is where they inculcate hatred of persons and groups outside the cultural community. An apparent majority of foreign policy and counter-terrorism experts see a connection – not one-to-one but nevertheless a connection – between the spread of Saudi-funded schools teaching Wahhabi doctrine and the multiplication of terrorist groups spreading mayhem in Pakistan, Bangladesh, Afghanistan, Indonesia, and the Arab world.[81] If they are correct about this connection, the West has persuasive grounds for refusing to license (much less to assist in funding, however indirectly) schools in which students are encouraged to avoid cooperating with members of other faiths, including other Islamic believers.

While declaring a right to free speech, not only does the Covenant make it subject to the usual qualifications; in addition, it imposes on states a positive obligation to prohibit "any advocacy of national, racial or religious hatred that constitutes incitement to discrimination, hostility or violence." Most European states have adopted legislation supposedly reflecting that obligation. France goes so far as to treat Holocaust denial as a form of hate speech, a measure that would be plainly unconstitutional in the United States, where a long line of Supreme Court decisions protects even the vilest expressions of racial and religious animosity and homophobia unless this speech urges the use of violence against their targets.

Up to a point, equal-treatment liberals like Bryan Barry and strong multiculturalists like Kukathas and Parekh would presumably agree on state assistance. Translators in criminal trials where the defendant cannot speak the national language are needed for due process. Equality of treatment also requires their availability for civil trials and for interactions with officials of the executive branch dispensing social benefits, licenses, and other public goods.

Arguably, minorities need assistance in preserving their legacy language, a central feature of most distinctive cultures. With the majority language regnant in the main organs of cultural reproduction – the media, the workplace, and the schools – and the key to social and economic opportunity, children are incentivized to use it at home as well. Moreover, children spend most of their waking hours either outside the home or watching television and their mobile phone or doing homework, while migrant parents need to spend most of theirs struggling for economic survival, particularly in a country like the United States where social benefits are closely tied to employment. Therefore, some migrant parents, anxious to preserve this element of their family's tradition, may want to have their children educated at least partially in their native language.

Bilingual programming in US public schools has proven to be more a technocratic than an ethical issue. The pressures of a laissez-faire economic system slightly leavened with exiguous public welfare programs drives migrant parents toward vehicles for the economic and social integration of their children in a harshly competitive environment. For them, bilingual education is a good thing only if it is in fact the most efficient means of positioning their children for academic success. Experts, like migrant families themselves, are divided over whether parallel classes are the most efficient means for transitioning migrants into the national-language stream.[82]

It is with respect to prayer spaces and prayer leaders that European Muslims are most in need of state assistance. While Wahhabis declare *collective* prayer to be an obligation of the faithful, mainstream Sunni doctrine does not censure individual prayer, a position consistent with the absence of clerical hierarchy in Sunni Islam. So it has been possible for a nomad wandering alone with his camels or a peasant laboring on his little plot of land to lay down a prayer rug, face Mecca, and demonstrate his piety in the sight of Allah. Still, where it is feasible, collective prayer in mosques at the call of imams is the cultural norm.

European Muslims have encountered various obstacles even in establishing appropriate prayer spaces, much less in building mosques. They are relatively late arrivals in the already congested urban spaces of countries which as a group began losing their postwar economic momentum four decades ago and like the Midwestern United States have been confronting the crisis of deindustrialization. Clustered for the most part in declining parts of the European economy, relatively deficient in the language and stylistic skills prized by the affluent sectors of the growing service sector, confronted by ethnic and religious discrimination, thus experiencing high rates of un- and under-employment, European Muslims as a group must strain to accumulate the capital required for mosque construction and maintenance sufficient to meet their needs comfortably. Moreover, at the local level where land use is generally regulated, they often face hostile officials and electorates whose enmity inhibits mosque construction even where the communities have the required capital.[83]

The Christian majority has had more than a millennium to build houses of worship and now has more than enough to accommodate a shrinking number of the actively faithful. In countries with state churches, public funds help to maintain them. In Germany, the state collects a religious tax from persons who identify with the Catholic and Protestant Churches and delivers it to their official representatives. Here again the relatively unstructured character of Islam and the variety of groups, beliefs, and practices existing under its broad umbrella complicate any effort states might undertake to assist in the provision of prayer spaces, other than overriding acts of local authorities who are arbitrarily hindering the development of mosques.

Another area where Muslim minorities seem to need "assistance to do those things the majority can do unassisted" is acquiring sufficient numbers of prayer leaders, particularly leaders who can help them navigate psychologically in an alien cultural setting. As Muslim immigrant communities expanded in the postwar decades, European states welcomed efforts by Saudi Arabia and the countries from which migrants came, primarily Turkey, Algeria, and Morocco, to staff such mosques as there were with prayer leaders selected and paid by them. Since very few of these imams were familiar with the language or the laws and practices of the countries to which they were sent, they were ill-prepared to help the faithful in negotiating the tensions between religious norms and traditional practices and the norms and practices of the secular capitalist, Christian-majority states to which economic incentives had driven them.

European governments were in general content to let Muslims look after themselves even after it became evident, as wives arrived and children multiplied, that most guest workers had no intention of going home. Authorities left mosque building and staffing in the hands of foreign states. Their satisfaction with this arrangement only began to dissolve when they began to apprehend an evolving jihadi subculture in some Muslim communities.

Violence-preaching Islamists operating from bases in Muslim-majority countries started using the internet to reach young men and women with an at least latent Muslim identity. They helped give political focus to the generalized angst of adolescence, the search for meaning and direction common to young men, and the special alienation of young Muslims with grim prospects at the bottom of socio-economic food chains. Along with the internet radicals urging violent struggle, there were local imams fertilizing the soil for violence by promoting a Manichaean world view in which there was little or no space for cooperation, much less friendly intercourse with, non-Muslims.

In light of their epiphany, governments began to appreciate the utility of developing an indigenous cadre of licensed teachers, prayer leaders, and theologians who, hopefully, could counter radical messaging. But this in turn required first the creation from scratch of an infrastructure of theological faculties and pastoral licensing like the Christian one which had been in place for centuries. In addition, governments would need to attract into that infrastructure able and educated young men who did not hold polarizing views.

Accepting prayer leaders from Muslim-majority countries has not so far been a problem in *all* cases. One striking feature of the terrorist networks uncovered in Europe has been the relative absence of Turkish participants. Causality as distinguished from coincidence is invariably hard to prove, but there is a logic behind the apparent difference between Turkish and other Muslim communities in this respect.

Migrants from North Africa do not in general seem to identify as strongly with their nation of origin as do those from Turkey. That is hardly surprising. Moroccans come in significant numbers from the long-neglected mountainous Berber region which has a history of latent or actual rebellion from the dominant Arab-speakers nearer the coast. Not all Algerians are likely to identify closely with a country ruled opaquely by a military-civilian elite which in 1994 blocked Islamist parties from political power following a contested election and then waged an extraordinarily barbaric counter-insurgency campaign against the succeeding no-holds-barred Islamist rebellion. Tunisians come from a small country of broad and deep poverty somewhat disguised by per capita income numbers and governed for decades before the Arab Spring by a corrupt secular authoritarian elite with close ties to the French government. It has generated per capita the largest number of ISIS recruits in the Arab world.

Turkey, by contrast, is a large country founded by a secular nationalist, Kemal Ataturk, who led the successful military resistance to post–World War I European attempts to divide and dominate Anatolian space. His heirs sturdily maintained Turkish political independence and territorial integrity through the long years of the Cold War in association with Western countries within the North Atlantic Treaty Organization (NATO). Now it is a regional power in which a party associated with Islam has governed for almost two decades of economic vitality. It is also a country which Turkish speakers can look to with feelings of pride and that may make them less susceptible to a virulently anti-Western pan-Islamic rather than nationalist identity. In addition, Turkey under both secular and Islamic-party governance has sent prayer-leaders to sustain the moderate version of Islam indigenous to Turkey. Up to now,[‡] they have not sought to reproduce in the contemporary world norms and practices modeled after life in seventh-century Arabia or to portray a Manichean division of the world into the faithful followers of the true Islam and dangerous and morally worthless infidels.

So, in this one case Europe may have benefited from the reception of non-European imams. Even if Turkey continues to service Turkish-origin Muslims, European governments have strong incentives to assist other Muslim communities in developing an educational infrastructure which will yield European imams better equipped to help Muslims navigate confidently through everyday life. Those imams will presumably tend to interpret the Qur'an and the sayings and practices of the Prophet in ways that foster cooperation with fellow citizens and respect for the law. It is, however, unlikely that new Europe-based Muslim theological faculties any more than the long-established Catholic ones will develop interpretations of the faith entirely compatible with liberal preferences.

To this point I have been speaking in general terms about the range of responses available to West European states for addressing the indisputable fact of cultural diversity stemming primarily from post–World War II migration. In Part II, I turn to the actual practices of exemplary states and their apparent results to date.

[‡] Where the country's increasingly authoritarian Islamist government will take it remains to be seen.

Exemplary National Experiences

PART II

Exemplar National Experiences

4

Nordic States

Sweden, Norway, and Denmark

Writing in 2006, the conservative journalist Christopher Caldwell heralded a dystopian future for Sweden.[1] He began his article by recalling a recent visit to the Bergsjon public housing project located five miles from the center of Gothenburg, Sweden's second largest city. Built originally to accommodate mostly Swedish workers in the city's then booming factories and shipyards, by 1996, Caldwell writes,

> it is inhabited mostly by immigrants ... Seventy percent of the residents were either born abroad or have parents who were. The same goes for 93 percent of the schoolchildren. You see Somali women walking the paths in hijabs and long wraps.... Forty percent of the families are on outright welfare, and many of the rest are on various equivalents of welfare that bear different names. Far below half the population is employed. There are reports of a rise in recruitment to criminal gangs – and to radical Islamic groups, too.... There are places like Bergsjon ringing the major cities across Sweden. They are all terra incognita to the vast majority of native Swedes.[2]

Sweden is considered by many to be one of the West's most successful societies. If we measure success by robust per capita income distributed more equally than in most advanced capitalist countries, low rates of crime and incarceration, high standards of education and health, ardent respect for human rights, and popular confidence in the country's political institutions, then the general impression is correct. In the form (possibly the spirit) of fair-minded journalism, Caldwell concedes that the public spaces are clean and that a native Swedish administrator, a woman who has worked in the development for a quarter-century, "says she has never ... felt insecure there," but he nevertheless concludes that "clearly, various experiments close to the heart of Swedish democracy and Swedish socialism have gone wrong.... A sobering realization is beginning to spread that the Swedish system cannot be easily adapted to a society in which a seventh of the working-age population is foreign-born." The principal experiment he has in mind is the country's "cradle-to-grave welfare state."[3] About half of the foreign-born, he fails to mention, come from member states of the European Union.[4]

Caldwell notes that in Sweden, as in other parts of Western Europe, immigration began as a guest worker program driven by the need for labor in the post–World War II economic expansion. This stage of postwar development came earliest in Sweden, which as a nominally neutral country had emerged from the war with an unscathed infrastructure and industrial base. The guest workers came first from Italy and Hungary, then from Yugoslavia and Turkey. Most of them surprised their hosts by staying. This first wave, according to Caldwell, "has been a success by any economic or cultural criterion you would care to use."[5]

When the boom stopped in the early 1970s, the government imposed restraints on workforce immigration, restraints which survive to this day. What remained as open doors for migration were political asylum and family reunification. The first entrants after the new restrictions on labor migration were Chileans fleeing the Pinochet dictatorship in the wake of the US-backed coup d'etat of 1973. They were the successors to the Greeks who had come in the 1960s to escape another thuggish right-wing, US-backed military regime. After them came Kurds fleeing persecution in various Middle Eastern countries, then Somalis and Bosnians escaping murderous internal conflicts in the 1990s, and, most recently, Iraqis, Syrians, and Afghanis. All of these groups were almost exclusively Muslim in their religious identity, like the Turkish workers who had preceded them. Of course, as in other European countries, these Muslims differed among themselves in the precise character and the strength of their Islamic identity.

While noting problems of physical isolation and discrimination, it is this Muslim identity, Caldwell implies, which is threatening Swedish society. After citing a report that non-Swedish citizens make up 26 percent of Swedish prison inmates and constitute about half of inmates incarcerated for serious crimes like murder, rape, and major drug dealing (figures, he adds, which "exclude the foreign-born who have become Swedes"), he states that "the association of crime and immigration is not a figment of the Swedish imagination."[6] From crime in general he slips immediately to terrorism, writing that "last summer, the left-leaning tabloid Aftonbladet *revealed* [my emphasis] that a number of Muslim extremist groups were recruiting in prisons":

> It is where crime interacts with the world of Sweden's hundreds of thousands of Muslims that people get most passionate. There can be few countries in Europe where natives know less about the way of the Muslims who live among them than Sweden [no citation is given]. The isolation of the apartments where immigrants mostly live has a lot to do with this. But even those who live and work in those areas find it hard to be precise about Muslim ways, and particularly about Islamist radicalism – although all are fairly sure that it is increasing.[7]

He concludes this subtle juxtaposition of crime, Muslim migrant families, and terrorism by quoting a police commissioner in a community with a large Muslim-migrant population: "We have some people here [who if] they went to the U.S., they would be imprisoned." So, Caldwell asks him, do the police have a pretty good idea of what's going on in the mosques? To which the commissioner responds "No."[8]

Reinforcing the implied growth of Islamic radicalism are quotations from Muslims he has encountered: a conservative imam who received death threats and "lost influence within his mosque" after condemning the London subway bombing carried out by Islamic terrorists, and an Iraqi-born writer "who added some horror stories of his own" including one about a prominent imam "who had been ostracized and condemned as 'a Jew who converted to Islam' because he had opposed suicide bombing."[9]

Is radicalization, to the extent it has in fact occurred, produced by discrimination and isolation? On this question, Caldwell equivocates. Yes, there probably is some discrimination, he appears to concede, but there is an element of self-isolation, caused, in the words of a Kurdish interlocutor, by "the racist, anti-Semitic honor culture that many of them live under."[10] But aggravating the problem of isolation and alienation, Caldwell seems to say, is a liberal discourse of such political correctness as to obscure either the existence of the problem or its sources. "Problems are constantly fudged in such a way as to establish no principles and offend no one."[11] For an example, he cites the taboo of openly questioning "the practice of second-generation Swedes returning to their ancestral countries to find husbands and wives ... In Sweden public discussion of this kind of endogamy is muted, although Swedes [how many?] complain in private that it slows integration and unacceptably widens the number of potential new immigrants."

A Kurdish immigrant who has become an author and television personality condemns recent government reports on problems of social and economic integra-tion because they shy away from any reference to pathological elements of immi-grant culture like anti-feminism. "The focus on discrimination," she tells Caldwell, "is a way of avoiding the real problem ... Because if the problem is not discrimin-ation, then the problem is the Swedish system itself."[12]

With the help of that observation Caldwell seems to arrive finally at the principal point of his clever conservative jeremiad. Yes, he seems to say, admitting large numbers of people, particularly Muslims, from the Global South, no doubt threatens public security, public finance, and public order. But the thickness of the welfare state aggravates the consequences of the country's migration policies. Socialist policies have produced a one-size-fits-all system which has "improved living conditions ... at the expense of limiting [citizens'] vital alternative choices."[13] Because the state has built the housing in which immigrants now congregate in large numbers, they can complain of state-imposed ghettoization. Because it plays so large a role in the economy, the state can be blamed for failures in economic integration. Because the state supplies migrant families with the economic essentials of a modestly comfortable life, they are not driven by necessity, as they would be in a rigorously laissez-faire capitalist state with very meager welfare assistance, to integrate themselves into the workplace. Caldwell concludes with lightly feigned uncertainty. "Maybe," he writes, "Sweden is now simply too diverse to benefit from the mass-produced prosperity and security that suited it so well for almost a century."

Nine years later, in November 2015, as the number of immigrants claiming asylum was doubling the 80,000 who had come in 2014, James Traub, a paragon of American liberal journalism, landed in Sweden to report on the country's response to the displaced persons pouring over its borders. In words reminiscent of his conservative predecessor, he heralded "The Death of the Most Generous Nation on Earth." "Little Sweden," he wrote in a post-trip article, "has taken in far more refugees per capita than any country in Europe. But in doing so, it's tearing itself apart."[14]

Unlike Caldwell, Traub did not fixate on refugees as a source of crime and potential terrorism. Nor did he note explicitly that for over 50 percent of the Swedish electorate, terrorism had vaulted into first place among issues deemed of greatest importance, leaving environmental concerns a distant second at 13 percent.[15] However, in his piece he shares Caldwell's concern about economic integration of the refugees because of both their number and their levels of education, which were lower, on average, than those of the Muslim Bosnians who arrived in the 1990s. Traub cites an informant he plainly trusts, who says that the Bosnian immigrants are nowadays "ministers in our government, they're our doctors, our neighbors." Traub wonders whether past is prologue, noting not only that the Bosnians "were better educated" but also that they practice "a more moderate version of Islam."[16]

Liberal though he is, Traub implies a concern shared with Caldwell and "many [Swedish] critics who were prepared to raise impolite questions" about the capacity of "a progressive and extremely secular country [to] socialize a generation of conservative Muslim newcomers," a concern heightened by the "New Year's Eve 2016 orgy of rape and theft in Cologne in which migrants [from the Middle East and North Africa] have been heavily implicated."[17]

For the conservative, Sweden's travails provide an occasion to indict the character of the welfare state, the elite's political correctness, and the intelligentsia's naiveté in sacrificing a long-established culture on the altar of diversity. The liberal, conversely, applauds the kindness and generosity of public officials and citizens alike in the face of "a moral test the likes of which Europe has not faced since the Nazis forced millions from their homes in search of refuge."[18] Traub plainly admires Sweden's building a system "designed to deliver to refugees the same extensive social benefits that Swedes gave themselves – housing, health care, high-quality education, maternal leave, and unemployment insurance."[19] He writes warmly of the "border police officials, unarmed, male and female, flawlessly proficient in English, and exceptionally polite," greeting refugees as they cross the border from Denmark and of "solicitous volunteers" waiting to help asylum-seekers at the central train station in Stockholm.[20]

Sweden, he concludes, "is the only country I have spent time in where the average person seems to be more idealistic than I am." But by the time he arrives, "the supply of good will [is] petering out."[21] The government announces that it will henceforth accept only a finite number of refugees and they must be vetted abroad by the UNHCR. To that end persons arriving from elsewhere in Europe will have to show proper documentation at the border, a step allowed under the Schengen Agreement as an emergency measure. The authorities also announce that they will begin a serious effort to deport persons whose asylum applications have been denied.[22]

Although, unlike Caldwell, the liberal Traub speaks with unreserved admiration for the social democratic model, he ends up appearing almost as doubtful about the capacity of Sweden to sustain the model if it continues to accept substantial numbers of migrants from conservative Muslim cultures. Indeed, he worries about the country's capacity to make the model work even with the existing body of immigrants. He cites an economist who says that while 82 percent of adult Swedes are in the workforce, the corresponding figure for immigrants from non-Western countries is 52 percent, and that immigrants are now absorbing 60 percent of all welfare payments. And despite his liberal instincts, he elides the opportunity to endorse "the official state ideology of integration, which asks Swedes as well as newcomers to integrate into a world that celebrates diversity, and thus casts Sweden as a gorgeous mosaic." In this vein he quotes uncritically the leader of the right-wing Sweden Democrats who asked him: "[A]re native Swedes to think of their own extraordinarily stable thousand-year culture as simply one among many national identities?"[23] Should they? Traub leaves the question unanswered.

The Integration Project

When Sweden became a favored European venue for humanitarian migrants, its government did not indulge the delusion that integration would occur spontaneously. On the contrary, it quickly elaborated and funded measures designed to enable refugees to integrate economically and navigate socially. Was economic integration likely to occur without a measure of cultural assimilation? Political and intellectual elites appeared to think so, since they enthusiastically invoked the vision of Sweden evolving seamlessly from a strikingly homogeneous into a vividly multicultural society.

The establishment of the Swedish Integration Board in 1969 and the introduction of free language training the following year are usually seen as the launch points of a formal integration system. As an OECD report notes, "over the following decade, the rights of immigrants were systematically extended to include access to most public jobs and (after three years of residence) the right to vote."[24]

The central element of the Swedish integration strategy remains a two-year introduction program for newly arrived humanitarian immigrants and their families which primarily emphasizes language training but includes something called "civic orientation." Initially the central government coordinated the program, while municipalities implemented it employing block grants from the center.

Measured in terms of employment or stimulation of continuing education, the results could be described as "disappointing" if the expectation were that by the end of the two-year period, rates of employment of migrant men and women in the fifteen to sixty-four age group would come close to approximating those of native Swedes. Even though the main responsibility for economic integration has been shifted to the national Swedish Employment Service, problems remain.

According to a 2015 OECD report, at the end of the program a large number of participants – particularly those who arrived with less than a high-school education – are neither working nor studying. Even a year after completing the program, "only 22% and 8% of low-educated participant men and women respectively were in employment," and a majority of them held positions in which their salaries were at least partially subsidized by the state. The low-educated constituted about 37 percent of recent refugee arrivals who now are almost exclusively from Africa (principally Somalia, Ethiopia, and Eritrea), Afghanistan, Iraq, and Syria.[25]

The employment challenge is particularly high in Sweden because it, like Norway and Denmark, has strikingly few jobs requiring less than a high school diploma or its equivalent. Such jobs account for roughly 5 percent of all jobs in the country. In Spain and the United Kingdom, low-skilled employment accounts for 14 percent and 9 percent of total jobs, respectively.[26] The small number stems partially from the long-established political relationship between capital and labor in these countries. Industrial wages in Sweden, bargained nationally, are high, and labor rights are strongly protected. So individual companies cannot lower their overall labor costs by hiring and training migrants willing to work thereafter at post-training wages substantially below those generally prevailing. Moreover, the character of private-sector activities in Sweden, an economy emphasizing technologically cutting-edge activities and the substitution of capital for labor, makes it difficult to train workers with a limited basic education. As of March 2018, 16 percent of people born abroad are unemployed. That is one of the highest rates among wealthy countries.[27] In Germany, by contrast, after fifteen years, refugees, normally more difficult to integrate economically than other migrants, enjoy an employment rate of 70 percent, just a tad below the native rate of 74 percent.[28] The difference appears explicable in terms of allowable local variation in wages and, in general, greater labor market flexibility.

Economic factors may contribute to one disturbing development in Sweden, namely, the sharp increase in gun violence perpetrated by criminal gangs competing in the market for illegal drugs. Between 2010 and 2015, people were killed by firearms at the same rate as in southern Italy. Gang members armed with Kalashnikovs and grenades have battled primarily among themselves, although an occasional grenade has been tossed at police stations. According to *The Economist*, over 70 percent of gang members are first- or second-generation migrants.[29]

The integration issues this strong society faces will not diminish. Consider only the population that identifies as Muslim. In 2016 its size was just over 800,000, which was approximately 8 percent of the country's inhabitants. In 2050, assuming no migration at all whether of refugees or persons seeking economic opportunity or persons entering under family-reunification policies (the "zero migration scenario"), the Muslim population is projected by the respected Pew Foundation's demographers to be 1,130,000. That would be 11.1 percent of the total. Under Pew's medium migration scenario, which assumes no new refugees, the Muslim component of Sweden's population would rise to 20.5 percent (2,470,000). And in the high migration scenario, which assumes a refugee flow comparable to the 2014–2016 pattern, that percentage increases to 30.6 percent (4,450,000).

With those numbers in mind, one can only hope that the Swedes' competent state, resilient economy, and idealistic self-image will enable them to manage the problems of integration the conservative Caldwell may exaggerate but the liberal Traub largely concedes. If they do manage successfully, then Sweden should continue to rank among the top ten in surveys of happiness levels within the globe's diverse states.[30]

NORWAY

Like its larger neighbor, beginning in the 1970s Norway sharply reduced labor migration, a policy that remained in place until the 1990s when, as a condition of free trade with EU countries, it accepted entry of EU citizens. Since the country had by that time, thanks to the efficient exploitation of its offshore oil resources, become the second richest country among OECD members (in terms of per capita income), it immediately became an attractive venue for East Europeans, particularly Poles, but also Lithuanians. They now constitute the two largest migrant-background groups in Norway.

After the door-narrowing migration policy of the 1970s, non-Europeans, other than those with valued skills or willing to fill very particular niches where there were local shortages, could enter and settle only under family-reunification criteria or in the role of asylum claimants. As in Sweden, Norway's political and intellectual elites, along with most of the electorate, imagined themselves as people peculiarly sympathetic to the travails of the persecuted and open to cosmopolitan experiences. They were also confident about the integrative capacity of their strong national culture and buoyant economy, and therefore kept the opening for asylum claimants relatively wide.

By 2014, out of a total population of approximately 5.4 million, just under 15 percent were either immigrants or children of recent immigrants and another 4.6 percent were born in Norway to one foreign-born parent; in short, by this definition migrants and their children constituted about 20 percent of the population and about half of that number had non-European antecedents. The single largest non-European national group was Somalis, numbering almost 35,000, followed closely by people from Pakistan, Iraq, and Afghanistan.[31]

In 2015, when the stream of persons fleeing to Europe from wars, persecution, and indiscriminately vicious governments became a churning torrent, Norway fulfilled its self-image by receiving over 31,000 asylum claimants, a number giving it in per capita terms the fourth place among European states. This still left it far behind Sweden, however, a country of about 9.5 million which admitted 163,000 people who filled and finally overflowed every available dwelling including makeshift ones from one end of the country to the other. As of 2016, refugees, who are almost exclusively from the Middle East, West Asia, or sub-Saharan Africa, make up 3.6 percent of Norway's population. The total identifying as Muslim was 160,000 in 2015, a number which probably grew substantially in 2016 when, as I noted above, more than 31,000 people entered the country to apply for asylum, at least 20,000 of whom were from the Muslim majority countries of Syria, Afghanistan, and Iraq. Under the high immigration scenario I mentioned above, 17 percent of its inhabitants will identify as Muslims in 2050.

Also like Sweden Norway has in place a robust set of policies and institutions dedicated to integrating migrants, policies and institutions which the country's long established parties, with the Social Democrats in the lead, have progressively tweaked. On entry, asylum claimants are immediately embraced by the welfare state, without prejudice to their inherited cultures. Until 2016 it helped them open a bank account into which the state deposited funds sufficient for purchasing food and other necessities. Now vouchers earmarked for the purchase of necessities have largely replaced the cash transfers. The state also provides claimants with temporary accommodations and free access to health services. Their children have the right to begin attending school. They themselves can apply for work permits, although the state does not guarantee a job. Meanwhile they can without cost take 250 hours of instruction in the Norwegian language.

All that is step one. Step two, intended to follow within at most a few months, is dispersal from the point of entry and initial settlement to those municipalities around the country which, in return for five-year block grants, have agreed to assume the obligation of integrating the arrivals into Norwegian economy and society.

Again, as in Sweden, the integration centerpiece is an introduction program consisting primarily of language instruction combined with a small dose of civic education intended to give the new arrival some sense of the country's political system and social values and practices. Municipalities, rather than civil servants dispatched from the capital, implement the program while assuming responsibility for social assistance to and housing for migrant families and preparing adults for participation in the country's labor markets. Preparation includes continued training in the Norwegian language up to a limit of 3,000 hours.

At least in theory each introductory program must be tailored by the municipality to the individual migrant taking account of level of education, practical skills, aspirations, and so on. The block grants are made for *delivery of services*; there is no reward to municipalities for *achieving superior results*. While endeavoring to make adult migrants literate in Norwegian, consistent with its stated goal of turning Norway into the "most inclusive society in the world," the government provides the children of migrants with the option of a primary education in their native language.

In terms of economic integration, what has Norway achieved? About 70 percent of the native born between the ages of sixteen and seventy-four participates in the labor market: 75 percent of men and 69 percent of women. Migrants from EU member countries roughly match those figures. The comparable numbers for Asian immigrants are 63 percent for men and 50 percent for women; for migrants from Africa they are 55 and 40 percent.[32] But within those broad regional categories outcomes differ profoundly, apparently as a result of two factors: the median level of each national group's education before migration and gender roles in the countries from which they have emigrated. Employment rates for women from Vietnam and Sri Lanka tend toward convergence over time with those of Norwegian natives. Convergence is much slower for women from Turkey and Pakistan, many of whom remain outside the labor force decades after settlement.[33] Rates of employment for Somali women are particularly low.[34] The limited participation of women from Africa, the Middle East, and West Asia in the Norwegian workforce may also be related to the state's provision of special financial assistance for women with young children. That "cash-for-care" subsidy is on top of the generality of social support payments.[35]

The numbers and policies I have sketched coincide with the progressive increase in Sweden and Norway and also in Denmark of electoral support for right-wing political parties. The party platforms emphasize limiting non-European immigration and maintaining the salience of traditional customs and practices, even ones seemingly so normatively trivial as including pork on school lunch menus. In addition to increasing their electoral support, right-wing parties have fostered a rightward shift in the discourse of the center and center-right parties as they attempt to halt the shrinkage of their traditional electoral base.

As in other European countries the gathering hostility to non-European and often explicitly to Muslim immigration is undoubtedly inspired by more than concern for the financial viability of the welfare state. I say "undoubtedly" because threats to social benefits are not the main ingredient of hot anti-immigrant campaigning rhetoric. The themes of anti-immigration advocates reference morality and national security more than economics. Ironically, what is expressed is the morality of liberal democracy: freedom of speech (so people can express their anger about aliens and Islam and the cultural traitors who praise diversity) and defense of the equality of women and their physical protection from the young men who predominate among asylum claimants.[36] Alongside the liberal-sounding rhetoric, however, is the communal one: the need to protect the legacy culture, with its imagined tradition of warm mutual respect and support, from persons supposedly determined to import their own inimical practices.

These appeals primarily find traction within the upper working and lower middle classes, among people in more rural areas and people without university degrees.[37] The robust welfare state and efficient management of the economy by political and bureaucratic elites have substantially buffered these groups from the blows of labor-saving technologies and global economic competition. For decades, many of them – at least among those who worked in manufacturing enterprises and the civil service – supported the left. But as political defeat drove conservatives to accept an unusually high measure of economic redistribution through the institutions of the welfare state and as technology and globalization drove the left toward more market-friendly policies, the traditional left–right divide narrowed along with gross inequality of condition. Meanwhile cultural divisions widened between the highly educated participants in an increasingly cosmopolitan and libertarian culture and the rest of the population.[38]

To be sure, the identity divide was not and is not a simple dualism. Opinions seem to range across a wide spectrum of attraction to or revulsion from a sunny, broadly tolerant hedonism. But hedonism is paired with a cosmopolitan idealism that is baked into Norwegian self-identity. It is reflected, among other ways, in its budgets, which establish Norway together with the other Nordic countries as the largest per capita contributors of humanitarian aid and development assistance among Western states.[39]

Everywhere in the West, populist identity politics, like the politics of class, combines envy and a sense of injustice. Wealth has traditionally been the primary measure of achievement in Western societies, but it has been displaced by an increasingly democratic celebrity culture. This, I believe, has aggravated feelings of resentment among the less educated members of the legacy population who, by virtue of their limited education, have in recent decades seen relatively small improvement in their standard of living. As immigrants from the Global South gain traction in European societies, their most talented members begin to appear as actors, athletes, models, musicians, news readers, style setters, or scholarly commentators on current events. Even if they are only a small fraction of the persons occupying those roles, their skin color makes them more conspicuous, multiplying their assumed numbers in the eyes of a viewer who grew up seeing only pale faces in glossy magazine advertisements and on television and movie screens. Add to celebrity as such the growth in its financial rewards and the pervasiveness of pictures of the homes and lifestyles those rewards finance and you have added catalysts for the politics of resentment.

Fear intensifies resentment. The only politically motivated mass-casualty assault ever to strike Norway was the massacre of seventy-seven people carried out by the Norwegian white fascist Anders Breivik in the name of defending traditional Western values. Nevertheless, the threat of Muslim terrorism looms larger in the national imagination. Norway is so integral a part of Europe that its people are bound to feel in their bones the effects of terrorist acts in Germany, France, Britain, Belgium, and Spain, attacks carried out in the name of one or another Islamic identity. Al Qaeda and ISIS and their affiliates claim, after all, to be at war with the West, not just this or that part of it. Osama bin Laden said that Sweden was not implicated in what he saw as the West's war against Islam and singled it out as a country against which he bore no ill will.[40] But who remembers that? Anyway, he is dead and he did not mention Norway or Denmark.

The images of the dead and dying on the streets of Berlin, Nice, and Paris obscure for many people the reality of Muslim families living within walking distance, who, having been uprooted from their homes by pitiless forces and barely surviving perilous journeys, are now desperately trying to construct a new life out of the broken pieces of their former one. Government officials and political leaders who sympathize with the often impoverished and not infrequently traumatized new arrivals have a two-fold task beyond preparing them for the workplace. One task is to demonstrate that a warmly compassionate response to migrants is compatible with an iron-fisted approach to national security. The other is to expend the financial and human capital needed to foster on a sustained and regular basis amiable and cooperative relationships between native and migrant families.

Contact, of course, is not an absolute guarantee of amity. White people in the southern United States had intimate daily contact with their black neighbors through all the long years of segregation and lynching. Intercommunal rage marked the introduction of African American kids into schools located in Boston's white ethnic neighborhoods.[41] Group rage propelled entrepreneurs of racial hostility onto that city's political heights in one of the most liberal states in America. Building a sense of shared community requires a far greater and more imaginative effort than even the strong, experienced, well-intentioned, and generally efficient Scandinavian state institutions have yet managed at least to the degree necessary to halt the rise of the right.

An extraordinarily moving conversation between a *New York Times* contributor and an Afghan asylum claimant illustrates both the isolation of some significant proportion of asylum-seekers and the redemptive possibilities of contact.[42] In 2011, the claimant was living with two other young Afghani men in the small Norwegian city of Kongsberg. The three of them shared a clothesline which stretched between a window in their apartment and one in an adjoining building. From time to time in the course of three years they saw the family with whom they shared that line, a father, mother, and daughter, but never did they share a word.

On July 22 the Afghan narrator is leaning out of his window hanging clothes and, in his account, worrying desperately about his fate because he has just heard on the television that a bomb had been set off in Oslo killing eight people. If the perpetrator turned out to be a Muslim, would he and other Muslims be rounded up by the police, perhaps expelled? Where could he go?

> Back in Kabul ... I had published a book on the Taliban, condemning terrorism.... A gang kidnapped me, held me ransom, beat and tortured me. I escaped ... [but] the threats kept coming. The gang found my home. They killed my father, my brothers and my sisters. My mother and I fled. We moved in with some friends. But it wasn't safe for me to stay in Afghanistan.[43]

Finally, he had made his way to Norway in the hope of finding refuge. After three years he still awaits a final resolution of his claim. Hanging his clothes, fearing the worst, he looks down and sees his neighbor arriving home from work. The man sees him. Apparently, he too had heard about the bombing. "'You people, you come here and ruin our country,' he yells. 'Norway is peaceful, and now you're destroying it! Go home. Make your own country crap. Leave ours alone.'"

> Actually, he said a lot worse than that. He kept shouting and shouting. But I stayed quiet. I just went on hanging my clothes. My hands were shaking.[44]

The narrator finishes hanging, sits down with his roommates. Fearfully they watch the television. "Suddenly all the headlines changed." The man responsible for the bombing has surrendered to the police after killing more than sixty young people on an island near Oslo. His name is Breivik, a Norwegian name.

Then there is a knock on the apartment door. The narrator thinks it's all right, for now everyone will know that the terrorist is not a Muslim. He opens the door:

> It was my neighbor. He was speaking very quickly, apologizing, telling me how ashamed he was for what he had said. He was crying. This big, pale, redheaded Norwegian man ... he had tears all down his face. He hugged me. He insisted that my roommates and I come to his apartment that night for dinner.... From that day on he opened his heart to us.[45]

DENMARK

"Open-hearted" is not exactly how one could characterize Denmark's response over the past fifteen years to Muslims generally, much less those seeking asylum. Despite (or is it because of?) being one of the most democratic and egalitarian countries in the world, a place where in the words of one writer, "bus drivers ... are paid like accountants,"[46] a country sturdy in defense of gay rights, generous in its foreign aid, and noted for its social cohesion alongside a "vigorous culture of social and political debate"[47] – despite, that is, being much like Norway and Sweden – Denmark was among the first European countries to shift hard right against acceptance of Muslim migrants whether they were searching for opportunity or refuge.

This spirit of implacable resistance, underscored by the government's sudden about-face in 2016 on a commitment to accept 1,000 Syrian refugees as its share of a proposed EU-wide dispersion, does not have a long history. Hugh Eakin, writing for the *New York Review of Books* in 2016, cites Danish observers in dating the anti-migrant shift to a parliamentary election in the immediate wake of the 9/11 terrorist attacks on the Pentagon and the World Trade Center. He implies that the attacks were a kind of tipping point for gathering unease about the country's Muslim population which, as the result of steady growth during the 1990s, had by 2001 become roughly 200,000 strong in a national population of about 5.3 million.

Muslim growth in the 1990s had been paralleled by growth in the then disreputable political margin of the openly anti-Muslim "Peoples' Party." The party appealed to the electorate with a platform combining unqualified support for the egalitarian policies pioneered by the Social Democrats with calls for protecting Danish popular government and integral society from EU bureaucrats and Global South migrants whom it envisioned as mostly Muslim. In the November 2001 parliamentary elections, the party's spinning wheels finally found traction. A third-place finish gave it sufficient weight in parliament to attract a somewhat anomalous alliance with the larger center-right Liberal Party – normally the champion of a smaller, less-active state – against the Social Democrats, who then took a bad beating. That was the beginning of a partnership which to this day has given the right a place in the coalition government.

Having helped make immigration the central issue of the 2001 campaign, the People's Party successfully pushed its partner to share its views on migration and to implement its policies. To reduce immigrant marriages as a quick path to citizenship for a foreign spouse, the parliament passed legislation requiring those spouses to be at least twenty-four years of age, together with a requirement that both spouses combined had to have spent more years living in Denmark than in any other country. In addition, social benefits for everyone were tied more closely to employment. Since migrants were more likely to be unemployed, this tweak in the welfare system fell disproportionately on them.

The rhetoric of political figures corresponded to the legislation. Distinguishing themselves from their Swedish and Norwegian cousins, Danish opinion-setters spurned the multicultural ideal. If you wanted to enjoy the comforts of being Danish, you needed to accept Danish culture. A leading Liberal Party politician declared in a newspaper interview: "All this talk about equality of cultures and equality of religions is nonsense."[48]

The governing coalition brought Danish foreign policy into alignment with its domestic one. Denmark embraced the Bush administration's "war on terrorism" and, for its size, has been remarkably active in Afghanistan, sustaining casualties relative to its population nearly twice those of the United States. Three years into this harsher ideological environment, hitherto low-profile Denmark achieved inter-national-culture-war prominence due to an editor's whim. According to Eakin, intrigued or provoked by hearing that a Danish illustrator had demurred from doing drawings for a book about Muhammad, Flemming Rose, of the center-right *Jyl-lands-Posten*, invited a dozen caricaturists to "'draw Muhammad as you see him.'"[49]

The results were by no means uniformly hostile to Islam, but several could easily be seen as insulting, particularly the memorable one depicting Muhammad wearing a bomb in place of a turban. In the event, the caricature functioned as a bomb, one with a slowly burning fuse. Initially the post-publication controversy was simply a Danish affair. Had the publication occurred in the United States, with its long-established constitutional norm protecting even the vilest speech from government sanction (as long as it did not constitute an appeal to violence), the Danish government could have responded to complaints from Muslim leaders simply by saying that constitutional law tied its hands. That answer was not available to the Danish authorities, since a law dating from 1939 prohibited "threatening, insulting or degrading speech."[50] The law, which apparently had been passed to protect the country's small Jewish population at a time of vicious and rampant anti-Semitism in most of Europe, was ignored. The government merely dismissed the Muslim community's complaints as if no such law existed.

Confronted with a government unwilling to accompany a defense of free speech with expressions of understanding for the community's concerns, community reli-gious leaders then took the matter international, first by appealing for support to the ambassadors in Denmark from Muslim-majority countries. Again, the government had an opportunity to differentiate its own views from those of certain private actors, and again it demurred. Indeed, it refused to meet with the ambassadors even to discuss their concerns, a refusal one of its foreign policy advisers would later acknowledge to have been a mistake.[51]

At that point, a group of Danish imams collected the original caricatures, along with several others that were arguably even more provocative, and prepared a dossier that described what the imams characterized as the chronic second-class treatment of Muslims in Denmark. The imams brought the dossier to the Middle East, from which steroidal versions of the dossier's contents quickly went viral throughout the Muslim world. They proved far more incendiary than the imams apparently expected or intended. Enraged crowds attacked Danish embassies in several coun-tries, and a boycott of Danish exports to the Middle East hurt several of Denmark's larger companies.[52]

The most serious consequence of the caricatures, however, was the addition of Denmark to the target list of jihadi terrorists. Western intelligence agencies aborted several plots. One, facilitated by an American convert to Islam who had previously assisted with the Mumbai slaughter of 2008, involved storming the building where the offending newspaper was published and massacring everyone who could be found inside it. A lone terrorist later murdered a guard outside the newspaper and one outside a synagogue before being shot dead. Raging threats on the internet propelled Danish police to organize round-the-clock protection for both the *Jyllands-Posten* editor, Flemming Rose, and the turban-bomb caricaturist.

Despite the country's traditional full-throated practice of free speech, retrospective support within the Danish establishment for publication was not uniform. Against Flemming Rose's insistence on the need for "'sarcasm, mockery, and ridicule'" in the face of an encroaching threat of totalitarianism that emanated from the Islamic world, the editor of *Politiken*, Denmark's more prestigious paper which shares a building and an owner with *Jyllands-Posten*, said that publication was like saying to a beleaguered minority: "'We don't respect your religion! You may think this is offensive but we don't think it's offensive, so you're dumb!'"[53]

There seems little doubt that publication and its aftermath reinforced the governing coalition's resistance to asylum claimants and indifference to the sensibilities of its Muslim minority. Most recently, aside from further cutting support payments for asylum claimants and insisting that they be contained in holding areas even if only tents are available, the government garnered international attention by adopting legislation calling for the seizure from refugees of cash and other valuables (other than those of sentimental significance) in excess of roughly $1,400 in order to offset the expenses of accommodating them. In addition, it took out advertisements in Lebanese papers warning potential refugees that they would not find Denmark a welcoming place. The message has apparently been communicated: in 2016, while tens of thousands of refugees from the Middle East, Africa, and West Asia sought asylum in Sweden and Norway, just over 7,000 applied to Denmark. Conceivably there is some relationship between the nation's hostility to Muslim immigrants, which has been communicated by the Danish state for almost fifteen years, and the fact that, per capita, Denmark ranks second or third among European countries in residents who have gone off to join ISIS in Syria.[54]

5

The United Kingdom

The United Kingdom and France are generally seen as the poles defining the range of rich-country migrant-integration policies, the former exemplifying a more laissez-faire response to the cultural diversity introduced by successive waves of migration, and the latter exemplifying official and societal intolerance of migrant cultural practices and norms at odds with local ones. This generalization, however, simplifies reality.

If the concept of race made any sense at all, one would have to say that Britain was an island of mongrels long before the post–World War II migrant waves began washing over the country's shores. It was a mix of Celts, Saxons, Norsemen, Romans (a multiethnic people themselves), Portuguese, Russians, Jews, Africans, and others. Each arriving at different times, the disparate cultures of these groups have blended over centuries into a recognizable cluster of norms and practices. Coincidentally they have acquired a common language and a shared identity of Britishness which coexists with self-conscious regional and class-defined subcultures like that of the London working-class cockney and the upper-class toff or the Cornishman and the Scot.[*]

THE GREAT REVERSE MIGRATION

In the centuries of British imperial power, adventurous Scots and the second and third sons of English aristocrats sallied forth into the empire to make their fortunes. In the wake of World War II, intrepid inhabitants of current or former colonies themselves sallied forth, this time to the United Kingdom, to make their fortunes or

---

[*] However, Paul Collier, citing B. Cunliffe's 2012 book *Britain Begins* (which drew on DNA data), writes that "around 70 percent of the current population of Britain are directly descended from ... the people who inhabited Britain in pre-Neolithic times" (in *Exodus* (New York: Oxford University Press, 2013), 59). Given the country's current demographic dynamics, that figure, however accurate, will change very substantially by 2050.

at least to manage a slightly better life than they could hope to find in the Caribbean, South Asia, or Africa. They did so as beneficiaries of the 1948 British Nationality Act, which allowed the many hundred millions of subjects of the British Empire (or of independent members of the Commonwealth) to live and work in the United Kingdom without needing a visa. Preceding them were roughly 100,000 Poles, many of whom had fought for the US–UK coalition against Germany and who shied from returning to a shattered country rocketing toward the status of a Soviet satellite. The British electorate seemed indifferent to, possibly even supportive of, their decision to remain in the country.

Economic migrants from the Commonwealth and dwindling empire were a mere trickle at first: roughly 3,000 in 1953. By 1961, the trickle had increased to an annual total of more than 130,000, a large proportion of whom were, at least in British eyes, "coloured." Although Africans and Afro-Caribbean people, together with migrants from the Asian subcontinent, helped staff the burgeoning British health service, London's underground, and the country's rail service, the native population did not uniformly welcome them. In a way reminiscent of the African-American experience in the northern United States following the great migration from the Jim Crow, lynch-mob South, black ghettoes formed in London and other large cities policed by an almost exclusively white force. Even as late as 1999, after a small measure of integration had occurred, a government-appointed investigative body found the Metropolitan Police Force to be institutionally racist.[1]

Long before the race riots and confrontations between police and young blacks, primarily Afro-Caribbeans, which marked the 1960s, concern about the potential influx of colored peoples was being voiced in government circles. As early as 1950 a Cabinet committee began considering "ways which might be adopted to check the immigration into this country of coloured people from British colonial territories."[2] By 1962, most of those territories had become sovereign states and the empire had morphed into the Commonwealth, an association of sovereign states with vestigial legal and sentimental ties to the United Kingdom.

The passage of "coloured peoples" from colonial subjects to citizens of independent states did not end the incentives for substantial numbers of them to settle in the United Kingdom. Introducing the UK government's first response to the growing phenomenon of movement from the periphery to the once omnipotent metropole, Rab Butler, the Conservative Government's Home Secretary, declared:

> The justification for the control which is included in this Bill ... is that a sizeable part of the entire population of the earth is at present legally entitled to come and stay in this already densely populated country. It amounts altogether to one-quarter of the population of the globe and at present there are no factors visible which might lead us to expect a reversal or even a modification of the immigration trend.[3]

Since the bill's requirement that persons seeking entry to settle must be found to meet the "labour needs" of the national economy did not appreciably diminish the migration numbers and in light of growing popular resistance, parliament in 1968 added the more stringent requirement that prospective migrants from Commonwealth members be connected by birth or ancestry to a UK national. This was not enough to satisfy a then important figure in the Conservative Party, Enoch Powell. Only a month after the act's passage he predicted in a speech which became an instant sensation that the continued migration of colored people would lead to "rivers of blood" in the streets of the nation. While Conservative Party leaders and the establishment more generally immediately condemned the man and his message, both resonated positively among at least a portion of the working class. Three days after Powell's speech some 2,000 dockworkers left work to march down to Parliament Square to protest Powell's banishment from the Shadow Cabinet. Almost three-quarters of persons polled by Gallup shortly after the speech stated their agreement with its thrust.[4]

The establishment's repudiation of Powell probably had several sources. In the first place, elites do not tend to view migrants as competitors for goods, services, or distinction. Migrants with money to invest or specialized skills figure to contribute to the economy and therefore to the well-being of its privileged sectors. Migrants without much money but with the above-average skills and drive and the ambition needed to uproot themselves in search of greater opportunity also appear as welcome additions to the structure, which dispenses and supports privilege. Moreover, unlike the British working class in the 1960s and even into the 1970s, migrants were not socialized from birth into the working-class culture of hostility to the managers of capital and support for the Labor Party.[5]

An additional factor, common to the British and French cases, was the hope lingering within the political class of maintaining among the peoples of the once far-flung empire a strong sense of connection to the metropole, the kind of felt connection which had previously brought nationals of sovereign Australia to fight and die for the United Kingdom at Gallipoli in World War I and their Canadian counterparts to bleed out on the Anzio beachhead in World War II. People of color from Africa and Asia and the Caribbean also had served the empire. Certain of the new states which now contained them – states like Nigeria, Ghana, Kenya, India, Pakistan – were important sites of British investment and had great potential value as consumers of British goods and services, particularly if Britain were to continue to enjoy privileged access to their markets. In short, displaying hostility to "coloured peoples" could not serve Britain's external interests as defined by the educated, relatively cosmopolitan strata of British society. Nor, as the dystopian US experience demonstrated, could it serve the country's internal interests to develop in its midst deeply alienated minorities defined by race.

Also, undoubtedly driving the establishment's repudiation of a racialized politics was a historically justified image of Britain as a tolerant liberal society, a self-image reinforced by the existential struggle with Nazi Germany. It was Britain, after all, that had outlawed the slave trade in the early nineteenth century and actually employed elements of the Royal Navy to hinder it. Britain was, moreover, the seedbed of modern liberal philosophy and the home of its seminal figure, John Stuart Mill.

Beginning in 1962, at the behest of its political leaders, parliament passed successive race relations acts. The acts gradually expanded prohibitions of racial discrimination beginning with public accommodations and over the decades coming to include employment in both the public and private sectors. As it expanded the scope of its prohibitions parliament created mechanisms for monitoring and enforcing compliance, most notably the Commission for Racial Equality, established in 1976.

In comparing Britain with Continental countries one noteworthy distinction about the British response to migration from poor countries is the early point at which migration became a political issue of some moment and its racial rather than primarily religious dimension at that point. Because of the variety of attitudes in Continental countries, the distinction is less sharp when one turns to the issue of migrant integration. By the second postwar decade, British political leaders saw cultural differences between the native and the rapidly growing migrant populations as a threat to the latter's integration into the national society. In response, the Labor government of the day declared its commitment to a policy of what would in later years be called "multiculturalism." In the words of the Home Secretary, the cosmopolitan intellectual Roy Jenkins, official policy should aim at "not a flattening process of assimilation but ... equal opportunity accompanied by cultural diversity in an atmosphere of mutual tolerance."[6]

As Jill Rutter notes in her fine study of migration, integration, and social cohesion in the United Kingdom,

> The 1960s saw a move ... towards policies ... which recognized the legitimacy of cultural diversity. Multi-faith religious education in schools was introduced at this time. There was also the first extensive public funding of community organizations working with specific groups of migrants. [What was missing, however, was a] clear or coherent policy agenda, and there was – and arguably still is – no consensus about the aims and nature of multiculturalist policy.[7]

Despite the steady tightening of criteria for entry and settlement, including limits on the annual intake of asylum claimants, migration from the poorer areas of the world, particularly the poorer states of the former empire, continued, in part because the door remained open for family reunion and foreign spouses, in part because Britain exerted cultural attraction for wealthy and skilled persons from countries like India, Pakistan, and Nigeria where elites learned English alongside their native tongues. In the 1990s, the accession to the European Union of former Soviet satellites in Central and Eastern Europe, all poor in comparison with the United Kingdom and the nations of Western Europe and able by virtue of accession to enjoy freedom of movement within the Union, produced a new migratory stream into the United

Kingdom, one which it could not control as long as it remained an EU member. Poles numbering in the hundreds of thousands came in the space of a few years, dwarfing the number who had settled after World War II. Asylum claimants also increased, drawn by an economy more open and less regulated than many of the Continental ones, particularly the French, and a society in which one could more easily move around and, if overstaying a visa, remain anonymous.

According to the 2011 national census, the net result of migration in the previous five decades was a foreign-born population constituting over 13 percent of the roughly 56 million people living in England and Wales, a substantial majority of whom were either "coloured" in the British sense of the word or mixed race. However, with respect to persons born outside the United Kingdom, according to 2015 figures, the second largest ethnic group was Polish. It numbered an estimated 700,000, just short of the 780,000 migrants who originated in India.

Precise figures for second- and third-generation migrants are harder to come by. The figures from the 2011 census on ethnicity show the following increases over the preceding decade in persons of Indian, Pakistani, and Bangladeshi background and in persons from sub-Saharan Africa and the Caribbean:

	2001 (in millions)	2011 (in millions)	Increase (%)
India	1,053	1,451	38
Pakistan	747	1,174	57
Bangladesh	283	451	59
Africa and Caribbean	1,149	1,904	65
Mixed	677	1,250	85

In terms of religious identity, the largest increase was in the Muslim population, from 1,591,000 in 2001 to 2,787,000 in 2011, an increase from 2.7 percent of the population to 4.41 percent. Under the Pew Foundation's zero, medium, and high migration scenarios for the year 2050, those percentages would increase to 9.7, 16.7, and 17.2, respectively.[8] In terms of color the country is already quite diverse. Non-white births in 2015 were just over one-third of the total.[9]

Do these numbers imply a growing challenge to the relatively liberal political and social culture, to the practices and norms most people think of as "British"? Or do they simply ensure that Britain will not experience the economic stagnation of the other highly developed island nation, Japan, a country long resistant to substantial immigration despite having one of the world's lowest birth rates, a country shrinking before our eyes with its current population of approximately 127 million projected to diminish to 107 million by 2050? Do the answers to those questions depend on the country's integration strategy and its implementation? Does it have a strategy, and, if so, what is it in actual fact? Before addressing those questions directly, I want to sketch the evolution of the migration issue in politics, public discourse, and public policy.

INTEGRATION ANXIETY: FROM RACE TO RELIGION

Black-youth-versus-police collisions in the 1960s and two infamous attacks on black-majority neighborhoods by white gangs[10] were only the first prominent signs of migrant integration problems. In the 1980s, a number of riotous fights between groups of young Asians and whites in northern cities enlarged the focus of public concern about integration. But the problem continued to be seen primarily as one of race, with anti-discrimination laws as the answer.

It was the aforementioned Rushdie affair in 1989 that started to shift the main focus of concern from race to religion, specifically to Islam. Concern intensified with the opening of sensational jihadist attacks on Western targets before taking a step-level jump following the 9/11 aerial assault on the Pentagon and the World Trade Center in the United States and the 2005 terrorist bombings in London, which killed 52 people and injured 700. Anxieties have remained high, sustained by a succession of aborted attacks in the United States and United Kingdom, brutally successful ones on the Continent, the horrific Manchester bombing in May of 2017 followed by the vehicle assaults on London and Westminster bridges, and the phoenix-like rise of ISIS out of what had a few years earlier appeared to be the dying remnants of Al Qaeda in Iraq.

The British government, like that of every other rich Western country, has wrestled essentially with three questions: What degree or kind of integration of migrant families should be the goal of public policy? How should it be attained? Can it be attained by means consistent with the liberal values which the government is ostensibly seeking to protect in part by fostering the integration of migrant families?

The variety of purposes integration policies are intended to serve complicate the search for answers. One is fiscal: governments want to maximize the contributions migrants and their descendants make to the economy and minimize the costs they impose on public services like education, medical and child care, and policing, and on the system of social protection including housing, welfare payments, and unemployment compensation. A second purpose is public safety: governments want to minimize the risk of migration raising the rate of ordinary crimes like robbery and rape, avoid violent confrontations between gangs of natives and migrants, and prevent politically or religiously motivated violence, violence now generally described as "terrorism." A third purpose is defense of what over the centuries have become core societal values, values which in the view of many define the national identity, values such as freedom of speech and religious practice, and equality of opportunity to participate in public life, to shape a personal identity, and to pursue self-defined success in economic and social realms.

The first two purposes are relatively clear and uncontroversial. The third is not, because even within the native population there is controversy about the proper limits of individual autonomy and the extent to which autonomy must be accompanied by duties to family and the wider community. After all, the native population includes libertarians, social democrats, religious conservatives, and, as contemporary politics on both sides of the Atlantic underscore, unashamed racial nationalists.

With each passing day, it is more difficult to identify confidently the defining elements of the national identity for which governments are the notional custodians. That is one problem pursuit of the third purpose needs to address. The other is resolving the question of whether pursuit is consistent with advancement of the other two purposes. Suppose, for instance, migrants are committed to patriarchal domination of the family, believe that wives must submit to their husband's sexual desires so marital rape is an oxymoron, deny a child's right to choose her husband, and endorse violent responses to blasphemy. Can the state criminalize actions consistent with these beliefs without affecting the spirit of cooperation between the concerned migrants and the security services? Or suppose the security services learn that the imam at a particular mosque, a non-citizen, declaims in fiery tones that Ahmadis, a minority Islamic sect often persecuted in Pakistan, are the instruments of Satan and an insidious threat to the unity of Islam. Consistent with the values of free speech and religion, must government refrain from deporting him as long as he does not urge his followers to kill Ahmadis at the first opportunity?

For decades after it was first enunciated, the official British approach to integration followed Roy Jenkin's dictum that government should seek "equal opportunity, accompanied by cultural diversity, in an atmosphere of mutual tolerance." Doubts about the wisdom of this proposition surfaced well before terrorism in the name of Islam became a central governmental concern, even before the Rushdie affair exposed harsh gaps in the area of free speech between general public opinion and the beliefs of a significant segment of the otherwise diverse Muslim "community."

Nevertheless, at least in comparison to France, Britain remained even into the first years of the present century a country with a multicultural approach to its non-Western migrants and their descendants. To a visitor from France the living proofs of this were the women promenading the streets of London in black-robed, fully veiled anonymity without drawing a glance from the natives. But as the establishment's rhetorical position, multiculturalism could not survive the rise of ISIS or the 800 or so UK citizens who went abroad to fight for the "caliphate," and the impact of successful terror attacks including those on other Western states.

Speaking in Munich at a conference on European security in February 2011, then Prime Minister David Cameron declared that "state multiculturalism" had encouraged Britons to live segregated lives, and, he seemed to imply, that segregation had created an environment conducive to the recruitment of a fraction of young Muslim men and women to the cause of jihad. The necessary alternative, he went on to argue, is a "muscular liberalism," which, according to a columnist for *The Economist*, "frankly confronts extremist ideas and promotes a British identity open to all."[11] Conservatives, the same columnist noted, took Cameron's words as root-and-branch rejection of multiculturalism in all of its forms and, presumably, its replacement by the goal of assimilation.

If carefully parsed, the column said, there was in fact nothing really new about Cameron's remarks:

> A year after the London bombings of July 2005 Ruth Kelly, then the Labour minister in charge of community policies, asked whether – in its anxiety to avoid imposing a single identity on diverse communities, multiculturalism had encouraged "separateness." In December 2006 Labour Prime Minister Tony Blair gave a speech on multiculturalism that reads like a list of Mr. Cameron's talking points. Both prime ministers called for tighter controls on Muslim groups receiving public funds, an entry ban on foreign preachers with sulphurous views, a tougher line on forced marriages and an expectation that all British citizens support common values from the rule of law to a rejection of discrimination.[12]

Hence the only thing arguably different about Cameron's speech was its implicit message. The message was that he had opted for one side in a debate that had been going on within successive governments for some time, namely, whether the government should fight terrorism by, among other means, working with ferociously anti-liberal Muslim ideologues who nevertheless opposed or at least claimed to oppose violence in the name of the faith.

"Working" with them meant including them among the faith groups receiving public moneys for carrying out educational or other philanthropic activities. Despite their fiery intolerance of any dissent from their very strict interpretations of Islam, despite their contempt for other faiths and sects, despite their positions on homosexuality (forbid) and blasphemy (punish), these ideologues had for years been included on the assumption that they enjoyed street credibility with those elements of the Muslim population most susceptible to recruitment by radicals capable of committing violence within the United Kingdom. Cameron, according to a source in government, had decided to embrace the "no" side in this debate by virtue of having come to accept the "conveyer belt" theory which posited that, whatever the intention of its practitioners, non-violent radicalism tended to groom people for passage to jihad.[13]

To *The Economist*, one of trans-Atlantic liberalism's most influential voices, the trouble with Cameron's speech was not its lack of novelty but its "muddle." The muddle, according to the journal's columnist, was not the conveyer belt theory, about which the author offered no opinion. Rather, it stemmed from Cameron's apparent belief, echoing his Labor predecessors Tony Blair and Gordon Brown, that a confident assertion of liberal values in every avenue of education and public discourse could combat the appeal of a ferocious version of Islam. That seems a fair interpretation of his claim that some young Muslims find it hard to identify with Britain "because we have allowed the weakening of our collective identity" and his equation of Britishness with belief in freedom of speech and worship, democracy, the rule of law, and equal rights regardless of race, sex, or sexuality.[14]

How, *The Economist*'s author asks, can this conception of Britishness be squared with the Prime Minister's "plans to deliver public services through community bodies, and especially his enthusiasm for faith schools"?[†] For it is not only some of the Islamic ones that explicitly or implicitly preach intolerance of conventional liberal views. The same accusation could be hurled at evangelical Christian, certain Hindu, and Orthodox Jewish schools.

If asked, Cameron might have responded that in these other cases of faith-based schools, their illiberalism cannot be a conveyer belt to terrorism, because at the present moment no significant organized fraction of their respective community of believers advocates its employment, at least against Western societies. While true, the response seems irrelevant. There is a fundamental contradiction in defining Britishness in terms of liberal values, while simultaneously using state funds to support the propagation of illiberal ones.

If nothing else Cameron's 2011 speech heralded continuing anxiety within the British establishment about the integration of Muslims, an anxiety regularly fueled by the tabloid press, by the prospective return of some of the estimated 800 or so persons who had gone abroad to fight for ISIS, and by multiplying instances of small-group and lone-wolf terrorist attacks in the United States, the Continent, and the United Kingdom itself.

Three months after Cameron's Munich speech, Trevor Phillips, a former head of the Equality and Human Rights Commission, the main governmental organ tasked with implementing non-discrimination laws, reinforced Cameron's remarks in a pamphlet on which the media feasted. Phillips was once a supporter of the Jenkins model and still an exemplar of "integration through tolerance and equal opportunity" by virtue of being a black man born in Guyana who has climbed the ladder of success. He warned in his pamphlet that by not facing up to the threat from multiculturalism, British politicians were "sleepwalking to disaster."[15]

His claim rested on an opinion poll of British Muslims commissioned by the BBC in connection with a documentary on Muslim integration. Some of the results were encouraging: a very large majority of respondents (88 percent) said they liked living in Britain and expressed a strong sense of belonging to Britain (86 percent). However, according to a BBC spokesperson, the poll evidenced "a chasm ... between those Muslims surveyed and the wider population ... on issues such as

---

[†] When founded in 2007, it incorporated among other public bodies the Commission for Racial Equality.

gender equality, homosexuality and issues relating to freedom of expression." Prominent among the numbers provoking the BBC and Phillips were the 52 percent who said homosexuality should be illegal, the 47 percent opposing the hiring of gays as teachers, and the 39 percent who agreed with the statement "wives should always obey their husbands."[16]

The absence of large majorities endorsing liberal values was only one cause of Phillips's alarm. The other was responses to questions designed to winkle out attitudes relating to religiously motivated violence and terrorism. Only about a third of respondents said they would contact the police if they knew someone was getting involved with terrorist groups in Syria. Roughly the same number refused to condemn people who took part in violence against persons mocking the prophet Muhammad. What these poll numbers signified to Phillips was the threat of "the establishment of a nation within our nation." So, what should be done? Seeming to echo David Cameron, Phillips called for a "muscular approach to integration."[17]

The Muslim Council of Britain, an umbrella group of Muslim organizations which had for years been the government's principal interlocutor on issues relating to the Muslim community, dismissed the polling numbers as the product of a deeply flawed methodology.[18] It noted that respondents had been drawn entirely from areas where Muslims predominated, in effect from ghettoes inhabited by the least successful and least integrated Muslims, while ignoring the large number of Muslims living in mixed neighborhoods.

In its report on the controversial poll and Phillips's comments, *The Economist* suggested that Phillips's pessimistic view of integration policy and its results were at best premature. Looking at post–World War II immigrants of color as a group, it called the evidence on how far Britain is actually integrating (a term it did not bother to define) as "mixed."[19] "On the positive side, the number of people claiming a mixed-race background doubled to 1.2 million, between 2001 and 2011." Moreover, it concluded, there had been a decline in racial prejudice, every ethnic community had become less ghettoized, and "black Africans, who used to be the most clustered, are spreading out the most quickly."[20]

Qualifying the good news about the shrinkage of single-ethnic clusters, however, was the finding in one scholarly study of the housing data that the result was not so much a mixing of native Brits and families with an immigrant background as the mixing of ethnic minorities in what the study's authors called "superdiversity."[21] It stemmed from a transit of whites out of areas as they became conspicuously more diverse: growth of the minority population to about 25 percent of the total seemed to trigger a marked uptick in white out-migration. To be sure, a percentage of whites often remained, but the net result was a good deal less mixing of minorities and native whites than one would anticipate if most native whites were essentially indifferent to the ethnic (as distinguished from the class) background of their neighbors.

That was one problem evidenced by the integration data. A second is "the stubborn but isolated non-integration of mainly Pakistan-origin groups in the former mill towns of the north such as Bradford, Oldham, and Burnley. Here, poverty and economic decline has led to the surly separation of a left-behind resentful white working class and an alienated Muslim minority."[22]

DOES THE UK HAVE AN INTEGRATION STRATEGY?

What grand strategic vision of how to achieve integration has inspired the succession of Conservative and Labor Party governments that have ruled the United Kingdom over the past six decades? After considering the smorgasbord of integration initiatives launched by Labor and Conservative leaders, a reasonable person might well agree with Jill Rutter that the British state has lurched along without benefit of a grand strategy even after its political leaders appeared to conclude, rightly or wrongly, that to a consequential degree integration had failed.

Would that person be right? The answer would probably be "yes" if we conceive of grand strategy as the central planning, funding, institutionalization, and execution of a consciously integrated cluster of actions reasonably calculated to achieve a measurable end, in this case the integration goals I listed above. No doubt the UK government's integration-related actions over the past few decades could be seen analogically as an extensive buffet concocted by capricious, mutually uncommunicative chefs with limited budgets, multiple uncertainties about who would like what, and insufficient oversight.

Responsibility for integration-related initiatives sprawled transiently among different ministries and quasi-independent commissions. Implementation was centralized, then largely decentralized, then partially recentralized. Budgets rose and fell in response to ministerial priorities, political imperatives, changes in government, a general squeeze from the Treasury.[23] Overall one senses messy improvisation, the absence of settled convictions about cause and effect, tactics without strategy.

But this impression may well be misleading. After all, integration was hardly the only issue governments had to address; by many reasonable measures it wasn't even the most important either to the voters or to the party leaders they elected to look after their interests. Compared with the perpetually strained National Health Service and the general state of the economy, it was decidedly secondary. Even as a security issue it hardly compared with the IRA in the 1970s and 1980s. Moreover, while integration of immigrants certainly registered among officials as a serious problem, it did not appear one at risk of metastasizing.

Being an island, the United Kingdom has more control over its borders than a country like France. Evidence of that control were the thousands of prospective migrants gathered over the better part of a decade in and around Calais, unable to complete the last twenty-six miles of their multi-thousand-mile ordeal. A country needs a grand strategy to meet threats of a near existential character, principally war, threats which, by trivializing the population's quotidian concerns, invest the government with broad discretion to concentrate resources and energy and provide it with a well-defined place to target them. Integration even after 9/11 and the London bombers of 2005 has not been seen as that sort of challenge. Whether the 2017 terrorist attacks in Manchester and London will catapult integration to the peak of the policy agenda, rather than simply intensifying surveillance by the security services, still remains to be seen.

If accused of underappreciating the need for greater investment and more active measures to force-march integration, UK leaders can take comfort from the experience of the United States, which absorbed without difficulty a quarter of a million refugees from Vietnam in the 1970s and continues to absorb millions from its poor southern neighbors and substantial numbers from elsewhere in the Global South without much effort or even the semblance of a national strategy. Like the United States, the United Kingdom has flexible labor markets compared with most Continental countries, a result of the Thatcherite revolution and the coincident weakening of trade unions. And although it has a more robust welfare state than the United States, outside the health service it is far more penny-pinching than its West European counterparts and thus provides new arrivals with an added incentive to find work.[24]

Those incentives seem unlikely to diminish at least while the Conservative Party rules. The shrinking of public services and social support for which Margaret Thatcher laid the intellectual foundations has accelerated during the current era of party rule. Despite being one of the ten richest countries in the world, if you compare per capita incomes, the United Kingdom, like the United States, has big chunks of people living in or on the margin of destitution.[25] According to a 2017 report of a House of Lords committee, approximately 1.7 million British residents do not even have a bank account.[26] An investigation of UK poverty conducted by the respected Joseph Rowntree Foundation found that roughly 14 million people live in it, that is, about one-fifth of the population, and the number has grown appreciably in the past five years of government cuts in social benefits and services.[27]

Rather than having a grand strategy, the governing elites of the United Kingdom, one could say, have had a general approach which breaks down into several elements. One element is to restrain new non-European migration by setting annual limits on family reunification entrants and imposing income requirements for the UK family members, denying spousal visas to mature men from the Global South with arranged marriages to young UK girls, issuing work visas only to persons with needed skills, and also by setting, arguably in violation of treaty obligations, strict annual limits on the entry and settling of asylum claimants.[28]

A second element is to incentivize the acquisition of language skills and entry into the workforce by creating the category of provisional settlement and making its renewal or the onward passage to citizenship dependent on the acquisition of functional English, a demonstrable effort to enter the labor force and participate in civic life, and an appreciation of British history and social and political norms. A third but closely related element is enforcement of anti-discrimination laws and the considerable incorporation of first- and second-generation migrants into the public service.

A fourth element consists of governmental acts and omissions calculated to signal respect for the Muslim minority and comfort with its presence in the United Kingdom. Prominent among the acts has been the funding of Muslim non-profit organizations to deliver services to their constituents. This has not been an uncontroversial policy. Arguably it encourages separation rather than integration. At least one city government has on that ground refused to fund any organization with an exclusive ethnic or religious remit.[29]

A second source of controversy had been the government's willingness to fund groups with very conservative leadership, a policy repudiated by Cameron in 2011. Conservative in this context means not only illiberal on cultural issues but also promulgating an interpretation of Islam inimical to cooperation with non-Islamic peoples on the basis of equal respect and furiously hostile to conflicting interpretations of the faith (seen as "heresy"), much less to those who leave it ("apostates"). A 2011 government policy paper described conservative Muslims as "extremist."[30] Driving this expansive conception of "extremist" is the solidifying assumption that acceptance of a fundamentalist theological position makes young men and women more susceptible to recruitment by jihadi groups or inspires them to homicidal rage.

That assumption had fueled criticism within British and certain European political circles of what was perceived as the reluctance of successive British governments to shut down mosques led by imams with anti-Western messages and conservative theological views and their failure to deny visas to foreign prayer leaders who attacked Western governments or other Muslims. A Muslim from northern England who stabbed to death an Ahmadi storekeeper in Glasgow in 2017 demonstrated that this concern is not entirely misplaced. The Ahmadis are a small Muslim sect which believes that a nineteenth-century Muslim living in what is now India succeeded Muhammad as the most recent instrument through which Allah has spoken to humanity. Fiery preachers from Pakistan, where Ahmadis currently suffer murderous persecution, have brought the anti-Ahmadi crusade to the United Kingdom where its theological warriors have created an organization with the single purpose of stamping out the heresy.[31]

Indifference to conspicuous manifestations of religious identity in the public workplace is another expression of an official policy guided either by principled tolerance of minority practices which don't directly threaten public order or by a calculated judgment about how best to integrate cultural minorities. There has, for instance, been no head-scarf controversy in the United Kingdom. In order to accommodate Sikhs, police departments have allowed Sikh recruits to wear turbans rather than the traditional caps and helmets. This approach to cultural diversity at the official level, backed by anti-discrimination laws, influences or perhaps simply expresses attitudes in the wider society. In the British sociopolitical atmosphere, it is unremarkable that a Muslim woman launches a business producing colorful, stylish head coverings[32] or that beard-wearing legacy-English hipsters purchase beard-softening oils from a business catering initially to Sikhs.[33]

MAKING MUSLIMS FEEL AT HOME: INTEGRATION AND THE COUNTER-TERRORISM PROJECT

According to some observers, government counter-terrorist programs have compromised efforts to make Muslims in particular feel at home in the United Kingdom. The focal point of this claim is the program called Prevent.[34] While the Labor Government launched Prevent in 2003, it took several years to acquire a tangible presence in British society. Prevent's stated purpose is to identify persons, primarily but not exclusively young people, at risk of being drawn to violent extremism. Once identified, they are encouraged to enter a program called Channel. The managers of Channel are tasked with coordinating personnel from all relevant agencies to the end of designing and implementing a deradicalization initiative custom-tailored to each entrant.

I will admit at the outset that Prevent generates feelings of ambivalence and consequent frustration in anyone, including me, who examines it with the greatest objectivity possible. The program is an effort to penetrate deeply into local communities in order to discover persons with thoughts about religion, politics, and society which could lead them to commit violent acts or to support violence by others. Its front-line instruments are deliverers of public services such as education, health, security, welfare, and also the managers of detention centers, that is, the people who come into direct contact with the country's inhabitants. They in turn are supposed to feed information to local committees chaired by a senior police officer operating within guidelines and under the broad supervision of the Home Office.[35] These committees determine, on the basis of the bits of information received from teachers, coaches, nurses, doctors, social workers, therapists, and others whether a given individual is in danger of "radicalization," the term government documents use to distinguish the mere holders of "extremist" ideas from those who are ready or have already begun to convert those ideas into action.

What follows from being identified as "a person at risk of being radicalized" is still not entirely clear. In theory, no one can be forced into the Channel program, although parents of a child determined to be at risk could, I assume, exercise their parental authority to press a son or daughter to participate. Presumably the names of persons identified as at risk will be entered into computers accessible by all the offices of government, including those concerned with recruitment into the military, the issuance of passports, and security clearance for a host of sensitive jobs, as well as by Scotland Yard and MI5. In addition, one presumes that some "at risk" adolescents and adults will be subject to covert surveillance of one or another degree of severity.

Following the Labor Party's defeat in the 2011 election, the new Home Secretary, Theresa May, commissioned a review of the program overseen by Lord Carlile, a distinguished lawyer and former senior figure in the Liberal Democratic Party.[36] The resulting report[37] submitted to parliament conceded certain flaws in the program, which had been conceived and implemented by the preceding Labour-led governments led successively by Tony Blair and Gordon Brown. One flaw was allowing Prevent to overlap with "community cohesion" programs intended to promote positive relations among British communities and between them and the state. The latter involved, among other things, state engagement with civil society organizations largely through the medium of grants. The report noted, gratuitously, that in attempting to promote cohesion the government had to some degree, and with good intentions, engaged with "extremist" organizations and implied that such engagement would not recur.

A second flaw was that "some problems have arisen notably from the feeling of some parts of the community that they have been the victims of state 'snooping.'"[38] Lord Carlile implied that a sharper focus on individual extremism with a rational connection to possible terrorist acts and better oversight would reduce this problem. In her own introduction to the report Theresa May touched on a related problem, namely, the feeling among many Muslims that Prevent was aimed peculiarly at them and that it stigmatized those Muslims with a conservative interpretation of the faith.

"[W]e must be clear," May wrote, "the ideology of extremism and terrorism is the problem; legitimate religious belief emphatically is not." Then, however, she went on to write that "we will not work with extremist organizations that oppose our values of universal human rights, equality before the law, democracy and full participation in our society."[39] She could thus be understood as equating extremism with belief, for instance, in the criminal punishment of homosexuality and insults to the Muslim religion, unequal rights for men and women in matters such as divorce and participation in civic life, in the supremacy of religious injunctions over democratic rule-making, in the heretical character of alternative interpretations of Islam, and more generally in an obligation of minimal cooperation with non-Muslims, beliefs championed by fundamentalist Muslims.

Unless she is implying that fundamentalist versions of Islam are not "legitimate" religious beliefs, one could fairly say that the line she attempts to draw between the "ideology of extremism" and "legitimate religious beliefs" is blurred. Her failure to draw a clear one stems, arguably, not from her choice of words but from the suspicion of a causal relationship between fundamentalist interpretations of the Qur'an and the Hadith and readiness for recruitment or self-recruitment to jihad.

The Prevent program by its very nature was bound to complicate relations between Muslim communities in the United Kingdom and the state. In the end, after all, Prevent is a hunt for people with bad thoughts, an additional task imposed on the hundreds of thousands of state employees with their various stereotypes and prejudices who deliver public goods to the general population. Even if the hunt were limited to identifying persons who were already disposed to commit or support the commission of violent acts, multiple cases of misidentification would be inevitable. But it is not so limited, since the stated purpose of the hunt includes identification of persons merely susceptible to becoming so disposed. Moreover, it is in the nature of the task that overzealousness in its execution will carry no sanction. The danger to one's career will arise only from failure to call to the attention of the authorities someone who later joins a terrorist group or performs a violent act and who it appears in retrospect showed signs of radicalization or susceptibility thereto.

Given the lack of operational criteria, the vast array of people of varying intellectual subtlety and prejudice obliged to forward observations of behavior or thought they deem alien, and the implicit career risks of failing to report, mistakes both sinister and ludicrous were inevitable.[40]

All in all, then, Prevent, whatever its virtues as a device for preempting terrorist attacks, was a recipe for sowing distrust and chilling speech. What statements are too rhetorically inflammatory to be tolerated? Would calling Israeli bombardment of Gaza a "crime against humanity" or Tony Blair a "war criminal" for initiating a "war of aggression" against Iraq qualify as signs of latent radicalization? How about a statement that acts of violence, even suicide bombing, are justified as a last resort against grave injustice or that acts of violence against persons mocking the prophet Mohammad should not be condemned? About one-third of participants took that latter position in a poll of Muslim opinion conducted for the BBC.[41]

Following a nine-month examination of the program, the Soros-funded Open Society Justice Initiative concluded in a report titled "Eroding Trust" that "[t]he current Prevent strategy suffers from multiple, mutually reinforcing structural flaws, the foreseeable consequence of which is a serious risk of human rights violations.... These violations include, most obviously, violations of the rights against discrimination, as well as the right to freedom of expression.... Prevent's structural flaws include the targeting of 'pre-criminality,' 'non-violent extremism,' and opposition to 'British values,' targeting which leads to governmental interference in everyday lawful discourse."[42]

For purposes of his assessment, the Open Society's principal investigator had selected certain recorded cases for close study. The one a *Guardian* reporter found most arresting described a four-year-old who drew a picture of a cucumber, which he then described to nursery school staff as a "cuker-bum." Creatively interpreting the child's phrase-making as a reference to a pressure-cooker bomb – the kind employed by the Boston Marathon killers – staff members had informed the child's mother that they were going to refer the child to the Channel program and that he might be taken away from her.[43] In the end, apparently, wiser heads prevailed.

The Open Society is hardly Prevent's only critic. After a three-day visit, the UN's special rapporteur on the right to freedom of assembly, a Kenyan lawyer, announced that Prevent had:

> created unease and uncertainty around what can be legitimately discussed in public ... I heard reports of teachers being reported for innocuous comments in class.... The spectre of Big Brother is so large, in fact, that ... some families are afraid of discussing the negative effects of terrorism ... fearing their children would talk about it at school and have their intentions misconstrued.

He concluded that by "dividing, stigmatizing and alienating segments of the population, Prevent could end up promoting extremism, rather than countering it." As an example, he quoted the mother of the four-year-old who drew his impression of his father cutting a cucumber: "I've never felt not British. And this made me feel very, very, like they tried to make me feel like an outsider. We live here. I am born and bred here.... I feel this Prevent duty is picking on you because you are Muslim, Asian, Pakistani, or whatever."[44] Despite criticism from these and other sources, including the institutional voice of British primary and secondary schoolteachers demanding that teachers be relieved of any obligation to report,[45] Prevent rolls on. Early in 2016, the National Police Chief Council reported that in the previous year 3,995 people, almost triple the number for 2014, were directed to Channel presumably through the Prevent network. According to government figures released in January 2016, among the 3,995 referrals, 415 were aged ten or under and 1,424 were in the eleven- to fifteen-year-old range.[46] In trying to explain the overall increase, a counter-terrorism researcher interviewed by *The Guardian* spoke of increased public discourse about "radicalization and the anxiety generated by the news that hundreds of young British Muslims, female as well as male, had joined ISIS." Conservative Party leaders have shared as well as contributed to the anxiety. When introducing the Counter-Terrorism Act of 2015, Theresa May, then Home Secretary, declared that ISIS had given "energy and a renewed sense of purpose to subversive Islamist organizations" in Britain.[47]

The anxiety of ordinary folk and political leaders is understandable. After all, by 2015, hundreds of young British Muslims had joined ISIS, a movement governing a territory as large as the country of Jordan and proclaiming a renewed caliphate. On November 13, 2015, fewer than a dozen jihadis coordinated by ISIS had murdered 130 and injured more than 350 people in Paris. Ten years earlier four young Englishmen without military training had contrived to murder 52 people and wound another 700 in London. In 2016, a man apparently inspired by ISIS managed to kill by truck 86 people and to injure more than 200, many of them critically, on Nice's seaside boulevard. That same year a lone gunman, also inspired by ISIS, slaughtered 49 people at an Orlando nightclub. The May 2017 suicide bomber at Ariana Grande's concert in Manchester, England, managed to kill 22 people and wound at least 120. One month later, a group of three murdered 7 and injured 48, 21 critically, with their combined van and knife attack on London Bridge and the nearby Borough Market. These slaughters by single individuals or tiny groups along with the episodic killing of one or two at a time in the name of Islam have occurred despite the tens of billions of dollars and thousands of personnel Western governments have dedicated to preempting them.

The question for Britain's current government is whether Prevent, despite its potential for aggravating feelings of mistrust between Muslims and the native population in general as well as the agencies of the British state, is an efficient means to the preemption end. Perhaps "efficient" sets an unreasonable standard. Perhaps it is hopeless to try and measure the relative utility of this security project against all the other ways in which the money and effort allocated to Prevent might be employed. For one thing, there is no way of measuring how many of the persons identified by means of Prevent would, *absent treatment in Channel*, have made the extraordinary leap from susceptible to terrorist. The Open Society's analyst, Amrit Singh, had no doubts about the program's inefficacy:

> [Its] targeting of non-violent extremism and "indicators" of risk of being drawn into terrorism lack a scientific basis. Indeed, the claim that non-violent extremism – including "radical" or religious ideology – is the precursor to terrorism has been widely discredited by the British government itself, as well as numerous reputable scholars.[48]

I think Singh overstates his case. It is true that most of the killers did not move at a studied pace from Muslim identity, whether or not pious, to embracing a fundamentalist Sunni interpretation of Islam, particularly concerning relations with other Muslims and non-Muslims, to a conviction of the need to express faith through murder. *But is that fact decisive?*

After most attacks, investigators have discovered signs of an ideologically targeted potential for homicidal rage, signs which either failed to appear on the radar screens of police and intelligence agencies before the massacre or were too comparatively slight to arouse the necessary degree of concern. Sometimes the signs accumulated over time. One of the four 7/7 London bombers, a migrant from Jamaica who had converted to Islam, had frequently and publicly raged against the British state. It turns out that months before the young Manchester bomber blew up himself and twenty-two other people, his public rants had driven fellow Muslims to report him on a counter-terror hotline. For some reason the security services appear to have concluded that he did not yet represent the kind of threat requiring close surveillance.[49]

Sometimes the conversion from alienation to dedicated killing machine appears to have been quick, catalyzed by some personal or vicarious experience often hard to locate even in retrospect. To this point we lack the algorithms needed to predict the incidence of conversion. So, we have to face the grim truth that the number of muddled or pathological adolescents and adults bristling with anger about the world and/or searching idealistically for a transforming identity and/or quietly aspiring to a moment of fame or a dollop of vengeance dwarfs the present or prospective number of security personnel needed to identify and then closely monitor – much less detain – them indefinitely. In the face of this reality, Singh and other critics conclude that programs like Prevent are misconceived. Indeed, they are deemed counter-productive because they yield so many false positives – the government itself reports that only 20 percent of those reported to Channel were found to be at risk – and add to the alienation of the Muslim community, thereby reducing the flow of useful intelligence and increasing the susceptibility to terrorist recruitment.[50]

The very lack of a predictive algorithm and the numerical insufficiency of the security services probably explain why, despite its critics, the British government persists with the program. What Prevent ideally does, May could argue, is conscript to the purposes of the security agencies huge additional numbers of public sector personnel, personnel whose jobs as teachers, health, and social workers bring them naturally into frequent, in some cases daily, non-threatening contact with the grass-roots of society. Add to that number neighborhood-patrolling coppers and also probation officers. They are the members of the public service in a position to notice small signs of change in attitudes or behavior which could, although in the vast majority of cases will not, signal a maturing or matured disposition to kill. They are as well the people most likely to notice the arrival in a neighborhood of new faces with obscure purposes.

Despite the increase in false positives, on balance the raw data the army of public servants could pour into the security services will make it somewhat more likely that they identify as imminently dangerous someone who has hitherto been off the radar or sharpen their concern for someone already in their computers but with only a metaphorical yellow flag by their names. In other words, it is not simply a matter of providing the security services with additional information; it is more importantly the quality of that information – the direct observations of public servants at the interface of relations with the wider society – that may make the effort worthwhile.

Because this argument has a certain persuasive force, not all of Prevent's critics have simply dismissed it as a politically driven, basically absurd and insidious response to domestic terrorism. Baroness Sayeeda Warsi is the daughter of a self-made Pakistani millionaire, who before the age of forty was propelled by David Cameron into the House of Lords, the co-chairmanship of the Conservative Party, and a ministerial position. Considered by many as integration's "poster child," she has criticized not the program itself but rather the absence of extensive consultation with the Muslim community's many elements during the program's design stage and its consequent launch as a legislative fait accompli.[51] This sentiment is echoed by, among others, Sir David Omand, the man who was the government's security and intelligence coordinator at Prevent's inception. "If you can persuade people of why it benefits everyone to do what you consider best," he has said, "you will get a more positive response than you would if you simply instructed them on what you want to do."[52]

In practice, as well as government rhetoric, Muslims are not the only target of Prevent and Channel. Fifteen percent of the persons referred to Channel were linked to far-right extremism, and, according to the official report on 2015 results, another 15 percent were linked to "other extremism," the forms of which were not specified.[53]

I appreciate that my discussion of Prevent has the generic structure of the lawyer's "on the one hand and on the other," a form of discourse so detested by former US President Harry Truman that, when told he needed a White House Counsel, he reputedly said be certain that the fellow has only one arm. It would be nice to reach a firm judgment on Prevent's efficacy. In time that might be possible. At this time it is not. I will return to the issues Prevent engages in Chapter 8, which elaborates a systematic national-liberal approach to migration and integration. For the moment, let me offer a last word on the integration project in the United Kingdom.

A WORK IN PROGRESS

Trying to summarize a phenomenon whose very definition is a matter of dispute is a Sisyphean task. How do we measure success when people do not agree on precisely what it is we are trying to measure and also on how to measure it? Take, for instance, the poll mentioned earlier of Muslim opinion generated by the BBC for purposes of a program on integration. Trevor Phillips, the former Committee on Race Relations chief, found in it signs of integration's failure.[54] There were the 52 percent of respondents saying homosexuality should be illegal, the 47 percent saying gay people should not work as teachers, the 39 percent who agreed with the statement "wives should always obey their husbands," positions he deemed in conflict with British values which he seems to equate with liberal interpretations of human rights. Yet similar views can be found among conservatives in every Western country. In Hungary the government itself espouses them.

Phillips also found ominous the mere one-third who said they would tell police if they knew someone who was getting involved with jihadi groups in Syria, the probably largely overlapping one-third who refused to condemn people who take part in violence against those who mock the Prophet Muhammad, and the nearly one-quarter who said they favored replacing the British legal system with Islamic law. Yet recall that 88 percent of the same survey participants thought that Britain is a good place for Muslims and that 86 percent reported a strong sense of belonging in Britain, a figure higher than the national average.[55] Certainly one could fairly argue that integration is pretty successful when most of its subjects believe they belong.

Raw facts about the economic and academic performance of the first- and particularly the second-generation minorities with a migrant background are another metric for assessing integration. Both those who feel integration has gone reasonably well and those who feel it is failing can find in those facts some support for their positions. The former can, for instance, invoke data on education. An analysis of country-wide tests of students completing their compulsory education at age sixteen found migrant children from several of the largest migrant groups doing appreciably better than the English mean. The mean difference for Indian students (mostly Hindu and Sikh) was +29.9 percent, for Nigerians +21.8 percent. Even Bangladeshi children whose parents on the whole arrived in the United Kingdom with weaker educational attainments than Indians and Nigerians tested slightly above the mean.[56]

By comparison, the children of migrants, mostly refugees, from the poor and conflict-ravaged states of Somalia and Afghanistan tested about 25 percent below the mean, approximately the same level as white Eastern Europeans. The lowest deviation from the mean belonged to the children of Portuguese immigrants. Their parents came with poor educational attainments and are concentrated in very low-wage jobs.

Relative achievement at the secondary-school level had, of course, follow-on effects: a 2014 survey of "black and minority ethnic" groups in Britain found that all minority groups compared with the white population have a higher proportion of students entering post-secondary education. Another relevant statistic: according to the OECD, "in contrast to most other European countries, the share of disadvantaged foreign-born students who succeed in school despite their background is higher than the share among disadvantaged native born."[57]

The economic data offer a more mixed picture but hardly offer an unambiguous boost to pessimists.[58] They might find some support in the fact that the unemployment rate among native-born children of migrants is almost twice as high as among youth without a migrant background. Optimists might respond that in the second generation, Pakistani and Bangladeshi women closed the employment gap between themselves and native English women by half. Pessimists will counter that the employment gap for males narrows hardly at all between the first and second generation.

The Dutch scholar Ruud Koopmans proposes measuring integration through a cross-national comparison of labor market participation, incarceration rates, and spatial segregation. According to the data he employs, the United Kingdom compared with other West European countries ranks at or near the top in the first two areas, less well with respect to spatial segregation. By contrast, when it comes to labor market participation and comparative rates of incarceration, Sweden, a European country much more receptive than the United Kingdom to the admission of refugees, has a relatively low ranking: fewer adult migrants of the first and second generations are in employment, and they constitute a relatively large percentage of the incarcerated.[59]

Koopmans speculates that these results are at least in part attributable to differences in social benefits between the two countries. Benefits are generous in Sweden, relatively parsimonious in the United Kingdom, and, of course, still thinner in the United States. The incentive to find work is correspondingly higher in the latter two and work is easier to find, particularly for people with limited education and/or fluency in the national language. Sweden's relatively low rank in labor-market integration may also derive from the fact that for several decades most of its migrants have been refugees coming, by definition, to escape from persecution or civil wars rather than in search of more profitable work. While refugees may include the highly educated, in recent decades the low-skilled have been numerous.[60] They constituted at least one-third of the refugees who entered Germany in 2015.[61]

As far as participation in the workforce is concerned, the utility of residential segregation as a marker of less integration is not entirely clear. In his study of economic integration in Britain, John Bowen concludes that Afro-Caribbeans, while less residentially concentrated, have overall been less successful economically than the generally more concentrated South Asians. Finding that self-employment in the form of small-scale entrepreneurship was substantially more common among South Asians, he speculates that residential concentration facilitated entrepreneurial activities, particularly those servicing the distinctive cultural tastes of ethnic communities.[62] The economic advantages of concentration, if they in fact exist, may be more than offset, however, by the lag in acquiring fluency in the national language for people surrounded by several generations of ethnic kin and perpetuation of traditional attitudes and practices, particularly relating to the role of women, inimical to economic progress for family units. Ethnic ghettoes, like the one in southern Sweden described by Christopher Caldwell, can also discourage employment by virtue of location in economically marginal areas.

Aside from their economic effects, ghettoes are dubious contributors to the social and psychological integration of migrant families into the national community. Ghettos seem unlikely to make a positive contribution even if the goal is not integration but rather the relaxed coexistence of culturally and socially distinct communities framed by a mutually accepted legal order and rubbing along more or less amiably in schools, pubs, and the workplace.

Voting patterns on the Brexit issue are suggestive in this respect. It is undisputed that for supporters of the leave referendum, migration (too much of it in their view) was the central issue.[63] Where were "Leave" voters concentrated? The concentration was particularly dense in the parts of England and Wales with relatively small numbers of migrants from the Global South and where migrants, many from Eastern Europe, work in low-wage jobs once held by people indigenous to England and live together in congested quarters. In London where there is the highest concentration and greatest variety of migrants, the overwhelming majority of voters supported remaining in the EU.[64] Migration thus failed as a wedge issue in a setting marked by the daily contact of natives and large numbers of first-, second-, and third-generation migrants of diverse origins in workplaces, streets, shops, restaurants, and parks. Migrant concentrations exist in the London metropolitan area but not to an extent which prevents daily intercourse on a large scale in a variety of spaces. In other words, people of different color and not infrequently different costumes than the native population are deeply integrated into the economic interactions and visual mosaic of everyday life.

Integration or merely an overarching sense of national identity together with relaxed inter-communal relationships, whichever you choose as your goal, is a bilateral relationship. Despite the Brexit vote, the relationship between the white majority and migrant-background population, though far from ideal, looks comparatively good and capable of getting better without extraordinary changes in public policy and popular narratives. In London's last mayoralty election, the son of a Pakistani bus driver, Sadiq Khan, decisively defeated a wealthy young conservative, Zac Goldsmith, who with support from then Prime Minister David Cameron had accused Khan of legitimizing Muslim radicals by appearing with a number of them on speakers' platforms. Khan, himself a supporter of gay rights and other positions despised by conservative Muslims, said that in his earlier career as a human rights lawyer, he had inevitably come into contact with radical Islamists despite his public rejection of their views.

For the most part, politicians are to the electorate what canaries were to miners in a low-tech age. So, the fact that some Conservative Party politicians distanced themselves from Goldsmith's charges reinforces the impression of a country where society is not polarized around relations between migrant-background families and the white native majority. An earlier tell in this respect was David Cameron's decision to grant Sayeeda Warsi a peerage to the end of bringing her into his government. Incongruously he was one Conservative who would subsequently support Goldsmith's attack on Khan. Perhaps he was merely showing solidarity with a fellow Etonian. Paradoxically, the anti-immigrant sentiments which drove the Brexit vote, when analyzed, contain a positive element, namely, the limited signs of color or religion rather than migration as such as the main drivers of the Leave vote.

After all, withdrawal from the EU could only affect immigration from white-majority, historically Christian countries. And some of the most intensely anti-EU voters were in parts of the country where EU nationals, particularly those from Poland, clustered.[65] Admittedly, in the course of the referendum campaign, some supporters of Brexit dog-whistled the religious issue with pictures of Turkish people notionally waiting to pour into the United Kingdom as if Turkish membership were imminent. Still, the voters' animus seemed directed not so much at the composition of migrant streams but at their effect on the legacy population's enjoyment of public goods like housing, schools, and the health service.[66] In addition, low-skilled natives complained about the impact of migration on wages and job openings. Whether many jobs in low-margin areas of the economy could have survived if employers had drawn on the native population by offering better wages is the sort of question more interesting to economists than the unemployed.

For those like myself who find newsworthy events as suggestive as big data about the emotional condition of a society, stories from 2018 support the view that Britain's indigenous white majority is overall becoming comfortable with the stark fact of racial and religious diversity. One is the generally positive public and media response to the marriage of Prince Harry to Meghan Markle, a mixed-race American actress with a demonstrably liberal social conscience. The second is the "Windrush" affair stemming from the Home Office's effort summarily to deport long-settled Afro-Caribbean residents who had arrived in the United Kingdom decades earlier, many as young children of the first wave of Caribbean migrants.

Under the UK law at that time, Commonwealth citizens could enter with their children at will. Many had come at the urging of the UK government to fill gaps in the labor force. In a 1971 law parliament had given all Commonwealth migrants indefinite leave to remain. Since at that point they had all the benefits of citizenship, some of them and even their children and grandchildren had never bothered to apply for naturalization papers. They simply went about integrating economically and socially. They became British. But then, in 2010, when the Conservative-Liberal Democratic Coalition came into office, the new Home Secretary, Theresa May, set about trying to grind down the country's net migration figures to the low level promised in the Conservative Party's Election Manifesto.

One means to that end was summary deportation with only an after-the-fact opportunity to appeal. A second means, made law by an act of parliament in 2012, was to require proof of legitimate presence in the country as a condition of obtaining employment, renting property, or accessing most social benefits including access to the health care system. Anyone renting, employing, or providing services without requiring such proof was subject to criminal penalties.[67]

In order to avoid being victimized by the new law and accompanying regulations and policies, survivors of the pre-1971 Afro-Caribbean migrant generation and their heirs had to show not only that they had arrived before the 1971 law granting permanent status but in addition that they had been continuously resident in the United Kingdom. A number yet to be clearly established could not satisfy even the first condition because in 2010 the landing cards they or their parents or grandparents had filled out on arriving at UK ports of disembarkation had been destroyed by a bureaucratic decision allegedly to reduce all sorts of old paper records.[68]

Empowered or driven by the zeal of their political masters, officers of the Border Agency launched a hammering campaign to identify and eject the undocumented. It fell with peculiar force on descendants of the early Afro-Caribbean migration and Caribbean islanders who had come a little later when entry was still almost at will and work plentiful. One predictable result of the campaign were poignant cases brought to the bar of public opinion by members of parliament, by the strongly institutionalized human rights and civil liberties movements, and the national press and found to be egregiously unjust.

In terms of British attitudes toward race, the Windrush affair had two arresting dimensions. One was the position taken by conservative newspapers and journals epitomized by an article in *The Spectator*, an impeccable organ of conservative opinion. Writing in April 2018, the columnist Brendan O'Neill decried what he characterized as the government's scandalous behavior:

> Windrush people who are effectively paperless – because they were told they could stay, because they were told they did not need papers, because they feel and *are* British – are now having their lives turned upside down.... Some of their stories are harrowing. The 66-year-old special-needs teacher who has been in Britain since he was nine years old and yet lost his job last year when he was judged to be an illegal immigrant. A 61-year-old woman who has been in Britain for more than 50 years and yet who was locked up in Yarl's Wood detention centre for a week and threatened with deportation to Jamaica – a country she hasn't visited for more than half a century. The man who has lived and worked in London for more than 40 years who was told he could no longer receive NHS care. He has prostate cancer.
>
> These people are as British as me. Or as Theresa May, indeed. It is as outrageous to threaten with deportation the 70-year-old woman who was born in Jamaica but who worked as a nurse and a mum in Britain for decades as it would be to throw May out of the country.[69]

"The Windrush scandal is a product of two things," O'Neill continues. One is "an entirely degraded understanding of what it means to be a citizen." It is not just a piece of paper or answers to a list of questions on some citizenship exam. "It is about feeling part of a nation and subscribing to that nation's values. It is about working and raising children and, in the process, keeping your society alive and prosperous. So many of the Windrush-era generation have done precisely this."

The other, he writes, is May's "great misreading of public concern about mass immigration as [if it equated with] public hostility to migrants ... The majority of British people ... want a greater democratic say over the immigration question, yes, but this doesn't mean they hate migrants or want them to suffer." As proof he then cites a recent poll which found that 60 percent of people oppose what the government has been doing to the Windrush migrants.[70]

The second arresting dimension of the scandal, one which reinforces O'Neill's view of public opinion, is the government's response to the hue and cry. Addressing parliament about the impact of her government's immigration policies on long-resident Afro-Caribbeans, Prime Minister May declared: "These people are British, they are part of us."[71] She promised that where damage had already been done, the government would compensate those who had suffered. Her successor as Home Secretary, Amber Rudd, initially resisted demands that she resign, in effect pleading an excess of zeal by lower-level bureaucrats. But when forced to reverse an earlier denial that regional offices of the Border Agency had been given hard targets for removal of the undocumented, targets which some parliamentarians assumed had inspired the blind zeal of Border Agency officials, she succumbed.

The third story grew out of the second. To replace Rudd as Home Secretary Prime Minister May chose a Muslim, Sajid Javid. Javid, the son of a man who arrived from Pakistan in 1961 with three pounds in his pocket and made his living as a bus driver, will preside over one of the three most important departments of the British government, the department with responsibility among other things for immigration. One of his first actions was to disown the Theresa May–authored "hostile environment" tactic for shrinking unauthorized residence. Another was promising to safeguard the rights of the Windrush generation and to compensate those of its members who have been injured by his predecessor's policies.

The fourth news story was about Mo Salah, an Egyptian soccer player who joined the Liverpool team in 2018. Scoring forty-three goals in forty-nine games, he drove the team to competitive heights it had not known for more than a decade, specifically to victory in the finals of the European Champions League, the most prominent tournament in soccer after the World Cup. For this achievement, he was voted England's player of the year by both his fellow players and the Football Writers' Association.[72]

In addition to being a remarkable scorer, Salah is a devout Muslim playing in a city not known as a center of the cosmopolitan elite. After scoring a goal, Salah first "runs to the fans closest to him, arms outstretched. He [then] stands stock still, soaking in the adulation."[73] Finally "he walks slowly back to the center circle ... raises his hands to the sky and then kneels on the field, prostrating himself in a deeply personal demonstration of his Muslim faith. 'The crowd goes a little quieter, allows him that moment of reflection, [there] is another roar as he stands up and then everyone celebrates again.'"[74]

In 2016, an *Economist* columnist who writes under the pen name Bagehot made a Christmas Eve visit to Ely, "a cathedral city sprouting from the prairies of eastern England, where thousands of central and eastern Europeans have moved to pick vegetables for low wages." Afterward the columnist proclaimed "a more cohesive society than the doom-mongers claim."[75] He goes to a food shop, the "White and Red" (colors of the Polish flag) owned by local Poles. It looks as if a little piece of Poland has been plopped down in the middle of the English plain but for one fact, namely, that Britons also shop there "lured by the garlicky sausage and crusty bread." Meanwhile "Poles are picking up British habits, like eating turkey and watching the queen's Christmas speech.... Without oaths, integration classes or other forms of state do-goodery, central European cultures are melding with local ones ... [with] children [in common schools] leading the way."

To the author, Ely is a miniature version of the larger picture:

Fully 82% of [Britain's] citizens socialize at least monthly with people from different ethnic or religious backgrounds; from 2003 to 2016 the proportion calling their vicinity "cohesive" rose from 80% to 89%; over half of first-generation migrants have friends of a different ethnicity (among their kids the proportion is nearer three-quarters); numbers of inter-ethnic marriages and households are rising; education and employment gaps are shrinking. The proportion of British–Pakistani households using English as their main language rose from 15% to 45% in the 13 years to 2010.

So, he concludes in ringing tones:

> The story of British life in 2017 is that new immigrants are enriching and combining with this mongrel culture as loyally as their predecessors once did. In pubs and churches, gyms and schools, Britishness is being made and remade not by political diktat but by an organic process of mixing and mingling.... In this troubled age let this diverse country take more pride in all that.[76]

The writer paints an uplifting portrait of contemporary Britain. He leaves the reader with the same good feeling as a bracing shower at the end of a hard day. But he also leaves unanswered two questions. One is whether, as the scholar/practitioner Jill Rutter implies, more ample government do-goodery, informed now by a considerable experience, could accelerate the "enriching and combining."[77] The other is whether a continuation of mass killing by terrorists invoking Islam will trigger that spiral of harsh profile-driven security measures that will throw a jammer in the works of integration. We can only hope that this journalist, an optimistic cosmopolitan, is not celebrating prematurely. Along with all those cited by Bagehot, one augury of successful integration and inspiring symbol of the process now under way is Eleanor Smith, whose mother emigrated from Barbados in 1954 to work in the National Health Service. Smith holds the parliamentary seat for Wolverhampton South West, the constituency adjacent to the one occupied by Enoch Powell in 1967 when he proclaimed that "rivers of blood" would flow through the streets of Britain if it did not close the doors to colored people.

6

France

THE UNFINISHED ROAD TOWARD FRATERNITY

France's response to its immigrant Muslim minority has been ethically confused and politically ambivalent, a fact personified by its once and probably not future president, the fiery bantam rooster Nicholas Sarkozy. In 2003, while serving as Minister of the Interior, he initiated formation of the French Council of the Muslim Faith in the hope that it would serve as a representative interlocutor for Islam in France. Responding to critics claiming that he was undermining the basic Republican idea of a nation constituted by equal and fraternal individual citizens rather than a cluster of separate communities, he said it would be "catastrophic [to deny] the cultural and religious identify of Muslims. An identity denied is an identity that radicalizes."[1] He went on to ask rhetorically:

> If you find Islam to be incompatible with the Republic, then what do you do with the five million people of Muslim origin living in France? Do you kick them out, or make them convert, or ask them not to practice their religion? ... With the French Council of the Muslim Faith, we are organizing an Islam that is compatible with the values of the Republic.[2]

Six years later, ensconced in the presidential palace, sensing a sharpening of anti-Muslim feeling in the electorate, Sarkozy's message became muddled. He appealed, on the one hand, for tolerance, but, on the other, warned that Muslims and all other members of religious faiths must embrace Europe's historical values and avoid "ostentation or provocation" in religious practice. Referring to the results of a recent Swiss referendum banning minarets on mosques, he said it should inspire reflection on the resentment felt by Swiss people and many other Europeans, "including the French people."[3] Then,

> [addressing my Muslim countrymen I] say I will do everything to make them feel they are citizens like any other enjoying the same rights as all the others to live their

faith and practice their religion with the same liberty and dignity. I will combat any form of discrimination.... But I also want to tell them that in our country, where Christian civilization has left such a deep trace, where republican values are an integral part of our national identity, everything that could be taken as a challenge to this heritage and its values would condemn to failure the necessary inauguration of a French Islam.[4]

Sarkozy's rhetoric grew sharper in the 2012 presidential election. Running behind in his bid for a second term and straining to draw votes from the extreme right candidate, Marine Le Pen, Sarkozy suddenly echoed her claim that meat ritually slaughtered according to Muslim norms (halal) was being sold surreptitiously to unsuspecting non-Muslim consumers and thus encroaching on the French way of life, a claim characterized by a *Guardian* journalist as the "secret Islamization of the dinner plate."[5] In what seemed an attempt to appropriate the issue, Sarkozy proposed that halal meat options be unavailable in state school canteens and that all meat sold in France be carefully labeled to distinguish halal cuts.

Defeated by Francois Holland in 2012, Sarkozy ran again in 2016, intensifying his criticism of Muslims. Having warned Muslims in 2009 not to be provocative in exercising their equal rights, he now denounced the "burkini," a modest, body-covering bathing suit popular among conservative Muslim women as a violation of his injunction. The "burkini," he asserted, was a "provocation" that supports radicalized Islam, adding that "[w]e don't imprison women behind fabric." France, he warned the electorate, had to fight to protect its "secular way of life." In this spirit, he slammed the "tyranny of minorities" and while reaffirming that Muslims in France are French people, "exactly like any other ones," he emphasized their duty as French nationals to assimilate. "Once you become French," he thundered, "your ancestors are the Gauls," a claim which moved Myriam El-Khomri, the Socialist labor minister and daughter of a Muslim family, to observe that "I too adore Asterix [a comic-strip muscle-man hero always battling the Roman occupiers of Gaul] but thankfully France is a much vaster idea than this particularly narrow-minded vision."[6] In the race for his conservative party's nomination Sarkozy succeeded in finishing third.

Did his electoral failure stem from his divisive rhetoric or from the nakedness of his ambition and the affectedly macho swagger in his soap-opera personal life? Or did it stem largely from the incontrovertible fact that he had failed during his time in office to invigorate the sclerotic economy, reduce unemployment, halt the decline of French influence within the EU, or reduce the cultural anxieties swirling within the native French community? The answer is unclear. What can at least be said is that his defeat was overdetermined.

Sarkozy, nevertheless, is not a French Trump. He was, after all, the first French politician to advocate something resembling American-style affirmative action as a means of hastening assimilation. Doing so meant taking a political risk. It cut against the Republican tradition exemplified by the fact that the government refuses to collect census data concerning religious and ethnic identity on the grounds that asking people to identify themselves as something more than "French" would be inconsistent with the nation's deepest value. For seeking such information could imply a country constituted by self-regarding communities living together under one constitutional roof.

In the past, to be a nationalist one had to reject that idea of France. For nationalists, the French state embodies the collective will and unique genius of its inhabitants. France as an ideal knits together past, present, and future generations; it is not and should not become a prosaic set of norms and institutions continuously negotiated among subgroups like capital and labor, Catholics and Protestants, Jews and Muslims, Bretons and Basques, the pious and the agnostic. Only an integral France, an organic France, can transcend all the latent conflicts native to modern societies.

Even Sarkozy's most notorious public statements contain mixed messages. A 2012 headline in *The Guardian* reads: "Nicholas Sarkozy: there are too many foreigners in France."[7] Taken alone those words could be lifted from a xenophobic tirade. In the context of the complete sentence – "we can no longer manage to find them [i.e., "foreigners"] accommodation, a job, [and] a school" – they suggest not intractable hostility to foreigners but rather belief that the size of migration in relationship to the existing capacities of the French state disable the latter from fulfilling its responsibility to give newcomers the social support owed to all French nationals. The implication of the sentence is that persons allowed to enter and settle should have the same rights as French people of ancient lineage.

The sum of his statements as I read them reveals a believer in a nation of individuals able to experience liberty and equality in the public realm, however great their diversity in private life, as long as they share a feeling of fraternity. Fraternity, however, requires a shared and prideful participation in the historical drama which is France: a history and a way of life. Fostering participation in that sense is part of the state's vocation. Embracing participation – that is, embracing the norms, practices, and values that constitute French culture and are manifest in its public spaces – is the migrant's duty and essential to successful integration.

FRANCE VERSUS THE UNITED KINGDOM

In the simplifying discourse of journalists and politicians, that conception of the obligations of the state and of the migrant (in particular, the Muslim migrant) makes France the polar opposite of the United Kingdom. But how well does this supposed opposition reflect reality? Imperfectly, I think it fair to say.

Certainly, there are manifest differences in the way the state and the native majority in each country relate to people who identify as Muslims. There has, for instance, been no controversy in the United Kingdom over women choosing to cover their hair, their entire bodies, or even their face. As for beach clothing, while a woman wishing to enjoy the chilly waters of the United Kingdom might well be fined should she wear nothing but her goose bumps, ordinances forbidding concealment of body parts, however comprehensively, are to the best of my knowledge unknown. The claim, were it ever made, that burkini-wearing threatened the integrity of British culture would have Brits of all political views falling all over each other in a fit of hysterical laughter.

Just as dress-code issues have found no traction in British political discourse, neither to any great extent has the creation and construction of prayer spaces and mosques, with or without minarets. Admittedly, this difference might conceivably stem from the fact that the English as a whole (and the Scots, for that matter) seem little interested in religion, despite having a national church.[8] In France, polling indicates a significant minority remains strongly attached to its inherited Catholic identity.[9] It is hard to see, however, how a residual Catholic identity as such would generate anxiety about halal food, another matter absent from the British political landscape. There was a time, I suppose, when one might have chalked this up to a general British indifference to culinary matters. After all, to paraphrase one wit, while the French dined the British grazed. But thanks to increased travel, growing national wealth, and the free movement of people – including chefs – within the EU, that distinction, such as it was, no longer holds.

In the United Kingdom, moreover, no taboo has prevented the collection of data on religion and ethnicity or denied public funding of non-profits that provide services exclusively to an ethnic or religious group. When David Cameron as prime minister hailed the end of multiculturalism, he was, it appears, referring not to sectarian organizations in general but only those promoting an identity inimical to amiable intercourse with other groups. Take, for instance, France's effort to erect a wall between religion and state institutions, an effort epitomized by the 1994 law banning the wearing of "ostentatious" religious symbols (head scarves, large crosses, yarmulkes) from public schools. In the United Kingdom, students and presumably teachers as well can adorn themselves as they wish. And objective descriptions of the major religious faiths are part of school curricula.

Another distinguishing feature of the approach to integration in the United Kingdom has been the very early adoption of anti-discrimination laws and subsequent toughening of them. French anti-discrimination legislation is of very recent origin. Consistent with the French reluctance to concede to its nationals any identity other than being French, affirmative action to facilitate entry of Muslims and others with a Global South migrant background into elite schools and the public service was a long time coming, and when it came, it arrived in the form of identification by neighborhood, rather than race or religion.[*]

[*] Still, by using geography as an unspoken proxy for minority status, in the past decade the French government has made an effort to reduce the isolation and alienation of immigrant ghettoes, which lie mostly on the periphery of Paris and other major cities, by channeling to

With respect to integration, then, the differences between the United Kingdom and France, while not precisely polar, have been profound in terms of discourse and significant in terms of practice. Like all political phenomena, they are rooted in history and have no single indisputable source. In one relevant respect, the countries are similar. Each was a great imperial power still dominating large swathes of the globe at the end of the World War II. In each a large proportion of postwar migrants came from the areas it once ruled and in many cases were able to speak the imperial language as well as their native one.

A second possibly relevant similarity is that both countries had an earlier experience of integrating migrants and providing asylum. Jews fleeing bigotry and pogroms in Eastern Europe found refuge in the United Kingdom and France, particularly during the nineteenth century. These refugees gradually acquired the full rights of citizenship as suspicion about their capacity for loyalty to the nation diminished. In the French case, Polish nationalists like Frederic Chopin, escaping persecution by Russian and German occupiers, were another migrant stream. Following them in the twentieth century were Spanish supporters of the secular Republic, who escaped across the Pyrenees into France after the fascist victory in their country's civil war. France in the pre- and also immediate post–World War II decades also provided a haven for a small number of African Americans, mainly writers and entertainers who sought a less racist home than the still profoundly segregated United States.

Beyond those two points of resemblance, one can add points they share with all the other wealthy European states: elected governments, relatively independent judiciaries, judicially enforceable political and civil rights, civilian control of the military, near universal literacy, and welfare states which at a minimum protect the vast majority of nationals from destitution and assure universal access to health care.

For all their similarities, the differences in their historical experiences are striking. One could say that Britain is the product of history, while France is the product of human will. The English language and the associated norms and practices which now distinguish most inhabitants of the British Isles evolved organically over millennia. English culture gradually absorbed regional norms and dialects and the distinctive tongues of Wales, Scotland, and Ireland. This was accomplished less by the sword (except in the Irish case) than by commerce, travel, and opportunities for public service in an explosively expanding empire. Also, undoubtedly fostering absorption was the success of the English elite in organizing a state which waged war successfully, built an enormous empire, and maintained a system of justice that gave a relatively large measure of security to private life, at least for the middle classes.

The gradual development of a rather homogeneous cultural order paralleled the gradual evolution of a political order that was responsive to changes in society and

them additional resources, an effort limited of course by the state's straitened finances despite high taxes. Straitened finances have correspondingly limited British efforts in this regard.

economy and, correspondingly, ideas about legitimacy. While over the centuries monarchical family lines changed with varying degrees of violence, aside from a very brief interregnum, the monarchy, although stripped of the power to govern, endures to this day as the focal point for an inclusive national identity. And because the rich and the landed in turn gradually expanded participation in the competition for power until it included the entire settled adult population, the United Kingdom has not had anything resembling a constitutional rupture for more than three centuries.

France's is a different story. The Revolution that began in 1789 achieved a complete rupture in the structure of authority. However much the inhabitants of the space then recognized as France liked or disliked a monarch, until the Revolution the monarchy and the Catholic Church were the fount of legitimate authority and therefore of order and predictability in day-to-day life. The Revolution's militants declared a new basis for legitimate authority. In one stroke, the French people were transformed from subjects to citizens, bonded by the values of liberty, equality, and fraternity. They became a new nation. To be sure, this was an ideal, a vision of literate anti-clerical thinkers and activists which had to be progressively sold and in certain cases imposed on what was then largely a peasant population that looked to a vast Catholic priesthood for moral guidance, an interpretation of life, and the celebration of birth, marriage, and death.

In 1814, a multi-country alliance finally defeated Napoleon, the Revolution's dictatorial guardian, and sat the guillotined monarch's brother on the vacant throne. But it could not reestablish monarchical legitimacy on enduring foundations, because it could not turn citizens back into subjects.

Such a dramatic political and ideological rupture, fiercely resisted by a very substantial part of the population and followed by the tumultuous economic and social transformations that accompanied the industrial revolution, delayed for at least half a century the crystallization of Republican legitimacy. Indeed, one could argue that the idea of electoral democracy as the sole basis for legitimate authority remained contested until the end of World War II and even then was fragile until the majority, led paradoxically by the former general and very Catholic traditionalist, Charles de Gaulle, promulgated the Fifth Republic in 1958. That was the moment of decisive defeat for the anti-democratic elements in society and the army.

Some Catholic clergy supported the initial stages of the Revolution. In short order, however, the revolution took a radical turn and its militants began identifying the Church and the priesthood with internal and external counter-revolutionary forces. Through an intensifying dialectic of hostility, France in the wake of the Napoleonic era became a place where the Catholic Church and the pious became an integral element of the royalist anti-democratic, politically reactionary fraction of France's population. Opposed to it was the secular state which in the form of the Third Republic began governing France in 1871, following Napoleon III's disastrous defeat in the Franco-Prussian War. Determined to strengthen the state whose weakness military defeat had exposed, its bourgeois leaders launched an ambitious project to educate the diverse peoples living within the internationally recognized boundaries of France into seeing the Republican government as the only legitimate source of authority.

To that end Republican elites made schooling free, abolished religious education in the public schools, forbade members of religious orders from teaching in them, and marched to the far corners of the land an army of schoolteachers committed to inculcating Republican values and constructing the sensation of belonging to the great fraternal association that was the French nation.[10] Since in 1871 well under half of the people living on French soil spoke French as their native language, achieving that goal meant weaning the next generation off regional languages like Basque, Bretton, and Occitan as well as loosening the population's connection to the Catholic clergy and through it to Rome. In the following decades, the teacher and the priest, the town hall and the parish church came to symbolize the ideological antipodes in towns and villages throughout the country. The final formal step in this cultural war was the laical law of 1905, so frequently invoked these days, which definitively declared the separation of church and state.

While the Republic won, its victory was far from total. Opposition to its secular liberalism, at all times simmering, would periodically come to a boil as it did, for instance, in the period 1894–1906 when French society erupted in a savage partisan conflict over the spurious conviction of captain Alfred Dreyfuss, one of the few Jewish officers in the French army, by a military court. Although Jewish emancipation had begun a century earlier and Jews had by the last years of the nineteenth century become prominent in public as well as commercial and intellectual life, anti-Semitism remained a club with which to batter Republican government.

The battering continued through the inter-war years. The spread of Communist ideology in the wake of the Bolshevik Revolution sharpened the hostility between capital and labor spawned by the industrial revolution in France. Fear of revolution led parts of the capitalist class to associate with the ultra-Catholic royalist military caste in a coalition which became explicitly anti-democratic when elections in 1936 brought to power a left-of-center coalition of liberals, socialists, and communists, the so-called Popular Front, led by Leon Blum. Bellowing the slogan "Better Hitler than Blum" (who was Jewish), fighting squads of the right battled trade unionists in the streets of Paris.

In the wake of the sudden and overwhelming defeat of the French army in 1940, they got their preference. The Third Republic fell, and Hitler's forces occupied Paris and negotiated satellite status with a regime of the French Right led by a former general, Philippe Petain, a hero of the country's Pyrrhic victory in World War I. Hitler's defeat and the coincident delegitimation of the collaborationist French Right allowed a Fourth Republic to emerge from the ruins of the Third only to shatter thirteen years later against the wall of Algerian nationalism. It then took Charles de Gaulle, the ardent Catholic and conservative nationalist, to establish the current Fifth Republic, to negotiate Algerian independence, and to organize the defeat of an attempted coup d'etat by military ultras and their civilian proto-fascist supporters.

By comparison to this history of repeated political rupture and often profound, sometimes murderous, social division, the United Kingdom is a paradigm of almost boring continuity, a nation growing organically out of the soil of history rather than one conscientiously built by elites willing its fabrication out of disparate fragments and struggling against other elites with very different visions of politics and society. To the secular political and intellectual elites of a country with France's history of bitter struggle against the enemies of Republican government and the liberal culture associated with it, the product of their grinding effort would naturally appear fragile. And because in the course of the struggle to maintain Republican government, the Catholic Church and the ardently pious were important elements of the enemy coalition, defenders of the revolutionary legacy – liberty, equality, fraternity – were virtually bound to experience hyper-sensitivity about any ardent manifestations of piety in public spaces.

When one takes the post-revolutionary history of France into account, the hostility of many politicians, some intellectuals, and swathes of the electorate to head scarves, burkinis, prayer in the streets, and demands for halal food in schools becomes more comprehensible. Moreover, the successive falls and renewals of Republican government and the gradual expansion of liberty and equality in the face of a reactionary Church and the unreconciled elements of the upper classes are not the whole of the historical narrative.

Differences between France and the United Kingdom with respect to migration and integration may also stem in part from the distinctive ways in which their colonial empires dissolved. For the latter, the dissolution was largely consensual. Pragmatism trumped nostalgia. Its people had been exhausted by two great wars in the space of thirty years, its state virtually bankrupted by the drain of World War II. It was pressured by its erstwhile ally, a US government determined to build a global free-trading system unhindered by imperial preferences. Confronted by increasingly mobilized colonial populations, the United Kingdom negotiated departures from its vast holdings rather than being forced into a bloody retreat, one country at a time. Labor and Conservative governments did the same sums: in the circumstances of the postwar world, colonialism no longer paid. There were one or two rear-guard actions like the brutal repression of the Kikuyu tribal revolt in 1950s Kenya,[11] but nothing on a grand scale.

France, by contrast, soaked its great recessional in gore, first in Indo-China and then, more terribly, in Algeria, where its effort to keep the country French by all means necessary failed, but only after three-quarters of a million of the indigenous Muslim population were killed.[12] Following that savage war, the settler population fled pretty much en masse into France, forming an electoral base for the neo-fascist National Front Party founded by a former French paratrooper in Algeria, Jean-Marie Le Pen. Savagery was not limited to Algeria. When Algerians living in Paris gathered to protest the war, French police massacred an estimated 200 of them by means that included hurling bound men into the Seine to drown.[13]

France's withdrawal from Algeria did not end its jagged relationship to the place and its people. In the 1990s, France like other Western states quietly supported the pitiless campaign waged by Algeria's secular authoritarian government against the Islamist insurgency that had been galvanized by the government's refusal to respect the results of an election when an Islamist party emerged victorious. Responding to French support for the Algerian authorities, during 1995 and 1996 an insurgent cell planted bombs in various parts of the Paris underground transportation system, killing eight and wounding nearly 160 people. Nevertheless, Algerians continued throughout the post–World War II decades to constitute the largest single source of Muslim migration to France.

The peculiarly uneasy relationship between the legacy French and the North African Muslim immigrants and their descendants antedates the Algerian war of independence and in retrospect made it inevitable. After conquering the territory of Algeria in a series of bloody campaigns, the French government eventually incorporated it into the French state, so that from the perspective of Paris, Algeria was both psychologically and politically as much a part of France as Provence. Incorporation distinguished it from the great bulk of other French-dominated territories including Algeria's North African neighbors, Tunisia and Morocco.

In the French political narrative, the territory of Algeria was a part of the French nation. But the same could not be said of its indigenous Muslim inhabitants. They were in a sense French "nationals," but they were not deemed "citizens" and thus formed a political as well as an economic underclass in the land of their ancestors. Until the Fourth Republic, citizenship was restricted to the Christians who had moved to Algeria from southern parts of France, Spain, and Italy and, after some delay, long-settled Sephardic Jews.[14] Collectively they formed a settler class which helped consolidate France's grip on the territory. Early in the Fourth Republic the government finally offered citizenship to indigenous Muslims, but only to those who agreed to accept the full application of French law, which would displace sharia law even with respect to family matters.[15] Most Muslims apparently regarded the initiative as one of conditioning citizenship on the surrender of their Muslim identity. A mere handful accepted the offer.

Algerian independence produced flight or expulsion of the one and a half million settlers, most of whom had opposed first equal rights for the Muslim population and then independence. The French soil to which they carried their grievances and hatreds was not virgin. In his memoir, *No Name in the Street*,[16] the great African-American writer James Baldwin recalls sitting in a Parisian sidewalk café one sunny afternoon in 1948, not long after moving to France. He "had watched the police . . . beat an old, one-armed Arab peanut vendor senseless . . . and had watched the unconcerned faces" of the French among whom he sat. "With a 'generous smile' Baldwin's friends reassured him that he was different from the Arabs" in that the black American is very evolved. So, he put to them a question he thought "very cunning: If so crude a nation as the United States could produce so gloriously civilized a creature as myself, how was it that the French, armed with centuries of civilized grace, had been unable to civilize the Arab?"[7]

Their answer was blunt. France had not succeeded in civilizing the Arabs because "'[t]he Arabs did not wish to be civilized.' They, the Arabs, had their own traditions, and 'the Arab was always hiding something; you couldn't guess what he was thinking and couldn't trust what he was saying. And they had a different attitude toward women, they were very brutal with them, in a word they were rapists, and they stole, and they carried knives." Recalling this memorable anecdote of Baldwin, Adam Shatz, the gifted former literary editor of *The Nation*, writes:

> Aside from ageing veterans of the French-Algerian war, no one in France talks about "the Arabs" any longer. Instead they speak of "the Muslims." But France's Muslims are the descendants of that Arab peanut vendor – and, all too often, targets of the same racist intolerance. Like the racism Baldwin encountered among his Parisian friends, it often wears an ennobling mask: anti-terrorist, secular, feminist.[18]

Of course, Baldwin's account is merely a single instant in one man's life. We have no measure of the depth or breadth of hostility to North African Muslims in the years before immigration became such a toxic issue in French politics and society. Certainly, anti-Muslim feeling was not uniform. Muslims had in large numbers fought and died for France in the World War I. As an expression of gratitude, the French government had supported the construction in Paris of the Grand Mosque, a Parisian landmark to this day. But if we are trying to appreciate why United Kingdom and French attitudes toward their respective Muslim populations differ so strikingly, the sordid history of French conquest and colonization in North Africa and the increasing association of Islam in France with North African immigration is strongly suggestive. Hostility to Islam among French intellectuals certainly has long roots. Following a trip to Algeria in 1839, Alexis de Tocqueville, famous to this day for the acute observations of the United States recorded in his book *Democracy in America*, wrote:

> I must say that I emerged convinced that there are in the entire world few religions with such morbid consequences as that of Mohammed. To me it is the primary cause of the now visible decadence of the Islamic world.[19]

The travails of building a common French consciousness after the Revolution and consolidating Republican government together with the very specific history of relations between France and the Muslims of North Africa, particularly Algeria, help to explain toxicity in the French majority's response to its Muslim minority. They are not, however, the entire story, but its other parts are not unique to France. For instance, the notorious ghettoization of migrant families on the rim of Paris and other major cities mirrors on a larger scale the evolution of Gothenburg's migrant ghetto. In both cases housing is cheap, provides basic amenities, but is relatively remote from current centers of economic activity. Other facets of the French problem – disproportionate presence of second-generation migrants in the prison system, very severe youth unemployment, job discrimination, harsh relations between migrant communities and the police – also mirror in varying degrees the experience of other EU members.

After ISIS seized a wide swathe of territory in the Middle East, there were news reports of young French men and women, including a considerable number of recent converts to Islam, leaving France to join "the caliphate."[20] Some of these recruits would then presumably become battle-hardened before returning to France. These stories aroused a tangible fear in the country that public security and order were at grave risk.

Still, this development was not unique to France. What did at first seem unique was the cascade of terrorist assaults beginning with the atrocities of a man called Mohammed Merah, who in March 2012 murdered three French Muslim soldiers in and around Toulouse, before slaughtering a teacher and three students in front of a Jewish school in Toulouse. One victim was a little girl he shot in the head after carefully turning her toward the school's surveillance camera to better record the terrifying tableau. According to the American academic Mark Lilla,[21] public concern was further escalated by a flurry of social media statements "by French Muslim sympathizers," which celebrated Merah's "heroism" after police discovered his hiding place and shot him dead. The number of these celebrants, and whether they were the work of many authors or a mere handful assuming different social media identities, is unclear.

Two years later, a Franco-Algerian petty criminal, Mehdi Nemmouche, walked into the Jewish Museum in Brussels with an assault rifle and murdered four people. This was a prelude to the January 2015 *Charlie Hebdo* and kosher-deli massacres which left seventeen dead in their wake. Over the next two years the human toll multiplied. Ten months later 130 were dead and 368 wounded in the bombing and shooting of Parisians at a football match in the suburbs of Paris and then at a concert hall and on streets in the heart of the city. Then Nice on Bastille Day, 2016, when one man with a nineteen-ton cargo truck plunged into celebrants strolling on the city's seaside promenade: 86 dead, dozens maimed.

Interspersed were micro-assaults: an elderly priest's throat slit in the church of a small town in Normandy by two young locals; a Muslim convert with a Facebook page brandishing radical Islamic material walking into a police station outside of Tours and, crying "Allahu Akbar," as he slashed three policemen with a long knife before being shot; the next day a Muslim man with the same cry-out crashed his car into Dijon's Christmas market, killing one person and injuring many more. Whether coordinated or examples of the contagious spread of violence, collectively these attacks conveyed the message any terrorist movement seeks to project: "No one anywhere is safe."

French intellectuals, empowered by the peculiar rock-star prominence big thinkers enjoy in France, made their own contribution to a political mood which, in light of the burkini affair, began to assume the proportions of panic not simply about physical security but also about the long-term survival of France as a cultural entity. Three preeminent media personalities seemed both to reflect and to sharpen this mood. One was the writer Michel Houellebecq. His novel *Submission*, released by uncanny coincidence on the day of the *Charlie Hebdo* killings, portrayed the election in 2023 of a Muslim president. This unlikely event occurs after the politician manages to finish as one of the top-two vote-getters in a multi-candidate first round of balloting, whereupon he leaps to victory in the second round against a far-right opponent after the more conventional candidates decide to back him as the lesser evil. Having assumed the presidency, the victor proceeds to replace French law with sharia.

In Houellebecq's telling, what makes the victory and its constitutional aftermath possible is the majority's apathy when confronted with the successful candidate's passionate confidence in the moral superiority of the Islamic normative tradition. Premised on the inability or unwillingness of Muslims to integrate, *Submission* implicitly indicts the majority's loss of will to defend its culture. It is a humanist satire in the great tradition of Voltaire's *Candide*.

Very few of the views expressed by the second figure in this triumvirate of Cassandras, Eric Zemmour, might fairly be deemed "implicit." Mark Lilla describes him as:

> less a journalist or thinker than a medium through whom the political passions of the moment pass and take on form. The son of North African Jews, he began his career writing editorials for *Le Figaro*,[†] then started appearing on television and radio where he would give intelligent and unpredictable commentary on the issues of the day. Though clearly on the right, he seemed like a fresh, affable voice, an *epateur* of the Voltairean sort in a new, McCluhan-cool style.

> That Zemmour is no more. Today he is an omnipresent Jeremiah who telegraphs the same message . . . on all available media: *France awake! You have been betrayed and your country has been stolen from you. . . .* He is a . . . counter intellectual of the sort the French right produced in the interwar years and who sees others in his guild [i.e., intellectuals] as the country's prime traitors. He is well educated, literary, stylish, light on his feet, a happy warrior who never raises his voice even when delivering bad news.[22]

In his best-selling 2014 broadside, *Le Suicide francaise*, Zemmour imputes what he sees as the suicidal decline of France to the emergence of the Muslim minority in the country's midst and to the moral flabbiness, if not outright treason, of an intellectual and political elite that has for decades betrayed its role as guardian of

---

† The long-time newspaper of relatively moderate conservatives.

the nation's autonomy, morality, and culture. He also flagellates the transnational elements of the capitalist class. Sources and manifestations of decline include, in Lilla's summary, "birth control, abandonment of the gold standard, speech codes, the Common Market, no-fault divorce, poststructuralism, denationalizing important industries, abortion, the euro, Muslim and Jewish communitarianism, gender studies, surrendering to American power in NATO, surrendering to German power in the EU, surrendering to Muslim power in the schools, banning smoking in restaurants, abolishing conscription, aggressive antiracism, laws defending illegal immigrants, and the introduction of halal foods in schools."[23] In short every social, political, economic, and speech act (like disparaging France's Vichy government and its colonial history) which in Zemmour's view weakened the state, eroded traditional moral convictions and social practices, undermined the cohesion and fecundity of French society, reduced the country's capacity to protect its borders by itself and project its power beyond them, every such act or omission, properly appreciated, has been one step in a process of collective suicide. Jihadi terrorism within France, along with what Zemmour describes as a "supportive context" reflected in Muslim youth delinquency and rebelliousness in the classroom, simply confirm the failure of the political establishment and the intellectual class to defend the nation.

Zemmour, who sounds like a French version of William Buckley in his early years, fuses issues and ideas which echo the ideological premises of the French inter-war alliance of neo-fascists and very conservative Catholic militants as well as the father Le Pen's National Front Movement. The same ideas resonate on American alt-right radio and websites.

The Guardian describes Alain Finkielkraut, the trio's third member, as one of the "media-savvy French intellectuals ... deemed the 'new reactionaries' for their political views and cultural conservatism."[24] But he is in fact difficult to classify. Unlike Zemmour, he is not a champion of the broad agenda of the trans-Atlantic right. He does not radiate hostility to international institutions and nostalgia for a bristling nationalism. On the contrary, many of his observations sound like those of a liberal despondent about what he sees as the failure to integrate Muslim immigrants into a society with liberal values worth defending.

It is hard, for instance, to imagine Zemmour declaring, as Finkielkraut did in a 2016 interview with Adam Nossiter of the *New York Times*, that "we can't compromise [with champions of multiculturalism] on the status of women" or, when asked if he could imagine voting for the National Front, responding, "No. I would never do that because this party appeals to people's base instincts and hatreds."[25] Nor, unlike members of the French right, does he advocate abolishing the right to French citizenship simply by virtue of birth on French soil regardless of the immigration status of the newborn's parents.

I noted earlier that liberalism can be practiced both as a formula for tolerance and as a militant faith. Finkielkraut is one of the faithful. Most of the time, the legacy he appears to be defending dates from the Revolution, not the Catholic patriarchal society that preceded it. "Back in 1989," he recalls in an interview,

> on the 200th anniversary of the revolution, I signed a petition against the Islamic headscarf. For me it had to do with the notion of secularism.... France believed at the time that this was a model for the world, and is today reminded of its distinctiveness. It is no longer a question of exporting our model. We have to remain modest, yet steadfast.[26]

So why is he, according to Nossiter, "the intellectual much of the French left loves to hate," putting aside the question of whether the "left" to which Nossiter refers is merely a few newspapers and journals and enough fellow intellectuals to fill, barely, a large ballroom? Principally because Finkielkraut is not reluctant to say that Islam, as it is currently practiced around the world including France, is not compatible with the Revolution's ideals, particularly the idea of equality. (I suspect he would add fraternity with others regardless of their faith or lack thereof.) When an interviewer asked him, "Hasn't Islam long since become a part of Europe?" he responded: "Islam may one day belong to Europe, but only after it has Europeanized itself."[27]

There has been, in his view, a gross failure to integrate Muslims into French culture. Ignoring the conventional dichotomy between the United Kingdom and France, he sees that failure stemming in part from the establishment's concessions to multicultural ideas which have infiltrated the educational system. It stems as well from the wilting defense of what is valuable in France's heritage and from what he sees as the fiercely exclusionist and anti-intellectual culture of contemporary Islam. Unlike Zemmour, he does not envision and by implication urge deportation of some part of the Muslim population. But he does believe that substantial numbers of French Muslims "hate" France and that there has been a gross failure to achieve integration. The acts of terrorism that flow from that failure thus require, if not deportation, then at least policies that limit further Muslim immigration to persons who are not conventionally pious. Those convictions do not make him Zemmour's ideological clone, but in terms of his impact on public opinion, "independent fellow traveler" would seem about right.

A striking feature of most scholars who have become polemicists and been taken up by the media is the loss of that attention to detail and nuance which made them respected scholars in the first place. Full of powerful convictions which they want a general audience to share, they tend to select reinforcing facts and ignore conflicting hypotheses about what the facts suggest. Finkielkraut has not entirely avoided this tendency. For example, when asked by one interviewer whether the failure of integration he treats as self-evident and the rage he imputes to young Muslims might be attributable to joblessness and discrimination, he simply ignores the question.[28]

The picture he paints of Muslims in France is done with large and vivid strokes. In his interviews, Finkielkraut sounds a bit like a scholar who has become bored with footnotes, especially the "but see" sort in which the serious scholar concedes that not all of his peers agree with him and not all of the ascertainable facts support his claims.

The Nossiter interview occurred in March 2016. Two months earlier the National Institute of Demographic Studies issued a 615-page report, the work of multiple investigators, which found that a majority of those French persons whose parents came to mainland France after World War II, mostly from former French colonies, embrace their French identity. One of the coordinators of the studies on which the report was based, the demographer Patrick Simon, said after the report's publication: "In a nutshell, they (the second generation) consider themselves French, but they feel they are not perceived as such."[29]

In interviews with the *Times* and *Der Spiegel*, Finkielkraut does not mention the report's findings, though in the latter he offers a hint of how he would have responded if pressed to comment on it. "Today the Muslims in France like to shout in an act of self-assertion: 'We are just as French as you!' It would never have occurred to my parents [Jewish immigrants] to say something like that. I would also never say that I am just as French as Charles de Gaulle was."[30] That is, to say the least, an ambiguous statement. It could be taken as an anodyne, though factually and conceptually dubious, anthropological observation to the effect that the still typical French person thinks in the French language, is white, descended from multiple generations of Christians, had an education suffused with French political history and the works of French novelists and poets, experiences a deep instinctive identity with France as a cultural and political entity, and feels a sentimental fraternity with people like himself.

The offspring of Jewish or Muslim immigrants, Finkielkraut seems to be saying, cannot feel that same instinctive identity and exclusive unqualified loyalty. Being French is possibly an important but it is not the exclusive constituent of their political and cultural identity and it does not define the limits of their feelings of fraternity. So, yes, his remark could be construed as a scholarly sociological observation, a detached hypothesis, but for the fact that he is not a sociologist and nothing he says in his present incarnation as a modern Cassandra is detached.

The other most grammatically plausible interpretation of his remark approaches self-contradiction and, in any event, locates him on the border of the nativist right wing of French politics. For if true "Frenchness" requires more than committing to the revolutionary ideal of "liberty, equality, and fraternity," requires more than recognizing the equality of women, then even if Islam may one day "Europeanize itself," its followers still will not be as authentically French as for instance the latest in an ancient line of rural conservative Catholic patriarchs who share his predecessors' views about Jews and gay people and thinks the Revolution was a malign rupture in the nation's history. Finkielkraut's intimation that the unreachably high bar to being truly French hovering over Muslims also towers above Jewish citizens like himself hardly softens his blow to the project of integration.

The dystopian vision of an existential Islamic threat to France and the coincident conviction that it demands radical measures of majoritarian self-defense is not limited to the far right. It exists as well in the center-right where Sarkozy was its most prominent voice and among major figures in the once powerful Socialist Party, now, in the wake of the 2017 parliamentary elections, reduced to a beleaguered rump. A measure of the remarkable moves and bedfellows this panic produces was the decision of Sarkozy and of Finkielkraut, reported in a piece on French Islamophobia by Adam Shatz, "to sign a petition in a far-right magazine protesting against the conversion of unused churches into mosques." Shatz notes ironically, "the defense of laicite now depends on the preservation of churches."[31]

If you read only Zemmour and Finkelkraut or listened to a host of prominent political figures like Marine Le Pen, Sarkozy, and the former Socialist prime minister, Manual Valls, you could easily conclude that France is in the grip of an existential cultural conflict in which the generality of Muslim residents are the aggressors. Investigative journalists actively seeking Muslim reaction to the intensifying clamor for action against the Islamic threat bring back a rather different picture of the Muslim condition.

Reporting from Nice three days after the Bastille Day truck massacre, Alissa Rubin of the *New York Times* spoke with a diverse group of residents. One was Feiza Ben Mohamed, a member of a Muslim non-profit, Muslims of the South, which is dedicated to fighting radicalization of Muslim youth. She told Rubin that Muslims and non-Muslim residents of Nice rarely mix except on days of special festivities like Bastille Day. Muslims were on the promenade when the Tunisian killer struck and some were among his victims. They also participated in the gathering two days later for collective mourning. She was among them. Afterward, standing by herself on the promenade, "reflecting on what had happened," a journalist approached her and asked "'if I was there to apologize in the name of Muslims.' I said to him, 'No, I came to weep for the dead like everyone else.'"[32]

Another of Rubin's interviewees is Samih Abid, a lawyer and longtime Nice resident. Abid tells her that because he wears Western clothes and works primarily on business law, when people first meet him they often do not recognize him as a Muslim. But when they hear his Arabic-sounding name, "I can see their looks change." He adds that "there is soft discrimination here, and I worry that it will harden now." To illustrate the soft discrimination, he notes that there are no mosques in the city itself and attributes this to the mayor's opposition. He also recounts walking near the promenade after the massacre and overhearing people who, on seeing Muslims praying before makeshift shrines on the promenade, saying: "Oh, look, they are praying here. Shame on them."

Boubakeur Bekri, an imam who has spoken out against radicalization, is another of Rubin's interlocutors. He worries about what he sees as a retreat into identity politics "in which Muslims were often the objects of 'black looks.'" What the Muslim community must do, he says, is "prevent those people who plot things from a million kilometers away from programming it [terrorist acts] and launching the torpedo."

When Rubin interviews him, the mayor himself sounds a concerned emollient note. "We must find the path that permits us to reconcile respect for religious values and republican values.... We can see from what happened on July 14 that the truck did not detect who was Muslim and who was not. There were victims of many nationalities and all religions."[33]

Aside from the question of mosque construction, some relatively comfortable working-class Muslim residents of the inner city complain of Muslims being pushed out to the city's far edge through a government-facilitated process of gentrification. Rubin chats with Lotfi Brick, a halal butcher from Tunisia, one of the surviving two in a neighborhood in which such butchers were once plentiful. "I have Charolais beef, the best meat in France, and reasonable prices.... That's why everyone shops here: Christians, Jews, Muslims." "He wants his street to remain a place where the two [Muslim and non-Muslim] meet," Rubin reports.[34]

Two reporters for Bloomberg record a similar tone among Muslims elsewhere in France.[35] A day after the butchery at the *Charlie Hebdo* satirical journal, they meet a youth worker, Mohamed, in a Paris suburb pasting up posters for a long-planned neighborhood party. His mood is bleak. "All we want is to live in peace with everybody and this is set to make things worse," he says. "My friends say they are being looked on as if they were responsible for what happened." According to the reporters, "Islamic leaders are urging people to ... avoid provoking other French people and to join protests against the killings."

Of course, anecdotes and "for examples" are not proof in the legal or scholarly sense. Still, good journalists have sensitive antennae for detecting group moods and base their accounts on many more interviews than the few that illustrate their published stories. By themselves these and other journalistic narratives undermine the Finkielkrautian narrative of a nation besieged by the approximately 8.8 percent of the population that identifies as Muslim. In fact, only a third of this group, according to polling data, are fully practicing, with another third essentially secular in the sense that they rarely pray, attend mosques, or adhere to religious dicta about dress, drinking, or eating.[36] There is even more evidence that counters Finkielkraut's fears. Empirically based scholarly accounts of French Muslim life like Jonathan Laurence's *The Emancipation of Europe's Muslims*[37] support the journalistic narratives of Muslim families aspiring to being accepted as French and struggling to build dignified lives in the midst of a torpid economy and an often-hostile majority.

THE TERRORISM ISSUE

Assuming the accuracy of that far more sanguine appreciation of French Muslim life, does it follow that we should dismiss Finkielkraut as a hysteric, still traumatized by the Holocaust? Should we repudiate politicians like Sarkozy as cynical entrepreneurs trying to induce a panic that will sweep them to power? And if we do dismiss them, should we correspondingly dismiss the widespread anxieties they channel? As the first part of this book makes clear, my answer is a qualified "no."

We can usefully think of the community dynamics that coexist with terrorist movements in terms of a pyramid.[38] At all levels of the pyramid are people who live inside a country and share an identity and related grievances that distinguish them from the rest of the population. At the pyramid's sharp peak is the very small number of incorrigible group members bursting with homicidal rage. Just below them is a slightly larger group, also deeply alienated, but not yet to the point where they themselves are ready to kill. Below them lies a larger but still relatively small group whose feeling of being victims of injustice makes them to varying degrees sympathetic to the declared ends of the terrorists *but opposed to their means*. Members of this third group may not be willing to assist the violent few in any way, but neither are they inclined to assist the government, by, for instance, helping the authorities identify or locate potential killers. Below them, at the base of the pyramid, are the great majority who oppose violence and repudiate those who advocate it in their name. One aim of the terrorists is gradually to invert the pyramid, at the very least to flatten it, that is, to swell their numbers and the ranks of their active supporters and passive sympathizers.

All figures about the Muslim population of France are rough estimates in part because of the prohibition on collecting data about religious and ethnic identity in the national census, in part because, even in the case of informal surveys using nation-of-origin or neighborhood as proxies for religious identification, the category of Muslim, like that of Christian in a very secular society, has porous borders. Is a religiously indifferent woman with parents who attend mosque very occasionally a Muslim? How about a young man who celebrates the beginning and end of Ramadan but does not fast? Are you a Muslim if, because of your name, you are so identified by the wider society and treated accordingly?

Numbers are not irrelevant. Polls confirm that popular majorities in all Western countries greatly exaggerate the size of their respective Muslim populations[39] and thereby self-aggravate the fears of "Islamization" echoed in Houellebecq's novel *Submission*. That said, 6–7 million appears to be a reasonable working number for France. Their median age is twenty-seven; for non-Muslims it is forty-three. Under the Pew Research Center's population projection scenarios I mentioned earlier, Muslims could make up anywhere from 12.7 to 18 percent of the French population in 2050.

Suppose only 1 percent of the current population in the dangerous age group of sixteen- to thirty-year-olds, perhaps 30,000 persons, stand at the pyramid's peak. Or, perhaps more plausibly, shrink that number down to 0.1 percent, roughly 3,000, and divide by two. Now consider that only nine young men executed the November 2015 attacks in Paris, including the assault on the Bataclan concert goers and the random mass shootings of Parisians who were out enjoying a stroll or a glass of wine that Friday evening. Those nine men, armed with guns and wearing suicide vests, killed 130 people and injured 413.

Among this terrorist unit were four ISIS members who had been hardened in the Iraqi–Syrian furnace. ISIS supplied them with their lethal automatic weapons. But in today's world the vast international arms bazaar is open to purely commercial criminal networks that can purchase (or steal) and move arms, as they move drugs and people, across the globe's mostly porous borders for sale to anyone, including sectarian fanatics. The pulverization of the ISIS caliphate will not enable the United States and its allies to recover the hundreds of millions in liquid assets its leaders have siphoned out of the peoples and lands in Syria and Iraq they once controlled. Nor, if the past is precedent, will they succeed in wholly blocking the flow of funds to jihadis from rich sympathizers in the Persian Gulf.

The availability of automatic weapons through ISIS or simply through common criminal networks is only part of the danger. After all, Mohamed Lahouaiej-Bouhlel, the Nice mass murderer, operated without benefit of any training or automatic weapons, and still killed eighty unsuspecting strollers in a matter of moments. In the United States, the right-wing terrorists Timothy McVeigh and Terry Nichols, former low-ranking soldiers in the US Army, fashioned out of common store-bought items and some explosives easily stolen from a quarry a truck bomb that shattered the nine-story federal building in Oklahoma City. The blast was so powerful it destroyed or damaged buildings in a sixteen-block radius, and killed 168 people, wounding at least 300.

So even if only 1,500 persons in France who identify as Muslim (plus a small fraction of the Christians likely to convert to Islam in the near future) are convulsing with homicidal rage, they can wreak havoc sufficient to shatter the Republic's foundations. They do not have to kill anything like the nearly 4,000 people who die annually on France's highways. Although the state could sharply reduce that toll by increasing highway patrols, imposing draconian penalties for speeding and driving under the influence, requiring cars to incorporate technology limiting speed, and making sobriety a condition for starting a vehicle, the people of France, like those of other countries, tolerate fatalities which could be sharply reduced by identifiable policies. Without evident stress, they accept those fatalities in part on the subliminal assumption that by virtue of their own driving skills and caution, they have a good chance of avoiding death by vehicle. They have, in other words, some sense of controlling their fate.

The same comforting sense restrains the public's response to the incidence of crimes like mugging and burglary committed for commercial rather than ideological reasons. You evade them, you think, by not strolling through parks at night, avoiding certain neighborhoods, triple-locking your doors, barring ground and first-floor windows, acquiring a loyal but otherwise surly hound, purchasing a home alarm system, and, in the United States, by maintaining in your residence a small armory of lethal weapons.

Terrorism works differently. Ideologically inspired crimes – unpredictable and indiscriminate attacks with no immediate purpose other than inspiring terror and expressing hatred of the target society – strip away that comforting feeling of being the manager of your risks. That is, after all, a core strategy of terrorism: to arouse in the first instance a feeling of individual helplessness. People who feel helpless turn to the state and demand that it fulfills its most essential duty: maintaining public security.

In a liberal democratic society, initially the political leadership will attempt to fulfill its duty by acting within constitutional limits designed to protect the citizenry from the abuse of state power. Those limits, however, allow in France and many other countries a range of special measures in the event of a "national emergency," measures like warrantless searches of residences and stopping and frisking persons who arouse suspicion. But if in the face of the first set of special measures terrorist attacks continue, even expand in frequency or destructiveness, measures which might at first have seemed excessive, like detention of people on grounds merely of "suspicion," will come to be seen as reasonable, even necessary. And step by step or possibly in one great leap, presumed efficacy can become the only measure of what is reasonable.

Where terrorists purport to act in the name of a discrete, recognizable minority, all of its members may be deemed suspect until they can prove their innocence. In extreme cases, where before the terrorist campaign the majority regarded the minority with suspicion or hostility, even the option of proving innocence may be largely abandoned as occurred in the analogous case of the United States with respect to citizens of Japanese ancestry following Japan's attack on Hawaii in 1941.[40]

If the Republican values of liberty, equality, and fraternity are the essential core of French culture, then Houellebecq has stood the existential threat on its head. The risk is not an Islamized France, but a Republican France broken by the fear of Islam. After replacing the smashed Republic, a proto-fascist government might largely succeed in exterminating jihadi cells. In the process it would deal harshly with all those perceived enablers of Islamic jihad – the intellectuals and journalists and teachers, the civil libertarians and social activists who defended multicultural tolerance or criticized extraordinary measures – unless they silence themselves and accept the new order. In the long term, that is the real risk to Republican France.

Although in an early stage, the process is under way. Writing in July 2016 the astute scholar/journalist Christopher de Bellaigue noted:

> the racial profiling and frisking of Arabs in the street, the police raids in the middle of the night ... Under the state of emergency, prefects have been able to order house searches, confine people to their homes, shut mosques, and ban assemblies without court order. The results of this expansion of police powers have been thin: five terrorist prosecutions have been launched as a result of the 3,500 house searches, while those being searched are stigmatized as suspect outsiders and would-be jihadists.

"Here," he concludes, "is the tension between the short-term imperative of preventing terrorism and the long-term need to integrate a large Muslim minority into society."[41]

The rightward drift of a scholarly humanist like Finkielkraut, once a man of the left, is a warning. While I am confident that he is in thrall to a delusionary scenario, he is correct in connecting the danger to a liberal France with the material and emotional relationship between the country's native majority and its Muslim minority. The question he does not attempt to answer, as if it were already too late, is: What should be done?

If terrorism is the prospective catalyst of extraordinary measures aggravated by the unofficial works of rightist thugs, then acquiring an accurate understanding of jihadi terrorism's sources is an important prelude to the formation of a grand strategy for defending the Republic.

DEBATING THE PSYCHOLOGICAL SOURCES OF ISLAMIC TERRORISM

On the question of the psychological development of Allah-invoking terrorists, two figures have acquired a commanding public presence: Giles Kepel and Olivier Roy, professors who have spent their professional lives studying Islam.

Former friends, Roy and Kepel have been driven into a harsh antagonism by their different views on the wellsprings of terrorism and their consequent rivalry in the campaign to shape public opinion and government policy in the febrile environment of contemporary France. When two erudite, polished scholars begin referring to each other with contempt,[42] one might suppose we are dealing either with the narcissism of small differences or with two men who agree on almost nothing. In fact, they agree on a good deal: that jihadis constitute a tiny fraction of France's Muslim population; that with respect to opportunities for employment, migrant families suffer heavy discrimination; that in spite of this a Muslim middle class has emerged in France; that unemployment in the ghettoes where a majority of young Muslims live is very high; that many Muslims have entered the political process as candidates and voters; that on social issues like gay marriage and teaching about gender equality in the public schools, the conservative views of many Muslims are identical to those of Catholic traditionalists; and that prisons are jihadist incubators.[43]

In spite of these broad and important areas of agreement, Roy's and Kepel's views have been reduced by journalists into a stark dichotomy: Roy as an advocate for the "Islamization of radicalism" versus Kepel's belief in the "radicalization of Islam." What informs the catchy headline?

Roy's is the more unconventional position and therefore the one requiring more unpacking.[44] He opens his analysis by rejecting what he calls the "cultural explanation" and the "Third World" one for the jihadist assault on Europe.

The first is that "recurring and nagging 'war of civilizations' theory: the revolt of young Muslims demonstrates the extent to which Islam cannot be integrated into the West, at least not so long as theological reform has not struck the call for jihad from the Qur'an."[45] The second interpretation evokes post-colonial suffering, the identification of these youths with the Palestinian cause, their rejection of Western intervention in the Middle East, and their exclusion from a French society that is racist and Islamophobic. "In short, the old song: So long as we haven't resolved the Israel–Palestine conflict, there will be a revolt."[46]

He then dismisses those two explanations on the not entirely persuasive grounds that if indeed they were the causes of radicalization, terrorists would not be such a tiny fraction of the Muslim population. They are not entirely persuasive because they assume the passage from anger and alienation to mass murder is psychologically easy; presumably there would be far more jihadists if it were not extraordinarily difficult.

Having in his judgment cleared the ground of implausible explanations, he offers his own. He arrives at it by examining the profiles of French jihadis and finding common elements:

> Nearly all the French jihadis belong to two very precise categories: They are either "second generation" French ... or they are "native" French converts (whose numbers have increased with time, but who already constitute 25 percent of radicals at the end of the 1990s).[47]

The number of converts among jihadis, he argues, reinforces the case against the two conventional explanations. For why would persons who themselves have "never suffered from racism, wish to brutally avenge the humiliation experienced by Muslims? [Moreover] ... many of these converts ... come from rural France and have little reason to identify with a Muslim community that for them exists only in theory."[48]

What is needed, then, according to Roy, is a theory which links second-generation Muslims and converts (and also explains why first- and third-generation Muslims rarely appear in the terrorist ranks). The common ground between the second generation and convert jihadis is rupture "with what their parents represent in terms of culture and religion."[49]

Members of the second generation who embrace jihad, he writes,

> do not adhere to the Islam of their parents, nor do they represent a tradition that is rebelling against Westernization. They are Westernized. They speak better French than their parents. They have all shared in the youth culture of their generation – they've drunk alcohol, smoked weed, flirted with girls in nightclubs. A large number of them have spent time in prison. And then, one morning, they are converted, choosing Salafi Islam, which is to say, an Islam that rejects the concept of culture, an Islam possessing of norms that allow them to reconstruct the self all by themselves. Because they want nothing of the culture of their parents or of the Western culture that has become a symbol of self-hatred.[50]

Why is the rupture peculiar to the second generation? "The key in [*sic*] this revolt," Roy answers, "is the absence of the transmission of a religion that is culturally integrated."[51] Members of the first generation, he argues, bring with them their national culture, a culture suffused by one or another version of Islam, which give firm shape and meaning to their lives. The move to a place with very different practices, normative premises, and interpersonal cues is an unsettling experience. Although the move jars their cultural identity, enough survives the journey to give them the psychological stamina to bear the challenges incident to transplantation into an alien culture. While the move does not immediately strip the first generation of its identity, the second generation is less fortunate in this respect.

Tension between the first and second migrant generations is a frequent incident of migrant life wherever the migration is from one cultural setting to another very different one. As I noted earlier, the first measures its conditions against those it left behind; the second by the pecking order into which it is born. In that latter hierarchy, their fathers' places in the hierarchical order are generally low and their own place and prospects are at best uncertain. Trying to wrench a living and make a stable place in a difficult alien world, the first generation tends to play by the rules, defer to authority in its various forms, and work very hard with rewards unlikely to impress the second with its different standard of success.

The rebelliousness of youth, particularly of male youth in a world undergoing change at a dizzying pace, is universally acknowledged and the inspiration for countless novels. But rebelliousness can coincide with a grudging respect for achievement. Hence in favorable circumstances fathers can still be role models even while resisted. In any event, parents frequently provide their children at an early age with a solid sense of identity and conventional moral parameters. What Roy seems to be saying, among other things, is that the austere conditions of life for poorly educated migrants to liberal European states make the first generation of migrants generally less successful in this respect. Their children may surpass them in fluency and almost certainly in street smarts at an early age. Seeing their parents' uncomplaining, meagerly rewarded effort, their awkward attempts to navigate minimally charted social and economic seas, children may look elsewhere for identity and direction.

A tiny fraction of those youths – by Roy's own account – find that identity in what they take to be a purified Islam, an Islam of absolutes that supports "the fantasy of heroism, violence, and death," that indulges "their desire for revenge for their suppressed frustrations," that allows them to reclaim, on their own terms, "an identity that, in their eyes, their parents have debased." It is an identity that empowers them in their own eyes by giving them the will to kill.[52]

Given Roy's generalizations about the second generation – its alienation from the first – the obvious question is why so few turn to jihad. He speaks of their "isolation from Muslim communities," their indifference to politics and social service, protest movements within the community, and their failure to attempt any serious study of Islam prior to their radicalization. Radicalization, he writes, occurs "within a small group of 'buddies' who met in a particular place (neighborhood, prison, sport club); they create a 'family,' a brotherhood." Not infrequently the brotherhood is literal, with one brother converting his sibling. "The religious leaders they eventually choose to follow are often self-proclaimed imams" reinforcing their fantasies.

Generational rupture, repressed rage, and social marginalization also, Roy argues, characterize the converts. Through the cyber fraternity of radical Islam they are liberated from their isolation and through its call to arms granted the power of the feared. Neither can be wooed by a "moderate" Islam, by one adapted to the circumstances of living in a country where Islam is a minority faith. The radicalism of fundamentalist Islam is what attracts them. In Roy's mind, it is the converts who reinforce his thesis that Islam is only a vehicle for the expression of a fierce nihilism: "*[The] converts choose Islam because it is the only thing on the market of radical rebellion. Joining the Islamic State offers the certainty of terrorizing*" (emphasis added).[53]

Roy finds additional reinforcement for his explanation of terrorism's wellspring in the paucity of the Turkish second generation among the jihadis. According to him, "the [cultural] transition has been smoother for the Turks, since the Turkish state took it upon itself to send teachers and imams to its overseas communities (which poses other problems but allows the Turks to avoid the adherence to Salafism and violence)."[54]

Standing alone, this explanation is unpersuasive. To begin with, many of the Turkish imams neither spoke a European language nor had prior experience of European culture. So they were hardly positioned to substitute for parents as cultural intermediaries. In addition, Turkey was hardly alone in sending teachers and imams. Algeria and Morocco also sent them. So did Saudi Arabia. The more plausible explanation for Turkish exceptionalism is the more moderate form of Sunni Islam native to Turkey, the country's lack of a colonial past, its psychological distance from the Arab world, the preceding Ottoman Empire's history of generally peaceful coexistence between the Muslim majority and the Christian and other minorities, and the mix of secular and religious elements in Turkish culture, at least since the nation's founding under the leadership of the aggressively secular Kemal Ataturk.

In any event, the Turkish component of France's Muslim population is sufficiently small[55] to make its behavior statistically irrelevant. But Roy seems to be making a point about jihadis in Europe, not simply France. So, if the under-representation of Turkish youth in jihadi circles occurs, as it appears to at this point, in countries with a large Turkish minority, most notably Germany, the phenomenon does at least nibble at the edges of Roy's theory about jihadism germinating in the first generation's difficulty helping the second one find a way of integrating itself comfortably as a conspicuous minority within the majority's cultural world.

The nibbling at the edges of Roy's distinction between Turkish and North African families will, of course, become a tearing at the middle if jihadi ranks begin to fill up with *third-generation* Muslim youth. That generation will be largely immune to the nihilistic impulse, Roy believes, because its members "speak French with their parents and ... have, thanks to them, a familiarity with how Islam can be expressed in French society."[56] Apparently parenthood (for those who live to be parents) will transform the supposedly frustrated, raging, and rupturing second generation into constructive cultural guides for their children.

That is an interesting proposition. Roy seems to assume that the great majority of the second generation will continue to resist the pull of the jihadi narrative; that its members will eventually find work, marry, and acquire a clearer and more relaxed sense of identity as they settle into the regularities of adult life; and that the boiling rage they experienced in their youth will cool. And because they will be fluent in French, as streetwise as their children, and more integrated into French life than their parents, they will be better equipped to help the third generation navigate psychologically through the shoals of a society in which they are a conspicuous minority. All this will occur, Roy seems to be saying, assuming that the majority does not drive Muslims into a defensive crouch.

One way the French state could contribute to belligerent self-isolation is by attempting to impose on Muslims a form of Islam with which the secular majority feels comfortable, an Islam which expresses itself quietly and does not challenge secular liberal values. It follows, for instance, that banning expressions of Muslim identity like head scarves in schools or, to take a more bizarre case, burkinis on the beach, is exactly what the state should not be doing.

At the root of contemporary French public policy, Roy argues, is the majority's own crisis of identity. What has become of France's national pride in the face of defeat in war; the long bloody colonial recession; the unraveling narrative of heroic resistance to the German occupation in World War II; more than three decades of economic stagnation; high unemployment (even for native youth); loss of European leadership to Germany; the drift of state power from Paris to Brussels; the hegemonic position achieved by the English language; empty churches and bulging mosques; the slow deterioration of life chances in smaller cities, towns, and the countryside; and the absence of any external threat to unify the nation? The loss of a proud and confident collective sense of self, the loss of national vitality especially in comparison to the adherents of Islam – that loss is precisely the theme of Houellebecq's novel.

What Roy sees in the veiling bans is an effort by the French state to define and reassert a threatened national identity through a certain interpretation of the revolutionary tradition. For the militants who made the French Revolution, the state was the incarnation of the French people united in liberty, equality, and fraternity. From their perspective, intermediate institutions, above all the Catholic Church, compromised the unity of people and state. The distrust of "sects" survived the move from rule by populist militants to Napoleonic dictatorship. It manifested itself in Napoleon's attitude toward the Jews: as a community, he is reported to have said, I give them nothing, but as individuals, they shall be equal.

Nevertheless, in a move that anticipated by two centuries Sarkozy's attempt to construct a representative voice for French Muslims by establishing the French Council of the Muslim Faith, Napoleon I convened an assembly of Jewish notables in 1806 and had them in turn call on Jewish communities around Europe to send representatives to a new entity to be called the Grand Sanhedrin after the main legislative and judicial body of the Jewish people in antiquity. When the representatives assembled, Napoleon notionally endowed them with the authority to give legal sanction to principles and rules Napoleon wanted to see Jews observe in their everyday life. Among them was the declaration that "every Israelite is religiously bound to consider his non-Jewish fellow citizens as brothers, and to aid, protect, and love them as though they were coreligionists."[57]

Following Napoleon's precedent, Sarkozy hoped to use the council, a body the state summoned into existence, as a means of influencing the practices of contemporary French Muslims, particularly Muslim youth.[58] Had he been asked, Roy would undoubtedly have advised Sarkozy that he was bound to fail in part because French Muslims are too diverse and in part because there is no authoritative hierarchy in Sunni Islam. Like fundamentalist Protestants, every believer feels entitled to form his own judgment about the meaning of the Qur'an and the sayings of the Prophet and their application to daily life. A Sunni Muslim may be influenced by one or another imam, but the influence derives from the imam's personal qualities rather than any formal authority. To Roy, government efforts to train imams are just another doomed effort to produce a "moderate" Islam, an Islam shorn of elements of dogma troubling the psychological tranquility and the security of secular France.

When in 1905 the Third Republic promulgated the doctrine of laicity, Roy argues, it intended to do no more than separate Church and state, to deprive the Catholic Church of a privileged position particularly in education. In trying at the present moment to revitalize French identity, the state rather than simply reaffirming separation is, according to Roy, aggressively intruding into the realm of religion. So laicity becomes more like an alternative faith with its own dogmas.[59]

The state's province is to make and enforce laws, not try and dictate what people believe. Of Muslims the state should ask not that they revise their views of dogma but only that they obey the law. Roy is confident that most will continue to do so without any dogmatic change, for dogma can be adapted to circumstances. For instance, the most famous advocate of a "European Islam," the Swiss academic Tariq Ramadan, grandson of one of the founders of the Muslim Brotherhood, concedes that the Qur'an calls explicitly for certain punishments such as amputation. Rather than dismissing this unambiguous language as a disposable relic of the religion's founding epoch, he simply calls for a moratorium on its application in the contemporary context.[60]

Muslims may take the abstract position that where the law of the state conflicts with God's law as revealed through Muhammad, the latter prevails, but many Christians feel the same way regarding the Bible. Indeed, reflecting the influence of its conservative Protestant base, the US Republican Party states in its platform that if "God-given, natural, inalienable rights" conflict with "government, court, or human-granted rights," the former must prevail.[61] Nevertheless, with tiny exceptions fundamentalist Protestants do not reach for a gun when they detect such a conflict. Instead, they run for office, vote for people with shared beliefs, challenge offensive legislation in the courts, and conduct peaceful demonstrations. French Muslims do the same. Some of those opposing gay marriage, for instance, joined with conservative Christians to peacefully protest when the National Assembly was considering the gay-marriage legislation.[62]

A version of Islam calling on Muslims to follow directly in the footsteps of the Prophet and his immediate successors and thus to purify themselves and make their isolation a cause for exultation cannot help but appeal to people with a peculiarly uncertain or reviled identity, people like the un- or under-employed youth of the banlieues, but also a scattering of young native French men and women who by dint of personal traits or family circumstances have lost their way.

In the epoch of the internet, even the powerful and autocratic Chinese state cannot entirely isolate its population from advocates of religious transformation.[63] A fortiori the French state cannot, no matter how many Salafist imams it might deport or bar from entering in the first place. Islam, Roy concludes, is not a culture. It takes different forms in different cultural settings. A European Islam or Islams will evolve over time. They will, Roy warns, not necessarily be on the whole "liberal" any more than European Catholicism is liberal in many (though by no means all) of its social values. But – and here we come to the essence of his convictions – its conservatism is not the avenue to jihad. Every generation has its violent nihilists. From the atmosphere they pluck whatever is at hand to rationalize their impulse to transform the story of their embittered lives into a heroic narrative.

Jihadists are hardly the first of their kind. Before them were the neofascists, whose bombs in Italian rail terminals and trains killed and crippled hundreds of travelers over more than a decade beginning in the late 1960s; in the 1970s the Italian Red Brigades and their German equivalent waged campaigns of assassination against "class enemies."

Both had nineteenth-century predecessors in the anarchist terrorists who attempted in 1894 to destroy the Royal Observatory in Greenwich Park, London, memorably limned in Joseph Conrad's novel *The Secret Agent*.[64] Terrorism in the name of some faith is not new.

It is precisely Roy's core conviction that Muslim theological fundamentalism, often described as "Salafism" or "Wahabbism," does not pave the pathway to jihad, which collides violently with the views of Giles Kappel, who believes that it does. Behind jihadism, Kappel writes, "looms the implantation of Salafism – a model for breaking with the values of the Republic and its secularism."[65] Salafists, he continues, "rely on a grand narrative promoting cultural separation from 'infidel' French society *and has become the norm in many places*" (emphasis added). While the radicalized activists among the children of postcolonial immigrants who have committed criminal acts "represent only a tiny minority, ... they constitute the avant-garde of a larger Salafist trend whose rapid expansion on French territory characterized the decade between 2005 and 2015," the period, he notes ominously, between the banlieue riots and the sudden clustering of terrorist assaults.[66] To be fair, he does not argue that all those who adopt "total Islam" as their way of being in the world will ascend to the top of the pyramid. Total Islam has "diverse forms, from overexcited identity politics to the descent into violence."[67]

While Roy optimistically views the attractions of jihad as a transient phenomenon, Kepel's analysis oscillates in tone from the merely uneasy to the lugubrious. Referring to what he calls the "Web 2.0 Revolution," he writes that the new generation of French citizens brought up in the banlieues finds in the internet "a privileged way of expressing and propagating its values. These values combine the search for an all-encompassing conception of Islam inspired by the Salafism of the Arabian Peninsula and a fervent consultation of a digital Islamosphere full of norms and injunctions breaking with the 'infidel' model of the West."[68]

Anxiety about the potential size of the minority which will adopt a radical version of Islam as its "sole identity" appears to produce in Kapel a corresponding anxiety about the size of the Muslim presence. While Roy estimates the Muslim population at 6 percent, Kepel prefers an estimate of 8 percent (just above the Pew Foundation estimate) and adds that the Muslim population is endowed with an "exceptionally dynamic demography in part because of conversions."[69]

Although he fears the numbers of violent and non-violent (but deeply alienated) Salafists will grow, Kepel's anxiety does not border on despair. The first jihadist massacre in France of the twenty-first century, Mohammed Merah's murder of Jewish children at their school in Toulouse, was "perpetrated ... in the name of this total Islam [Salafism], but coincided, Kepel notes favorably, with "an over-whelming majority of French Muslim citizens participating consequentially in a Presidential election."[70]

At the end of his book, *Terror in France*, he reflects on his recent visit to a small city, Lunel, which has exported a disproportionate number of its Muslim inhabitants to do jihad in the Middle East and where young people with an immigrant background have an unemployment rate estimated at 40 percent. From that visit he retains "the image of a single place where all the city's components live together in a 'friendship' ... that allows them, through work and shared values, to move beyond atavism and communalism."[71] In Lunel, that place is the *lycee*, the French high school, which in his view is blessed with inspirational leadership, a quality he finds generally lacking in the French elite. In order to achieve that same "friend-ship" which he found in this one school, what France needs, he concludes, is the refounding of public education, "from the nursery school to the university." It must be refounded because, "as the result of a blameworthy incompetence on the part of the whole political class," it has fallen into poverty.[72] Thus Kepel places himself in the great Republican tradition of constructing fraternity in order to sustain liberty.

His tone, however, strikes me as rather elegiac, unnecessarily so at this point in time. Yes, there are grounds for concern about the integration project; there are also grounds for optimism despite many past mistakes like the burkini nonsense. As the Mohamed Salah phenomenon suggests the potential for amiable interfaith relations in the United Kingdom, Mahmoud M'seddi, a baker, does the same for France.

M'Seddi, whose father migrated from Tunisia more than thirty years ago, is the 2018 winner of the Grand Prize for Best Parisian Baguette, that "long crusty stick that," in the words of Adam Nossiter of the *New York Times*, "announces its nationality like no other bread."[73] Rejecting indignantly any implication that the fact of his immigrant background is significant in relation to this particular award, M'seddi declared in an interview, "I'm French. This is my home.... People like to remind me of it [his background], yeah sure.... Me, I don't make these distinctions. I couldn't care less about it.... I grew up here. I pay my taxes here. It's true that Tunisians call me, after I won. They're proud. But the Parisians are proud, too."[74] M'Seddi was not the first Muslim to outbake the indigenous French. The 2017 winner also was the son of a Tunisian immigrant. And three years ago a baker of Senegalese origin, Djibril Bodian, became a two-time winner.

After wading through the extensive literature about integration in France, and considering the flow of events, it seems clear to me that the great majority of Muslims in France desire to be seen and treated as French. The policies of France's government at every level will help to determine whether that desire is fulfilled.

Hard Choices

Hard Choices

7

Migration and Integration

Options for the Liberal State

THE PURPOSES AND PROBLEMS OF A "GRAND STRATEGY"

Great problems call for grand strategies. To formulate such strategies, political leaders and the administrators and analysts directed by them must set goals, propose solutions, and eventually arrive at some consensus about how to achieve an enduring success. Unfortunately, strategists too often forget the sage dictum of former heavyweight boxing champ Mike Tyson: "Everyone has a plan until they get punched in the mouth."[1] Reality inevitably intrudes on even the most thoughtful strategy.

Devising the right mix of policies to address complex societal issues is an intimidating challenge. Several difficulties urge caution. One is that the real causes of any social phenomenon are never self-evident and hence always subject to debate. Consider just one small example: Why does an indolent, religiously indifferent, boozing, woman-chasing young punk suddenly have a come-to-Muhammad moment and then morph into a raging jihadi? This is not an uncommon event in the annals of Islamic terrorism. But how do you explain it? Does it start with subtle theological grooming? Does intense piety precede jihad? Is there in each case some transforming idiosyncratic moment? Thoughtful and careful students of the phenomenon offer competing hypotheses. We have no labs for controlled testing of them.

A second difficulty is the nature of reality. It is a stream in which, as the Greek philosopher Heraclitus is reputed to have said, you can only step once. The next time you do so, it is a different stream. At any point in time, for instance, the values, narratives, and practices that constitute a culture can seem fixed. Some are sticky; others can change with stunning and unpredictable speed. Think of attitudes in the West toward gay marriage and interracial love. Some practices are integral; others are little more than loose threads that can be pulled out without the slightest damage to the whole. After the fact, we may know. Before, we guess and sometimes we guess wrong.

Additionally, reality intrudes because social life is interwoven in so many complex ways that even where policy inputs generate the predicted outputs they also generate some measure of unpredicted side effects. The side effects can add to the predicted costs or in the longer term nullify the desired outputs or create new problems demanding new inputs with outputs which will in their turn have unintended side effects. For instance, the 2003 US invasion of Iraq had the intended effect of removing a dictator who no longer served US interests in the Middle East. Its unintended side effects included destabilizing the entire region.

Still, elected governments are by their nature unlike the philosopher's donkey starving to death midway between two equally succulent-looking bales of hay. In order to survive, politicians avoid the appearance of paralysis by moving in one direction or the other. Action may seem improvised, a hurried response to some event that traumatizes the public, but even when there is no officially articulated grand strategy, improvisation by long-serving senior bureaucrats and political leaders from mainstream parties occurs within a framework of settled priorities and assumptions about inputs and outputs, cause and effect, which together constitute an implicit grand strategy, however misconceived.

Governments do not simply invest in strategies, they sell them. The better the selling, the harder it generally is to say, "Oops, we were wrong." So, the United States goes on thrashing about in Afghanistan just as it once did in Vietnam. Nor is it simply a matter of a reluctance to admit error. In acting, one changes the thing acted on or the things to which it turns out to be connected. So bad policies cannot simply be walked back to the place where improvisation first occurred. That place no longer exists.

Were the electorate composed of philosophers, policymakers might acknowledge that they act on the basis of hypotheses, not certainties, and, moreover, that the great issues of public life, the great dangers to the welfare and security of the population, are subject at best to mitigation, not resolution. A grand strategy may be little more than a cluster of hypotheses about how to achieve goals that may themselves require reconsideration as their true costs unfold. Nevertheless, it offers some hope of greater mitigation than mere serendipity would produce. But if it becomes rigid, if it ceases to be a rough guidebook through poorly explored territory, if it conceals error from illumination by reality, then it could easily prove worse than improvised responses to diurnal manifestations of deeper forces wracking the national body.

I am going to begin with some general analysis of the strategies available to Western, principally European governments wrestling with two questions. First is the question of what guidelines should governments employ in order to determine which and how many aspiring migrants to admit and under what conditions. The second question is what governments should do to facilitate the integration of new migrants from the Global South and the several generations that have preceded them to the extent that parts of the latter remain poorly connected to the economy and the country's civic and social life. As a prelude, however, I want to restate the nature and source of the ends which shape the means I will propose in Chapter 8.

My highest priority is the survival of liberal democracy, an outcome by no means assured. Nothing in modern history persuades me that tolerance for unconventional views and minority lifestyles, commitment to real equality of opportunity regardless of gender or race or sexual preference, and support for protecting all citizens from unearned destitution is reflexive among the generality of people in contemporary Western society. The norms codified in the Universal Bill of Rights have, over the past seventy years, come to dominate the political rhetoric of rich Western countries. But domination has come by means of unceasing struggle and along a route littered with martyrs. The norms remain a work in progress, a progress now slowed, even halted in some places, by political leaders of the populist right scorning what they describe as "politically correct" speech.

Anxiety mixed with blind enmity toward migrants from the Global South, particularly toward Muslims, is not the only source of the anti-liberal surge in Western politics. Other often-noted forces[2] have helped fuel a rancid populism and a parallel decline of trust in government institutions, the mainstream media, and traditional political elites. The benefits of stunning technological change and globalized production have been very unevenly distributed. There have been many losers, their losses being relative in some cases, absolute in others.[3]

What has been lost is not merely income or the secure anticipation of progressively improving lives. What has been lost for many is a felt way of life. In 2018, a *New York Times* correspondent revisiting lesser cities of provincial France after the passage of decades is struck by the dusty somnolence of their centers.[4] Once people filled the streets, moving among the multitude of small shops, the little kingdoms of an entire class of retailers. There were butchers and bakers and sellers of a hundred varieties of cheese. Now pedestrians are far fewer and so are the shops, the great majority having been replaced by big-box retailers that dominate the sprawling crowded malls on the edge of towns. In less than a lifetime, the look, the feel, the smells of everyday life have faded like sepia prints of our great grandparents. What may underscore the sense of loss of a way of life experienced by a not trivial number of French people and their counterparts in other countries is the sight of veiled women trailing children and closely attended by men of color in streets still familiar but no longer yours.

Renaud Camus, a wealthy French writer now popular in North American as well as European alt-right circles, tells an interviewer from *The New Yorker* about his political awakening. In the course of writing a travel book commissioned by the French government, he visits the department of Herault in southern France whose capital is the beautiful ancient city of Montpellier. "Traveling through medieval villages," Camus tells the interviewer, "you would go to a fountain, six or seven centuries old, and there were all these North African women with veils!" Camus laments the policies of centrist liberals like France's Emanuel Macron, which, he believes treat people as "interchangeable" units within a larger social whole. "People are not just things. They come with their history, their language, with their looks, with their preferences."[5]

Camus sees immigration as one dimension of a globe-encircling process that has devalued so many traditional things, from cuisine to landscapes. "'The very essence of modernity', according to Camus, 'is that fact that everything ... can be replaced by something else, which is absolutely monstrous.'"[6]

For someone with Camus's views, the appropriate question is not how many should be admitted over how long a period of time and on what conditions, but rather how to bar the doors. The logic of his view would actually take him further, to the question of how we can reduce the number already here.

Fortunately, this is still plainly the view of a small minority, although one that politicians like Donald Trump; Marine Le Pen; Victor Orban, the Hungarian Prime Minister; and Mario Salvini, the Italian Minister of the Interior, have drawn out of the shadows into the public space. If it does not dominate, it certainly is present in the French parliament's second largest party and the third largest in its German counterpart. While migration is the right's contemporary calling card, a broader illiberalism is its guiding spirit, for Camus's sentiment is incompatible with the idea of a plural society. The kind of society that already exists in the West[7] cannot be made into a unitary one without first suffering the destruction of liberal institutions and norms.

Unlike its American counterpart, the European right is not anti-statist. It wants to preserve the welfare state.[8] Indeed, one of the objections to migration is its supposed threat to the welfare state's survival. European electorates in general see the state as a necessary mechanism for protecting their economic along with their physical security; the latter is also seen to be threatened by migration.

Judging from polls and from the rhetorical appeals of right-wing political entre-preneurs, the liberal center is vulnerable on three counts: a lack of candor in its communication with the electorate, a lack of a clear and detailed vision for addressing the problems arising from migration (along with globalization and technological change), and an overall failure to exercise vigorously the instruments of power. All these political vices were on display when leaders like Cameron and Merkel disavowed multiculturalism without explaining precisely what they were repudiating, why they had supported it previously (whatever in their view it was), and what they intended to do concretely in light of their epiphany.

The center should hold if its leaders have coherent goals, rational policies, the demonstrated will to implement them, and the courage to revise them openly when reality intrudes. As I conceded at the outset, not all the methods for addressing migration issues are readily compatible with liberal ideals. The challenge for defenders of the liberal project will be to identify the point at which compromise of their ideals becomes defeat.

Whether a more restrictive position on migration and a more demanding approach to integration by centrist parties in the rich European states will keep the right from power indefinitely is, I concede, debatable. Euro-populism was growing before the 2008 financial crisis and the refugee surge beginning in 2015. A recent study of the phenomenon conducted by Yascha Mounk, of Harvard University, and others found the right-wing populist vote growing on average within the EU as a whole from 8.5 percent in 2000 to 24.1 percent in 2017.[9] Coopting some of its themes, as centrist parties have done already, could backfire, since cooption arguably makes rightist rhetoric more normal, hence more respectable. In the words of one British scholar, it "primes the electorate for the radical right's message."[10]

For Rita Chin, the American author of a magisterial history of the word "multiculturalism" in European politics, coopting any rightist themes in the name of what David Cameron called a "muscular liberalism" is both a strategic and moral error. "[I]t is simply irresponsible," she writes,

> for European states to continue to allow significant segments of their populations to be driven by nostalgia for homogeneity. There is no longer room to pretend that European countries will return to some imagined, idealized state of ethnic and cultural sameness. To continue to do so is to condone and ultimately perpetuate the perception of immigrants as aliens, interlopers, and enemies.[11]

What Europe needs in the first place from its political leaders, she argues, is a "forceful, positive argument (beyond ... demographic needs) for multiethnic coexistence as a defining feature of their society ... The real danger here ... is that [their] silences and disavowals have created a democratic deficit, a situation in which immigrants are effectively written out of the social body." Signaling that ethnic minorities do not belong "fuels disaffection, giving those most embittered greater incentive to join the growing number of extremist groups eager to expand their international ranks."[12] Multiculturalism, Chin concludes, is not a particular political program. It is, rather, the acceptance of minorities as legitimate participants in the ongoing democratic struggle to shape each national society's social blueprint and in the process "produce new ways of thinking about European diversity."[13]

The question which Chin does not really attempt to answer is what should be the content of the "forceful, positive argument" she believes political leaders should make on behalf of "multiethnic coexistence." Leaders, she argues, need to appeal to more than their societies' "naked demographic needs,"[14] by which I assume she refers to care for the aged and performance of other services from crop-picking to street-sweeping at wages which repel the native working class even where members of it are theoretically available. But what beyond an appeal to material self-interest is the plausible substance of the argument she would have leaders make? In Chapter 8 I will suggest how the argument she urges might be framed.

To underscore a point I made earlier, from the government's perspective integration is a success when migrants (1) are making a net contribution to the gross national product; (2) are paying more into government coffers than they withdraw, whether directly through welfare, disability, pension, and other direct payments or indirectly through utilization of the various services the state provides (health, housing, policing, courts, etc.); (3) are not by their actions disproportionately threatening public order; and, more controversially, (4) are not behaving or encouraging behavior that threatens or actually violates those conventional moral norms which are a defining feature of national identity as it is appreciated by the great majority of legacy citizens.

Liberal idealists naturally define success in terms not of the government's interests but rather of the individual migrant's. Jill Rutter is a representative of the human rights perspective: "The definition I use for integration is the *capability of migrants to achieve social inclusion and well-being.*"[5] These differences in perspective are not necessarily at odds.

If, for instance, in order to feel socially included a migrant family must have at least one member in the workforce, then the integrated family is making at least some contribution to the GNP and, by virtue of having taxable income, is contributing to the costs of government. And if its members have a sense of well-being, almost by definition they are unlikely or at least less likely than members of an alienated family to engage in behavior threatening to public order or national security.

Whether a family could achieve social inclusion and a sense of well-being while engaging in practices offensive to public morality as defined by the legacy population is a trickier question. Could a family unit practicing polygamy and the genital mutilation of young girls, a unit in which the wife accepted her husband's injunction to walk about with a full-face veil or never to go outside without being accompanied by him, and in which girls hardly in puberty were affianced by paternal diktat to cousins or rich older men in a distant land – could such a unit at the same time be socially included and enjoy Rutter's "sensation of well-being," assuming one or several of these practices had to be hidden from the eyes of neighbors and the state? Would not the felt need to conceal coincide with a sense of majority disrespect for the family's culture? If by "well-being" Rutter means, as I assume she does, that the migrants feel at home in the society receiving them, then is it plausible to believe that a family feeling the hostility of the surrounding national society will enjoy a sense of well-being?

In order to integrate, Rutter asserts, migrants "must be supported by facilitators: *attributes and resources* which may include English language fluency, as well as … permanent housing, a job and workplaces that support social mixing."[6] Her entirely plausible claim of what is necessary implies that a daunting amount of financial and human resources would need to be applied to the task of integration. Achieving anything close to language fluency, for example, can take a newly arrived adolescent two to five years, depending on aptitude, resolve, intensity of training, and degree of interaction with native speakers outside the classroom.[17] It takes even longer for most adults. Some never manage the feat. Since the majority of migrants arrive with very limited funds and refugees often arrive virtually penniless, language training will have to be heavily subsidized. So will housing migrants while they acquire the skills which could ultimately make them self-sufficient.

INTEGRATION AND BORDER CONTROL

To achieve the goals of integration that I listed above, what are the strategic options available to Western governments and what are the considerations which should influence their choices? Let's start with the second question. One consideration is the possible impact of integration strategies on future levels of pressure on the border. Every wealthy country aspires to regulate the flow of persons across its borders. A country that provides generous financial support for migrants virtually from the moment they arrive seems bound to attract more migrants, especially if they stand to enjoy the same social benefits enjoyed by natives. A wealthy country becomes more attractive still if it eases entry for family members left behind, and accommodates distinctive lifestyles, even those alien to the native culture. Certainly, that very plausible reasoning has driven Denmark's decidedly cold response to new arrivals, which appears to have been successful in diverting asylum-seekers from its doors. Denmark does not shun migration; it simply wants to limit the inflow to those likely to make the country richer and those who are willing to assimilate voluntarily into the national culture. It is looking, in short, for those who will need little to no help in getting to feel "at home."

There is a tension between facilitating border control and facilitating integration of those already settled in a country, and it haunts other policy options. Generous policies on family reunification, including recently acquired spouses, guarantee further migration from the diasporas' countries of origin. Allowing for larger family units should generally be a plus for migrants' "well-being." But it might not always be advantageous for the state. Older parents, much less grandparents, will normally have far greater difficulty than the young in learning enough of the local language to be able to work. They will generally have much greater need to use the health services. And they will retire in many cases long before their contributions to government revenues even begin to match the cost of their pensions. Where the law or political pressure sets annual fixed limits on total entries, a preference for family members will limit selective migration. In a given year the country would thereby get more sclerotic grandfathers and fewer software engineers, but hypothetically happier and on that score possibly more easily integrated migrant families.

There is more at stake here than the happiness of migrants. Families generally exert a calming influence on young men and women, including those who by dint of circumstance or character are peculiarly vulnerable to the temptations of the criminal economy or, more dangerously, to recruitment for crusades against the West. As convenience stores and ethnic restaurants in North America and Western Europe demonstrate in their vast multiplicity, families also facilitate entrepreneurial activity by pooling resources and reducing labor costs.

The "integration" case for spousal migration, a subset of family reunification, is particularly strong. Young men without wives or advanced education are the most volatile element in any population. They are also, usually, the foot in the door of a new country, since they are best equipped to navigate the perilous route to the West. Admitting them while maintaining a privileged position for family reunification – even if "family" is limited to parents and juvenile siblings – is a commitment to admitting two, three, four, or more times their number. Nevertheless, the moral, legal, and instrumental case for giving core family reunification a certain priority among the criteria for admission and settlement is strong.

INTEGRATION AND THE ELECTORATE

The connection between integration policies and border control is one source of policy dilemmas. Another source is the connection between integration policies and popular support for them. Support is necessary not only for the government's political survival but also for the integration project itself, since the parts of the population alienated by measures they deem unfair are hardly likely to welcome newcomers into their neighborhoods or accept them cordially as workmates, much less open to them the networks through which many private-sector jobs are allocated.

Alienation can occur in diverse ways. Consider the case where there is a waiting list for public housing and a point system that takes into account family size, availability of other residential options, and the length of time a family has been waiting. Imagine a three-bedroom apartment opens for new occupancy and one claimant is a two-child, two-parent native family that is currently occupying a more expensive, cramped, and generally less attractive apartment. Because they have been waiting for many years, they are first in line for the new home. However, the government is trying to settle a recently arrived refugee family with six children and negligible resources. This family is currently housed with other refugees in an abandoned factory on the outskirts of the capital far from schools and potential jobs which the government has equipped as a temporary shelter.

Neither the location nor the conditions in which the refugee family are living are conducive to integration. As long as the family members are stuck there, language and skills training for adults and education for children are not likely to be very effective. The economic dimension of the integration project cannot begin. That is one incentive for giving the apartment to the refugees. Another is that though they are far from the front of the queue in terms of time spent waiting, when one considers family size and housing alternatives, they may have the superior claim.

After all, the native family is already in permanent housing with access to jobs and schools. So, the government would not be manipulating the established rules of the public housing game if it ordered the municipality to give the refugees precedence, a fact unlikely to mitigate the native family's sensation of injury and injustice.

Governments can fuel anti-immigrant sentiment even by doing nothing. In the absence of government placement policy, migrants will tend to cluster, selecting areas with relatively low rents, public transportation, potential jobs, and already settled families from their country of origin. As they concentrate they will stress local public services, including education and health care. A sudden, large infusion of migrants can mean soaring teacher–student ratios, longer lines in emergency rooms, and longer waiting times for appointments with primary-care physicians. Concentration in areas where migrants with a common ethnicity are already settled may reduce the *need* for new arrivals to interact with the native population. Inability to speak the national language will reduce the *possibility* for interaction in public spaces like parks, schools, shops, and playing fields.

So, a national government that prioritizes integration must act exigently to reduce the stress on local resources and to facilitate contact between migrants and natives. It needs to divert resources in order to increase the supply of public services in migrant-impacted areas, to improve the spaces where positive interaction could occur, and to help migrants acquire the national language quickly. It may also need to expand job opportunities for everyone in the area to minimize the risk of migrants being seen to put downward pressure on wages or actually displace native workers. But steering job opportunities to areas with large minority populations could provoke voters in areas where migrants are sparse.

To minimize ghettoization, governments might try to disperse new migrants around the country with special emphasis on areas whose public facilities like schools are underutilized. Unfortunately, a dispersal strategy, like every solution to integration dilemmas, arrives in the administrative mind freighted with problems of its own. To begin with, the government would need to overcome the new arrivals' natural desire to locate adjacent to ethnic kin or co-religionists. Moreover, unless the government subsidizes housing initially, new migrants will, as I noted above, filter toward the low-rent areas which attracted their predecessors.

Officials will need either to coerce or to incentivize dispersal. Given legal authority, they could coerce by making entry or right to work or access to social benefits conditional on settling in designated areas of the country. Enforcing those conditions beyond a short period, however, might be found to conflict with human rights provisions of the ICCPR and the European Convention embedded in national law. There is, for instance, a right to move at will within the national borders except under extraordinary circumstances where movement can be shown to be a danger to public health and safety.[18] It is doubtful that a court would construe the right as limited to citizens. Whether courts would uphold any waiver of rights extracted as a condition of entry or as a condition of access to generally available social benefits is less clear. At best officials might make access *to the full range of benefits* conditional on accepting location by governmental fiat for a fixed period of time. What it seems clear they cannot do is threaten migrants with destitution if they do not settle where directed. A British court ruled out that option as a means of pressing persons found not qualified for asylum to self-deport.[19]

If I am correct in predicting what the courts would currently allow, a dispersal strategy would have to rely largely on incentives, and any special incentives program runs the risk of enraging parts of the electorate. Aside from that difficulty, dispersal may conflict with the government's interest in the efficient orientation of new arrivals to the end of achieving rapid integration. It might be less costly to deliver high-intensity language and vocational training programs when participants are geographically concentrated. The reverse may, however, be true, because in ghetto-like conditions, migrants are more likely to speak their native languages not only at home but also in shops and day-to-day intercourse with neighbors. Web-based language-training may resolve this particular dilemma.

Then there is the matter of shelter. No government has yet found the political will and public support to marshal the resources needed to build even modest apartment blocks scattered among various towns and cities on a scale sufficient to house the intake in recent years. Makeshift arrangements have proven to be the rule and seem likely to remain so. Anything better would again raise the question of whether new arrivals were getting accommodations superior to those available for many members of the working and lower middle class.

Being settled for any length of time in uncomfortable structures with little privacy encourages migrants to slip away in search of something better. Even very shabby housing in low-rent areas may represent improvement. To secure it, family members who have not yet acquired a working ability in the language or lack vocational training will seek out ethnic kin who may employ them at mere survival wages or may help them navigate onto the welfare rolls. In countries where welfare benefits increase with the number of young children, even without anyone working large migrant families might survive with much greater comfort than they had experienced in their native lands.

One way governments can influence the residential, work, and other choices of new migrants is by requiring them to pass through a stage of provisional settlement during which they need to fulfill various conditions before securing permanent settlement short of citizenship. Access to the latter stage can in turn be subjected to similar or new conditions. And even after the migrant becomes a full-fledged citizen, depending on a country's national and international legal obligations, governments might use the ongoing threat of denationalization to influence behavior. This might run afoul of constitutional protections, however. The French government, for instance, attempted unsuccessfully to annul the French citizenship of persons with dual citizenship who went abroad to join ISIS, an attempt thwarted by the judiciary.[20]

Although the International Refugee Convention appears to preclude giving migrants provisional status after a claim for asylum has been found valid,[21] several European states have nevertheless assigned this status for all new migrants whether or not they are refugees.[22] Putting legality aside, the public policy issue is whether, on balance, provisional status serves the purposes of integration.

Some argue that uncertainty about the future incident to provisional settlement spurs refugees to intensive study of the local language, to find employment, or to do whatever else the state may require as conditions for renewal of status or advancement to permanent settlement. The counterargument is that the risk of expulsion might discourage migrants from investing time and energy in learning a language, particularly if they need to pay for the lessons out of their meager resources, or if the time allotted for achieving a working knowledge of the language appears insufficient. They might instead focus on finding an alternative country of refuge or devote their waking hours to whatever jobs are available in order to acquire funds to cushion their next move. Moreover – pace Dr. Johnson[23] – the anxiety caused by the looming threat of expulsion may disorient rather than concentrate their minds on their studies.

At a minimum, provisional and rigorously conditioned status may slow the psychological process by means of which the migrant transitions to a new national identity. A migrant might not retain warm feelings for the country he left, but it should be remembered that he had other identities, perhaps a transnational one like religion and almost certainly one to an extended family or some sort of clan. Under the circumstances, one or another of those identities could intensify for want of appealing alternatives. In short, provisional status is a sharp-edged tool which demands carefully calibrated use lest it turn in the hand.

This merely suggestive list of policy options has touched only incidentally on what is the most challenging item on my list of integration's purposes: achieving compliance with the majority's cultural norms. It is problematical because (1) people within the native majority are likely to disagree about the content of those norms and (2) not everyone agrees that achieving compliance is an appropriate state purpose or at least an important one. Obviously, any discussion of this purpose draws us back to the multicultural debate.

Previously I emphasized the moral issues surrounding the debate, in particular the question of what position in the debate liberals may feel required to take by virtue of their defining values. Now I want to put the moral questions to one side in favor of the public policy ones. Imagine a government concerned only with economic growth, public finance, public order, and national security issues, a government that does not see itself as enforcer of the majority's moral norms. Would this somewhat narrower focus lead to different policies than the ones a government committed to the defense of the majority's moral norms would adopt?

On the one hand, liberalism implies respect for each culture, however illiberal its practices, because a culture provides individuals born into it with a stable identity and a means for orienting themselves in an otherwise confounding thicket of unmediated experience. On the other hand, being a faith, liberalism inspires resistance to practices that violate its tenets. So if a government's assessment of its strictly economic and security interests led it to incentivize or even compel migrants to shuck off illiberal practices carried with them from their countries of origin, that choice would coincidentally advance the crusading side of liberalism and also, ironically, advance the program of those members of the European right who imagine or at least pretend to imagine themselves defenders of female autonomy, gay rights, and free speech.[24]

Is tolerance of an illiberal minority's practices the surest way of "integrating" minorities to the end of advancing economic and security goals? One could argue that my way of phrasing the question is at best confusing. Suppose a minority lives a cultural life apart from the mainstream. It lives apart because its religious convictions or cultural norms discourage social contact outside the workplace. And suppose, in addition, it sends its children to parochial schools designed to propagate its distinctive cultural values. And suppose finally that the minority's religious leaders express abhorrence of majority culture. Where those not entirely hypothetical conditions prevail, is the minority in any meaningful sense "integrated" even if it picks the country's crops, sweeps its streets, and services its nursing homes?

In the period just after World War II, Germans would not have described their guest workers as "integrated" despite the large role they played in the German economy. The very fact that Germans called the large contingent of workers they imported from Turkey as "guests" and made no effort to incorporate them into the country's political and social orders underscores the absence of any expectation of or desire for their integration. In other words, Germans in those days did not see any organic or instrumental relationship between the incorporation of foreigners into the economy and their integration into society. Neither did the guest workers, even after they brought over their families and settled in for the indefinite duration. Most of that first generation retained Turkish citizenship and there is little evidence that they would have seized the opportunity for German citizenship had it been offered.

Assembly line, crop-picking, and construction jobs are the work of the first generation. They don't require fluency in the native language or interpersonal skills like the accurate reading and appreciation of other persons' expectations, needs, desires, preferences, offers of friendship, or intimations of hostility. Such skills arise more or less gradually from informal contact in public spaces like bars, parks, and sports centers, and structured contact in military units and schools, and from a shared media experience. Sophisticated interpersonal skills are required for effective performance in the bulk of jobs in the service sector, now by far the largest piece of the economy, even in an export dynamo like Germany.[25] That in itself suggests that the goal of optimizing the economic contribution of migrant-background residents requires a considerable measure of social integration.

Arguably, social integration does not require holding a broad range of social values in common. Any liberal golfer can testify to having amicably played eighteen holes with a partner who abhors the very idea of gay marriage, believes in the inerrancy of scripture, and who would outlaw abortion altogether. To be sure, one of the canons of golf is "avoid discussion of politics and religion." That is easy enough to do when people spend only four hours together every now and then. It is rather less easily managed when they occupy the same workspace eight or more hours a day. Moreover, political values bleed into social ones. The bleeding occurs because politics never has been concerned solely with the distribution of income and wealth. It has also been about the distribution among groups of status and respect. Both are closely connected to group identity.

A group's practices and values are the external signs of its identity.[*] To the extent those practices violate majority norms and either are manifested in public (by the wearing of face-concealing veils, for example) or become public knowledge (as when an affianced child escapes to a women's shelter), they tend to spread through the gossip of daily encounters in the workplace and public spaces as well as the anonymous intimacy of social media.

The politics of cultural conflict can get very personal, and technocrats would prefer to consign such issues to the private sphere. But they cannot easily evade them. Evasion is problematical because personal and group hostility stemming from incompatible cultural practices seem likely to affect adversely the minority's employment prospects, the education and social integration of their children, and its relationship with the police and intelligence services. *Therefore, whatever the personal preferences of technocrats and political leaders and however narrowly they conceive of their stewardship of the public interest, they cannot avoid factoring cultural conflicts to some degree into their design of integration strategies and their tactics for implementing them.*

Accepting that conclusion does not, however, determine strategic and tactical choices. There is no indisputably best way to wean people away from practices and values alien to the resident majority. Should they be nudged or driven? Should integration be left largely to the seductive pressure of the majority culture that dominates the mass media and the environment of schools and the workplace? Should incentives and disincentives be left largely to the discretion of local governments or should they be closely managed by central government departments?

---

[*] So, when governments disparage or outlaw practices and values of a group, they cannot avoid being seen as disrespecting the group and its individual members. But if for that reason a government abstains from outlawing practices the majority finds abhorrent, it will be seen as limiting the dominant group's freedom to engage in politics. Seen by whom? Seen by every reader of the tabloids in countries like the United Kingdom, by the audience for aspiring media personalities hoping to soar on the current of some popular passion, and by an electorate anxious to be told that the source of its anxieties and pains is not impersonal structures but rather people unlike themselves. In short it is very difficult to defang politics by trying to isolate it from cultural conflicts.

How can governments avoid driving culturally distinct migrants into a defensive crouch in which they furiously embrace every feature of their legacy culture instead of gradually relaxing their grip? What adjustments, if any, should be made in school curricula, school lunches, and public holidays?

Should governments design and fund programs which bring people from minority cultures into contact with the majority outside the workplace? How can they ensure that the contact is positive? Moreover, even accepting the proposition that cultural differences should be factored into government responses to the challenge of integration, what degree of importance do they demand? Are cultural differences a principal source of social conflict or is the long-resident population alienated principally by the perceived negative impact of migration on its economic well-being and access to public housing and medical care?

INTEGRATION AND COMMUNICATION

Friction between natives and newcomers makes societies less happy, less efficient, and less orderly. Friction may boost the careers of shameless politicians and sincere xenophobes, but it burdens governance. Therefore, governments have strong incentives to eliminate sources of friction, to ease the friction when preemption fails, and, above all, to avoid being themselves one of its sources. Liberal governments have, in addition, a value-driven incentive to make relative newcomers and their families feel at home.

Among the principal means for achieving these ends is improved communication, particularly with migrants whose cultural background makes it difficult for them to slip comfortably and unobtrusively into Western societies. Communication serves two functions. One is to inform the government about migrant minority concerns and to identify influential community members and factions. The other is to express respect for those concerns if only by explaining why it is unable to address them as fully as migrant communities would like. Humiliation is one of the most powerful drivers of human behavior. A community ignored, a community that experiences public policy as diktat, is humiliated.

Contemporary West European constitutional systems do not for the most part formalize representation in legislative, judicial, or executive institutions for religious, racial, and ethnic minorities. But in most countries a rough-and-ready kind of representation occurs when party elites place persons from minority communities in favorable positions. This might happen through their inclusion on electoral lists and their appointment to cabinet and sub-cabinet positions by party leaders or their selection by local constituency committees in first-by-the-post parliamentary systems.

The logic of electoral politics drives the established parties to select Muslim candidates in districts where Muslims are concentrated and eligible to vote. Rafaela Dancygier, a particularly acute student of Muslims in European politics, notes that thanks to a combination of chain migration, available housing stock, immigrant preferences, and discrimination, areas of Muslim concentration are commonly found in run-down city centers.[26][†] These urban enclaves "are more likely to feature conservative and religious Muslims."[27] The local leaders able to turn out a bloc vote are older than the average Muslim and strongly patriarchal in orientation. Since residents of the enclaves tend to be relatively poor, parties of the left might seem their natural home. But their social values coincide in large measure with those that have traditionally been found on the right. So, their incorporation into parties of the left inevitably produces internal tensions, since those parties are normally led by liberal cosmopolitans. The result can be increasing programmatic incoherence.

Informal methods of representation work best where social entrepreneurs within minority communities have managed to build organizations able to express the real desires, needs, and identity of their members. Organizational leaders can then counsel national political elites about selecting representative candidates for inclusion in government. Moreover, by their sheer existence such organizations provide a prism through which elites can identify representative figures. The highly developed institutions of Jewish communities in countries like Germany, France, and Great Britain exemplify the self-organization of a religious group for purposes of communicating its special concerns to political leaders and officials.

In terms of their capacity to achieve the same end, Muslims in Western Europe are at a distinct disadvantage. As I have previously noted, Sunni Islam, the faith of roughly 80 percent of Muslims, is not hierarchically organized. It is rather the reverse. Persons can self-identify as religious leaders and authoritative expositors of religious obligation and then seek followers. Also complicating the question of representation are differences among Muslim migrants in country of origin, in inherited language, in schools of interpretation to which they adhere, in levels of education and wealth, and in customs and practices peculiar to their own or their parents' or grandparents' original home. The Muslim faith is the dominant religion in countries as varied as Indonesia and Albania, Afghanistan and Somalia. So where organs of the state want to communicate with what they think of as the "Muslim community," they have had difficulty finding interlocutors who can authoritatively speak for Muslims generally or even for an indisputably large fraction of them except at the municipal level where migrants from a single small area in one country sometimes cluster.[28] Muslims, conversely, have not been famously successful in building channels for communicating their aggregated desires and needs to the government and the public.

When the first wave of Muslim immigrants arrived in Europe, representation was not an issue because governments and perhaps the workers themselves assumed they were transients and remained citizens of their respective countries of origin. Even after workers' families joined them and it became clear that most of them were not

---

[†] France tends to be something of an outlier in this respect in that most of its most problematic ghettoes are on the urban fringe.

going home, European states continued a policy of indifference to the desires, needs, and to a large extent the practices of their Islamic populations. Indifference morphed into concern only when demands for labor dwindled, migrant unemployment multiplied, prisons began to fill with members of the second generation, and, following one or another dramatic incident, governments began to perceive migrants from Muslim-majority countries as a potential source of violence. It was then that a number of governments began an active search for legitimate interlocutors.

For liberals, the search was driven by ethical values reinforced by security concerns. One difference between liberal and illiberal champions of elected governments is the former's conception of society as a congregation of groups competing through shifting alliances for public and private goods *according to rules precluding winner-take-all outcomes*. Of course, participation is far more than a matter of periodic elections. Competition for public goods – subsidies, licenses, permits, space, guarantees, regulations, laws, and so on – is incessant and occurs not only in offices and legislative halls at local, regional, and national levels but also in the media. Voice, facts, theories, friendships, networks, studies, appeals to identity and values, electoral promises or threats: competitors use whatever they have in the way of tools. Only citizens can vote, but even that tool can be useful to settled non-citizens since they are *potential* members of the electorate. By contrast, champions of illiberal democracy regard a majority vote as a mandate for the untrammeled exercise of executive power to implement the majority's agenda, which may include the disablement of its perceived enemies.

Consultation whether with migrant or any other large and complex minority is easier to propose than to conduct. Suppose there are grave divisions within the minority over the essential features of its contemporary identity. Consider a Western country containing large numbers of first-, second-, and third-generation migrants from various Islamic-majority countries in Africa, the Middle East, and Asia. Even those families that originated in the same country may be Sunni or Shia in their faith. If they are Sunni, they may be Salafi or Sufi or adherents of other variations of the Sunni division of Islam. They may be divided among the four major schools of interpretation of sharia. They may disagree over whether a contemporary cultural practice is integral to their faith as Muslims or a tradition peculiar to the tribe or region from which they moved to the West. For an instance of the latter, consider the removal of a young girl's clitoris and labia, infibulation – what we in the West often refer to as "female genital mutilation" or "female circumcision." Among Somalis and some other peoples in the Global South, it is a deeply rooted practice, although it is not mentioned in the Qur'an or commanded by sharia. Not surprisingly, then, it is not practiced in all Muslim-majority countries.

Migrant-background minorities may also be divided between the religiously indifferent and the fervently faithful, between those anxious to preserve inherited practices and norms and those who wish to adapt them to the majority cultural setting. So, who "speaks" for the minority community? Who, indeed, constitutes the minority community since every person has multiple loyalties and affective identities? Is it simply those within the minority who struggle to preserve the practices and norms brought with them from the countries in which they or their parents or grandparents originated? What if the cultural practice being defended is the maintenance of a traditional, patriarchal organization in which women are silenced and daughters-in-law are forced by custom to live under the command of their husband's mother?

Consistent with their controlling concerns, conservatives among the majority would probably say: "We ought to recognize as community interlocutors those persons who (1) appear to us (the majority) as actually possessing authority and power among groups from which enemies of the state seem able to recruit supporters and (2) are willing to cooperate with us in restraining recruitment, in identifying the recruited, and then in helping us to deradicalize the recruited, where that is possible, or in imprisoning them where it is not. However, where a community lacks established leaders, we should select those who are willing to cooperate and have leadership potential and then help them, as subtly as possible, to become leaders."

Liberalism arguably imposes an obligation at least to listen to every voice and to allow minority communities a certain autonomy in selecting their leaders. Hence liberals should feel more ambivalent about actively fostering collaborators willing to enforce majority interests in return for the majority's facilitating their dominance within the minority.

Only in villages, however, can every voice be heard. In the real world of massive urbanized populations, democratic governments at the national level need representatives with whom to consult. If because of its poverty, divisions, or for any other reason a minority community lacks effective representation, governments may then have to work with such communities to create structures able to aggregate and express community interests. But communities of any size and complexity will almost never speak with a single voice.

Interest groups are a principal vehicle in democracies for continuous communication between a country's inhabitants and their government. When they are well organized and financed, they do far more than communicate demands, preferences, incentives, and threats. They also help initiate, shape, and block laws and regulations. As the great political scientist Robert Dahl argued years ago, the democratic process can best be understood as the interplay of interest groups – their competition, compromises, shifting coalitions, power-seeking – operating within the framework constitutionally established to make, interpret, and execute the law.[29] He saw in the multisided play of interest groups the genius of real democratic representation.

In time Dahl came to recognize the flaw in this genius. It is the absence from the game of persons with shared interests who, however, lack the means to organize themselves.[30] The first generation of migrants, who often come from peasant and working-class backgrounds, illustrates this problem. They arrive as strangers in a strange land, often with limited skills and assets. The daily struggle to find permanent shelter and employment can leave them exhausted and demoralized. If they come as refugees or guest workers, their status is fragile, their long-term settlement contingent. They are not citizens, may not even be regarded as settled. Hence, they often are disqualified from voting even in local elections. As poor migrants they have common interests, but they are likely to be divided, rendered strangers to each other by color, sect, national origin, history, and culture. Under these circumstances, large-scale organization into an effective interest group happens over time, if it happens at all.

Once governments recognize the need for interlocutors, they face difficult choices. They should be looking for leaders with both the capacity to influence their notional followers and the willingness to strike deals which on balance advance the government's goals. The balance can be delicate. For every leader, there is an aspirant eager to displace him by painting compromise, indeed anything other than imperious demands, as surrender. Then there is the matter of style. Officials are drawn to interlocutors who look and sound like themselves. Those will be members of the migrant community who by virtue of fluency in the national language, inherited or acquired wealth, and/or possession of a highly valued skill have already integrated. Unfortunately, the very qualities which make them appealing interlocutors may make them less credible to their ostensible constituents and vulnerable to ambitious and clever rhetoricians bursting out of the poorly integrated mass.

In deciding with whom to talk governments also need to account for generational tensions. It is a commonplace among students of migration that because the first generation measures its progress against the conditions it in most cases fled, it is likely to feel relatively satisfied. Its children, by contrast, having naturally adopted the native population's definition of success, feel in most instances dissatisfied. Their superior fluency in the national language and culture aggravates their frustrated ambitions. They may also have a limited capacity to appreciate the rigors of their parents' passage from the parched farms, dreary slums, and torture chambers of the old country to the lower rungs of the new one, thus eroding their respect for the first generation's accomplishments and sacrifices. What follows is that the leaders acknowledged by the first generation may not enjoy credibility with the second one.

The bottom line is that governments navigate across obscure terrain in trying to find interlocutors who can actually speak on behalf of enclaves expanding vigorously within the nation's borders. Credibility in politics often proves volatile. The government itself may taint the brand of leaders by appearing to anoint them. One plausible way for a government to avoid that outcome and to learn who are its best interlocutors is to encourage competing claimants for the minority leadership mantle to associate. They associate by sending representatives to a kind of higher council which the government can consult and through which it can indirectly communicate to the minority base.

To incentivize association, it can offer community development funds which association members can in turn dispense both as patronage and as authentic contributions to education, entrepreneurship, and other ends, serving both the community and the state. Of course, this, like any other targeting of funds or services to minorities, may exact political retribution from less advantaged sectors of the native electorate. Well, no one ever said governing is easy. Government leaders have to persuade the electorate that they are not pandering to minorities but are rather working to make them net contributors to the economy and collaborators in the struggle against terrorism.

As I proposed above, communication in the form of respectful dialogue does more than inform. It is a substantive good in that it publicly signifies respect and acceptance and thus helps to incorporate minority persons into the ongoing national narrative. Public incorporation reduces vulnerability. Like christening a national holiday or park or battleship after a historical figure associated with the minority or naming a contemporary one to a cabinet post, it implicitly encourages officialdom in general to treat newcomers with respect and encourages the private-sector employer to give them a fair chance.

In material terms, manifestations of respect are one of the least expensive ways of responding to the needs, desires, and demands of all minorities, including migrants. They are potentially costly to centrist political establishments only to the extent that the self-respect of a significant electoral faction is invested, however unconsciously, in a sense of ethnic or religious or racial superiority. Having seen itself as by virtue of birth at least one rung above new arrivals or more generally people of color, some natives may feel a loss of status as a consequence of public manifestations of respect for relative newcomers of a different color and religious identity as well as by their increasing appearance in the media as celebrities of the music, cinematic, sports, and business worlds. This nativist fragment's anger over a sensed loss of status will show up more readily in elections than polls until a compelling enemy of "political correctness" arrives to celebrate the nativists' virtues and dog-whistle their bigotry.

8

A Model

Problematic Means for Liberal Ends

To govern is to choose. So far, I have merely sketched a range of options for political actors committed to the defense of liberal norms, practices, and institutions. The immediate threats to them come from the political strivers who surf the fear and rage of cultural conservatives, anti-government ideologues, racists, Islamophobes, and, most significantly, people left behind by changes in technology, culture, and markets. Incidents of jihadi violence add impetus to this electoral challenge from the political right.

The longer-term threat is the loosening of the bonds of society. The fragmentation of social identity, the decline of social trust, tolerance, compassion, and empathy could reach a point where the borders of Western countries do not enclose nations but a congeries of mutually antagonistic groups. Public services like the provision of health care, education, roads, bridges, parks, and security shrink because citizens divided by race, ethnicity, religion, and ideology refuse to cooperate; they prefer battling for a bigger share of the shrinking pie to enlarging the pie. Cultural pessimists would add another threat, namely, the replacement of personally liberating norms, practices, and institutions by ones that constrain individual choice and brutally punish deviance from conventional thought and practice within each human enclave.

Laying out the buffet of policy choices is the strategist's first task. Then comes the risky task: choosing. In this final chapter, I, viewing myself as a defender of liberal democracy in a bad time, offer a model I believe may be the best suited for addressing (1) the pressure on the borders of rich liberal states, (2) the integration of those who have entered over the past seven decades, and (3) the terroristic attacks on Western society that have been carried out either in the name of imported faiths or as furious nativist responses to the migrant presence. Generalizations are cheap. Reality is in the details.

As a thought experiment, imagine we are all citizens of a country with a demographic profile that falls somewhere between France, Germany, and the United

Kingdom. We will call it Netherfranc. A young, charismatic politician has just become head of the government, carried into office on the shoulders of a new party, "Citizens Forward," which she describes as "liberalism without tears and conservatism without hate." Imagine further that she has campaigned with a manifesto promising to defend the country's borders, its welfare system, its commitment to equal opportunity regardless of race or gender, its social cohesion, and the security of its streets. She promises to pursue this course with the same zeal that she would bring to defending Netherfranc's liberal institutions and the European project which had ended the Continent's history of fratricidal wars.

On her first day in office, she asks you – a friend, a longtime political adviser, and an expert on issues of migration and integration – for a detailed plan of action to implement her manifesto. The plan, she warns you, must plausibly lead to shrinkage in the undocumented population, including persons whose applications for asylum have been denied.

Since you share her liberal values, her lack of dogmatism about means, and her determination to keep the xenophobic, authoritarian right out of power, you propose a plan with the overall theme of enhancing state capacity (1) to detect and abort threats to public safety, (2) to increase equality of opportunity and access to social benefits while preserving the fiscal integrity of the welfare state, (3) to encourage and facilitate work and entrepreneurial activity, (4) to increase social cohesion, and (5) to limit unauthorized presence within the national frontiers. This plan would take into account the existing minority communities formed by seven decades of migration from the Global South. Those communities constitute at least 7 percent of the national population and 18 percent of youth under the age of twenty-one. Numbers are only approximate because, according to unofficial estimates, there are as many as 200,000 undocumented persons in the country. The numbers do include more than 150,000 people awaiting decisions on their asylum claims. The native population's birth rate is well below replacement, let us say, 1.5. The migrant population's birth rate is 2.9, having dropped from 3.4 ten years ago.

THE PLAN: A MEMORANDUM TO THE
HEAD OF GOVERNMENT (CONFIDENTIAL)

INTRODUCTION

Most of our fellow citizens recognize or can be prodded into recognizing that they are not reproducing at a rate sufficient to maintain a tolerable ratio of the economically active to the inactive who are, primarily, the rapidly growing number of retired persons. Many also appreciate or you can help them to appreciate that, as demonstrated by Japan, a decreasing and aging population leads to economic stagnation and insufficient care for the sick and the aged, particularly those in the final years of their lives.

Our population is about half the size of Germany's and has proportionately similar needs. Today Germany lacks more than 100,000 nurses and caregivers.[1] Netherfranc lacks about 50,000 and the number will grow over the next decade. In a major address to the nation celebrating a new political era, you trash the right's claim that migration threatens the welfare state. The truth, you will point out, is that carefully regulated migration is needed to save it. After all, the majority of persons seeking entry are relatively young. If we admit primarily young adults in numbers corresponding to our employment needs, including the employment opportunities their arrival will generate, their contributions to welfare state funding will for decades far exceed their need to draw on government support. To illustrate what could happen if, for instance, we fail to import caregivers, mention the recently reported cases of Japanese men and women in understaffed retirement communities lying dead in their little flats until the smell of their corpses announces their passing.[2]

To reassure those who have been persuaded that migrants will drain the system of social support, note that initially the state will provide them only with the means to integrate rapidly into the economy. Until they are employed we will provide relatively meager benefits. There will be ample incentive to work. But you must also emphasize the ways in which new arrivals can help our very slow-growth economy to accelerate. Cite the American experience of migrants of the first and second generations playing a crucial role in entrepreneurship. In Silicon Valley, the center of America's high technology industry, they have founded half the start-ups.[3] In order to attract enterprising people, you should argue, we need to provide a welcoming environment.

Electorally we are on safe ground. According to our polling data, a majority of the electorate, moved by a sense of self-interest supplemented to varying degrees by a feeling of humanitarian responsibility (the "Good Samaritan" impulse stemming, perhaps, from our Christian traditions) favors a modest annual intake of new residents, most of whom will inevitably come from the Global South, since the legacy population of Eastern European countries is shrinking just like our own.

At the same time, however, a good part of our electorate is ambivalent. Yes, more people are needed, they concede, but they fear a large influx of immigrants will threaten revolutionary change in the character of our society. As it is, a good part of our electorate feels disoriented by the pace of cultural change and the manifest presence of people with exotic beliefs and customs. They are easily aroused by generally false reports that migrants are getting more support from the state than they are, as well as the sometimes-accurate experience of strain on our housing market and our health and education systems. Despite the objective reality of a decline in violent crime,[4] wary citizens are ready to believe claims that migrants are uniquely dangerous, claims lent credence by terrorist attacks. One thing that makes them feel less secure and more dubious about public institutions is the indisputable gap, a veritable chasm, between, on the one hand, successive governments' promises to regulate and limit entry and remove illegal entrants and, on the other, the results of our predecessors' efforts such as they have been.

Finally, there is a broad discomfort caused by a perceived erosion of national identity, the loss of a sense of belonging to a historically defined community, Netherfranc. Many people instinctively associate the erosion with migration, ignoring the effects of urbanization, the internet, social media, the decline of religious or ideological conviction, and, more broadly, the post-industrial culture of feverish consumption and cultivation of the auto-celebrated self. As the Harvard Professor Robert Putnam famously put it, too many of us go bowling alone. We live narcissistically, without a sense of obligation or higher purpose. Trying to address the problems of integrating strangers may coincidentally impel us to address that anomie and atomization of society which would beset us, however high our border walls.

The following is what I propose for your consideration.

CONTROLLING THE BORDER

Identity Cards and Deportation

The state will issue a biometric identity card to every resident and every person entering the country through an authorized entry point.[*] Parliament will prohibit employing and providing goods or services, other than emergency medical assistance, to any person unable or unwilling to produce the card. Violations by providers would lead to severe fines or forfeiture of property, the severity increasing with the number and willfulness of the violations. In extraordinary circumstances providers could apply to a designated local official for a waiver. Depending on its gravity and the absence of unusual mitigating circumstances, violation of the prohibition by a non-citizen could be enforced through expulsion from the country.

Most Continental countries already have identity cards, but their presentation is not a condition for receiving most goods and services in the private sector.[†] Under this plan, a card-less person could not buy or be given even a banana without placing the provider at risk. Since cards could be lost or stolen, we would authorize police substations to issue new ones on the spot after verifying the applicant's identity with an iris scan. Cards could also be lent or sold. In the longer term we would replace cards with a national biometric database which could be accessed by cell phone. Instead of presenting a card, someone seeking to obtain a good or service would simply allow the supplier to snap a picture of their eye and transmit it to the national

---

[*] India has managed a very broad distribution of such a card in order to reduce corruption in the distribution of its welfare payments.

[†] The United Kingdom precludes provision of services like renting to the undocumented, but it does not have a card system to help enforce the prohibition.

biodata register, which would automatically verify and respond. In the short term we would deter lending or selling cards by treating those acts as crimes punishable by fines and property confiscations.

Once the identity-card system is in place, persons who enter the country without documentation or who overstay visas will be much more easily located, then deported and banned for ten years from participating in the migration lottery I will describe next. We must, however, provide for the cases where persons overstay their visas because of dangers in their home countries which arose during their stay here. (Consider, for instance, the impact on female Afghan students of the Taliban seizing control of the Afghan state.) Under those circumstances we should grant them temporary settlement if they apply for it within a reasonable time after the visa expires. In addition, obviously we will not expel persons while they are undergoing treatment for a life-threatening condition.

Despite the efficacy, even necessity, of the identity-card system for controlling our borders in the coming decades, it is the one among my various proposals that causes me the most unease. For it undoubtedly expands the state's ability to invade private space. It does so at a time when that space is already being shrunk by the operations of social media and state surveillance mechanisms including ubiquitous cameras and enhanced facial recognition capacity. Therefore, we need stringent safeguards to prevent us creating the conditions that would enable a government of the right to drag us into the dystopian world George Orwell imagined in his novel 1984. In that world of total surveillance, private life would survive only in our dreams.

Here are the safeguards I envision. First, we would recognize a defense of "humanitarian emergency" for anyone accused of giving a good or service without demanding display of an identity card. I think, for instance, of a doctor treating an injured person or a Samaritan feeding a famished child. However, I would place on the accused service-giver the burden of showing by a preponderance of the evidence that the emergency was real. Moreover, the person giving the good or service would have to report the incident after the fact. Second, to minimize abuse of the augmented power the card system would give to the state, we would create an independent oversight body with punitive power composed of persons nominated by our principal human rights and civil liberty organizations and approved by the parliament. In addition, we will need to deter use of the system for any purpose other than to identify the presence of undocumented persons. Private use by government personnel must be punished severely.

The identity-card system will undermine minority integration and aggravate minority-youth alienation if the government allows municipalities to enforce it with "stop-and-identify" policing. Inevitably police will concentrate on people with darker skins or unconventional clothing. So, in the legislation establishing the system we should specify that absent a declared emergency, police must obtain a judicially issued warrant in order to demand production of an identity card except in the course of an arrest made pursuant to a judicially issued warrant or an observed serious crime (not, for instance, a traffic stop). Moreover, we need to establish at the municipal level an inspector-general's office independent of the police to which residents can bring claims of improper stops and empower that office to hold hearings, issues subpoenas, and, where appropriate, impose heavy administrative sanctions.

In order to make deportation of unauthorized persons a real option, we must create a deportation service with its own logistical arrangements and personnel committed to the task. In addition, we must incentivize the countries that are the principal sources of undocumented entrants to allow their deported nationals to return. Clearly if EU members negotiate collectively with those countries the chances of success will be much enhanced. We or again, ideally, the EU as a whole must also find countries willing to admit though not necessarily to retain indefinitely those deportees who would be persecuted if we returned them to their home countries or who are stateless or have made themselves appear stateless. Like Israel, we could provide deportees with a small stipend sufficient to enable them to travel on to a country they prefer. Obviously, the stipend would be substantially less than the going rate for smuggling people into Netherfranc. We hardly want to make it profitable to have yourself smuggled here and then deported. To enable deportees to move on we would provide them with a temporary passport that expires within a short period, cannot be used to reenter Netherfranc, and is not subject to renewal.

Deportation of the entirety of the existing undocumented population is not feasible, humane, or consistent with our society's interests. Large numbers of the undocumented are now so integrated into the economy and the social life of many communities that their expulsion would seriously damage certain economic sectors, impede delivery of social services, and make our existing political divisions more acrimonious. So we should institute a one-time amnesty for all those who have not been convicted of a serious crime, who agree to pay a special tax out of future earnings as a contribution to the welfare state (except where they are already long-time contributors through tax and social security payments), and, if they are not currently employed, who agree as well to perform community service within the framework of the national service program I will describe below or participate in our fast-track training programs.

Those amnestied would be granted provisional settlement status which would evolve into an opportunity for citizenship if, over a period of years, they fulfilled all the obligations incorporated into individual settlement agreements between the presently undocumented and the state. That would leave a small minority, one small enough to be detained and then expelled expeditiously. I am confident that we can secure strong public support for an amnesty with these features if accompanied by the border-control measures I will describe next.

Offshore Immigration and Asylum-Claim Processing Centers

Applications for entry or asylum must be made abroad at either consulates or special centers established with the permission of the host country, which we would no doubt have to secure through financial incentives or other instruments of statecraft. Ideally the EU would fund the centers and manage them in partnership with the office of the United Nations High Commissioner for Refugees (UNHCR).

Formally, they would exist as organs of the UNHCR or the UN itself, both familiar presences in poor countries. Unlike some existing refugee centers, they would operate like real communities with schools, shops, factories, and sports fields open to participation by residents of the host country. The UN flag, together with a diversity of races and ethnicities in management and administration, is essential. It would shelter the centers from the charge that they are neocolonial intrusions reminiscent of the European-controlled concessions carved out of the coast of China in the nineteenth century. Since most if not all of the centers I envision would be in Africa north and south of the Sahara, we should seek to reinforce the symbolism of the UN flag with a statement of support for the centers from the African Union. I think we might induce its support by presenting the centers (accurately, I believe) as nodules of development as well as humanitarian relief and preparation of persons for integration into Netherfranckish society.

Both locals and asylum claimants could apply to participate in the point-system and lottery which would determine who could enter Netherfranc or other EU countries. We would create a cadre of asylum assessors and rotate them through these centers so that asylum judgments could be made on the spot. A favorable judgment would count heavily in the point system, but it would not be decisive in all cases. Under Macron, the French have recently initiated on a very small scale an asylum-assessment center in Niger.[5] Persons found to qualify are flown directly to France and given state support and access to language training. In addition, it appears that the French are paying the government in Niger to put the people-smugglers out of business. The numbers crossing the Sahara in the past year have dropped noticeably.[6] Unhappy by-products of the French initiative are loss off income for the considerable number of Nigerian citizens involved in or indirectly benefiting from the semi-clandestine movement of people from Niger through the desert to Libya and the shift to routes more dangerous for both drivers and migrants.

At the EU migrant-processing centers I envision, Netherfranckish members of the EU-funded staff would familiarize applicants with the laws, values, and customary practices of our country and would provide them with language instruction, facility in the language being another element of the point system. Since many of our citizens already speak English as a second language, we could weight English competency almost as heavily as fluency in Netherfrancish. English-language competence would make it easier for people to move on to places like the United

Kingdom, Canada, the United States, Australia, and New Zealand if, for instance, they failed to find employment in Netherfranc or to satisfy the conditions in their initial-settlement agreements.

As a next step, Netherfranckish consular officials would interview lottery winners to the end of determining family size and age distribution, whether they appear psychologically prepared to respect the laws and practices of our country, their level of skills relevant to employment in Netherfranc, and more generally the prospective ease of integrating them into our society. On the basis of these interviews our officials will assign points to the lottery winners that will cumulate with points they might already have as persons with legitimate asylum claims and points stemming from their language test scores.

We would also conduct lotteries for prospective economic migrants in countries without refugee centers. The prospect of someday winning and the risk of summary expulsion for unauthorized presence in Netherfranc and long-term exclusion from participation in lotteries should help deter prospective migrants from attempting the perilous and expensive journey through the people-smuggling system.

Point System

You, as head of government, will establish a committee composed of representatives of the political parties and the private and non-profit sectors, assisted by experts from government agencies, think tanks, and universities. It will help you to develop a migration point system and to set annual limits on entry. You will task the committee members with estimating the number of migrants needed to meet our country's present and projected employment needs which cannot be satisfied out of our current population supplemented by foreign workers on seasonal or limited-term contracts. They will also consider the impact of migrants of varying numbers, skills, and ages on government expenditures for education, health, unemployment, and disability compensation, and other features of our welfare state.

On the basis of the committee's conclusions, you would obtain perhaps biennial parliamentary approval of an annual cap for entry and provisional-settlement visas and approval also of your proposed hierarchy of qualities (language fluency, satisfaction of criteria for asylum, close family connections in Netherfranc, successful establishment perhaps in cyberspace of a mentoring relationship with unrelated Netherfranckish citizens, readiness to accept Netherfranckish social norms, etc.) to be reflected in the point system that will govern the allocation of a given year's visas. You could soften the cap by insisting on discretion, reviewable from time to time by parliament, to admit persons in desperate need of refuge for whom there was no space at that moment in the refugee-processing centers. There should also be an exception for persons prepared to make job-expanding investments and persons who have demonstrated exceptional qualities as artists, designers, scholars, and scientists, indeed, creators and innovators of all kinds.

Also, outside the cap – but naturally influencing its size – would be persons entering on fixed-term contracts with specific employers. A hospital with a chronic shortage of nurses, for instance, could recruit persons with the necessary skills or sufficient education to enable them to be trained up quickly once they arrive in Netherfranc. Since one of the necessary skills is a working knowledge of our language or of English, these will be persons who, having become aware of our term-contract arrangement, choose to learn the language using materials provided by our consulates or cultural missions.

I envision contracts of around four years. Compensation would be equal to that of Netherfranckish practitioners, and, like natives, contract workers would pay a portion of their income into our national retirement fund where it would be matched by the employer's contribution. However, at the end of the contract period, as the contract employee prepares to depart, he or she, as the case may be, will receive both their own and the employer's contribution plus their share of whatever funds earned during the contract period. While contracts could be terminated prematurely for cause, employers would still have to pay for the employee's passage home. Once back in their home country, the guest worker could participate in the lottery or, after the passage of a stipulated period of time, perhaps two years, could seek a renewal of contract employment. If we allow contracts to be renewed immediately, they will become a back door to permanent settlement, thereby undermining the carefully negotiated cap.

INTEGRATION

Margaret Thatcher once controversially remarked that "there is no such thing as society, there are just individual people."[7] Our core electoral base *instinctively* rejects that view. You and I *consciously* reject it, in the first place because it is an insidiously misleading statement about reality. We are social animals. People will inevitably group together on some basis: an imagined identity of blood, religious conviction, ideology, myth of origins, preferred soccer team, whatever. To try and govern without taking account of group identities is a recipe for failure.

Of course, people have multiple identities. If identity with the country where they live is not high among them, that country is in trouble. At least so you and I believe. Trouble stems from the fact that Netherfranckish society, like all others, has potential lines of conflict: between the agnostic and the pious, between people of different faiths, between capital and labor, white and colored, urban and rural, and so on. Without an overarching sense of shared national identity, the potential becomes real. At best its toxicity weakens the government's authority and capacity.

When citizens cease to trust and respect public institutions, the consequences can be dire. If those institutions cease to attract into their ranks the best and the brightest, they will have progressively less capacity to mediate conflict. The best way to minimize group competition is to produce more public goods and to facilitate private-sector initiative. A stagnant economy or difficulty in starting businesses on top of a reduction in public goods like health care, education, and affordable housing will increase group competition over the diminishing supply. Fractures then widen, capital flees, tax revenue drops, and public goods shrink further. At some point the fractures become chasms. Instead of a virtuous circle we have a vicious one. Then it is the time of the demagogues and the end of liberal democracy.

The Narrative

Some of Netherfranc's liberal utopians associate the twentieth century with the rise of human rights discourse. But that came in the last third. You and I, having specialized in twentieth-century history at university, think more about its first three decades, when communist and fascist gangs battered each other, spattering the grand boulevards of our cities with blood. We recall the Austrian army in the employ of capital turning the workers' quarters of Vienna into rubble. If this time around the state fails to build or reinforce a sense of national community that transcends our natural lines of fracture, we will not get street battles. Instead, we will get a violently repressive paranoid state which in the service of society's most powerful groups casts off the restraints of liberal values and institutions even as it purports to be preserving them from terrorists and their fellow-travelers. That sort of state will include in its definition of fellow-travelers those who dare to question the state's methods for keeping order.

That prospect is only one reason we instinctively resist the vision of the good liberal society as a "cultural archipelago," to quote Professor Kukathas. To be fair, he believed that respectful accommodation of norms and practices that are grossly alien to the Western way of life is not only ethically correct, but also the best or only means for achieving internal tranquility. We believe he is wrong, although not totally. A respect for difference is a vital lubricant for a society that is already somewhat heterogeneous. But Kukathas takes the idea too far. He takes it to the point where it intrudes on the national narrative all should share.

I speak of "narrative" not because the term is now fashionable, but because it describes something real and essential. Even you and I understand life through stories. Unlike factoids, stories have themes. They openly or subtly distinguish good and evil. They are our ethical and epistemological guides. They carry emotional punch. So, it is not enough that people who migrate here profess to respect Netherfranc's constitution and the laws adopted thereunder. They must appear susceptible to internalizing one grand national narrative, a heroic ongoing story in which everyone, however new to our shores, can participate. The narrative would be what an American historian, Thomas Bender, called "a history in common," which, he rightly said, "is fundamental to sustaining the affiliation that constitutes national subjects." Nations, he went on to say, "are among other things, a collective agreement ... to affirm a common history as the basis for a shared future."[8]

What I am proposing is that the narrative should follow the Swedish and Norwegian examples. They bake into their national identities a "good Samaritan" image, the image of a people of unusual generosity who do good works at home and abroad. We should fit the overseas migration-assessment centers into that image, so they do not appear as a cynical exercise in self-defense. I spoke of the electorate's ambivalence. We can evoke its idealism if we simultaneously demonstrate firmness in protecting its economic and security interests.

The French have gotten this narrative creation, like so many other non-culinary things, wrong. Can you imagine anything more fatuous than demanding of Algerian migrants that if they want to be accepted as French, they need to associate themselves mentally with the Gauls, or Louis XIV, or that other self-glorifying butcher, Napoleon, or some colonial general who murdered their ancestors? We should ask migrants to identify only with those people in Netherfranc's past who have helped shape the narrative which all of us can share, the narrative of a people engaged in the ongoing project of building a free and fair society, a generous society but also one prepared to act forcefully in defense of its interests.

You and I are in certain respects conservative, but in no way like that foppish French fanatic, Renaud Camus, who resents the appearance of dark-hued women around ancient fountains in worn-out towns he almost never deigns to visit. We are the ideological descendants of Edmund Burke as much as of John Stuart Mill. We accept change as inevitable and often desirable. We don't aspire to stand athwart history and shout "Stop!" We prefer gradual change, change that doesn't threaten to rupture society. And, like that quintessential centrist former US President Barack Obama, we believe that, at least in the West, the arc of change at least since World War II has bent toward the discourse of moral equality, which is a discourse of respect for all persons settled on our national soil.

That discourse has evolved gradually, in a sense organically. As pragmatic liberals (which means that we have a dash of Burkean conservatism in our ideas and feelings), we are the custodians of continuity in the national story. And so now we are defenders of that discourse. Above all we are the enemies of rupture, and at this time the greatest danger of rupture comes from the fundamentalist and xenophobic right. Rupture opens the way to tyranny.

Now I think you see where I am going. That arc, with its bend toward equal dignity, is a historical narrative in which theoretically all can participate. Of course, neither the secular fanatics of the European right – like the Norwegian slaughterer Anders Breivik – nor the sundry religious extremists scattered round the world want to participate in this story. Fortunately for us the ranks of the murderous zealots in our country are still thin. They are not, however, the only opponents of the moral-equality narrative. Arrayed behind them are tens of million traditionalists in Africa, the Middle East, and West Asia: believers in rigid patriarchy, who are intolerant of the agnostic and the gay and the heretic and the apostate.

Tough struggles over time, and a shift in the Western zeitgeist, have reduced the size of our legacy fundamentalists to a small but still consequential fraction. Migration from the Global South is one of the many targets of their animus, along with atheism, feminism, and homosexuality. So, my old friend, what we have here is a triple irony. Our native fundamentalists hate the great majority of our migrants because they are often poor and non-white (as our white nationalists define "white") and hate with particular virulence those who identify as Muslims. That visceral hatred prevents them from welcoming migrants even though many will bring with them the same anti-liberal views that infect the right's electoral base.[‡] You and I, as custodians of authority and continuity, defend the liberal narrative all the fundamentalists detest, and we do so whether the attack is from the first or fiftieth generation on our soil. Meanwhile, a fraction of the liberal left, its ardent multiculturalist wing, indicts us as bigots because we want to carefully manage migration and lack a full measure of tolerance for the illiberal views of recent and prospective migrants. Amusing, no?

As guardians of the progressive narrative, we should vet prospective migrants not only for their capacity to contribute to our economy but also, following the Dutch precedent, for their cultural compatibility. By this I mean, at a minimum, we should demand their readiness to recognize the equal right of people to shape their own lives. Limiting the rigor with which we can enforce that test is the fact that for seven decades or so we have done without it. A certain fraction of our existing migrant communities could not have passed the test had the test existed when they entered. Some could not pass it today. Note in this connection the UK poll finding a greater hostility to gay marriage among British Muslims than within the general population.[9] I suspect that a poll of Christian migrants from Uganda would produce similar results.

So, we don't legislate on a blank slate. The results of past migration policies, or lack thereof, cannot be easily isolated from the ones we adopt today. Suppose a very traditionalist set of Netherfranckish Muslim parents engage their daughter to a second cousin who lives in their ancestral village and, when vetted by our consular officials, seems to embrace his prospective in-laws' views about gays and the position of women and participation with atheists in cooperative ventures. Or suppose they want to bring over their aging parents who also fail the cultural test. Do we say "no"

[‡] To be sure, some politicians have tried to veil their anti-Muslim electoral base by declaring themselves the true defenders of women, gays, and free speech in the face of threats from Islam and the spineless permissiveness of the established parties of the center-right and center-left. (I think, for instance, of the Dutchman Pim Fortuyn, murdered in 2002 by an animal rights fanatic who, by the way, has been just released from prison after a mere eighteen years.) Our version of "muscular liberalism" should thwart any effort to appropriate liberal values and deploy them on behalf of a fundamentally illiberal fragment of the electorate.

to family reunion in one case and to marriage in the other? Denying a visa in either case would doubtless strike not only the Netherfranckish parents but also many members of their diaspora community as discriminatory and disrespectful, and hardly consistent with the progressive national narrative we want to inculcate in all of our nationals. Moreover, it is an indisputable fact that a stable family unit contributes to social order and the development of human capital.

How do we navigate around the difficulties associated with a policy of intolerance of the intolerant? I propose we ease the incidental damage in two ways. First, through dialogue at both the national and municipal levels with members of the diasporas as well as the white majority. Unlike Macron before he was scarred by the yellow-vest protests, you won't issue televised manifestos from behind that enormous desk in your splendid office where you would seem the arrogant embodiment of elite distance and privilege. Instead, now while you are the focus of hope from an electorate hungry for a government sensitive to its multiple anxieties, you should move around the country on what you can bill as a "listening tour," although you plan to speak as well as listen.

In city halls, community centers, and wherever else you can convene the right-sized assembly of local people, you explain frankly the principled nature of our policy, underscoring for diasporas the advantage of our emphasis on equal dignity and our corresponding intention to strengthen enforcement of anti-discrimination laws against employers and landlords and lenders. You will emphasize your determination that no group be profiled by the police and that policies will be applied evenhandedly. We will deny long-term visas to a gay-hating fundamentalist Christian preacher from the United States just as firmly as to a gay-hating mullah from Bangladesh. (Parenthetically, I would deny both of them any visa at all.) Moreover, rather than making judgments about prospective ease of social integration an absolute bar, we will incorporate it into the point system. Culture would count without being decisive in every case.

We have another card to play with the diasporas. Being in general nearer the bottom than the top of our socioeconomic hierarchy, they, like less-skilled sectors of our legacy population, have a vested interest in protecting the welfare state and in limiting competition for jobs. So, in our consultations with them we emphasize our intent to manage migration so as to protect the welfare state and to increase the economic opportunities of relatively recent arrivals. Polling in other countries reveals that while eager to unite families, diaspora communities are not uniformly enthusiastic about open borders.[10] The main exceptions are ethnic politicians looking to increase their electoral base. We can soften their opposition by incorporating more of them into our party and then helping them win elective office.

Cultural tests (by which I mean detecting whether prospective migrants are ready to cooperate with people whose beliefs and personal lifestyles are at odds with their own) are only a minor element of our larger project: to build an inclusive national identity through which all of our "tribes" or, if you prefer, "sects" can be reconciled and into which new migrants can be incorporated. That identity requires, as I have said, a widely shared narrative of struggle toward equal respect, equal opportunity, and compassionate assistance to those who, through no fault of their own, have fallen behind. This narrative of struggle toward a society in which all enjoy equality of respect in turn will help us in our role of custodians of the national interest, which requires that we enhance public safety and defend the core elements of the welfare state.

In order to be widely accepted, the narrative must be consistent with the real lived experience of migrant families. We have yet to achieve the requisite consistency. You have a second-generation Moroccan in your cabinet. Migrants like him have thrived, but they are conspicuously underrepresented in politics, the private sector, the universities, the professions, the police, and the security services. They are also greatly overrepresented in our prisons, our underclass, and the unemployed. Polling results confirm a widespread feeling, particularly among Muslim migrant families, of discrimination and exclusion. Coincidentally an ominously large slice of our legacy electorate views migrant families as remote, hostile, parasitic on the welfare state, and potentially dangerous. The British counterpart of that slice voted for Brexit; its German one made the far-right AFD party the third largest in parliament. Ironically the constituents of that slice tend to be those people who have had the least quotidian contact with migrants.[11]

The fracture in our body politic will increase if we don't address it. Nationals from the Global South are still reproducing far faster than the legacy population, a fact which will strengthen the far-right narrative of replacement,[12] and its visceral fears of cultural invasion and occupation. Growing hostility from the legacy population will be reciprocated by the migrant one and that hostility will color the views of the new migrants you and I agree we will need.

It is hard to believe that an increasingly polarized political environment will not increase the incidence of terrorist acts emanating from both sides of the chasm. They in turn will widen the split beyond the point where belated public policies can bridge the gap. That is why we need to take unprecedented steps now. We need to take immediate action not only because of our integration problems, but also to increase the civic spirit, the dynamism, and the creativity of the entire society. These steps will also reduce the growing inequality and political fracturing within the legacy population, increasingly divided as it is between, on the one hand, the highly educated upper-middle-class cosmopolitans frolicking in the globalized culture and, on the other, all those who have experienced relative economic decline, loss of social status, and the normalization of practices like gay marriage and adoption rights for gay couples which collide with their inherited moral norms.

How do we halt the momentum of disintegration in our national society? How do we simultaneously recharge its batteries? We need to do both just to hold onto the less-than-satisfactory political, economic, and social status quo and to take control of our frontiers.

Sponsorship and Mentoring

In 2016, Mouhamad al-Hajj, a virtually illiterate Syrian refugee and former farmer, arrived in Canada with his wife, Wissam, and four children. Waiting for them in Toronto were a small group of Canadians – grandmothers, retirees, and book club friends – who along with hundreds of other such groups had volunteered through a government sponsorship program to help finance and guide a Syrian family through the first year of its immigrant life. They had assumed responsibility for a penniless family that spoke not a word of English and was unfamiliar with the most basic skills required to live in a Western nation. They had never used a bank and had very little idea of how to manage money, much less how find a place to live, insert their children in schools, navigate public transportation, or find employment.

Together the group had pooled resources to raise more than $22,000 which, together with a small government subvention, would allow the family to rent a small apartment in the Toronto area, move about the city on public transport, and purchase the necessities of existence. A Palestinian-Canadian friend of the group found employment for Mouhamad at minimum wage in a restaurant owned by a former immigrant from Egypt. Outside his working hours, Mouhamad, who could neither read nor write in Arabic, struggled to learn English.

A sixty-nine-year-old hockey enthusiast among the sponsors introduced the three oldest children to the sport. One of the sponsors would drop by the apartment almost daily to give English lessons to Mrs. Al-Hajj, who was tending to her infant daughter. One or more would drop by in the evening to help the children with their homework from a public school where, in special classes, they were learning English and French. Collectively the Canadians functioned as doting grandparents for a year, never sure whether they were making the family too dependent on them, never sure whether after only a year, the family could survive largely on its own.

Financially, between Mouhamad's minimum wage and a government subsidy for low-income families, they could. Beyond that, as of the thirteenth month, it remained to be seen. The school-age children had begun to read children's books in English. They had gone without school for almost three years while the two eldest had worked for one dollar a day in Lebanon, the family's first place of refuge. Their father was beginning to be able to read signs. The children had begun to evidence future prowess on the rink. Emotionally committed to the family they had nurtured, the sponsors still hovered, feeling the family's need for a safety net.

The *New York Times* journalists who studied this case and the Canadian experience generally concluded:

The early results of private sponsorship of Syrians looked a lot like Mr. Hajj's progress – still tentative, but showing forward motion. According to early government figures, about half of privately sponsored adults were working full or part time.... As a group they were outpacing the thousands more refugees who did not have sponsors and were being resettled by the government – only about 10 percent of them had jobs (on the whole, they were less educated and had higher rates of serious health problems and other needs).... Many resettlement veterans argued that it was unrealistic to expect refugees to be self-sufficient after a year and that the real test would be the fate of their children.[13]

Canada is a huge country with a relatively low population, the journalist wrote, and immigration is seen as "necessary fuel" for occupying the land and, presumably, continuing to grow the economy. Therefore "many Canadians [are] willing to make a generational investment."[14] While obviously Netherfranc is a very different place, I am confident that we can find individuals willing to serve as sponsors, particularly if we do not require a financial contribution (although we will be happy to accept them!). After all, a growing number of our citizens are at the age of grandparents and families are small.

So, we should make a concerted effort to find sponsors. What I propose, however, is that we blend the sponsorship idea with local community consultation. The community could be a village, a town, or, in urban areas, a neighborhood. We would need to organize a cadre of sympathetic officials who work through local social organizations to meet people in areas where we think migrants can best fit and contribute quickly with the least strain on local amenities. A cadre member would explain our reasoning, assure the locals that we have earmarked central government funds to offset the impact of any increased use of public services, and describe the careful vetting we have done. She would also explain the point system we are employing and how we anticipate migrants contributing to the well-being of the society, giving illustrations from this and other countries.

Then we would ask not only for comments and ideas but also for volunteers who would help introduce migrants into Netherfranckish cultural life. Thus, we would implicitly convey the message that we are not advocates for a cultural archipelago. We would stress that we advocate respect for different beliefs but not for practices at odds with our culture of equal opportunity and protection of individual rights.

The Stages of Integration

We can also prepare the ground and reassure our electorate by legislating two broad steps on the road to the ultimate prize of citizenship, steps which would underscore our commitment to the idea that citizenship must be well earned. Step one we would call "Provisional Settlement." Each adult member of a migrant family would sign an individualized agreement detailing actions we expect them to take (going to school, attending Netherfranckish language classes, accepting any job identified by the integration counsellor we would provide, etc.). The family would receive income sufficient to cover austerely basic necessities (in conjunction with whatever resources it had) and could access the health system and the public schools. It would live in an area we would designate in light of our consultations and any sponsorship the family might have. If any adult member of the family is convicted of a serious crime, he or she would be punished and then deported.

Provisional Settlement might last for something like three years. At the end of each year, however, the family counselor would have to certify that the family was making "satisfactory progress" in fulfilling the obligations spelled out in the initial agreement. If overall progress was unsatisfactory, the family – or, if failure was attributable to one member, then that member – would be subject to deportation. In any event, the family would remain only provisionally settled.

Assuming satisfactory progress, the family would move into the category of "settled." In that category, it could access all of the services of our social support system but would be subject to a tax surcharge to support the system and would be subordinate to the rights of full citizens with respect to family reunification requests other than for parents of working age, spouses meeting certain requirements, or children. We would structure advancement to citizenship through the medium of another point system, one which would encourage employment, skills acquisition, study of the country's history, language competency, entrepreneurship, general education, and community activities such as parent–teacher associations, sports clubs, and organizations that help integrate new migrants.

I think it would, on balance, be an error to require applicants for citizenship to relinquish their present one. Countries vary on this question of dual citizenship[15] and it is somewhat controversial in the electorate. The self-proclaimed nationalists who oppose it insist that citizenship is a token of loyalty. One cannot be loyal to two states. What if they go to war with each other? By its nature citizenship demands an exclusive loyalty. Either one has managed the psychological transition from one national identity to another or one has not. The person who desires dual citizenship is saying implicitly that he or she has not.

Often concealing a visceral hostility to migrants, this argument is notable for its abstractness, its pretense to logical force, and its indifference to lived experience. The desire to retain citizenship in one's country of birth while acquiring Netherfranckish citizenship does not necessarily signify divided loyalty to the state or the absence of a feeling of fraternity with nationals of Netherfranc. There are practical reasons having to do with everyday life, not necessarily primal loyalties, that fuel the preference of some people for duality. For instance, the inheritance and other laws relating to property and economic opportunity of most countries favor citizens over non-citizens to some degree. Migrants may own or have the hope of inheriting property from kin in the countries they have left. They may own businesses there. In addition, if the country of birth and Netherfranc do not have an agreement for free movement between them, Netherfranckish immigrants would need to obtain visas whenever they wished to visit family and friends in the country they left or to oversee property or businesses.

For those prosaic reasons, a migrant who feels very much at home in Netherfranc and desires to be regarded as a loyal citizen might nevertheless wish to retain his or her legacy citizenship while acquiring ours. Conversely those migrants who readily relinquish formal citizenship in their countries of birth and swear allegiance to ours may for all we know be going through a merely ritual transfer of loyalties without any change in emotional commitments. Citizenship is more than a piece of paper and a formulaic arrangement of words. We should look to actual behavior of applicants for citizenship during their period of settlement to decide whether they truly want to join the nation. If formal citizenship were a crucial test of loyalty, the US armed forces would not be enlisting into their ranks migrants who have not yet acquired US citizenship.

Why, moreover, should we be concerned if migrants feel some residual connection to the countries where they were born and where members of their extended families may still live? This concern with loyalty is appropriate to a world divided into blocks of mutually hostile states always in or on the edge of war. That is not our present or prospective condition at least insofar as the relations between Europe and the states from which the great bulk of prospective migrants currently live are concerned.

Education

First, we should follow the French Third Republic's policy of using the schools to disseminate the national narrative of progress through the centuries toward an equal-opportunity and equal-dignity society and more generally to promote patriotism. I propose that we lower the starting age of compulsory schooling to three. The sooner we can get children into the system, the easier it will be to offset parochial loyalties and to inculcate respect for the institutions of the state and the national narrative. In addition, early schooling should enhance learning and increase opportunities for social mobility.[16] Recent studies confirm the positive impact of early schooling when properly done on the life chances of children of the poorer classes.[17] It improves their performance in primary and secondary school and therefore gives them a better chance to compete, and it should increase the entire country's pool of talent.

Where geography and logistics permit, we would consciously integrate legacy and migrant-family children. Where we cannot integrate the children to any great extent, we can integrate the instructors or, drawing on the national service program I will get to in a moment, at least the teaching assistants. When students reach the age where they can travel alone on public transport, then we can integrate economic and ethnic groups, students from native and migrant families, if not comprehensively then at least selectively through magnet schools with various emphases like the performing arts and science and technology using family income and residential location to assure proportional representation of all sectors of the national population. These magnet schools should be gender mixed. Out of respect for conservative Muslims (and in order to encourage them to use the state schools) and consistent with what was once common practice in Netherfranc for schools established by Catholic dioceses, we should offer single-gender schools beyond the primary level.

Although constitutional and international legal norms prevent us from prohibiting private schools, we should require them to deliver a core curriculum identical to the one in public schools using the same textbooks. That core will include a comparative religions course covering the history of all of the major faiths in as neutral a way as possible. Officials of the Ministry of Education will work with scholars and religious leaders in designing the text.

National Service

Another integrative mechanism we should employ, arguably the keystone of all my proposals, is compulsory national service for one year. Participants would have considerable latitude to choose the form of service – for example, teaching pre-school classes, teaching Netherfranckish in our overseas migrant reception centers, taking civilian support roles in the police or the military, building shelters for the homeless, coaching youth sports teams in the police-organized athletic leagues – and the precise time between, let us say, the ages of eighteen and twenty-one to undertake this civic responsibility. Participants would work in small groups, again integrated by economic class and family background. Each group would also constitute a team to compete in sports and video and board games against other national service groups. To overcome traditionalist objections, we would allow participants to choose between single and mixed-gender teams. Israel exemplifies the integrative power of national service. Unlike Israel, however, we will use national service to integrate rather than to isolate our Muslim population.

In all European countries, Netherfranc being no exception, social networks continue to influence access to employment and therefore to social mobility. In Sweden, according to an OECD report, up to two-thirds of all vacancy fillings in the private sector involve some form of informal contacts.[18] In Norway only 40 percent of all private-sector vacancies have been formally published prior to being filled.[19] By integrating classrooms and national service teams, we will draw the first migrant generation's heirs into the social networks from which their backgrounds now exclude them unless they are remarkably talented or have the good fortune to be the offspring of the wealthy or highly educated. Simultaneously we will help to turn the opaque threatening stranger into a "mate," as the Australians amiably refer to each other.

While we will pay national service participants only a small stipend, the institution will not serve our integrative purpose unless we create a cadre of mature, culturally sensitive team leaders. Leadership would be a profession like teaching and its members would have to receive middle-class salaries. In addition, of course, we would have to find funds for housing, feeding, and transporting national service members. So, despite the minimal compensation for the rank and file, the project will require either new sources of state income or shifts within the extant national and municipal budgets.

Building electoral support and the human and material infrastructure for a comprehensive system of national service will take years. We can, however, begin now with a voluntary demonstration program starting with the recruitment and training of a cadre of team leaders. We would recruit them from all sectors of society – urban and rural, the banlieues and the central city, the pious and the atheist – and different generations. We would appeal to their idealism and sense of adventure in launching a great national project. For the retired we could offer an income supplement and a relief from aimlessness. For those already in the work-place, we would need guarantees from their employers if they work outside the state sector that they could return after a certain time without prejudice to their prospects. To that end we would want to establish a board of advisers for the project that would incorporate private-sector luminaries, as well as directors in the non-profit sector, and political and religious leaders across a broad ideological spectrum. Once we have a trained cadre, we would recruit young men and women for the service teams, again appealing to a sense of adventure and self-interest.

Macron has recently mooted a one-month program of national military service, a proposal reportedly greeted with appropriate dismay by the military.[20] Increased Russian friskiness has led Sweden to restart military conscription for a term that is to be somewhere between three and six months. I believe that nothing less than a year of service would suffice to advance our goals of building networks crossing the lines of class, color, and religion; staffing the offshore migration centers; assisting teachers in difficult schools; and supplementing the state bureaucracy's capacity to penetrate disadvantaged communities and help them access welfare-state programs and gen-erally to experience the state as a caring presence.

Fiscal challenges of one degree or another shadow national service and the other initiatives I have so far proposed: the new schools and the offshore migration centers. We can address them at least in part by shifting funds from those parts of our foreign aid budget which are not used for immediate humanitarian relief or to in effect purchase cooperation in damming the migrant flow. In addition, by setting up processing centers in lower-wage countries and using national-service members to help staff them, we will save money currently spent on feeding and housing and trying to keep track of asylum claimants here in high-wage Netherfranc. Further savings can flow from ideas I have about how to handle integration and public security and to refine the distribution of social benefits in the immediate future while we are building up the national service and offshore processing institutions. In the long term, the preparation and selection of migrants and their increased participation in the workforce will translate through taxation and social benefit contributions into increased revenue and could accelerate overall economic growth and hence generate still more revenue.

In addition, having been almost as fiscally conservative as the Germans up to now, we should be prepared to run up the maximum budgetary deficit allowed by EU rules for a number of years and we may persuade other governments including the German to modify the deficit rules for a time. Failure to control the borders of the EU and to achieve the economic and social integration of our migrant-background families will endanger the very survival of the liberal democratic project and of the EU itself. In times of national emergency – and it is close to being such a time – deficits take a back seat.

Short-Term Steps

The big institutional initiatives I have proposed – national service, compulsory preschool, integrated secondary schools, the use of the schools to inculcate an inclusive national narrative and a concomitant patriotism – will, as I said, take time to implement, not decades but years. What can we do in the immediate future to foster economic and social integration and at the same time reduce the friction between our legacy citizens and our Global South, primarily Muslim migrant communities?

Policing

One indisputable need is to alter the character of relations between the police and the inhabitants – particularly the youth – of areas with high concentrations of relatively poor migrant families, our ghettoes. The acrimony in the police–ghetto relationship long predates large-scale migration. You could say it begins with industrialization and urbanization in the West. For the nineteenth-century European state dominated by the wealthy, the semi-pauperized workforce drawn from or impelled to leave the countryside into the city constituted the "dangerous classes," so called because of their presumed threat to the owners of property. The dangers they presented to each other were a matter of secondary import. The state created the police to contain the danger. At least to the young men in working-class areas, always a community's most volatile element, the police appeared as an occupying force, and to a large measure appearance coincided with reality.

In this respect, not enough has changed either in the United States or Netherfranc. Though not generally thought of as one of the "helping professions" like social work, policing can be more than the deterrence and punishment of crime. We need to raise the salience of policing's helping dimension and lower the salience of its repressive features. To accomplish that we should elevate the incidence and quality of neighborhood foot patrols in the migrant-family areas of high youth unemployment and pervasive alienation. We should also incorporate "helping activities" into neighborhood policing. I see a distant analogy to counter-insurgency doctrine with its theoretical emphasis on winning hearts and minds, although this is an analogy I would not be inclined to publicize.

Community patrolling by officers with the cultural sensitivity and personality traits required to build trust with neighborhood people could help to increase the transparency of neighborhoods, which is important for both counter-terrorism and more efficient delivery of social services. The requisite trust will grow if the police protect the population from its more predatory and bullying members and patrol with civilian auxiliaries trained to mediate disputes within the community and between the community and state institutions and serve as a source of information about how to access state services or private ones subsidized by the state. These auxiliaries should be recruited from the minority communities themselves

The US military theoreticians of counter-insurgency emphasize the need to make life better in the neighborhoods, towns, and villages the troops are sent out to protect. That should be the mantra of our police at every level. How can we equip them to make their neighborhoods better?

To begin with, we must spend more. The police are, after all, the front line of the entire system not simply of justice but of government. They make daily decisions on whether to overlook minor transgressions or give a warning or make an arrest. They may interact with the locals either abrasively or courteously. They may choose to ignore conflicts among youth or neighbors or spouses or to intervene. So, they can personify a caring, an indifferent, or an actively hostile state, a just or an unjust one.

I need hardly say that it is in our government's interest to be seen as just and caring. So, our police must be carefully vetted for empathy and understanding as well as integrity and physical courage. Their tasks are more complicated in certain respects than those of our soldiers. They need at least as much training and perhaps even more education. Very few governments invest as much in the training of police as in the training of professional soldiers. That is a mistake, one we have been making since the inception of policing.

Ideally every neighborhood patrol unit would include an officer or a civilian originally if not currently from the area and fluent in one or more of the migrant languages that predominate at least among the first generation. The patrol would stop in and visit with shopkeepers, have lunch in local restaurants. It would operate out of a local police substation with a widely publicized emergency number. A second number could be called to receive information from members of the auxiliaries about social benefits for which local people might qualify. And a third one would receive tips about appearances of criminal activity. The patrols would visit schools, get to know the teachers, and speak about the profession of policing to classes, particularly in the lower grades where distrust of the police is less likely to have hardened. At regular intervals paramedics or medical students would be available at the substation to examine people of any age who felt they or their children needed treatment.

The most difficult relationship to manage is with the neighborhood's youth. To promote a positive relationship with them, every police substation should be co-located with a leisure and sports center equipped with large screen TVs showing soccer games from around the world, media-game rooms, a basketball court, and a gym. Policemen supplemented by young men and women with appropriate skills doing national service would coach and organize teams that would then compete with teams from other neighborhoods building toward regional and then national championships. Each substation would also have a nearby soccer pitch under its control where police athletic league competitions would be held.

In order to strengthen the training of police and particularly to recruit from migrant communities, I believe we should include among our magnet schools at least one in each city which prepares students for fast-track careers in the police and the intelligence services. Since we now allow the police and the military to retire with pretty decent pensions after twenty years of service, students could anticipate moving thereafter to a second career in either public administration or the private sector. To heighten anticipation, we would legislate a preference for retired officers in competition for public-sector jobs and encourage employers' associations to announce a similar preference in their areas of the economy.

Crime, Punishment, and Terrorism

In order to improve the police–community dynamic we also need to reconsider crime and punishment. Existing policy is both too soft and too harsh. It is too harsh in its response to non-violent crime, particularly the retail distribution of marijuana. As long as there is demand for a prohibited product, it will be supplied. Prohibition simply elevates the price and allows market entry to persons without the skills or contacts to secure other forms of employment.

Very high levels of unemployment among ghetto youth guarantee its involvement in marijuana distribution. We should legalize production and distribution of mari-juana within the country and channel retail sales operations to neighborhood residents. We would help them open outlets by providing micro-lending and entrepreneurship courses run after hours in local schools.

Marijuana legalization is obviously not a panacea, but I think it will help. One of the ways it will help is reducing incarceration. Prisons have been an important recruiting ground for jihadists. We can also reduce incarceration of the young by not jailing them for non-violent crimes. Instead, we should use confiscation (phones, other electronic articles, vehicles, and cash) and community service combined with much more intense programs of counseling and vocational training for jobs identi-fied by the private sector.

Where I think we are not harsh enough – and this is true of all West European states – is in handling chronically violent criminals in general and jihadis and neofascists in particular. The human rights conventions declare that the main purpose of incarceration must be rehabilitation.[21] We take a different view. When it comes to serious violence, for us the main purposes of incarceration include deterrence, isolation (to protect the community from renewed assaults), and retribution. Since you have asked me to counsel you about migration and integration, not crime in general, and since the crime our electorate most fears and associates with migration is terrorism, that will be my focus.

Ideally, we will become better at detecting radicalization before it leads to action. Neighborhood policing along the lines I have described should help. In addition, I recommend we follow the English precedent and marshal all the elements of the public service – primarily educators and social and medical workers – to assist in identifying people who have become or seem to be in the process of becoming radicalized, whether by jihadists, xenophobes, or nihilists. To help overcome resistance from educators and caregivers, instead of having them report potential terrorists to the police, we would channel reports to a local committee on which police or security-organization personnel would serve alongside caregivers, psychologists, religious leaders, and persons designated by our principal human rights NGOs.

The local committees would shape an individualized deradicalization program. In order to limit the alienation of migrant communities who may see a Prevent-type program as aimed particularly at them, we need to consult with community leaders to emphasize the advantage of prophylaxis in saving their children from imprisonment or death and minimizing incidents that will strengthen the far right. We would also emphasize the program's contribution to protecting them by reducing the recruiting capabilities of violent xenophobes. They are as much a target of our efforts as are Al Qaeda and ISIS.

Deflecting the probably reflexive opposition of the Muslim community, the minority likely to feel targeted, is important for many reasons, the most important being that the community is, finally, the best source of intelligence about latent or actual terrorists and the best source of rebuttal to the jihadi narrative. How well we succeed in isolating jihadists from the community they claim to be defending will be a function of its overall relationship to the state.

Despite our Herculean efforts to keep the most disaffected and alienated migrants from morphing into killers, a few will so morph and be joined by the odd pathological convert. How should we deal with those who embrace violent jihad, whether we capture them in the conspiracy, the attempt stage, or after they have struck? Where should we put them and how long should we keep them there?

We do not want them in the general prison population, by definition an alienated group and therefore more liable to recruitment by the already converted. So, I see two options. One is a prison modeled on the US maximum security prisons where terrorists and other very dangerous criminals are held under conditions of nearly solitary confinement for life or at least until they are dotards.

We would also hold out the bare possibility of parole after a very long minimum period on appeal to the Minister of Justice or a person or committee established by us for this purpose. Parole would be denied if it were found that the prisoner still constituted a risk to the public. The twenty-one-year sentence imposed on the unspeakable Anders Breivik, who methodically murdered seventy-seven people and said he regretted not killing more, would be laughable in its lenience were it not possible for his sentence to be extended as long as he is found to be a continuing threat.

Sentences in most West European states for very violent crimes are ludicrously brief and therefore unresponsive to the totality of reasons for punishment. In 2017 an Afghan refugee living in a small German city stalked and ultimately stabbed to death in plain sight a teenaged girl he had once dated. A judge sentenced him to eight years and six months in prison. Given parole policies, this killer may serve half that time.[22] Meanwhile the girl's family has suffered a life sentence. Is it any wonder that the German right has weaponized the case?

Very high-security prisons are very expensive. The annual cost per prisoner in the US state of Illinois's so-called supermax is estimated at $62,000, never mind the initial capital cost.[23] However, as long as the numbers of terrorists remains small, the cost is not prohibitive. Still, we will be removing not only the perpetrators from society. We will also want to imprison those who are found to aid them as well as those we discover in the conspiracy stage. These numbers may force us to consider the options of a remote island or outsourcing imprisonment, whether of nativist right-wing or migrant-family terrorists, to a low-wage foreign country.

To avoid sovereignty issues, the prison would be owned and managed by a company nominally private but with a board whose members we would appoint. It would recruit staff locally; provide them with housing, schools, and clinics; stable employment at wages high by the standards of a country like the Democratic Republic of the Congo; meritocratic advancement; and a pension at the end of service. Further to encourage loyalty, we would give them migration points which would offer them the prospect of migrating to Netherfranc with their families when they retire. For enhanced security, we would rotate special force units through the prison guard community, nominally seconding them to the prison corporation.

Another option would be to extradite migrant-background terrorists to countries where they or their families originated. No doubt we would need to provide those countries with financial or other incentives to receive and incarcerate the persons we convict. Even where the terrorists are not citizens, a policy of extraditing them to their native countries after conviction will encounter legal obstacles. Both the European Human Rights Convention and our own constitution ban cruel treatment. The average prisons in countries like Algeria, Morocco, and Tunisia – not to mention those in sub-Saharan Africa – probably make the prisons of Netherfranc look like rest homes. (The same could not be said of many prisons in the United States.[24]) Defense lawyers will argue that we are violating not only the prohibition of cruel treatment but also the principle of non-refoulement, which prohibits sending people to countries where they are likely to experience violations of any of their core human rights.

We could pay governments for some upgrade in normal prison conditions for persons we outsource and negotiate agreement for occasional visits by our consular officials to allow us to confirm that conditions, while austere, are not plainly brutal. Still, to avoid litigation in the European Court of Human Rights, we might have to add reservations to our treaty ratification to deny the application of the Convention to non-citizen migrants convicted of terrorist offenses. We might also have to amend our own constitution, since with respect to individual rights it largely mirrors the European Convention.

We would confront even higher barriers, political as well as legal, if we attempted to outsource the incarceration of Netherfranckish citizens. To overcome political resistance, we would have to persuade the electorate that the decision to murder and mutilate your fellow citizens in the name of some alien authority or imagined community is an implicit renunciation of the bond with fellow nationals and the state which citizenship connotes. Terrorists, in other words, should be deemed to have voluntarily renounced their citizenship. If attacks multiply, I think such an argument could gain traction in the polity and ultimately the courts.

The case of persons with dual citizenship is easier from the legal perspective. Even if we in effect strip them of citizenship, they are not stateless, a condition disfavored by international law. In this connection consider that the United Kingdom has revoked the citizenship of about 150 UK dual citizens who went abroad to fight for ISIS.[25]

As you know, about 300 Netherfranckish nationals – some still in their adolescence, the others mostly between twenty and thirty – have gone abroad over the past few years to fight for ISIS or, as some claim, simply to live in the caliphate pictured as an ideal Muslim community. Some have been killed; a number we believe are hiding along with other ISIS members at various points along the Syria–Iraq border. A few have already returned and are presently in detention while we sort out what to do with them. More, we believe, are hoping to return.

You will recall that after the 2005 terrorist attack in London, Britain's parliament passed legislation making it a crime to join or conspire to assist or to support a terrorist organization wherever it is based and wherever it operates. It included a conventional definition of terrorism and assigned to the prime minister responsibility for promulgating and periodically updating a list of terrorist organizations. It established a minimum prison term of ten years for membership or support for listed organizations. Netherfranc already has a virtually identical statute. Your predecessor put ISIS on the list years ago.

We could argue in court that leaving Netherfranc to live in the so-called caliphate makes one at least a supporter of ISIS. After all, we can show that ISIS vetted persons wishing to enter the territory it controlled. Allowing them in meant that ISIS officials concluded that they were supporters. Moreover, we can in many cases offer as evidence of loyalty to ISIS and support for its aims emails and other kinds of messages sent by these persons to friends and family back here.

In quite a few instances parents of the returnees have pleaded the youth of their children and urged their placement in a deradicalization program as an alternative to prosecution and long-term incarceration. I propose we try deradicalization programs for those returnees who did not serve as either fighters or enforcers and, as far as we can tell, did not commit vile acts like taking captured women as sexual slaves. As for those who were combatants or helped control the population of territories occupied by ISIS or committed atrocious acts, when you take into account the devastation and misery ISIS inflicted on the populations of captured territory, you must conclude that they should be deemed beyond redemption.

Consider the account of a twelve-year-old Yazidi girl captured by ISIS and then assigned to one of its fighters. Questioned by a journalist in a refugee camp to which she escaped after months in captivity, she recounted how, before he raped her, the fighter bound her hands and gagged her. "Then he knelt beside the bed and prostrated himself in prayer before getting on top of her. 'I kept telling him it hurts – please stop,' said the girl, whose body is so small an adult could circle her waist with two hands. 'He told me that according to Islam he is allowed to rape an unbeliever. He said that by raping me, he is drawing closer to God.... When he finished he knelt again to pray.'"[26] Retribution, my friend, is a legitimate purpose of the criminal law. We believe that and so do our voters.

Toward a Mutually Respectful Environment: Opportunities and Challenges

One indisputable reality of contemporary Netherfranckish society is a great diversity of piety and practice among people who identify as Muslim. People from Muslim backgrounds differ also in the relative importance they attach to that identity among all the others they feel, including their Netherfranckishness. What the state and the legacy majority can accomplish, however, through actions and omissions that manifest hostility, condescension, or even contempt, is to fuse this great disparate collection of people into a mass bristling with anger and angst. Quite aside from any moral imperative to treat Muslims with the respect we owe all of our nationals, we obviously have a prudential one.

In working toward a national unity transcending religious and cultural differences, we can learn from French mistakes. The banning of head scarves in schools and so-called burkinis on beaches are acts of a stupidity almost beyond comprehension. People should feel free to express their religious identity. To prevent far-right mayors from imposing local bans as has happened in France in the matter of the burkinis, we must pass legislation at the national level forbidding localities from adopting measures aimed at or having the effect of limiting expressions of religious identity which do not conflict with the exercise of other people's protected liberties. We should then follow up with letters from your office or from the appropriate minister to the mayor and the chief of police in every municipality stating that head scarf and burkini bans are prohibited and any efforts to enforce them will be met with severe administrative sanctions. We should see to it that the letters are well publicized.

The one matter of apparel where we might not defer to minority cultural practices, in this case a very small subgroup, is full-face veiling. In arguing successfully before the European Court of Human Rights, the French government justified its prohibition on the grounds that the veil inhibited social intercourse and thus constituted a barrier to fraternity among its people.[27] While I am marginally sympathetic to that argument, I propose that if we ban the niqab (as the full-face veil is often called), we do so purely on security grounds. If veils are allowed, we would argue, wanted criminals and suspected terrorists could possibly walk the streets undetected.

I must admit, however, that the security argument is not entirely convincing. To begin with, full-face veiling is unusual among Muslims in our country, a sign that it derives from the strict patriarchal customs of certain places rather than from the Islamic religion, which calls only for "modest" clothing. So, a veiled face in a public place will attract the attention of the police, attention a terrorist or common criminal would want to avoid. In addition, a more common feature of dress among pious Muslims, the full-bodied flowing burqa, arguably constitutes a greater security risk, since it could easily conceal weapons and explosive devices. But banning it would affect many Muslim women and thus aggravate relations between the community and the state. Moreover, some non-Muslim women wear clothing which could conceal weapons. Furthermore, weapons can also be concealed in backpacks, in shopping bags, and some of the gargantuan purses certain women seem to like. In short, I don't see how we could word a proscription of baggy, body-covering clothing that was as a practical matter enforceable. No doubt that is why even the French have not tried to proscribe the burqa.

We also need to end the manipulation of land-use laws and notional traffic regulations by certain municipalities to hamper the construction of mosques. Right-wing demagogues deplore the sprawl of praying Muslims over city sidewalks, even into the street. At the same time, they do everything possible to block the creation of proper prayer spaces. In the French case we even have the absurdity of intellectuals and politicians signing a petition urging that Muslims be denied the right to purchase excess Christian churches for conversion to mosques. They are not speaking simply of churches with particular aesthetic or symbolic value which could be protected on historical preservation grounds from sale for any purpose. Their petition is aimed directly at the Muslim community.

A feeling of humiliation is one of the most powerful human emotions. Nothing is more likely to cause it than the perception of intentionally unequal treatment and contempt for a group or its icons. In our battle for hearts and minds, we as representatives of the state must constantly strive to show respect for those with migrant backgrounds.

One important way of displaying official respect for the Muslim faith is through well-publicized efforts to prevent workplace discrimination. Since we are making new migration conform to present and prospective workplace needs that cannot be satisfied internally, the unions should be willing to help us design programs for the economic integration of new migrants. Sharp differences in access to work and opportunity to move up in the workplace will undermine other efforts to heighten a spirit of national unity.

As youth unemployment is high for unskilled and semi-skilled native youth, we cannot expect the unions to help with the still higher unemployment of youth in minority ghettoes. Their rank-and-file would revolt over affirmative action programs and quotas. What they might support, if it did not affect their present membership, and what the government could introduce into public employment, is a lowered minimum wage for new workers in general, knowing that the bulk of them will come from the ranks of migrant families. Lower wages for young employees should enable both the public and private sectors to absorb more workers. People with little education and low-level skills must be able to price themselves into jobs. At a certain price, jobs will materialize. The hostility of Swedish trade union leaders to this approach helps to explain Sweden's poor performance at economically integrating its huge refugee intake during the period 2013–2016. The foreign-born in Sweden are three times as likely to be unemployed as the native-born.[28]

Migration at current levels, whether of asylum claimants or those simply seeking a better life, is adding to the stress on our welfare state.[29] In this matter the right, while exaggerating grossly, is not altogether wrong. That is one reason we want migrants to enter the workforce quickly and to stay there. The young men who have predomin-ated in recent migrant streams share our desire. Most of them, being asylum claimants, are chafed by our legal restraint on employment before their claims are adjudicated, restraints avoided by some of the undocumented who have found work at sub-minimum wages often in the businesses of settled migrants.

Lifting those restraints would not solve the problem of integrating economically the one-third or more of claimants in the last two years' intake who have little education and meager if any competence in our language. They will join the ranks of our native youth suffering from an unemployment rate of 20 percent for those under twenty-five who have no special skills. We could improve that figure if we follow the US practice in the face of labor union resistance and make labor markets more flexible, by ending, for example, uniform nationwide wage and salary scales and benefit contributions. We should also lower the barriers to firing workers in order to encourage hiring them in the first place. More flexible labor markets will not be enough, however, because like the Scandinavian countries, the number of jobs in the economy available for the poorly educated is low, particularly compared with the United States. Since we cannot let them starve or freeze under our bridges, admitting people with sparse chances of entering the workforce will add to the pressure on our system of social support – until we have succeeded in giving them the needed skills, that is.

Among the obstacles to economic integration is the abrupt cutoff of housing subsidies and other state benefits as soon as a person's income exceeds the poverty level, a regulation your predecessor failed to reform. That cutoff can mean a loss of income almost as great as the gain from working. It operates, therefore, as a huge marginal tax rate. What we need to legislate is a gradual reduction in benefits as income from work increases. The reduction will function as a moderately progressive income tax.

You will recall that one criterion I have proposed for accession first to permanent settlement and then to citizenship is employment. As I suggested above, we should have a point system for obtaining citizenship as well as for entry. A family could get additional points in cases where both the husband and the wife enter the workforce. Among other things, that would incentivize husbands in traditionalist families to allow their wives out of the house. Looking at the experience of other countries, I see that among certain ethnic communities, female migrant participation in the workforce is much lower than men's.[30] At the same time, we want to eliminate disincentives for female workforce entry. One obvious disincentive is our present child support program which increases payments to families for each additional birth without limit. Being limitless, it encourages men from patriarchal traditions to turn their wives into secluded engines of reproduction.

The original intention of the child bonus was to raise our birth rate toward the population-replacement level. It had sunk below 2.1. Census data indicate that it has had little effect on the birth rate of the native population. It is migration that has increased our population. The higher birth rate of migrant families could carry us beyond the point where we want to go demographically. In any event, big migrant families agitate our voters by increasing pressure particularly on the schools in certain areas and by aggravating fears of replacement, fears which writers like Camus encourage. So, I propose that we cap the payment increases for new births at two.

Speaking of work, an issue all employers have found difficult to handle is fitting the Quranic injunction to pray five times a day into the rhythms of the workplace. Many businesses of any size and factories are willing to provide a prayer space equipped with water for the required ablutions. We have them in most government buildings. What may not be practicable in some settings is having a part of the workforce suspending its labors in the middle of the afternoon or early evening.

What we need on this matter is a fatwa from eminent Islamic religious authorities authorizing Muslims where they are a minority community to complete the obligatory five daily prayers by increasing the number of evening prayers or through additional prayers on the weekend. We also need to solicit authoritative fatwas to deal with the problem of Friday as the Muslim day of rest and the day when under normal circumstances collective prayer at a mosque is essential for the pious. Some jobs can be configured so a fraction of employees take off Friday but work on

Saturday or Sunday. Others as a practical matter cannot. I have doubts about the government dictating solutions to private employers. If we make the employment of pious Muslims onerous, employers will be even less inclined than they are now to hire them. Both the current government of Egypt and the driving force for modernization in Saudi Arabia, the tyrannical Crown Prince Mohammed bin Salman, have the power to obtain those fatwas from religious authorities. I believe they will be inclined to help us. Actually, a few congregations have already initiated Sunday prayer in order to accommodate those who must work on Friday.[31]

A second way of manifesting respect is having you as head of government break bread with Muslims on days of special religious significance, the most important being Eid Al-fitr when Muslims feast to celebrate the end of Ramadan, the month of daytime fasting. You might host a number of ordinary Muslim families at your official residence. Consistent with our emphasis on equal regard for all nationals, whatever their religious identity, you would then have to hold similar dinners for some typical Christian families at Christmas or Easter, and Jewish and Hindu families as well on appropriate days.

A third way in which the state can manifest respect is by equal application of laws affecting speech. European Muslim leaders have on occasion called for the criminalization of insults to the faith, insults usually directed at the person of Muhammad but not unreasonably seen as a disparagement of Muslims generally and an incitement to hostility and discrimination. French Muslims have complained bitterly that, while scatological references to Muhammad are passed off as free speech, Holocaust denial or even minimization is treated as a criminal expression of anti-Semitism.

Laws criminalizing criticism of religious doctrines or cultural practices cannot be squared with Western values. Indeed, the state with all its might should defend critics against private threats and aggressions from enraged members of minority communities or partisans of the majority when their idols are perceived to be abused. The more difficult case is speech intended to incite hostility to a minority as such by suggesting that its members engage in vile practices or are a threat to public order. Such speech with Muslims as its principal target is now commonplace in Western countries. With every new terrorist outrage, its impact on popular opinion grows even as millions of Muslims, of all generations, peacefully attempt to find their way in increasingly hostile societies. If the spiral of mutual resentment and fear does not halt, the jihadi aim of irretrievably dividing indigenous majority and migrant communities will move at growing speed toward its target.

By virtue of their differences, normative and prudential, about how best to manage national societies containing liberal and illiberal cultures, the more ardent multiculturalists and liberal universalists will tend to disagree over where the line should be drawn between free speech, however tainted by bigotry and paranoia, and speech unacceptable by virtue of its encouragement to discrimination, enmity, and violence. What cannot be justified on either ethical or prudential grounds is unequal application of hate speech laws.

Every government imposes certain limits on speech. There is a broad continuum. At one end lies the United States where only direct incitement to violence seems prohibited. At the other are countries like China where even calls for equal application of the law can be dangerous. We Europeans have never indulged the pretty illusion that the best corrective for speech encouraging hatred and discrimination always is more speech. The International Covenant on Civil and Political Rights, whose provisions are now largely incorporated into our legislation, reflects our views, not the American ones. You may remember that it requires states to prohibit "any advocacy of national, racial or religious hatred that constitutes incitement to discrimination, hostility or violence."[§] Consistent with that obligation we, like the French, have made Holocaust denial a crime and have over the years actually prosecuted a couple of people for it. Under the broader statute which mirrors the language of the Covenant, we have never prosecuted slurs on Muslims or their faith, such as claims that Muslims in general have a proclivity for terrorism.

The group libel – for that is what it is – has taken the form of pictures as well as words. If we are going to enforce the law against denying the Holocaust, we should prosecute these anti-Muslim slurs. I propose some exemplary indictments focusing on the newspapers or magazines which publish this trash and a sharp increase in fines.

The more dangerous venues for incitement are the social media. We should follow the German example of legislating punitive fines for social media companies like Facebook and Twitter which do not eliminate hate-speech postings within twenty-four hours of a complaint.[32] We should also press the EU to push the companies to improve algorithms designed to identify and block xenophobic and racist rants. In addition, we should establish a social media office which would promote the national narrative through social media channels while constantly scanning the internet for hate speech. When possible, it would expose and disparage those seeking to use Facebook, Twitter, Instagram, and other popular digital platforms to spread misinformation and discord.

Our commitment, captured in our national narrative, to protect the human rights of every human being who lives in Netherfranc will necessarily place limits on our respect for cultural differences. We must not tolerate, for instance, brutal cultural practices like female genital mutilation. Instead, we must punish such outrages severely. Deportation and the confiscation of assets of non-citizens who perform this ritual should be the normal response, one we publicize widely. The relatives who organize it should also be severely punished. However, we should be open to a cultural compromise, namely, a ceremonial drawing of blood from the labia of babies, a pinprick performed by a midwife or nurse. That is the kind of flexibility we

---

[§] Of course, the wording is maladroit in that advocacy of national, racial, or religious hatred is always intended or will predictably have the effect of inciting discrimination, hostility, or violence.

are already demonstrating, as when we exempted Sikhs in the police from wearing the traditional caps.

You asked for a detailed set of proposals that address the main issues on the migration agenda and are roughly consistent with our political values and what we believe to be our electoral needs. I hope you find my suggestions helpful. As you consider them, you might usefully recall Francis Fukuyama's foreboding conclusion to his famous 1989 article entitled "The End of History?" "What we may be witnessing," the American scholar wrote, "is not just the end of the Cold War, or the passing of a particular period of postwar history, but the end of history as such: that is, the end point of mankind's ideological evolution and the universalization of Western liberal democracy as the final form of human government."[33]

Was this, according to Fukuyama, a reason to rejoice? No! On the contrary, he continued,

> The end of history will be a very sad time. The struggle for recognition, the willingness to risk one's life for a purely abstract goal, the worldwide ideological struggle that called forth daring, courage, imagination, and idealism, will be replaced by economic calculation, the endless solving of technical problems, environmental concerns, and the satisfaction of sophisticated consumer demands.... I can feel in myself, and see in others around me, a powerful nostalgia for the time when history existed. Such nostalgia, in fact, will continue to fuel competition and conflict even in the post-historical world for some time to come. Even though I recognize its inevitability, I have the most ambivalent feelings for the civilization that has been created in Europe since 1945, with its north Atlantic and Asian offshoots. *Perhaps this very prospect of centuries of boredom at the end of history will serve to get history started once again.*[34] (emphasis added)

I believe that our youth, probably youth everywhere, feel in varying degrees that desire to display daring and courage and to find some higher purpose. I intuit this restless desire particularly among the great majority who cannot realistically envision themselves rising to the heights of power and celebrity through the normal grinding of the current political economy. The leaders of ISIS saw that desire. They shaped their propaganda accordingly and drew to their malign ranks thousands of young people, perhaps a quarter of them converts from an inherited Christianity. The neofascists appeal to the same passions in their recruitment efforts.

Assuming I am correct, then we stand on dangerously unstable ground if, when defending our position, we appeal only to self-interest and the unbridled pursuit of individual comfort. We must not be seen as the defenders of a national project that offers nothing grander than sophisticated consumerism. A sunny hedonism does not stir the soul. Instead, we should insist that liberalism is but a name for the legacy culture of the West, and that we must defend it from all barbarians, not only those who attack it in the name of Islam. If the center does not itself crusade, it will not hold. We, too, must speak of duty to the nation and we must provide outlets for those who most yearn for risk and challenge. Should we fail to express rhetorically and programmatically an ardent liberal nationalism, then, in the American historian Jill Lapore's graphic image, nationalism, rather than dying, will eat liberalism.[35]

That is why I think national service is so important. If we had it in place when Bin Laden first called for jihad against the West, we could have allowed a choice of tasks and let those most in need of the demonstration of courage, most in search of a higher purpose, to volunteer for teams doing dangerous work like delivering assistance inside Middle Eastern and West Asian war zones or assisting doctors struggling to isolate an Ebola epidemic. That is also why we must have a narrative with heroes and martyrs. And, finally, that is why, in cases where reform and discourse fail, we must be pitiless with the enemies of the liberal project whether their roots are in the second or the fiftieth generation of Netherfranckish inhabitants. The passion of defenders of liberal democracy and their readiness to defend it must match the passion and courage of its enemies.

Respectfully submitted.

Last Thoughts (but still thinking)

Theresa May, prime minister of the United Kingdom at the moment I write, has declaimed that if you are a citizen of the world, you are a citizen of nowhere.[36] She doubtless believes, erroneously, she has thus dismissed the cosmopolitans with that one Trumpian slash. She is probably right, however, in her political calculation that we in the rich countries have yet to reach the point, indeed will probably never reach the point, where what guides the majority's generosity is a perceived hierarchy of need rather than one of identity. To put the point in another way, the time has not yet come when the majority of the rich feel to a deeply consequential degree the pain which brings the persecuted and the poor to its door.

The world is as it is. We save what we can by means not always in harmony with our ends. Meanwhile, we hope that when, decades from now, people look back on what the governments of the West did at the end of the second decade of the twenty-first century in order to preserve liberal democracy, they will not at the same time recall what an American officer is supposed to have said in the midst of the Vietnam War: "We destroyed the village in order to save it."

Notes

INTRODUCTION

1 Laura Dean, "With Senegal's Fishermen," *London Review of Books* blog, May 16, 2017, www.lrb.co.uk/blog/2017/05/16/laura-dean/with-senegals-fishermen/#more-25696.

2 Ibid.

3 United Nations, Office of the High Commissioner on Human Rights, *International Covenant on Civil and Political Rights*, G.A. Res. 2200A(XXI), March 23, 1976, accessed April 7, 2018, www.ohchr.org/en/professionalinterest/pages/ccpr.aspx.

4 See Helena Rosenblatt, *The Lost History of Liberalism: From Ancient Rome to the Twenty-First Century* (Princeton: Princeton University Press, 2018).

5 Samuel Moyn, *Not Enough: Human Rights in an Unequal World* (Cambridge: Belknap Press of Harvard University Press, 2018). See also Pankaj Mishra, "The Mask It Wears," *London Review of Books*, www.lrb.co.uk/v40/n12/pankaj-mishra/the-mask-it-wears.

6 Amartya Sen, "Equality of What?," in *The Tanner Lectures on Human Values*, edited by Sterling McMurrin (Cambridge: Cambridge University Press, 1980).

7 Despite a suggestion to that effect in Ralph Gaebler, Review of *Is Liberal Nationalism an Oxymoron?*, by Yael Tamir, *Indiana Journal of Global Legal Studies* 3 (1995): 283–293.

8 Patrick Kingsley, *The New Odyssey: The Story of the Twenty-First-Century Refugee Crisis* (New York: W. W. Norton, 2017), 126.

9 Ibid., 134.

10 Gaia Pianigiani, "Mafia in Italy Siphons Huge Sums from Migrant Centers," *New York Times*, July 17, 2017, www.nytimes.com/2017/07/17/world/europe/italy-migrants-mafia-edoardo-scordio.html.

11 "Americans Express Increasingly Warm Feelings toward Religious Groups," Pew Research Center, last modified February 15, 2016, www.pewforum.org/2017/02/15/americans-express-increasingly-warm-feelings-toward-religious-groups/pf_17-02-15_feelingthermometer_gp200px/.

12 Ana Gonzalez-Barrera, "More Mexicans Leaving than Coming to the U.S.," Pew Research Center, November 19, 2015, www.pewhispanic.org/2015/11/19/more-mexicans-leaving-than-coming-to-the-u-s/.

13 Maurizio Bussolo, Jonathan Karver, and Luis-Felipe López-Carva, "Is There a Middle-Class Crisis in Europe?," Brookings Institution, March 22, 2018, www.brookings.edu/blog/future-development/2018/03/22/is-there-a-middle-class-crisis-in-europe/.

14 Terence Hogarth et al., *Technology, Globalisation, and the Future of Work in Europe: Essays on Employment in a Digitised Economy*, edited by Tony Dolphin, Institute for Public Policy Research, March 2015, www.oxfordmartin.ox.ac.uk/downloads/academic/technology-globalisation-future-of-work_Mar2015.pdf.

15 Joseph Halevi and Peter Kriesler, "Stagnation and Economic Conflict in Europe," *International Journal of Political Economy* 34 (2004): 19–45.

16 Robert Guest, "Generation Uphill," *The Economist*, January 23, 2016, 4–6.

17 George S. Tolley, "Urbanization and Economic Development," in *The Robinson Rojas Data Bank*, www.rrojasdatabank.info/econurb87/econurbp27-43.pdf.

18 Louise Shelley, *Human Smuggling and Trafficking into Europe: A Comparative Perspective*, Transatlantic Council on Migration, Migration Policy Institute, February 2014, www.migrationpolicy.org/sites/default/files/publications/BadActors-ShelleyFINALWEB.pdf.

19 Saskia Sassen, *Expulsions: Brutality and Complexity in the Global Economy* (Cambridge: Belknap Press, 2014).

20 Douglas Murray, *The Strange Death of Europe: Immigration, Identity, Islam* (London: Bloomsbury Press, 2017). See also Christopher Caldwell, *Reflections on the Revolution in Europe: Immigration, Islam, and the West* (New York: Anchor Books, 2010).

21 Murray, *Strange Death*, 3.

22 Abby Ohlheiser, "Uganda's New Anti-homosexuality Law Was Inspired by American Activists," *The Atlantic*, December 20, 2013, www.theatlantic.com/international/archive/2013/12/uganda-passes-law-punishes-homosexuality-life-imprisonment/356365/.

23 Pew Research Center, "Religion and Education around the World," December, 13, 2016, http://assets.pewresearch.org/wp-content/uploads/sites/11/2016/12/21094148/Religion-Education-ONLINE-FINAL.pdf; Caryle Murphy, "Q&A: The Muslim-Christian Education Gap in Sub-Saharan Africa," Pew Research Center, December 14, 2016, www.pewresearch.org/fact-tank/2016/12/14/qa-the-muslim-christian-education-gap-in-sub-saharan-africa/.

CHAPTER 1

1 Rod Norland, "A Mass Migration Crisis, and It May Yet Get Worse," *New York Times*, October 31, 2015, www.nytimes.com/2015/11/01/world/europe/a-mass-migration-crisis-and-it-may-yet-get-worse.html.

2 "Don't Panic," *The Economist*, September 24, 2014, www.economist.com/news/2014/09/24/dont-panic.

3 "World Population Projected to Reach 9.8 Billion in 2050, and 11.2 Billion in 2100," Department of Economic and Social Affairs, United Nations, June 21, 2017, www.un.org/development/desa/en/news/population/world-population-prospects-2017.html.

4 Paul Harris, "Population of World 'Could Grow to 15bn by 2100,'" *The Guardian*, October 22, 2011, www.theguardian.com/world/2011/oct/22/population-world-15bn-2100; Reuters, "World's Population Unlikely to Level off Anytime Soon – May Hit 12 Billion by 2100," *Washington Post*, September 22, 2014, www.washingtonpost.com/national/health-

science/worlds-population-unlikely-to-level-off-anytime-soon-may-hit-12-billion-by-2100/
2014/09/22/aa668900-3f68-11e4-9587-5dafd96295f0_story.html?noredirect=on&utm_
term=.a4d49a7db29c.

5 "UNICEF Report: Africa's Population Could Hit 4 Billion by 2100," National Public
   Radio, August 13, 2014, www.npr.org/sections/goatsandsoda/2014/08/13/340091377/unicef-
   report-africas-population-could-hit-4-billion-by-2100.

6 Claire Provost, "Nigeria Expected to Have Larger Population than US by 2050," *The
   Guardian*, June 13, 2013, www.theguardian.com/global-development/2013/jun/13/nigeria-
   larger-population-us-2050.

7 Jennifer M. Ortman and Christine E. Guarneri, "United States Population Projections:
   2000 to 2050," United States Census Bureau, 2009, www.census.gov/content/dam/Census/
   library/working-papers/2009/demo/us-pop-proj-2000-2050/analytical-document09.pdf.

8 Ivana Kottasova, "Biggest Populations in 2050: Move over Russia and Mexico. Here Comes
   Africa," CNN Money, August 18, 2015, https://money.cnn.com/2015/08/18/news/countries-
   with-biggest-populations/index.html.

9 Joel Kotkin, "Death Spiral Demographics," *Forbes*, February 1, 2017, www.forbes.com/
   sites/joelkotkin/2017/02/01/death-spiral-demographics-the-countries-shrinking-the-fastest/
   #3d5ee250b83c.

10 "Africa vs. Asia: The Population Dimension," *The Globalist*, September 16, 2015,
   www.theglobalist.com/africa-asia-nigeria-population/.

11 Shelly Walia, "Finally, India's Population Growth Is Slowing Down," *Quartz*, December
   24, 2014, https://qz.com/317518/finally-indias-population-growth-is-slowing-down/.

12 United Nations, Department of Economics and Social Affairs, Population Division,
   World Population Prospects, 2017 Revision, https://esa.un.org/unpd/wpp/publications/
   Files/WPP2017_KeyFindings.pdf.

13 Ibid.

14 Patrick Clawson, "Demography in the Middle East: Population Growth Slowing, Women's
   Situation Unresolved," *Middle East Review of International Affairs* (March 2009), www.washing
   toninstitute.org/policy-analysis/view/demography-in-the-middle-east-population-growth-
   slowing-womens-situation-un.

15 Ibid.

16 Patrice Clawson, "Demography in the Middle East: Population Growth Slowing,
   Women's Situation Unresolved," Washington Institute (March 2019), www.washingtonin
   stitute.org/policy-analysis/view/demography-in-the-middle-east-population-growth-slowing-
   womens-situation-un.

17 Alexander Betts and Paul Collier, *Refuge: Transforming a Broken Refugee System* (New
   York: Oxford University Press, 2017), 81–82.

18 "Middle East and North Africa: Youth Facts," Youth Policy Labs, accessed January 19,
   2019, www.youthpolicy.org/mappings/regionalyouthscenes/mena/facts/; Regional Bureau
   for Arab States, "Arab Human Development Report 2009," United Nations Development
   Programme (2009), accessed January 18, 2019, www.arab-hdr.org/publications/other/ahdr/
   ahdr2009e.pdf.

19 Navtej Dhillon, "The Middle Eastern Marriage Crisis," interview on PBS, July 11, 2008,
   www.pbs.org/now/shows/427/Middle-East-Marriage.html.

20 Ragui Assaah and Farzaneh Roudi-Fahimi, "Youth in the Middle East and North Africa: Demographic Opportunity or Challenge?," PRB (April 2007), accessed January 18, 2019, www.prb.org/youthinmena/.

21 The World Bank, "Middle East and North Africa Fact Sheet," 2013, http://go.worldbank.org/GI3KGTOOOo.

22 Hiroyuki Hino, "Youth and Unemployment in Sub-Saharan Africa," Seminar Report, African Economic Research Consortium Senior Policy Seminar XV, 19.

23 Kwabena Gyimah-Brempong and Mwangi S. Kimenyi, "Youth Policy and the Future of African Development," Working Paper 9, Africa Growth Initiative, Brookings Institution, April 2013: 7.

24 John Page, "Africa's Job Gap," Brookings Institution, March 4, 2013, www.brookings.edu/opinions/africas-jobs-gap/.

25 Kingsley Ighobor, "Africa's Youth: A 'Ticking Time Bomb' or an Opportunity?," *Africa Renewal*, May 2013, www.un.org/africarenewalmagazine/magazine/may-2013/africa's-youth.

26 See, for instance, Indermit Gill and Homi Kharas, *An East Asian Renaissance: Ideas for Economic Growth* (Washington, DC: World Bank, 2007).

27 Hiroyuki Hino and Gustav Ranis, eds., *Youth and Unemployment in Sub-Saharan Africa: Working but Poor* (New York: Routledge, 2014), 18.

28 "Few and Far Between," *The Economist*, October 22, 2015, www.economist.com/middle-east-and-africa/2015/10/22/few-and-far-between.

29 "Europe Is Sending African Migrants Home. Will They Stay?," *The Economist*, March 28, 2018, www.economist.com/middle-east-and-africa/2018/03/28/europe-is-sending-african-migrants-home.-will-they-stay.

30 World Bank, "Record High Remittances to Low- and Middle-Income Countries in 2017," April 23, 2018, www.worldbank.org/en/news/press-release/2018/04/23/record-high-remittances-to-low-and-middle-income-countries-in-2017.

31 Caroline Freund and Nikola Spatafora, "Remittances: Transaction Costs, Determinants, and Informal Flows," World Bank Policy Research Working Paper Series, No. 3704: 1.

32 Leandro Medina, Andrew Jonelis, and Mehmet Cangul, "The Informal Economy in Sub-Saharan Africa: Size and Determinants," IMF Working Paper 17/156 (2016).

33 The World Bank, "GDP Per Capita Growth (Annual %)," International Labour Organization, ILOSTAT Database, https://data.worldbank.org/indicator/SL.UEM.1524.MA.ZS?locations=ZQ&view=chart.

34 World Bank, "Unemployment, Total (% of Total Labor Force) (Modeled ILO Estimate)," International Labour Organization, ILOSTAT Database (September 2018), https://data.worldbank.org/indicator/SL.UEM.TOTL.ZS?locations=FR&view=chart.

35 World Bank, "Unemployment, Youth Male (% of Male Labor Force Ages 15–24) (National Estimate)," International Labour Organization, ILOSTAT Database (September 2018), https://data.worldbank.org/indicator/SL.UEM.1524.MA.NE.ZS?locations=FR.

36 Elaine Sciolino, "Why Is France a Target? Look to Its Alienated Muslim Youth," PBS, November 18, 2015, www.pbs.org/newshour/show/why-is-france-a-target-look-to-its-alienated-muslim-youth.

37 "Labour Force Survey (Annual Data 1975–91, Quarterly Data 1992–2010)," Centre for Economic Performance, LSE (accessed February 22, 2019), http://cep.lse.ac.uk/pubs/

download/cp338.pdf; "Unemployment Rate (Aged 16 and over, Seasonally Adjusted),"
Office for National Statistics (released February 19, 2019), www.ons.gov.uk/employmen
tandlabourmarket/peoplenotinwork/unemployment/timeseries/mgsx/lms.

38 World Bank, "Unemployment, Total (% of Labor Force) (Modeled ILO Estimate)," and
"Unemployment, Youth Total (% of Total Labor Force Ages 15–24) (National Estimate),"
International Labor Organization, ILOSTAT Database, November 2017, https://data.world
bank.org/indicator/SL.UEM.TOTL.ZS?end=2014&start=1991; https://data.worldbank.org/
indicator/SL.UEM.1524.NE.ZS?end=2014&locations=EU&start=1983.

39 See, for example, Ekrame Boubtane et al., "Immigration, Growth, and Unemployment:
Panel VAR Evidence from OECD Countries," *Labour* 27 (December 2013): 399–420;
Vincenzo Bove and Leandro Elia, "Migration, Diversity, and Economic Growth," *World
Development* 89 (2017): 227–239; J. Muysken and T. H. W. Ziesemer, "A Permanent Effect
of Temporary Immigration on Economic Growth," *Applied Economics* 45 (2003):
4050–4059.

40 Consider Steven A. Camarota, "The Effects of Immigration on the Earnings of Low-
Skilled Native Workers: Evidence from the June 1991 Current Population Survey," *Social
Science Quarterly* 78 (June 1997): 417–431; Pia M. Orrenius and Madeline Zavodny,
"Does Immigration Affect Wages? A Look at Occupation-Level Evidence," *Labour
Economics* 14 (2017): 757–773.

41 Lionel Shriver, "Why Mass Immigration Explains the Housing Crisis," *The Spectator*,
March 17, 2018, www.spectator.co.uk/2018/03/why-mass-immigration-explains-the-housing-
crisis/.

42 "Boon or Burden?," *The Economist*, June 13, 2013, www.economist.com/finance-and-
economics/2013/06/15/boon-or-burden.

43 James Lubitz and Ronald Prihoda, "The Use and Costs of Medicare Services in the Last
2 Years of Life," *Health Care Financial Review* 5 (Spring 1984): 117–131.

44 Brian Wheeler, "Net Loss: Anatomy of a Pledge," BBC, February 26, 2015, www.bbc.com/
news/uk-politics-31638180.

45 Ibid.

46 Alan Travis, "Net Migration to UK Hits Record High of 330,000," *The Guardian*,
August 27, 2015, www.theguardian.com/uk-news/2015/aug/27/net-migration-predicted-
to-hit-record-level.

47 Charles Clarke, "Immigration," in The *Too Difficult Box: The Big Issues Politicians Can't
Crack* (London: Biteback Publishing, 2014).

48 See Robert A. Dahl, *Preface to a Democratic Theory* (Chicago: University of Chicago
Press, 1956).

49 Alan L. Feld, "The Shrunken Power of the Purse," *Boston University Law Review* 89
(2009): 487–497.

50 It is estimated that the cost of deporting a single denied asylum applicant from the United
Kingdom is £25,000. Jill Rutter, *Moving up and Getting On* (Bristol: Policy Press, 2016),

51 However, according to a recent study by Margaret Peters, neoliberal policies (enabling
firms to move their operations to low-skilled workers abroad rather than having to bring
those workers to the rich-country site of those operations) together with automation have
sharply reduced the incentives for corporations to invest political capital in support of

relatively open borders: *Trading Barriers: Immigration and the Remaking of Globalization* (Princeton: Princeton University Press, 2017).

52 Micheline Ishay, "The Socialist Contributions to Human Rights: An Overlooked Legacy," *The International Journal of Human Rights* 9 (2005): 225–245.

53 Neel Kashkari, "Immigration Is Practically a Free Lunch for America," *Wall Street Journal*, January 18, 2018, www.wsj.com/articles/immigration-is-practically-a-free-lunch-for-america-1516320376.

54 Philip Legrain, "How to Convince Sceptics of the Value of Immigration?," *The Economist*, June 1, 2018, www.economist.com/open-future/2018/06/01/how-to-convince-sceptics-of-the-value-of-immigration.

55 Joan Walsh, "The New Trump Immigration Plan Is Anti-American," *The Nation*, January 26, 2018, www.thenation.com/article/the-new-trump-immigration-plan-is-anti-american/.

56 Paul Collier, *Exodus: How Migration Is Changing Our World* (Oxford: Oxford University Press, 2013), 42–53.

57 Manuel Orozco et al., "The Continued Growth of Family Remittances to Latin America and the Caribbean in 2015," The Dialogue Leadership for the Americas, February 2016, www.thedialogue.org/wp-content/uploads/2016/02/2015-Remittances-to-LAC-2122016.pdf.

58 Consider Christopher Woolf, "A Brief History of America's Hostility to a Previous Generation of Mediterranean Migrants – Italians," Public Radio International, November 26, 2015, www.pri.org/stories/2015-11-26/brief-history-america-s-hostility-previous-generation-mediterranean-migrants.

59 Albeit gradually and arduously. See Joshua Zeitz, "The Real History of American Immigration," *Politico*, August 6, 2017, www.politico.com/magazine/story/2017/08/06/trump-history-of-american-immigration-215464.

CHAPTER 2

1 Lynda E. Boose, "Crossing the River Drina: Bosnian Rape Camps, Turkish Impalement, and Serb Cultural Memory," *Journal of Women in Culture and Society* 28 (2002): 74.

2 Robert M. Hayden, "Imagined Communities and Real Victims: Self-Determination and Ethnic Cleansing in Yugoslavia," *American Ethnologist* 23 (1996): 783–801.

3 Giuseppe Mazzini, "Foreign Intervention and National Self-Determination," in Stefano Recchia and Nadia Urbinati, eds., *A Cosmopolitanism of Nations* (Princeton: Princeton University Press, 2009), 194.

4 James Joll, "Mussolini's Roman Empire," *New York Times*, June 20, 1976, www.nytimes.com/1976/06/20/archives/mussolinis-roman-empire-the-trouble-was-trying-to-keep-up-with-the.html.

5 See, generally, Timothy Snyder, "Hitler's World," *New York Review of Books*, September 24, 2015, www.nybooks.com/articles/2015/09/24/hitlers-world/.

6 Cas Mudde, "Europe's Populist Surge," *Foreign Affairs* 95 (November–December 2016): 25–30.

7 For example, Anthee Carassava, "Attack on Migrants 'Planned by Far-Right Party' Golden Dawn in Greece," *The Times*, June 20, 2017, www.thetimes.co.uk/article/attacks-on-migrants-planned-by-far-right-party-in-greece-90jd7nssb.

8 See Mark Lilla, "Two Roads for the New French Right," *New York Review of Books*, December 20, 2018.

9 James Traub, "The Death of the Most Generous Nation on Earth," *Foreign Policy*, February 10, 2016, https://foreignpolicy.com/2016/02/10/the-death-of-the-most-generous-nation-on-earth-sweden-syria-refugee-europe/.

10 Alice Schwarzer, "The Current Outrage Is Very Hypocritical," interview by Christian Hoffmann and René Pfister, *Spiegel Online*, January 21, 2016, www.spiegel.de/inter national/germany/german-feminists-debate-cologne-attacks-a-1072806.html.

11 Hannah Hartig, "Most Americans View Openness to Foreigners as 'Essential to Who We Are as a Nation,'" Pew Research Center, October 9, 2018, www.pewresearch.org/fact-tank/2018/10/09/most-americans-view-openness-to-foreigners-as-essential-to-who-we-are-as-a-nation/.

12 Compare Christopher Heath Wellman and Phillip Cole's justification for debating the ethics of immigration largely in terms of theory rather than more instrumental consider-ations like economic impact: "It is the role of theory . . . to challenge 'common sense.' And we can at least shift it out of the consciousness of those who engage in this debate at the theoretical level. . . . Theory is the use of the imagination to construct possibilities, and we can only critically examine our beliefs if we are prepared to imagine other possibilities." *Debating the Ethics of Immigration: Is There a Right to Exclude?* (New York: Oxford University Press, 2011), 8–9. Compare the position of Chandran Kukathas. After conceding that a campaign for open borders is politically untenable, he goes on to encourage theorizing about and coming to recognize the case for them.

13 Paul Collier, *Exodus: How Migration Is Changing Our World* (Oxford: Oxford University Press, 2013), 16.

14 Alan E. Steinweis, "German Cultural Imperialism in Czechoslovakia and Poland," *The International History Review* (August 1991): 470.

15 United Nations, Charter of the United Nations, Art. 3, Para. 4, 1 UNTS XVI, October 24, 1945, accessed July 10, 2018, www.un.org/en/sections/un-charter/un-charter-full-text/.

16 United Nations, *Charter of the United Nations*, Art. 2, Para. 4, 1 UNTS XVI, October 24, 1945, accessed July 10, 2018, www.un.org/en/sections/un-charter/un-charter-full-text/.

17 United Nations, Office of the High Commissioner on Human Rights, International Covenant on Civil and Political Rights, G.A. Res. 2200A(XXI). March 23, 1976.

18 Ibid.

19 Consider Joseph H. Carens, *The Ethics of Immigration* (Oxford: Oxford University Press, 2013); Michael Huemer, "Is There a Right to Immigrate?," *Social Theory and Practice* 36 (2010): 429–461; Bryan Caplan, "Why Should We Restrict Immigration?," *Cato Journal* 32 (2012): 5–24.

20 Utkarsh Anand, "Need to Relocate Evicted Slum Dwellers," *The Indian Express*, February 12, 2010, https://indianexpress.com/article/cities/delhi/need-to-relocate-evicted-slumdwellers/.

21 "In Much of Sub-Saharan Africa, Cell Phones Are More Common than Access to Electricity," *The Economist*, November 8, 2017, www.economist.com/graphic-detail/2017/11/08/in-much-of-sub-saharan-africa-mobile-phones-are-more-common-than-access-to-electricity.

22 Fiona Govan, "Spain Admits Firing Rubber Bullets at Migrants Swimming to Enclave," *The Telegraph*, February 14, 2014, www.telegraph.co.uk/news/worldnews/europe/spain/10638607/Spain-admits-firing-rubber-bullets-at-migrants-swimming-to-enclave.html.

23 "Ceuta and Melilla: Spain Wants Rid of Anti-immigrant Razor Wire," BBC News, June 14, 2018, www.bbc.com/news/world-europe-44485995.

24 Elisabetta Povoledo, "In Rome, Violent Eviction of Migrants 'Touched a Nerve,'" *New York Times*, September 4, 2017, www.nytimes.com/2017/09/04/world/europe/italy-rome-migrants-eviction.html.

25 Sarah Poppleton and Linda Rice, "Programmes and Strategies in the UK Fostering Assisted Return to and Reintegration in Third Countries," *UK Border Agency Home Office* (February 25, 2010), https://ec.europa.eu/home-affairs/sites/homeaffairs/files/what-we-do/networks/european_migration_network/reports/docs/emn-studies/assisted-return/27._united_kingdom__national_report_assisted_return__re-integration_study_final_version_31march_201_en.pdf.

26 Alasdair Clark, "Being a 'Failed Asylum Seeker' Leads Directly to Homelessness on the Streets of Glasgow," *New Statesman*, August 2, 2018, www.newstatesman.com/politics/uk/2018/08/being-failed-asylum-seeker-leads-directly-homelessness-streets-glasgow.

27 "Europe Migrant Crisis: EU Blamed for 'Soaring' Death Toll," BBC, July 6, 2017, www.bbc.com/news/world-europe-40515054; Lizzie Dearden, "EU Accused of 'Willfully Letting Refugees Drown' as NGOs Face Having Rescues Suspended in the Mediterranean," *The Independent*, July 29, 2017, www.independent.co.uk/news/world/europe/refugee-crisis-ngo-rescue-ships-mediterranean-sea-italy-libya-eu-code-of-conduct-deaths-2300-latest-a7866226.html.

28 Melissa Eddy, "Violent Backlash against Migrants in Germany as Asylum-Seekers Pour in," *New York Times*, August 13, 2015, www.nytimes.com/2015/08/14/world/europe/germany-migrants-attacks-asylum-seekers-backlash.html.

29 Federal Republic of Germany, Federal Ministry of Justice, *Basic Law of the Federal Republic of Germany (Grundgesetz, GG)*, Art. 1–19, www.gesetze-im-internet.de/englisch_gg/englisch_gg.html#.

30 Jörg Faust and Melody Garcia, "With or without Force?: European Public Opinion on Democracy Promotion," German Development Institute, 2013, www.die-gdi.de/uploads/media/DP_10.2013.pdf.

31 Sean Byrne, "Defenders of Inequality: Milton Friedman and Robert Nozick," *Studies: An Irish Quarterly Review* 75 (1986): 186–195.

32 Consider Goran Sunajko, "Rawls and Piketty: The Philosophical Aspects of Economic Inequality," *The Journal of Philosophical Economics* 9 (2016): 71–84.

33 Joseph H. Carens, *The Ethics of Immigration* (Oxford: Oxford University Press, 2013), 226.

34 Ayalet Shachar, *The Birthright Lottery: Citizenship and Global Inequality* (Cambridge, MA: Harvard University Press, 2009), 2–3.

35 Sven Beckert, *Empire of Cotton: A Global History* (New York: Alfred A. Knopf, 2014).

36 Ibid.

37 Andre Gunder Frank, *The Development of Underdevelopment* (Boston: New England Free Press, 1966).

38 Wellman and Cole, *Debating the Ethics of Immigration*, 67.

39 United Nations, Office of the High Commissioner on Human Rights, *International Covenant on Civil and Political Rights*, Art. 12, Para. 4.

40 Lawrence Peters, "Sovereignty: The UN and the Westphalian Legacy," in *The United Nations: History and Core Ideas* (New York: Palgrave Macmillan, 2015).

41 Roland Burke, *Decolonization and the Evolution of International Human Rights* (Philadelphia: University of Pennsylvania Press, 2010), 51–57.

42 United Nations, 2005 World Summit Outcome, A/RES/60/1, October 24, 2005, accessed June 6, 2018, www.un.org/en/development/desa/population/migration/generalassembly/docs/globalcompact/A_RES_60_1.pdf.

43 Wellman and Cole, *Debating the Ethics of Immigration*, 29.

44 A. Mark Weisburd, "The International Court of Justice and the Concept of State Practice," *University of Pennsylvania Journal of International Law* 31 (2009): 295–372.

45 Alexander Betts, "What Europe Could Learn from the Way Africa Treats Refugees," *The Guardian*, June 26, 2018, www.theguardian.com/commentisfree/2018/jun/26/europe-learn-africa-refugees-solutions.

46 Rana F. Sweis, "Jordan's Open Door Is Now Only Cracked, Leaving Syrians Stranded," *New York Times*, November 19, 2014, www.nytimes.com/2014/11/20/world/middleeast/jordans-open-door-is-now-only-cracked-leaving-syrians-stranded.html.

47 Adam Taylor, "Germany's Small Yet Important Change to the Way It Deals with Syrian Refugees," *Washington Post*, August 26, 2015, www.washingtonpost.com/news/worldviews/wp/2015/08/26/germanys-small-yet-important-change-to-the-way- it-deals-with-syrian-refugees/?utm_term=.7166a8b37b86; Chris Morris, "Sweden's Asylum Offer to Refugees from Syria," BBC, October 23, 2013, www.bbc.com/news/world-europe-24635791.

48 Ashley Fantz and Becky Anderson, "Refugee Crisis: Why Aren't Gulf States Taking Them In?," CNN, September 8, 2015, www.cnn.com/2015/09/08/world/gulf-states-syrian-refugee-crisis/index.html; James Kanter, "EU Moves against 3 Countries That Don't Take Refugees," *New York Times*, June 13, 2017, www.nytimes.com/2017/06/13/world/europe/eu-refugees-czech-republic-hungary-poland.html; Jan Cienski, "Why Poland Doesn't Want Refugees," Politico, May 21, 2017, www.politico.eu/article/politics-nationalism-and-religion-explain-why-poland-doesnt-want-refugees/.

49 Alan Greenblatt, "What's Causing the Latest Immigration Crisis? A Brief Explainer," National Public Radio, July 9, 2014, www.npr.org/2014/07/09/329848538/whats-causing-the-latest-immigration-crisis-a-brief-explainer.

50 Russell Berman, "The New Crackdown on Migrant Families," *The Atlantic*, January 5, 2016, www.theatlantic.com/politics/archive/2016/01/the-obama-administrations-crackdown-on-central-american-migrants/422550/.

51 Hurst Hannum, *Autonomy, Sovereignty, and Self-Determination: The Accommodation of Conflicting Rights* (Philadelphia: University of Pennsylvania Press, 1990), 39–40.

52 Ernest Gellner, *Nations and Nationalism* (Ithaca: Cornell University Press, 1983), 7.

53 Benedict Anderson, *Imagined Communities: Reflections on the Origin and Spread of Nationalism* (London: Verso, 2006), 16.

54 Ernest Renan, "What Is a Nation?," conference delivered at the Sorbonne, March 11, 1882, trans. Ethan Rundell, http://ucparis.fr/files/9313/6549/9943/What_is_a_Nation.pdf.

55 Ibid.

56 See Chris Noack, "Europe's Citizenship Tests Are So Hard Not Even Citizens Can Pass," *Washington Post*, July 12, 2016, www.washingtonpost.com/news/worldviews/wp/2016/07/13/europes-citizenship-tests-are-so-hard-not-even-citizens-can-answer-the-questions/?utm_term=.407a35ffb5cc.

57 Michael Walzer, *Spheres of Justice: A Defense of Pluralism and Equality* (New York: Basic Books, 1983).

58 Michael Walzer, *Just and Unjust Wars*, 2nd ed. (New York: Basic Books, 1991), xxviii; Aristotle, *Politics*, in *Introduction to Aristotle*, ed. Richard McKeon (New York: Random House, 1947), 556–557.

59 Robert Putnam, "*E. Pluribus Unum*: Diversity and Community in the Twenty-first Century," *Scandinavian Political Studies* 30, no. 2 (2007): 137 at 165.

60 Alexander Betts and Paul Collier, *Refuge: Transforming a Broken Refugee System* (New York: Oxford University Press, 2017).

61 "Refugees Bear Cost of Massive Underfunding," United Nations High Commissioner for Refugees, October 9, 2018, www.unhcr.org/news/briefing/2018/10/5bbc57d94/refugees-bear-cost-massive-underfunding.html.

62 Betts and Collier, *Refuge*, 55.

63 This figure is disputed in Christopher Bertram, "Reforming Refuge," *New Humanist*, August 29, 2017, https://newhumanist.org.uk/articles/5224/reforming-refuge.

CHAPTER 3

1 "Immigrants or Children of Immigrants Make up 12% of Congress," Pew Research Center, August 21 2018, www.pewresearch.org/fact-tank/2018/08/21/immigrants-or-children-of-immigrants-make-up-at-least-12-of-congress/; Tess Sohngen, "9 Children of Immigrants Who Fundamentally Changed the US," Global Citizen, September 5, 2017, www.globalcitizen.org/en/content/children-of-immigrants-who-changed-the-us/.

2 Kenan Malik, "The Failure of Multiculturalism: Community versus Society in Europe," *Foreign Affairs* 94, no. 2 (2015): 21.

3 Ernest Gellner, *Nations and Nationalism* (Ithaca: Cornell University Press, 1983), 7.

4 Paul Kelly, "Defending Some Dodos: Equality and/or Liberty?," 66.

5 David Miller, *Justice for Earthlings: Essays in Political Philosophy* (Cambridge: Cambridge University Press, 2013), 99.

6 Paul Kelly, "Defending Some Dodos: Equality and/or Liberty?," in *Multiculturalism Reconsidered*, 66.

7 Eugen Weber, *Peasants into Frenchmen: The Modernization of Rural France 1870–1914* (Stanford: Stanford University Press, 1976).

8 Seyla Benhabib, *The Claims of Culture: Equality and Diversity in the Global Era* (Princeton: Princeton University Press, 2002), ix.

9 Consider, for example, on the one hand, David Cameron, "PM's Speech at Munich Security Conference," Prime Minister's Office, February 5, 2011, www.gov.uk/government/speeches/pms-speech-at-munich-security-conference; and, on the other, Alan Patten, *Equal Recognition: The Moral Foundation of Minority Rights* (Princeton: Princeton University Press, 2014).

10 See Muslim Brotherhood, "Muslim Brotherhood Statement Denouncing UN Women Declaration for Violating Sharia Principles," Ikhwan Web, March 14, 2013, www.ikhwan web.com/article.php?id=30731.

11 Ibid. A spokesperson for Egypt's National Council for Women condemned the Brotherhood's statement shortly after it was issued.

12 Gustav Niebuhr, "Southern Baptists Declare Wife Should 'Submit' to Her Husband," *New York Times*, June 10, 1998, www.nytimes.com/1998/06/10/us/southern-baptists-declare-wife-should-submit-to-her-husband.html.

13 "Where the Public Stands on Religious Liberty vs Nondiscrimination," Religion and Public Life, Pew Research Center, September 28, 2016, www.pewforum.org/2016/09/28/where-the-public-stands-on-religious-liberty-vs-nondiscrimination/.

14 Bichara Khader, "Muslims in Europe: The Construction of a 'Problem,'" in *The Search for Europe: Contrasting Approaches* (Birmingham: BBV, 2016), 312; "Europe's Growing Muslim Population," Religion and Public Life, Pew Research Center, November 29, 2017, www.pewforum.org/2017/11/29/europes-growing-muslim-population/.

15 "Support for Same-Sex Marriage Grows, Even among Groups That Had Been Skeptical," U.S. Politics and Policy, Pew Research Center, June 26, 2017, www.people-press.org/2017/06/26/support-for-same-sex-marriage-grows-even-among-groups-that-had-been-skeptical/; "One-in-Seven New U.S. Marriages Is Interracial or Interethnic," Social and Demographic Trends, Pew Research Center, June 4, 2010, www.pewsocialtrends.org/2010/06/04/marrying-out/.

16 Gretchen Livingston and Anna Brown, "Intermarriage in the U.S. 50 Years after Loving v. Virginia," Social and Demographic Trends, Pew Research Center, May 18, 2017, www.pewso cialtrends.org/2017/05/18/intermarriage-in-the-u-s-50-years-after-loving-v-virginia/.

17 Dionne Searcey, "A Quiet Revolution: More Women Seek Divorces in Conservative West Africa," *New York Times*, January 7, 2019, www.nytimes.com/2019/06/world/africa/niger-divorce-women.html?emc=edit_th_190107&ni=todaysheadlines&nlid=410168840107.

18 Ibid.

19 Ibid.

20 Maria Abi-Habib, "Pakistan Dispatch: They Once Danced for Royalty. Not It's Mostly for Leering Men," *New York Times*, January 6, 2019, www.nytimes.com/2019/01/05/world/asia/pakistan-lahore-dancing-girls-html?emc=edit_th_190106&nl=todaysheadlines&nlid=410168840106.

21 United Nations, Office of the High Commissioner on Human Rights, *International Covenant on Civil and Political Rights*, Art. 18, Para. 4.

22 Ibid., Art. 20, Para. 2.

23 Chandran Kukathas, *The Liberal Archipelago: A Theory of Diversity and Freedom* (Oxford: Oxford University Press, 2003), 257–270.

24 Chandran Kukathas, "The Life of Brian, or Now for Something Completely Difference-Blind," in *Multiculturalism Reconsidered*, 194–199.

25 Will Kymlicka, *Multicultural Citizenship: A Liberal Theory of Minority Rights* (Oxford: Clarendon Press, 1995), 75.

26 Michael Walzer, "Response to Kukathas," Ethnicity and Group Rights: Nomos 39 (1997): 105–111.

27 Ibid., 108.

28 Tom Farer, *Confronting Global Terrorism and American Neo-Conservatism*, (New York: Oxford University Press, 2008), 131–132.

29 See Samuel Huntington, *The Clash of Civilizations and the Remaking of World Order* (New York: Simon & Schuster, 1996), 134–168.

30 Michael Walzer, *Ethnicity and Group Rights: Nomos XXXIX* (New York: NYU Press, 1997)

31 "The Elusive 90% Solution," Pew Research Center, March 11, 2011, www.pewresearch.org/2011/03/11/the-elusive-90-solution/.

32 See, for instance, Brennan Hoban, "One Year after Charlottesville, Has American Learned to Reckon with Its Racist History?," Brookings Institution, August 10, 2018, www.brookings.edu/blog/brookings-now/2018/08/10/one-year-after-charlottesville-has-america-learned-to-reckon-with-its-racist-history/.

33 Robert Schlesinger, "Poll on Birthers: Most Southerners, Republicans, Question Obama Citizenship," *U.S. News*, July 31, 2009, www.usnews.com/opinion/blogs/robert-schlesinger/2009/07/31/poll-on-birthers-most-southerners-republicans-question-obama-citizenship.

34 Humphrey Taylor, "'Wingnuts' and President Obama," Harris Poll, March 24, 2010, https://theharrispoll.com/wp-content/uploads/2017/12/Harris-Interactive-Poll-Research-Politics-Wingnuts-2010-03.pdf.

35 U.S. Politics and Policy, "Public Remains Divided over Use of Torture," Pew Research Center, April 13, 2009, www.people-press.org/2009/04/23/public-remains-divided-over-use-of-torture.

36 Ibid.

37 On the phenomenon of "racial apathy," see Maria Krysan and Sara Moberg, "A Portrait of African American and White Racial Attitudes," University of Illinois, Institute of Government and Public Affairs, September 9, 2016, https://igpa.uillinois.edu/programs/racial-attitudes.

38 "Political Polarization in the American Public," U.S. Politics and Policy, Pew Research Center, June 12, 2014, www.people-press.org/2014/06/12/political-polarization-in-the-american-public/.

39 Alasdair McIntyre, *After Virtue: A Study in Moral Theory*, 3rd ed. (Notre Dame: University of Notre Dame Press, 2007), 253.

40 Michael Walzer, *Politics and Passion: Towards a More Egalitarian Liberalism* (New Haven: Yale University Press, 2004), 135.

41 Avishai Margalit and Moshe Halbertal, "Liberalism and the Right to Culture," *Social Research: An International Quarterly* 71, no. 3 (2004): 529–548.

42 "Changing Attitudes on Gay Marriage," Religion and Public Life, Pew Research Center, June 26, 2017, www.pewforum.org/fact-sheet/changing-attitudes-on-gay-marriage/.

43 Pamela Constable, "Afghanistan's 'American Idol' Is the Voice of a New Generation – And Muslim Clerics Aren't Happy about It," *Washington Post*, December 1, 2017, www.washingtonpost.com/world/asia_pacific/afghanistans-american-idol-is-the-voice-of-a-new-generation–and-muslim-clerics-arent-happy-about-it/2017/11/30/cd65ba96-ca1d-11e7-b506-8a10ed11ecf5_story.html?noredirect=on&utm_term=.812143ffbe32.

44 Lyman Stone, "The Beginnings for the American Church," *Medium*, April 21, 2017, https://medium.com/migration-issues/the-beginning-for-the-american-church-6bb5654a91fc;   Pew

Research Center, Religion and Public Life, "America's Changing Landscape," Pew Research Center, May 12, 2015, www.pewforum.org/2015/05/12/chapter-1-the-changing-religious-composition-of-the-u-s/.

45 Melanie Phillips, "After the Rushdie Affair, Islam in Britain Became Fused with an Agenda of Murder," *The Guardian*, May 27, 2006, www.theguardian.com/commentis free/2006/may/28/religion.islam.

46 Alasdair Palmer, "Multiculturalism Has Left Britain with a Toxic Legacy," *The Telegraph* (February 11, 2012), www.telegraph.co.uk/news/uknews/immigration/9075849/Multicul turalism-has-left-Britain-with-a-toxic-legacy.html.

47 Martin Amis, "Fear and Loathing," *The Guardian*, September 18, 2001, www.theguardian .com/world/2001/sep/18/september11.politicsphilosophyandsociety.

48 Bhikhu Parekh, *Rethinking Multiculturalism: Cultural Diversity and Political Theory* (Basingstoke: Macmillan, 2000), 296–297.

49 Ibid., 298.

50 Ibid., 298–299.

51 Derek McGhee, *The End of Multiculturalism? Terrorism, Integration and Human Rights* (New York: Open University Press, 2008), 31.

52 Parekh, *Rethinking Multiculturalism*, 299.

53 Ibid., 304.

54 Ibid., 304–305.

55 Ibid., 310–311.

56 Ibid., 306–307.

57 Will Kymlicka, *Politics in the Vernacular: Nationalism, Multiculturalism, and Citizenship* (Oxford: Oxford University Press, 2001), 33.

58 Brian Barry, *Culture and Equality: An Egalitarian Critique of Multiculturalism* (Cambridge: Polity, 2001), 6.

59 Brian Barry, "Second Thoughts – And Some First Thoughts Revived," in *Multiculturalism Reconsidered*, 205.

60 Ibid.

61 Kwami Anthony Appiah, *The Ethics of Identity* (Princeton: Princeton University Press, 2005), 135.

62 Barry, "Second Thoughts," 228.

63 *Masterpiece Cakeshop v. Colorado Civil Rights Commission*, 138 S. Ct. 1719.

64 See Parekh, *Rethinking Multiculturalism*, 337: "[D]ialogue is possible only if each culture accepts others as equal conversational partners, who need to be taken seriously as sources of new ideas and to whom it owes the duty of explaining itself."

65 Ibid., 336.

66 Ibid., 337: "Since each culture is inherently limited, a dialogue between them is mutually beneficial. It both alerts them to their biases . . . and enables then [sic] to reduce them and expand their horizons of thought."

67 Ibid. Emphasis added.

68 Ibid., 141: "Given the differences in their history, traditions and moral culture, it is both inevitable and desirable that different societies should differently interpret, prioritize and realize great moral values and integrate them with their own suitably revised thick and complex moral structures."

69 Ibid., 137: "Although East Asian countries differ in important respects, most of their citizens do cherish such 'Asian' values as social harmony, respect for authority, orderly society, a united and extended family and a sense of filial piety."

70 Seyla Benhabib, *The Claims of Culture: Equality and Diversity in the Global Era* (Princeton: Princeton University Press, 2002), emphasis added.

71 Parekh, *Rethinking Multiculturalism*, 314.

72 Ibid., 319.

73 Ibid., 320.

74 Ibid., 336.

75 Dave Phillips, "Sikh Captain Says Keeping Beard and Turban Lets Him Serve U.S. and Faith," *New York Times*, April 1, 2016, www.nytimes.com/2016/04/02/us/sikh-army-captain-simratpal-singh.html.

76 Tom Brune, "Refugees' Beliefs Don't Travel Well," *Chicago Tribune*, October 28, 1996.

77 Deborah A. Phillips et al., "Puzzling It Out: The Current State of Scientific Knowledge on Pre-Kindergarten Effects," Brookings Institution, April 17, 2017, www.brookings.edu/research/puzzling-it-out-the-current-state-of-scientific-knowledge-on-pre-kindergarten-effects/.

78 *Meyer v. State of Nebraska*, 262 U.S. 390 (1923).

79 Donald P. Kommers et al., *American Constitutional Law: Essays, Cases, and Comparative Notes*, 2nd ed. (Lanham: Rowman & Littlefield, 2004), 263.

80 Holmes expressed this opinion in the context of *Bartels v. Iowa*, a case very similar to, and argued on the same day as, *Meyer v. Nebraska*. See Max Lerner, ed., *The Mind and Faith of Justice Holmes: His Speeches, Essays, Letters, and Judicial Opinions* (New York: Routledge, 2017), 320.

81 Consider William Dalrymple, "Inside Islam's 'Terror Schools,'" *New Statesman*, March 28, 2005, 15; Patrick Cockburn, *Rise of the Islamic State: ISIS and the New Sunni Revolution* (London: Verso, 2015), 155, 166.

82 For example, see Diane Dagenais and Marianne Jacquet, "Valuation of Multilingualism and Bilingual Education in Immigrant Families," *Journal of International Migration and Integration* 1 (October 2000): 389–404; Matthew Wright and Irene Bloemraad, "Is There a Trade-Off between Multiculturalism and Socio-Political Integration? Policy Regimes and Immigrant Incorporation in Comparative Perspective," *Perspectives on Politics* 10 (March 2012): 77–95; Gary M. Stern, "Controversy: Immigrant Parents Challenge Bilingual Education," *The Hispanic Outlook in Higher Education* 6 (January 1996): 6.

83 "Constructing Conflict," *The Economist*, April 30, 2007, www.economist.com/international/2007/08/30/constructing-conflict; Gabriela Baczynska, "Mosque Building Brings Islam Fears to Poland," *Reuters*, April 1, 2010, www.reuters.com/article/us-poland-mosque/mosque-building-brings-islam-fears-to-poland-idUSTRE6302VN20100401.

CHAPTER 4

1 Christopher Caldwell, "Islam on the Outskirts of the Welfare State," *New York Times Magazine*, February 5, 2006, www.nytimes.com/2006/02/05/magazine/islam-on-the-outskirts-of-the-welfare-state.html.

2 Ibid.

3 Ibid.

4 Tom Turula, "Sweden's Foreign-Born Population Is Nearing 1.7 Million," *Business Insider*, https://nordic.businessinsider.com/swedens-foreign-born-population-is-nearly-17-million-people — finns-are-the-biggest-group-2017-3.

5 Christopher Caldwell, "Islam on the Outskirts of the Welfare State," *New York Times Magazine*, February 5, 2006, www.nytimes.com/2006/02/05/magazine/islam-on-the-out skirts-of-the-welfare-state.html.

6 Ibid.

7 Ibid.

8 Ibid.

9 Ibid.

10 Ibid.

11 Ibid.

12 Ibid.

13 Ibid. Quoting Mauricio Rojas, a liberal economist who migrated from Chile.

14 James Traub, "The Death of the Most Generous Nation on Earth," *Foreign Policy*, February 10, 2016, https://foreignpolicy.com/2016/02/10/the-death-of-the-most-generous-nation-on-earth-sweden-syria-refugee-europe/.

15 Ibid.

16 Ibid.

17 Ibid.

18 Ibid.

19 Ibid.

20 Ibid.

21 Ibid.

22 Ibid.

23 Ibid.

24 Organisation for Economic Cooperation and Development, *Working Together: Skills and Labour Market Integration of Immigrants and Their Children in Sweden*, OECD, March 13, 2016, 46.

25 Ibid., 42, 99.

26 OECD, "Getting Skills Right: Good Practice Adapting to Changing Skill Needs," in *OECD Library* (Paris: OECD Publishing, 2017), www-oecd-ilibrary-org.du.idm.oclc.org/docserver/9789264277892-en.pdf?expires=1550970961&id=id&accname=ocid177442&checksum=5F519E7ED99EF342C47E7AF5794269EC.

27 "Why Are Young Men in Sweden Shooting Each Other?," *The Economist*, March 8, 2018, www.economist.com/europe/2018/03/08/why-are-young-men-in-sweden-shooting-each-other.

28 *The Economist*, "Integrating Refugees," *The Economist*, April 21, 2018, www.economist .com/international/2018/04/21/refugees-need-not-be-a-burden-if-they-are-allowed-to-work.

29 "Why Are Young Men in Sweden Shooting Each Other?"

30 John F. Helliwell, Richard Layard, and Jeffrey D. Sachs, "World Happiness Report," New York: Sustainable Development Solutions Network, 2018, http://worldhappiness.report/.

31 "Persons with Immigrant Background by Immigration Category, Country Background and Gender," Statistics Norway, January 1, 2012, https://web.archive.org/web/20130206040422/http://www.ssb.no/english/subjects/02/01/10/innvbef_en/tab-2012-04-26-04-en.html.

32 OECD, "Jobs for Immigrants: Labor Market Integration in Norway." www.oecd.org/els/mig/43247521.pdf, 17.

33 Ibid., 48.

34 Ibid., 43.

35 Ibid., 49.

36 Tjitske Akkerman and Anniken Hagelund, "'Women and Children First!' Anti-immigration Parties and Gender in Norway and the Netherlands," *Patterns of Prejudice* 41 (2007): 197–214.

37 Pippa Norris, "The 'New Cleavage' Thesis and the Social Basis of Radical Right Support," paper for presentation at American Political Science Association Annual Meeting, September 2, 2015, 14–15.

38 David Runciman, "How the Education Gap Is Tearing Politics Apart," *The Guardian*, October 5, 2016, www.theguardian.com/politics/2016/oct/05/trump-brexit-education-gap-tearing-politics-apart.

39 Gregory Korte, "Obama Greets Nordic Leaders, Saying They 'Punch above Their Weight,'" *USA Today*, May 13, 2016, www.usatoday.com/story/news/politics/2016/05/13/obama-nordic-leaders-summit-punch-above-t heir-weight/84330852/.

40 Osama bin Laden, "Full Transcript of bin Ladin's Speech," *Al Jazeera*, November 1, 2004, www.aljazeera.com/archive/2004/11/200849163336457223.html.

41 Bruce Gellerman, "It Was Like a War Zone: Busing in Boston," WBUR News, September 5, 2014, www.wbur.org/news/2014/09/05/boston-busing-anniversary.

42 Will Boast, "Blaming Muslims, at First, in Norway," *New York Times Magazine*, June 24, 2016, www.nytimes.com/2016/06/26/magazine/blaming-muslims-at-first-in-norway.html.

43 Ibid.

44 Ibid.

45 Ibid.

46 Hugh Eakin, "Liberal, Harsh Denmark," *New York Review of Books*, March 10, 2016, www.nybooks.com/articles/2016/03/10/liberal-harsh-denmark/.

47 Ibid.

48 Rik Rutten, "Assimilation or Alienation? Denmark Mulls 'Ghetto' Laws Targeting Immigrants," *World Politics Review*, November 12, 2018, www.worldpoliticsreview.com/articles/26741/assimilation-or-alienation-denmark-mulls-ghetto-laws-targeting-immigrants.

49 Flemming Rose, "Why I Published Those Cartoons," *Washington Post*, February 19, 2006, www.washingtonpost.com/wp-dyn/content/article/2006/02/17/AR2006021702499.html; Hugh Eakin, "Denmark's Surprising About-Turn on Refugees," *Financial Review*, March 11, 2016, www.afr.com/news/world/europe/denmarks-surprising-aboutturn-on-refugees-20160229-gn61bf.

50 William Drozdiak, *Fractured Continent: Europe's Crises and the Fate of the West* (New York: W. W. Norton, 2017).

51 Mikael Rothstein and Klaus Rothstein, *The Bomb in the Turban* (Copenhagen: Tiderne Skifter, 2006), 32.

52 Jytte Klausen, *The Cartoons That Shook the World* (New Haven: Yale University Press, 2009), 35; Hassan M. Fattah, "Caricature of Muhammad Leads to Boycott of Danish Goods," *New York Times*, January 31, 2006, www.nytimes.com/2006/01/31/world/mid dleeast/caricature-of-muhammad-leads-to-boycott-of-danish-goods.html.

53 Ibid.

54 Christina Capatides, "Which European Countries Have Produced the Most ISIS Fighters?," CBS News, January 26, 2016, www.cbsnews.com/news/isis-terror-recruiting-europe-belgium-france-denmark-sweden-germany/.

CHAPTER 5

1 William Macpherson, *The Stephen Lawrence Inquiry*, parliamentary paper (London: Home Office, February 24, 1999), www.gov.uk/government/publications/the-stephen-lawrence-inquiry.

2 United Kingdom, House of Commons, "Immigration," *Hansard Parliamentary Debates*, 6th ser., vol. 401, cols. 270–94WH, March 19, 2003.

3 United Kingdom, House of Commons, "Commonwealth Immigrants Bill," *Hansard Parliamentary Debates*, 5th ser., vol. 649, cols. 687–819, November 16, 1961 (Rab Butler, Home Secretary).

4 "Dockers on the March for Powell," *Evening Times*, April 23, 1968, https://news.google.com/newspapers?id=zudYAAAAIBAJ&sjid=AosMAAAAIBAJ&pg=1643,7221622.

5 E. P. Thompson, *The Making of the English Working Class* (London: Penguin Books, 1980).

6 Eliot Joseph Benn Rose and Nicholas Deakin, *Colour and Citizenship: A Report on British Race Relations* (Oxford: Oxford University Press, 1969).

7 Jill Rutter, *Moving up and Getting On* (Bristol: Policy Press, 2016).

8 "The Size of the European Muslim Population in 2050 Depends Largely on the Future of Migration," Pew Research Center, December 1, 2017, www.pewresearch.org/fact-tank/2017/12/04/europes-muslim-population-will-continue-to-grow-but-how-much-depends-on-migra tion/ft_17-12-04_muslimpopulation_thesize_1/.

9 "Birth Characteristics in England and Wales," Office for National Statistics, released October 21, 2016, www.ons.gov.uk/peoplepopulationandcommunity/birthsdeathsandmar riages/livebirths/bulletins/birthcharacteristicsinenglandandwales/2015.

10 "The 1958 Race Riots of Notting Hill," My Notting Hill, www.mynottinghill.co.uk/the-1958-race-riots-of-notting-hill/; "1976: The Notting Hill Carnivals," libcom, posted September 19, 2006, https://libcom.org/history/1976-the-notting-hill-carnival-riots.

11 Adrian Wooldridge (Bagehot), "Muscle v Multiculturalism," *The Economist*, February 10, 2011, www.economist.com/britain/2011/02/10/muscle-v-multiculturalism.

12 Ibid.

13 Ibid. According to *The Economist*, as far back as 2009, the then Labour Government had resolved to abandon the "'covenant of security' under which authorities left the Islamists alone as long as they did not plan domestic attacks."

14 Ibid.

15 Trevor Phillips et al., *Race and Faith: The Deafening Silence* (London: Civitas, 2016), 2–4.

16 Frances Perraudin, "Half of All British Muslims Think Homosexuality Should Be Illegal, Poll Finds," *The Guardian*, April 11, 2016, www.theguardian.com/uk-news/2016/apr/11/british-muslims-strong-sense-of-belonging-poll-homosexuality-sharia-law.

17 Trevor Phillips, "This Life and Death Struggle: In a Stark Analysis, Former Equalities Chief Reveals How Extremist Ideas Have Been Allowed to Flourish," interviewed by the *Daily Mail*, April 10, 2016.

18 Liam Stack, "Poll of British Muslims Reveals Startling Views, but Some Question Methodology," *New York Times*, April 14, 2016, www.nytimes.com/2016/04/15/world/europe/poll-british-muslims.html.

19 "Integration Nation," *The Economist*, May 21, 2016, www.economist.com/britain/2016/05/21/integration-nation.

20 Ibid.

21 Ibid.

22 Ibid.

23 Rutter, *Moving up and Getting On*, 44–63.

24 Neil Johnson, "The Rise of the Precariat," *Economia*, ICAEW, June 2, 2017, https://economia.icaew.com/features/june-2017/the-rise-of-the-precariat.

25 Lords Select Committee, "Time to Act on 'Unacceptable' Level of UK Financial Exclusion," March 25, 2017, www.parliament.uk/business/committees/committees-a-z/lords-select/financial-exclusion/news-parliament-2015/financial-exclusion-report-published/.

26 Helen Barnard, "UK Poverty 2017," Joseph Rowntree Foundation, December 4, 2017, www.jrf.org.uk/report/uk-poverty-2017.

27 Joseph Rowntree Foundation, "UK Poverty 2018," JRF Analysis Unit, December 4, 2018, www.jrf.org.uk/report/uk-poverty-2018.

28 Ibid., 21–23; Adrian Wooldridge (Bagehot), "Of Foreigners and Families," *The Economist*, October 15, 2011, www.economist.com/britain/2011/10/15/of-foreigners-and-families.

29 "Integration Nation." *The Economist*, May 21, 2016, www.economist.com/britain/2016/05/21/integration-nation.

30 United Kingdom, Home Office, "Prevent Strategy," policy paper, HM Government, June 2011, www.gov.uk/government/uploads/system/uploads/attachment_data/file/97976/prevent-strategy-review.pdf.

31 "Preparing for the Worst," *The Economist*, May 21, 2016, www.economist.com/britain/2016/05/21/preparing-for-the-worst.

32 "10 Stylish Hijabs Made by and for Muslim Women," *Elle*, August 1, 2016, www.elle.com/uk/fashion/news/a28848/10-stylish-hijabs-made-by-and-for-muslim-women/.

33 "Modesty Sells," *The Economist*, June 2, 2016, www.economist.com/britain/2016/06/02/modesty-sells.

34 United Kingdom, Home Office, "Prevent Strategy."

35 Catherine Fieschi and Nick Johnson, "Islam and Muslim Communities in the UK: Multiculturalism, Faith and Security," *The International Spectator* 48 (2013): 97–100.

36 United Kingdom, Home Office, "Prevent Strategy."

37 Lord Carlile, "Report to the Home Secretary of Independent Oversight of Prevent Review and Strategy," HM Government, 2011.

38 Ibid., 3.

39 Ibid., 1.

40 Adrian Wooldridge (Bagehot), "Battlefields of the Mind," *The Economist*, June 7, 2016, www.economist.com/britain/2016/01/07/battlefields-of-the-mind. "Suspicion among Muslims is matched by bewilderment among public servants. London teachers whom Bagehot asked about their new role said they felt overwhelmed: the complexity of modern British Islam."

41 "Most British Muslims 'Oppose Muhammad Cartoon Reprisals,'" BBC, February 2015, www.bbc.com/news/uk-31293196.

42 Ian Cobain, "UK's Prevent Counter-Radicalisation Policy 'Badly Flawed,'" *The Guardian*, October 18, 2016, www.theguardian.com/uk-news/2016/oct/19/uks-prevent-counter-radicalisation-policy-badly-flawed.

43 Ibid.

44 Damien Gayle, "Prevent Strategy 'Could End Up Promoting Extremism,'" *The Guardian*, April 21, 2016, www.theguardian.com/politics/2016/apr/21/government-prevent-strategy-promoting-extremism-maina-kiai.

45 Sima Kotecha, "More Than 400 Children under 10 Referred for 'Deradicalisation,'" BBC *News*, January 21, 2016, www.bbc.com/news/uk-35360375; Nation Police Chief's Council, 000026/16, March 7, 2016.

46 Rachel Shabi, "Deradicalising Britain: The Activists Turning Young Muslims away from Extremism," *The Guardian*, March 18, 2016, www.theguardian.com/uk-news/2016/mar/18/deradicalising-britain-the-activists-turning-young-muslims-away-from-extremism.

47 Theresa May, "Counter-Terrorism," speech, November 24, 2014, Home Office, www.gov.uk/government/speeches/home-secretary-theresa-may-on-counter-terrorism.

48 Cobain, "UK's Prevent Counter-Radicalisation Policy 'Badly Flawed.'"

49 Robert Mendick et al., "Security Services Missed Five Opportunities to Stop the Manchester Bomber," *The Telegraph*, June 6, 2017, www.telegraph.co.uk/news/2017/05/24/security-services-missed-five-opportunities-stop-manchester/.

50 Cobain, "UK's Prevent Counter-Radicalisation Policy 'Badly Flawed.'"

51 Sayeeda Warsi, "Sayeeda Warsi on New UK Counter-Extremism Chief: 'She's Not Going to Change Hearts and Minds,'" interviewed by Julia Rampen, *New Statesman America* (January 26, 2018), www.newstatesman.com/politics/uk/2018/01/sayeeda-warsi-new-uk-counter-extremism-chief-she-s-not-going-change-hearts-and.

52 Ibid.

53 Simon Hooper, "Exclusive: UK Government to Introduce 'Mandatory Deradicalisation' Scheme," *Middle East Eye*, July 22, 2016, www.middleeasteye.net/news/exclusive-uk-government-introduce-mandatory-deradicalisation-scheme-746303354.

54 Perraudin, "Half of All British Muslims Think Homosexuality Should Be Illegal."

55 Ibid.

56 Rutter, *Moving up and Getting On*, 141.

57 "Indicators of Immigrant Integration 2015: Settling in," Organisation for Economic Cooperation and Development, 2016, www.oecd.org/els/mig/press-note-UK.pdf.

58 "Native-Born Unemployment," Organisation for Economic Cooperation and Development data, 2016, www.oecd.org/els/mig/press-note-UK.pdf.

59 Ruud Koopmans, "Trade-Offs between Equality and Difference: Immigrant Integration, Multiculturalism and the Welfare State in Cross-National Perspective," *Journal of Ethnic and Migration Studies* 36 (2010): 14–18.

60 Ibid., 7–9.

61 Stefan Trines, "Lessons from Germany's Refugee Crisis: Integration, Cost, and Benefits," WENR, May, 2, 2017, https://wenr.wes.org/2017/05/lessons-germanys-refugee-crisis-integra tion-costs-benefits.

62 John R. Bowen, *On British Islam: Religion, Law, and Everyday Practice in Shari'a Councils* (Princeton: Princeton University Press, 2016), 16.

63 Adrian Wooldridge (Bagehot), "Let the Work Permits Flow," *The Economist*, January 21, 2017, 48.

64 "Straws in the Wind," *The Economist*, July 16, 2016, www.economist.com/britain/2016/07/16/straws-in-the-wind.

65 Employment and Social Affairs, "UK Chooses Brexit," chart, StatistaCharts, June 27, 2016, www.newslettereuropean.eu/united-kingdom-more-divided-than-ever-after-brexit-referen dum/; Oliver Hawkins and Anna Moses, "Polish Population of the United Kingdom," House of Commons Library, CBP7660, July 15, 2016.

66 Wooldridge (Bagehot), "Let the Work Permits Flow," 48.

67 Theresa May, "2012 Speech on Immigration," December 12, 2012, Home Office, www.ukpol.co.uk/theresa-may-2012-speech-on-immigration/.

68 James Slack, "Windrush Crisis: Home Office Admits Destroying Thousands of Migrant Landing Cards amid Deportation Fears," *The Guardian*, April 12, 2018, www.theguardian.com/uk-news/2018/apr/17/home-office-destroyed-windrush-landing-cards-says-ex-staffer.

69 Brendan O'Neill, "Why Theresa May Is to Blame for the Windrush Scandal," *The Spectator*, April 17, 2018, https://blogs.spectator.co.uk/2018/04/why-theresa-may-is-to-blame-for-the-windrush-scandal/.

70 Anthony Wells, "Where the Public Stands on Immigration," YouGov, April 27, 2018, https://yougov.co.uk/topics/politics/articles-reports/2018/04/27/where-public-stands-immigration.

71 "Windrush: Theresa May Hits Back at Labour over Landing Cards," BBC, April 18, 2018, http://bbc.com/news/uk-politics-43806710.

72 Rory Smith, "Mo Salah of Liverpool Breaks Down Cultural Barriers, One Goal at a Time," *New York Times*, May 2, 2018, www.nytimes.com/2018/05/02/world/europe/mo-salah-liverpool-champions-league.html.

73 Ibid.

74 Ibid. Rory Smith quoting Neil Atkinson, who hosts a Liverpool fans' podcast.

75 Adrian Wooldridge (Bagehot), "Pierogi and the British Genius," *The Economist*, January 7, 2017, 36.

76 Ibid.

77 Ibid; Rutter, *Moving up and Getting On*, 305.

CHAPTER 6

1 Jonathan Laurence, *The Emancipation of Europe's Muslims* (Princeton: Princeton University Press, 2012), 121.

2 Nicolas Sarkozy, speech at the French Interior Ministry, 2003.

3 Ian Traynor, "Sarkozy Defends Switzerland Minaret Ban," *The Guardian*, December 8, 2009, www.theguardian.com/world/2009/dec/08/sarkozy-sympathises-minaret-ban-switzerland.

4 Paul Mirengoff, "Sarkozy's Message to France's Muslims – The Good, the Bad, and the Ugly," *Powerline*, December 10, 2009, www.powerlineblog.com/archives/2009/12/025126 .php.

5 Angelique Chrisafis, "Nicolas Sarkozy: There Are Too Many Foreigners in France," *The Guardian*, March 7, 2012, www.theguardian.com/world/2012/mar/07/nicolas-sarkozy-too-many-foreigners.

6 Henry Samuel, "Nicolas Sarkozy Says Immigrants Must Accept 'Your Ancestors Are the Gauls,'" *The Telegraph*, September 20, 2016, www.telegraph.co.uk/news/2016/09/20/nico las-sarkozy-says-immigrants-should-live-like-the-french/.

7 Angelique Chrisafis, "Nicolas Sarkozy: There Are Too Many Foreigners in France," *The Guardian*, March 7, 2012, www.theguardian.com/world/2012/mar/07/nicolas-sarkozy-too-many-foreigners.

8 Harriet Sherwood, "More than Half UK Population Has No Religion, Finds Survey," *The Guardian*, September 4, 2017, www.theguardian.com/world/2017/sep/04/half-uk-popula tion-has-no-religion-british-social-attitudes-survey.

9 Sylvie Kauffmann, "God Is Back – In France," *New York Times*, January 26, 2017, www.nytimes.com/2017/01/26/opinion/god-is-back-in-france.html.

10 Consider John E. Craig, *Scholarship and Nation Building* (Chicago: University of Chicago Press, 1984); Stephen L. Harp, *Learning to Be Loyal: Primary Schooling as Nation Building in Alsace and Lorraine, 1850–1940* (DeKalb: Northern Illinois University Press, 1998).

11 Chris McGreal, "Shameful Legacy," *The Guardian*, October 13, 2006, www.theguardian .com/politics/2006/oct/13/kenya.foreignpolicy.

12 Alistair Horne, *A Savage War of Peace: Algeria 1954–1962* (New York: New York Review of Books, 2006).

13 George Packer, "The Other France," *The New Yorker*, August 31, 2015, www.newyorker .com/magazine/2015/08/31/the-other-france.

14 Paul Lewis, "The Jews of France," *New York Times*, October 9, 1983, www.nytimes.com/ 1983/10/09/magazine/the-jews-of-france.html.

15 Frederick Cooper, *Citizenship between Empire and Nation: Remaking France and French Africa, 1945–1960* (Princeton: Princeton University Press, 2014), 15–16.

16 Adam Shatz, "How Did We End Up Here?," *London Review of Books* blog, April 5, 2016, www.lrb.co.uk/blog/2016/04/05/adam-shatz/how-did-we-end-up-here/.

17 Ibid.

18 Ibid.

19 Quoted in Joan W. Scott, *The Politics of the Veil* (Princeton: Princeton University Press, 2007) 46.

20 Mark Lilla, "France: A Strange Defeat," *New York Review of Books*, March 19, 2015, www.nybooks.com/articles/2015/03/19/france-strange-defeat/.

21 Ibid.

22 Ibid.

23 Ibid.

24 Angelique Chrisafis, "Right-Wing 'New Reactionaries' Stir Up Trouble among French Intellectuals," *The Guardian*, October 9, 2015, www.theguardian.com/world/2015/oct/09/right-wing-new-reactionaries-stir-up-trouble-among-french-intellectuals.

25 Mathieu von Rohr and Romain Leick, "There Is a Clash of Civilizations," interview with Alain Finkielkraut, *Spiegel Online*, December 6, 2013, www.spiegel.de/international/world/interview-french-philosopher-finkielkraut-on-muslims-and-integration-a-937404-2.html.

26 Ibid.

27 Ibid.

28 Ibid.

29 Celestine Bohlen, "Study Finds Children of Immigrants Embracing 'Frenchness,'" *New York Times*, January 25, 2016, www.nytimes.com/2016/01/26/world/europe/study-finds-children-of-immigrants-embracing-frenchness.html.

30 Mathieu von Rohr and Romain Leick, "There Is a Clash of Civilizations," interview with Alain Finkielkraut, *Spiegel Online*, December 6, 2013, www.spiegel.de/international/world/interview-french-philosopher-finkielkraut-on-muslims-and-integration-a-937404-2.html.

31 Shatz, "How Did We End Up Here?"

32 Alissa J. Rubin, "Attack on Nice Turns Spotlight on City's Religious Divisions," *New York Times*, July 17, 2016, www.nytimes.com/2016/07/18/world/europe/muslims-nice-france-terrorism.html.

33 Ibid.

34 Ibid.

35 Jean-Philippe Ksiazek, "After Charlie Hebdo Attack, 'Panic' over Future Spreading in Poor Muslim Suburbs of Paris," *National Post*, January 9, 2015.

36 Michael Cosgrove, "How Does France Count Its Muslim Population?," *Le Figaro*, April 7, 2011, http://plus.lefigaro.fr/note/how-does-france-count-its-muslim-population-20110407-435643.

37 Jonathan Laurence, *The Emancipation of Europe's Muslims* (Princeton: Princeton University Press, 2012), 121.
   Nicolas Sarkozy, speech at the French Interior Ministry, 2003.

38 Tom Farer, "Terrorism, Communalism and Democracy: The Limits of Tolerance," in *Confronting Global Terrorism and American Neo-Conservatism: The Framework of a Liberal Grand Strategy* (Oxford: Oxford University Press, 2008), 128–157.

39 George Packer, "The Other France," *The New Yorker*, August 31, 2015, www.newyorker.com/magazine/2015/08/31/the-other-france.

40 Ron Grossman, "When Japanese-Americans Were Sent to Internment Camps," *Chicago Tribune*, February 9, 2017, www.chicagotribune.com/news/opinion/commentary/ct-japanese-internment-camps-war-trump-roosevelt-flashback-perspec-0212-jm-20170208-story.html.

41 Christopher de Bellaigue, "France at War," *New York Review of Books*, July 21, 2016, www.nybooks.com/daily/2016/07/21/france-at-war-after-nice-rightward-shift/.

42 Adam Nossiter, "'That Ignoramus': 2 French Scholars of Radical Islam Turn Bitter Rivals," *New York Times* (July 12, 2016), www.nytimes.com/2016/07/13/world/europe/france-radical-islam.html.

43 Olivier Roy, *Secularism Confronts Islam* (West Sussex: Columbia University Press, 2007); Gilles Kepel, *Terror in France: The Rise of Jihad in the West* (Princeton: Princeton University Press, 2017).

44 Mark Lilla, "France: Is There a Way Out?," *New York Review of Books*, March 10, 2016, www.nybooks.com/articles/2016/03/10/france-is-there-a-way-out/.

45 Olivier Roy, "France's Oedipal Islamist Complex," *Foreign Policy* (January 7, 2016), https://foreignpolicy.com/2016/01/07/frances-oedipal-islamist-complex-charlie-hebdo-islamic-state-isis/.

46 Olivier Roy, "The Islamization of Radicalism," *Rosa Luxemburg Stiftung – North Africa Office*, June 2016.

47 Ibid.

48 Ibid.

49 Ibid.

50 Ibid.

51 Roy, "France's Oedipal Islamic Complex."

52 Ibid.

53 Ibid.

54 Ibid.

55 An estimated 800,000 out of a total Muslim population of 4.7 million. See Statista, "Population in France in 2010 by Religious Affiliation," 2018, www.statista.com/statistics/459982/population-distribution-religion-france/; Pierre Vermeren, "Faced with Islam of France, from Denial to Paralysis," *L'express*, June 3, 2014, www.lexpress.fr/actualite/face-a-l-islam-de-france-du-deni-a-la-paralysie_1548482.html.

56 Roy, "France's Oedipal Islamic Complex."

57 Cyrus Adler, *The Jewish Encyclopedia: A Descriptive Record of the History, Religion, Literature, and Customs of the Jewish People from the Earliest Times to the Present Day* (New York: Funk & Wagnalls, 1907).

58 Karina Piser, "A New Plan to Create an 'Islam of France,'" *The Atlantic*, March 29, 2018, www.theatlantic.com/international/archive/2018/03/islam-france-macron/556604/.

59 Myriam Francois, "Olivier Roy on Laicite as Ideology, the Myth of 'National Identity' and Racism in the French Republic," *Jadaliyya*, May 20, 2015.

60 Ian Buruma, "Tariq Ramadan Has an Identity Issue," *New York Times Magazine*, February 4, 2007, www.nytimes.com/2007/02/04/magazine/04ramadan.t.html?mtrref=www.google.com&gwh=17EFC77183F116A84465D9D62B9914A6&gwt=pay.

61 The American Presidency Project, "2016 Republican Party Platform," July 18, 2016, www.presidency.ucsb.edu/ws/index.php?pid=117718.

62 Tom Heneghan, "French Muslims Join Opposition to Same-Sex Marriage," Reuters, January 7, 2013, https://uk.reuters.com/article/uk-france-marriage-muslim/french-muslims-join-opposition-to-same-sex-marriage-idUKBRE9060IX20130107.

63 Ian Johnson, "How the State Is Co-opting Religion in China," *Foreign Affairs*, January 7, 2019, www.foreignaffairs.com/articles/china/2019-01-07/how-state-co-opting-religion-china.

64 Joseph Conrad, *The Secret Agent* (Hertfordshire: Wordsworth, 1993).

65 Kepel, *Terror in France*, 2.

66 Ibid., 66.

67 Ibid.

68 Ibid., 21.
69 Ibid., 5.
70 Ibid., 66.
71 Ibid., 198.
72 Ibid.
73 Adam Nossiter, "Sons of Immigrants Prop up a Symbol of 'Frenchness': The Baguette," *New York Times*, May 14, 2018, https://nyti.ms/2GejGcE.
74 Ibid.

CHAPTER 7

1 Mike Berardino, "Mike Tyson Explains One of His Most Famous Quotes," quoted in *Sun Sentinel*, November 9, 2012, www.sun-sentinel.com/sports/fl-xpm-2012-11-09-sfl-mike-tyson-explains-one-of-his-most-famous-quotes-20121109-story.html.
2 Shadi Hamid, "The Rise of Anti-liberalism," Brookings, February 21, 2018, www.brookings.edu/blog/order-from-chaos/2018/02/21/the-rise-of-anti-liberalism/.
3 Daron Acemoglu, "Technology and Inequality," National Bureau of Economic Research (2003), www.nber.org/reporter/winter03/technologyandinequality.html.
4 Adam Nossiter, "As France's Towns Wither, Fears of a Decline in 'Frenchness,'" *New York Times*, February 28, 2017, www.nytimes.com/2017/02/28/world/europe/france-albi-french-towns-fading.html.
5 Quoted in Thomas Chatterton Williams, "The French Origins of 'You Will Not Replace Us,'" *The New Yorker*, December 4, 2017, www.newyorker.com/magazine/2017/12/04/the-french-origins-of-you-will-not-replace-us?mbid=ni_Daily%20112817%20Subs&CNDID=29104.
6 Ibid.
7 Tony Judt, "What Have We Learned, if Anything?," *New York Review of Books*, May 1, 2008, www.nybooks.com/articles/2008/05/01/what-have-we-learned-if-anything/.
8 "In Europe, Right-Wing Parties Are Offering Bigger Handouts than Traditional Ones," *The Economist*, January 25, 2018, www.economist.com/europe/2018/01/25/in-europe-right-wing-parties-are-offering-bigger-handouts-than-traditional-ones.
9 Charlie Cooper, "Tony Blair Institute: 'Wave of Populism Not Yet Peaked,'" *Politico*, December 29, 2017, www.politico.eu/article/tony-blair-institute-wave-of-populism-not-yet-peaked/.
10 Tim Bayle of Queen Mary University in London, quoted in "A Dangerous Waltz," *The Economist*, February 3, 2018, 19.
11 Rita Chin, *The Crisis of Multiculturalism in Europe: A History* (Princeton: Princeton University Press, 2017), 304.
12 Ibid., 305.
13 Ibid.
14 Ibid.
15 Jill Rutter, *Moving up and Getting On* (Bristol: Policy Press, 2016), 72.
16 Ibid., 6.

17 Stefan Trines, "Lessons from Germany's Refugee Crisis: Integration, Cost, and Benefits," WENR, May 2, 2017, https://wenr.wes.org/2017/05/lessons-germanys-refugee-crisis-integra tion-costs-benefits.

18 United Nations, Office of the High Commissioner on Human Rights, *International Covenant on Civil and Political Rights*, Art. 12, Para. 1.

19 *R (Kiarie) v. Secretary of State for the Home Department*, [2017] UKSC 42.

20 Krishnadev Calamur, "The End of the Plan to Strip French Terrorists of Their Citizen- ship," *The Atlantic*, March 30, 2016, www.theatlantic.com/international/archive/2016/03/ france-citizenship-law-dropped/475980/.

21 United Nations, Office of the High Commissioner for Refugees, *Convention Relating to the Status of Refugees*, Art. 1, Sec. D, G.A. Res. 429(V), December 14, 1950, accessed July 10, 2018, www.unhcr.org/en-us/3b66c2aa10.

22 Johanna L. Wiese and Katharine Thorpe, "Temporary and Circular Migration: Empirical Evidence, Current Policy Practice and Future Options in EU Member States," UK Border Agency, https://ec.europa.eu/home-affairs/sites/homeaffairs/files/what-we-do/networks/euro pean_migration_network/reports/docs/emn-studies/circular-migration/27._united_king dom_national_report_circular_migration_final_version_15_april_2011_en.pdf, 13–15.

23 "When a man knows he is to be hanged in a fortnight, it concentrates his mind wonderfully," according to Samuel Johnson, in James Boswell, *The Life of Samuel Johnson* (London: Penguin Classics, 2008), 612.

24 Mark Lilla, "The End of Identity Liberalism," *New York Times*, March 18, 2018, www.nytimes .com/2016/11/20/opinion/sunday/the-end-of-identity-liberalism.html; Margot Wallström, "Cul- ture Is Not an Excuse for Oppressing Women," *The Economist*, June 25, 2018, www.econo mist.com/open-future/2018/06/25/culture-is-not-an-excuse-for-oppressing-women.

25 Statista, "Germany: Share of Economic Sectors in Gross Domestic Product (GDP) in 2017," 2018, www.statista.com/statistics/295519/germany-share-of-economic-sectors-in-gross- domestic-product/.

26 Rafaela Dancygier, *Dilemmas of Inclusion: Muslims in European Politics* (Princeton: Princeton University Press, 2017), 51–63.

27 Ibid., 52.

28 Jytte Klausen, *The Islamic Challenge: Politics and Religion in Western Europe* (Oxford: Oxford University Press, 2005).

29 Robert A. Dahl, *Preface to a Democratic Theory* (Chicago: University of Chicago Press, 1956).

30 Robert A. Dahl, *On Democracy* (New Haven: Yale University Press, 1998), 76–77.

CHAPTER 8

1 "Can Refugees Help to Plug Europe's Skilled-Labour Gaps?," *The Economist*, June 14, 2018, www.economist.com/finance-and-economics/2018/06/14/can-refugees-help-to-plug-europes- skilled-labour-gaps.

2 Norimitsu Onishi, "In Japan, the Elderly often Live, and Die Alone," *Seattle Times*, November 30, 2017, www.seattletimes.com/nation-world/in-japan-the-elderly-often-live- and-die-alone/.

3 "52% of Startups in Silicon Valley Founded by at Least One Immigrant," Becker & Lee LLP, 2019, www.blimmigration.com/52-startups-silicon-valley-founded-least-one-immi grant/.

4 John Gramlich, "5 facts about Crime in the U.S.," Pew Research Center, January 3, 2019, www.pewresearch.org/fact-tank/2019/01/03/5-facts-about-crime-in-the-u-s/.

5 Adam Nossiter, "At French Outpost in African Migrant Hub, Asylum for a Select Few," *New York Times*, February 25, 2018, www.nytimes.com/2018/02/25/world/africa/france-africa-migrants-asylum-niger.html.

6 Ibid.

7 Margaret Thatcher, interview for *Woman's Own*, October 31, 1987, Margaret Thatcher Foundation, www.margaretthatcher.org/document/106689.

8 As quoted in Jill Lepore, "A New Americanism," *Foreign Affairs* 98, no. 2 (March/April 2019): 10, at 11.

9 Trevor Phillips, "Poll: What Muslims Really Think," *ICM Unlimited*, April 2016, www.icmunlimited.com/polls/icm-muslims-survey-for-channel-4/.

10 Aida Just and Christopher J. Anderson, "Dual Allegiances? Immigrants' Attitudes toward Immigration," *The Journal of Politics* 77 (January 2015): 188–201.

11 Chris Lawton and Robert Ackrill, "Hard Evidence: How Areas with Low Immigration Voted Mainly for Brexit," The Conversation, July 8, 2016. http://the conversation.com/hard-evidence-how-areas-with-low-immigration-voted-mainly-for-brexit-6.

12 World Bank, "Fertility Rate, Total (Births per Woman)," International Labour Organiza-tion, *ILOSTAT Database*, accessed March 23, 2019, https://data.worldbank.org/indicator/sp.dyn.tfrt.in.

13 Jodi Kantor and Catrin Einhorn, "Canadians Adopted Refugee Families for a Year: Then Came 'Month 13,'" *New York Times*, March 26, 2017, https://nyti.ms/2nPCn11.

14 Ibid.

15 See Randall Hansen and Patrick Weill, eds., *Towards a European Nationality: Citizenship, Immigration and Nationality Law in the EU* (New York: Palgrave, 2001) p. 17.

16 Richard Alba and Nancy Foner urge this move in their important work *Strangers No More: Immigration and the Challenges of Integration in North America and Western Europe* (Princeton: Princeton University Press, 2015), p. 242.

17 Lillian Mongeau, "Why Does America Invest so Little in Its Children?," *The Atlantic*, July 12, 2016, www.theatlantic.com/education/archive/2016/07/why-does-america-invest-so-little-in-its-children/490790/.

18 OECD "Jobs for Immigrants: Labour Market Integration in Norway," www.oecd.org/els/mig/43247521.pdf, 63. This study draws on 2008 figures. Since there has been heavy humanitarian migration in the past eleven years and humanitarian migrants tend to have much more difficulty integrating than economic migrants, the relevant numbers could easily be worse today since there has not been a fundamental change in the methods and institutions for integration.

19 Ibid.

20 David Chazan, "Macron's National Service Programme Dismissed as 'Big Teenagers' Party,'" *The Telegraph*, October 27, 2018, www.telegraph.co.uk/news/2018/10/27/macrons-national-service-programme-dismissed-big-teenagers-party/.

21 United Nations, Office of the High Commissioner on Human Rights, *International Covenant on Civil and Political Rights*, Art. 10, Para. 3.

22 Yascha Mounk, "How a Teen's Death Has Become a Political Weapon," *The New Yorker*, www.newyorker.com/magazine/2019/01/28/how-a-teens-death-has-become-a-political-weapon?mbid=nl_Daily%20012319&CNDID=29190489.

23 Jacob McCleland, "The High Costs of High Security at Supermax Prisons," National Public Radio, June 19, 2012, www.npr.org/2012/06/19/155359553/the-high-costs-of-high-security-at-supermax-prisons.

24 See, e.g., Shaila Dewan, "The Violence of Prison," *New York Times*, March 30, 2019, A19.

25 Press Association, "UK 'Has Stripped 150 Jihadists and Criminals of Citizenship,'" *The Guardian*, July 30, 2017, www.theguardian.com/uk-news/2017/jul/30/uk-has-stripped-150-jihadists-and-criminals-of-citizenship.

26 Rukmini Callimachi, "ISIS Enshrines a Theology of Rape," *New York Times*, August 13, 2015, https://nyti.ms/1TucUEA.

27 Uzma S. Burney, "European Court of Human Rights Upholds France's Ban on the Full-Face Veil," American Society of International Law, *Insights* 19 (2015), www.asil.org/insights/volume/19/issue/3/european-court-human-rights-upholds-frances-ban-full-face-veil.

28 *Financial Times*, March 26, 2017, www.ft.com/content/838d60c2-0961-11e-97d1-5e720a-267716.

29 Assaf Razin, "The Aging, Crisis-Prone Welfare State Must Confront the Problem of Welfare Migration," *Business Insider*, October 27, 2010, www.businessinsider.com/assaf-razin-on-us-demographics-2010-10.

30 "Sweden Is in a Strong Position to Integrate Refugees, but Support for the Low Skilled Needs to Be Strengthened," Organisation for Economic Cooperation and Development, May 13, 2016, www.oecd.org/sweden/sweden-in-a-strong-position-to-integrate-refugees-but-support-for-the-low-skilled-needs-to-be-strengthened.htm.

31 "The Little Noticed Transformation of Islam in the West," *The Economist*, February 16, 2019, www.economist.com/leaders/2019/02/16/the-little-noticed-transformation-of-islam-in-the-west.

32 Melissa Eddy and Mark Scott, "Delete Hate Speech or Pay up, Germany Tells Social Media Companies," *New York Times*, June 30, 2017, www.nytimes.com/2017/06/30/business/germany-facebook-google-twitter.html.

33 Francis Fukuyama, "The End of History?," *The National Interest* 16 (Summer 1989): 17–18.

34 Ibid.

35 Jill Lapore, "A New Americanism: Why a Nation Needs a National Story," *Foreign Policy*, March 2019, www.foreignaffairs.com/articles/united-states/2019-02-05/new-americanism-nationalism-jill-lepore.

36 Max Bearak, "Theresa May Criticized the Term 'Citizen of the World.' But Half the World Identifies That Way," *Washington Post*, October 5, 2016, www.washingtonpost.com/news/worldviews/wp/2016/10/05/theresa-may-criticized-the-term-citizen-of-the-world-but-half-the-world-identifies-that-way/?utm_term=.3903b255d208.

Bibliography

Adler, Cyrus. *The Jewish Encyclopedia: A Descriptive Record of the History, Religion, Literature, and Customs of the Jewish People from the Earliest Times to the Present Day*. New York: Funk & Wagnalls, 1907.

Akkerman, Tjitske and Hagelund, Anniken. "'Women and Children First!' Anti-immigration Parties and Gender in Norway and the Netherland." *Patterns of Prejudice* 41 (2007): 197–214.

Alba, Richard and Foner, Nancy. *Strangers No More: Immigration and the Challenges of Integration in North America and Western Europe*. Princeton: Princeton University Press 2015.

The American Presidency Project. "2016 Republican Party Platform." July 18, 2016. www.presidency.ucsb.edu/ws/index.php?pid=117718.

Amis, Martin. "Fear and Loathing." *The Guardian*. September 18, 2001. www.theguardian.com/world/2001/sep/18/september11.politicsphilosophyandsociety.

Anand, Utkarsh. "Need to Relocate Evicted Slum Dwellers." *The Indian Express*. February 12, 2010. https://indianexpress.com/article/cities/delhi/need-to-relocate-evicted-slumdwellers/.

Anderson, Benedict R. O'G. *Imagined Communities: Reflections on the Origin and Spread of Nationalism*. Rev. ed. London: Verso, 2006.

Aristotle. Politics. In *Introduction to Aristotle*, edited by Richard McKeon. New York: Random House, 1947.

Assaah, Ragui and Roudi-Fahimi, Farzaneh. "Youth in the Middle East and North Africa: Demographic Opportunity or Challenge?" PRB (April 2007). Accessed January 18, 2019. www.prb.org/youthinmena/.

Baczynska, Gabriela. "Mosque Building Brings Islam Fears to Poland." *Reuters*. April 1, 2010. www.reuters.com/article/us-poland-mosque/mosque-building-brings-islam-fears-to-poland-idUSTRE6302VN20100401.

Bagehot. "Battlefields of the Mind." *The Economist*. June 7, 2016. www.economist.com/britain/2016/01/07/battlefields-of-the-mind.

"Of Foreigners and Families." *The Economist*. October 15, 2011. –www.economist.com/britain/2011/10/15/of-foreigners-and-families.

"Let the Work Permits Flow." *The Economist*. January 21, 2017.

"Muscle v Multiculturalism." *The Economist*. February 10, 2011. www.economist.com/britain/2011/02/10/muscle-v-multiculturalism.

"Pierogi and the British Genius." *The Economist.* January 7, 2017.

Barry, Brian. *Culture and Equality: An Egalitarian Critique of Multiculturalism.* Cambridge: Polity, 2001.

"Second Thoughts – And Some First Thoughts Revived." In *Multiculturalism Reconsidered: Culture and Equality and Its Critics,* edited by Paul Kelly, 205–238. Cambridge: Polity, 2002.

BBC. "Ceuta and Melilla: Spain Wants Rid of Anti-Migrant Razor Wire." BBC News. June 14, 2018. www.bbc.com/news/world-europe-44485995.

"Europe Migrant Crisis: EU Blamed for 'Soaring' Death Toll." July 6, 2017. www.bbc.com/news/world-europe-40515054.

"Most British Muslims 'Oppose Muhammad Cartoon Reprisals.'" February 2015. www.bbc.com/news/uk-31293196.

"Windrush: Theresa May Hits Back at Labour over Landing Cards." April 18, 2018. http://bbc.com/news/uk-politics-43806710.

Bearak, Max. "Theresa May Criticized the Term 'Citizen of the World.' But Half the World Identifies That Way." *Washington Post.* October 5, 2016, www.washingtonpost.com/news/worldviews/wp/2016/10/05/theresa-may-criticized-the-term-citizen-of-the-world-but-half-the-world-identifies-that-way/?utm_term=.3903b255d208.

Becker & Lee LLP. "52% of Startups in Silicon Valley Founded by at Least One Immigrant." Becker & Lee LLP. 2019. www.blimmigration.com/52-startups-silicon-valley-founded-least-one-immigrant/.

Benhabib, Seyla. *The Claims of Culture: Equality and Diversity in the Global Era.* Princeton: Princeton University Press, 2002.

Berman, Russell. "The New Crackdown on Migrant Families." *The Atlantic.* January 5, 2016. www.theatlantic.com/politics/archive/2016/01/the-obama-administrations-crackdown-on-central-american-migrants/422550/.

Berry, Mike, et al. "Press Coverage of the Refugee and Migrant Crisis in the EU: A Content Analysis of Five European Countries." United Nations High Commissioner for Refugees. December 2015. www.unhcr.org/56bb369c9.pdf.

Bertram, Christopher. "Reforming Refuge." *New Humanist* (Autumn 2017). https://newhumanist.org.uk/articles/5224/reforming-refuge.

Betts, Alexander and Collier, Paul. *Refuge: Transforming a Broken Refugee System.* New York: Oxford University Press, 2017.

bin Laden, Osama. "Full Transcript of bin Ladin's Speech." *Al Jazeera.* November 1, 2004. www.aljazeera.com/archive/2004/11/200849163336457223.html.

Boast, Will. "Blaming Muslims, at First, in Norway." *New York Times Magazine.* June 24, 2016. www.nytimes.com/2016/06/26/magazine/blaming-muslims-at-first-in-norway.html.

Bohlen, Celestine. "Study Finds Children of Immigrants Embracing 'Frenchness.'" *New York Times.* January 25, 2016. www.nytimes.com/2016/01/26/world/europe/study-finds-children-of-immigrants-embracing-frenchness.html.

Boose, Lynda E. "Crossing the River Drina: Bosnian Rape Camps, Turkish Impalement, and Serb Cultural Memory." *Journal of Women in Culture and Society* 28 (2002): 71–96.

Boubtane, Ekrame, et al. "Immigration, Growth, and Unemployment: Panel VAR Evidence from OECD Countries." *Labour* 27 (December 2013): 399–420.

Bove, Vincenzo and Elia, Leandro. "Migration, Diversity, and Economic Growth." *World Development* 89 (2017): 227–239.

Bowen, John R. *On British Islam: Religion, Law, and Everyday Practice in Shari'a Councils.* Princeton: Princeton University Press, 2016.

Bunch, Lonnie G. "Emancipation Evoked Mix of Emotions for Freed Slaves." *Washington Post.* September 7, 2012. www.washingtonpost.com/lifestyle/style/emancipation-evoked-mix-of-emotions-for-freed-slaves/2012/09/07/57ad5184-f15a-11e1-892d-bc92fee603a7_story.html?utm_term=.3480a8e4b31e.

Burney, Uzma S. "European Court of Human Rights Upholds France's Ban on the Full-Face Veil." American Society of International Law. *Insights* 19 (2015). www.asil.org/insights/volume/19/issue/3/european-court-human-rights-upholds-frances-ban-full-face-veil.

Buruma, Ian. "Tariq Ramadan Has an Identity Issue." *New York Times Magazine.* February 4, 2007. www.nytimes.com/2007/02/04/magazine/04ramadan.t.html?mtrref=www.google.com&gwh=17EFC77183F116A84465D9D62B9914A6&gwt=pay.

Bussolo, Maurizio, et al. "Is There a Middle-Class Crisis in Europe?" Brookings Institution. March 22, 2018. www.brookings.edu/blog/future-development/2018/03/22/is-there-a-middle-class-crisis-in-europe/.

Byrne, Sean. "Defenders of Inequality: Milton Friedman and Robert Nozick." *Studies: An Irish Quarterly Review* 75 (1986): 186–195.

Calamur, Krishnadev. "The End of the Plan to Strip French Terrorists of Their Citizenship." *The Atlantic.* March 30, 2016. www.theatlantic.com/international/archive/2016/03/france-citizenship-law-dropped/475980/.

Caldwell, Christopher. "Islam on the Outskirts of the Welfare State." *New York Times Magazine.* February 5, 2006. www.nytimes.com/2006/02/05/magazine/islam-on-the-out skirts-of-the-welfare-state.html.

    Reflections on the Revolution in Europe: Immigration, Islam, and the West. New York: Anchor Books, 2010.

Callimachi, Rukmini. "ISIS Enshrines a Theology of Rape." *New York Times.* August 13, 2015. https://nyti.ms/1TucUEA.

Camarota, Steven A. "The Effects of Immigration on the Earnings of Low-Skilled Native Workers: Evidence from the June 1991 Current Population Survey." *Social Science Quarterly* 78 (June 1997): 417–431.

Cameron, David. "PM's Speech at Munich Security Conference." Prime Minister's Office. February 5, 2011. www.gov.uk/government/speeches/pms-speech-at-munich-security-conference.

Capatides, Christina. "Which European Countries Have Produced the Most ISIS Fighters?" CBS News. January 26, 2016. www.cbsnews.com/news/isis-terror-recruiting-europe-bel gium-france-denmark-sweden-germany/.

Caplan, Bryan. "Why Should We Restrict Immigration?" *Cato Journal* 32 (2012): 5–24.

Carassava, Anthee. "Attack on Migrants 'Planned by Far-Right Party' Golden Dawn in Greece." *The Times.* June 20, 2017. www.thetimes.co.uk/article/attacks-on-migrants-planned-by-far-right-party-in-greece-90jd7nssb.

Carens, Joseph H. *The Ethics of Immigration.* Oxford: Oxford University Press, 2013.

Carson, Clayborne and Garrow, David J. *The Eyes on the Prize Civil Rights Reader: Documents, Speeches, and Firsthand Accounts from the Black Freedom Struggle.* New York: Penguin, 1991.

Chazan, David. "Macron's National Service Programme Dismissed as 'big Teenagers' Party.'" *The Telegraph.* October 27, 2018. www.telegraph.co.uk/news/2018/10/27/macrons-national-service-programme-dismissed-big-teenagers-party/.

Chrisafis, Angelique. "Nicolas Sarkozy: There Are Too Many Foreigners in France." *The Guardian.* March 7, 2012, www.theguardian.com/world/2012/mar/07/nicolas-sarkozy-too-many-foreigners.

"Right-Wing 'New Reactionaries' Stir Up Trouble among French Intellectuals." *The Guardian*. October 9, 2015, www.theguardian.com/world/2015/oct/09/right-wing-new-reactionaries-stir-up-trouble-among-french-intellectuals.

Cienski, Jan. "Why Poland Doesn't Want Refugees." *Politico*. May 21, 2017. www.politico.eu/article/politics-nationalism-and-religion-explain-why-poland-doesnt-want-refugees/.

Clarke, Charles. "Immigration." In *The Too Difficult Box: The Big Issues Politicians Can't Crack*. London: Biteback Publishing, 2014.

Clawson, Patrick. "Demography in the Middle East: Population Growth Slowing, Women's Situation Unresolved." *Middle East Review of International Affairs* (March 2009). www.washingtoninstitute.org/policy-analysis/view/demography-in-the-middle-east-population-growth-slowing-womens-situation-un.

Cobain, Ian. "UK's Prevent Counter-Radicalisation Policy 'Badly Flawed.'" *The Guardian*. October 18, 2016. www.theguardian.com/uk-news/2016/oct/19/uks-prevent-counter-radicalisation-policy-badly-flawed.

Cockburn, Patrick. *Rise of the Islamic State: ISIS and the New Sunni Revolution*. London: Verso, 2015.

Collier, Paul. *Exodus: How Migration Is Changing Our World*. Oxford: Oxford University Press, 2013.

Conrad, Joseph. *The Secret Agent*. Hertfordshire: Wordsworth, 1993.

Constable, Pamela. "Afghanistan's 'American Idol' Is the Voice of a New Generation – And Muslim Clerics Aren't Happy About It." *Washington Post*. December 1, 2017. www.washingtonpost.com/world/asia_pacific/afghanistans-american-idol-is-the-voice-of-a-new-generation--and-muslim-clerics-arent-happy-about-it/2017/11/30/cd65ba96-ca1d-11e7-b506-8a10ed11ecf5_story.html?noredirect=on&utm_term=.812143ffbe32.

Cooper, Charlie. "Tony Blair Institute: 'Wave of Populism Not Yet Peaked.'" *Politico*. December 29, 2017. www.politico.eu/article/tony-blair-institute-wave-of-populism-not-yet-peaked/.

Cooper, Frederick. *Citizenship between Empire and Nation: Remaking France and French Africa, 1945–1960*. Princeton: Princeton University Press, 2014.

Cosgrove, Michael. "How Does France Count Its Muslim Population?" *Le Figaro*. April 7, 2011. http://plus.lefigaro.fr/note/how-does-france-count-its-muslim-population-20110407-435643.

Craig, John E. *Scholarship and Nation Building*. Chicago: University of Chicago Press, 1984.

Dagenais, Diane and Jacquet, Marianne. "Valuation of Multilingualism and Bilingual Education in Immigrant Families." *Journal of International Migration and Integration* 1 (October 2000): 389–404.

Dahl, Robert A. *On Democracy*. New Haven: Yale University Press, 1998.

Preface to a Democratic Theory. Chicago: University of Chicago Press, 1956.

Dalrymple, William. "Inside Islam's 'Terror Schools.'" *New Statesman*. March 28, 2005.

de Bellaigue, Christopher. "France at War." *New York Review of Books*. July 21, 2016. www.nybooks.com/daily/2016/07/21/france-at-war-after-nice-rightward-shift/.

de Tocqueville, Alexis. *Democracy in America and Two Essays on America*. London: Penguin, 2003.

Dean, Laura. "With Senegal's Fishermen." *London Review of Books Blog*. May 16, 2017. www.lrb.co.uk/blog/2017/05/16/laura-dean/with-senegals-fishermen/#more-25696.

Dearden, Lizzie. "EU Accused of 'Willfully Letting Refugees Drown' as NGOs Face Having Rescues Suspended in the Mediterranean." *The Independent*. July 29, 2017. www.independent.co.uk/news/world/europe/refugee-crisis-ngo-rescue-ships-mediterranean-sea-italy-libya-eu-code-of-conduct-deaths-2300-latest-a7866226.html.

Dhillon, Navtej. "The Middle Eastern Marriage Crisis." Interview on PBS. July 11, 2008. www.pbs.org/now/shows/427/Middle-East-Marriage.html.

Dierenfield, Bruce. *The Civil Rights Movement*. Rev. ed. New York: Routledge, 2013.

Eakin, Hugh. "Liberal, Harsh Denmark." *New York Review of Books*. March 10, 2016. www.nybooks.com/articles/2016/03/10/liberal-harsh-denmark/.

The Economist. "A Dangerous Waltz." *The Economist*. February 3, 2018.

"Boon or Burden?" *The Economist*. June 13, 2013. www.economist.com/finance-and-eco nomics/2013/06/15/boon-or-burden.

"Can Refugees Help to Plug Europe's Skilled-Labour Gaps?" *The Economist*. June 14, 2018. www.economist.com/finance-and-economics/2018/06/14/can-refugees-help-to-plug-eur opes-skilled-labour-gaps.

"Constructing Conflict." *The Economist*. April 30, 2007. www.economist.com/inter national/2007/08/30/constructing-conflict.

"Culture Is Not an Excuse for Oppressing Women." *The Economist*. June 25, 2018. www.economist.com/open-future/2018/06/25/culture-is-not-an-excuse-for-oppressing-women.

"Don't Panic." *The Economist*. September 24, 2014. www.economist.com/news/2014/09/24/ dont-panic.

"In Europe, Right-Wing Parties Are Offering Bigger Handouts than Traditional Ones." *The Economist*. January 25, 2018, www.economist.com/europe/2018/01/25/in-europe-right- wing-parties-are-offering-bigger-handouts-than-traditional-ones.

"Europe Is Sending African Migrants Home. Will They Stay?" *The Economist*. March 28, 2018. www.economist.com/middle-east-and-africa/2018/03/28/europe-is-sending-african- migrants-home.-will-they-stay.

"Few and Far Between." *The Economist*. October 22, 2015. www.economist.com/middle- east-and-africa/2015/10/22/few-and-far-between.

"Integration Nation." *The Economist*. May 21, 2016. www.economist.com/britain/2016/05/ 21/integration-nation.

"The Little Noticed Transformation of Islam in the West." *The* Economist. February 16, 2019. www.economist.com/leaders/2019/02/16/the-little-noticed-transformation-of-islam- in-the-west.

"Lost Boy Found." *The Economist*. March 3, 2018. 28.

"Modesty Sells." *The Economist*. June 2, 2016. www.economist.com/britain/2016/06/02/ modesty-sells.

"In Much of Sub-Saharan Africa, Cell Phones Are More Common than Access to Electri- city." *The Economist*. November 8, 2017. www.economist.com/graphic-detail/2017/11/08/in- much-of-sub-saharan-africa-mobile-phones-are-more-common-than-access-to-electricity.

"Preparing for the Worst." *The Economist*. May 21, 2016. www.economist.com/britain/2016/ 05/21/preparing-for-the-worst.

"Straws in the Wind." *The Economist*. July 16, 2016. www.economist.com/britain/2016/07/ 16/straws-in-the-wind.

"Why Are Young Men in Sweden Shooting Each Other?" *The Economist*. March 8, 2018. www.economist.com/europe/2018/03/08/why-are-young-men-in-sweden-shooting-each- other.

Eddy, Melissa. "Violent Backlash against Migrants in Germany as Asylum-Seekers Pour In." *New York Times*. August 13, 2015. www.nytimes.com/2015/08/14/world/europe/germany- migrants-attacks-asylum-seekers-backlash.html.

Eddy, Melissa and Scott, Mark. "Delete Hate Speech or Pay up, Germany Tells Social Media Companies." *New York Times*. June 30, 2017. www.nytimes.com/2017/06/30/business/ germany-facebook-google-twitter.html.

Elle. "10 Stylish Hijabs Made by and for Muslim Women." *Elle.* August 1, 2016. www.elle.com/uk/fashion/news/a28848/10-stylish-hijabs-made-by-and-for-muslim-women/.

Evening Times. "Dockers on the March for Powell." *Evening Times.* April 23, 1968. https://news.google.com/newspapers?id=zudYAAAAIBAJ&sjid=AosMAAAAIBAJ&pg=1643,7221622.

Fantz, Ashley and Anderson, Becky. "Refugee Crisis: Why Aren't Gulf States Taking Them In?" CNN. September 8, 2015. www.cnn.com/2015/09/08/world/gulf-states-syrian-refugee-crisis/index.html.

Faust, Jörg and Garcia, Melody. "With or Without Force?: European Public Opinion on Democracy Promotion." German Development Institute, 2013. www.die-gdi.de/uploads/media/DP_10.2013.pdf.

Federal Republic of Germany. Federal Ministry of Justice. Basic Law of the Federal Republic of Germany (Grundgesetz, GG). www.gesetze-im-internet.de/englisch_gg/englisch_gg.html#.

Feld, Alan L. "The Shrunken Power of the Purse." *Boston University Law Review* 89 (2009): 487–497.

Fernández-Huertas Moraga, Jesús and Rapoport, Hillel. "Tradable Immigration Quotas." *Journal of Public Economics* 115 (2014): 94–108.

Fieschi, Catherine and Johnson, Nick. "Islam and Muslim Communities in the UK: Multiculturalism, Faith and Security." *The International Spectator* 48 (2013): 86–101.

Francois, Myriam. "Olivier Roy on Laicite as Ideology, the Myth of 'National Identity' and Racism in the French Republic." *Jadaliyya.* May 20, 2015.

Freund, Caroline and Spatafora, Nikola. "Remittances: Transaction Costs, Determinants, and Informal Flows." World Bank Policy Research Working Paper Series, No. 3704.

Fukuyama, Francis. "The End of History?" *The National Interest* 16 (Summer 1989): 3–18.

Gaebler, Ralph. "Review: Is Liberal Nationalism an Oxymoron?" *Indiana Journal of Global Legal Studies* 3 (1995): 283–293.

Gayle, Damien. "Prevent Strategy 'Could End Up Promoting Extremism.'" *The Guardian.* April 21, 2016. www.theguardian.com/politics/2016/apr/21/government-prevent-strategy-promoting-extremism-maina-kiai.

Gellner, Ernest. *Nations and Nationalism.* Ithaca: Cornell University Press, 1983.

Gill, Indermit and Kharas, Homi. *An East Asian Renaissance: Ideas for Economic Growth.* Washington, DC: World Bank, 2007.

The Globalist. "Africa vs. Asia: The Population Dimension." *The Globalist.* September 16, 2015. www.theglobalist.com/africa-asia-nigeria-population/.

Gonzalez-Barrera, Ana. "More Mexicans Leaving than Coming to the U.S." Pew Research Center. November 19, 2015. www.pewhispanic.org/2015/11/19/more-mexicans-leaving-than-coming-to-the-u-s/.

Goodman, Peter. "In Britain, Austerity Is Changing Everything." *New York Times.* May 28, 2018. www.nytimes.com/2018/05/28/world/europe/uk-austerity-poverty.html?action=click&module=Ribben&pgtype=Article.

Govan, Fiona. "Spain Admits Firing Rubber Bullets at Migrants Swimming to Enclave." *The Telegraph.* February 14, 2014. www.telegraph.co.uk/news/worldnews/europe/spain/10638607/Spain-admits-firing-rubber-bullets-at-migrants-swimming-to-enclave.html.

Gramlich, John. "5 Facts About Crime in the U.S." Pew Research Center. January 3, 2019. www.pewresearch.org/fact-tank/2019/01/03/5-facts-about-crime-in-the-u-s/.

Greenblatt, Alan. "What's Causing the Latest Immigration Crisis? A Brief Explainer." NPR. July 9, 2014. www.npr.org/2014/07/09/329848538/whats-causing-the-latest-immigration-crisis-a-brief-explainer.

Guardian Press Association. "UK 'Has Stripped 150 Jihadists and Criminals of Citizenship.'" *The Guardian*. July 30, 2017. www.theguardian.com/uk-news/2017/jul/30/uk-has-stripped-150-jihadists-and-criminals-of-citizenship.

Guest, Robert. "Generation Uphill." *The Economist*. January 23, 2016.

Gyimah-Brempong, Kwabena and Kimenyi, Mwangi S. "Youth Policy and the Future of African Development." Working Paper 9. Africa Growth Initiative. Brookings Institution. April 2013.

Halevi, Joseph and Kriesler, Peter. "Stagnation and Economic Conflict in Europe." *International Journal of Political Economy* 34 (2004): 19–45.

Hamid, Shadi. "The Rise of Anti-liberalism." Brookings. February 21, 2018, www.brookings.edu/blog/order-from-chaos/2018/02/21/the-rise-of-anti-liberalism/.

Harp, Stephen L. *Learning to Be Loyal: Primary Schooling as Nation Building in Alsace and Lorraine, 1850–1940*. DeKalb: Northern Illinois University Press, 1998.

Harris, Paul. "Population of World 'Could Grow to 15bn by 2100.'" *The Guardian*. October 22, 2011. www.theguardian.com/world/2011/oct/22/population-world-15bn-2100.

Hayden, Robert M. "Imagined Communities and Real Victims: Self-Determination and Ethnic Cleansing in Yugoslavia." *American Ethnologist* 23 (1996): 783–801.

Heneghan, Tom. "French Muslims Join Opposition to Same-Sex Marriage." Reuters. January 7, 2013. https://uk.reuters.com/article/uk-france-marriage-muslim/french-muslims-join-opposition-to-same-sex-marriage-idUKBRE9060IX20130107.

Hino, Hiroyuki. "Youth and Unemployment in Sub-Saharan Africa." Seminar Report. African Economic Research Consortium Senior Policy Seminar XV.

Hino, Hiroyuki and Ranis, Gustav. *Youth and Unemployment in Sub-Saharan Africa: Working but Poor*. New York: Routledge, 2014.

Hoban, Brennan. "One Year after Charlottesville, Has American Learned to Reckon with Its Racist History?" Brookings Institution. August 10, 2018. www.brookings.edu/blog/brookings-now/2018/08/10/one-year-after-charlottesville-has-america-learned-to-reckon-with-its-racist-history/.

Hogarth, Terence, et al. *Technology, Globalisation, and the Future of Work in Europe: Essays on Employment in a Digitised Economy*, edited by Tony Dolphin. Institute for Public Policy Research. March 2015. www.oxfordmartin.ox.ac.uk/downloads/academic/technology-globalisation-future-of-work_Mar2015.pdf.

Hooper, Simon. "Exclusive: UK Government to Introduce 'Mandatory Deradicalisation' Scheme." *Middle East Eye*. July 22, 2016. www.middleeasteye.net/news/exclusive-uk-government-introduce-mandatory-deradicalisation-scheme-746303354.

Horne, Alistair. *A Savage War of Peace: Algeria 1954–1962*. New York: New York Review of Books, 2006.

Huemer, Michael. "Is There a Right to Immigrate?" *Social Theory and Practice* 36 (2010): 429–461.

Huntington, Samuel. *The Clash of Civilizations and the Remaking of World Order*. New York: Simon & Schuster, 1996.

Ighobor, Kingsley. "Africa's Youth: A 'Ticking Time Bomb' or an Opportunity?" *Africa Renewal*. May 2013. www.un.org/africarenewal/magazine/may-2013/africa%E2%80%99s-youth-%E2%80%9Cticking-time-bomb%E2%80%9D-or-opportunity.

Ishay, Micheline. "The Socialist Contributions to Human Rights: An Overlooked Legacy." *The International Journal of Human Rights* 9 (2005): 225–245.

Jan, Tracy. "White Families Have Nearly 10 Times the Net Worth of Black Families. And the Gap Is Growing." *Washington Post*. September 28, 2017. www.washingtonpost.com/news/wonk/wp/2017/09/28/black-and-hispanic-families-are-making-more-money-but-they-still-lag-far-behind-whites/?utm_term=.8b2ba15ffd24.

Johnson, Samuel. In Boswell, James. *The Life of Samuel Johnson*. London: Penguin Classics, 2008.

Joll, James. "Mussolini's Roman Empire." *New York Times*. June 20, 1976. www.nytimes.com/1976/06/20/archives/mussolinis-roman-empire-the-trouble-was-trying-to-keep-up-with-the.html.

Judt, Tony. "What Have We Learned, if Anything?" *New York Review of Books*. May 1, 2008. www.nybooks.com/articles/2008/05/01/what-have-we-learned-if-anything/.

Just, Aida and Anderson, Christopher J. "Dual Allegiances? Immigrants' Attitudes toward Immigration." *The Journal of Politics* 77 (January 2015): 188–201.

Kanter, James. "EU Moves against 3 Countries That Don't Take Refugees." *New York Times*. June 13, 2017. www.nytimes.com/2017/06/13/world/europe/eu-refugees-czech-republic-hungary-poland.html.

Kantor, Jodi and Einhorn, Catrin. "Canadians Adopted Refugee Families for a Year. Then Came 'Month 13.'" *New York Times*. March 26, 2017. https://nyti.ms/2nPCn11.

Kashkari, Neel. "Immigration Is Practically a Free Lunch for America." *Wall Street Journal*. January 18, 2018. www.wsj.com/articles/immigration-is-practically-a-free-lunch-for-amer ica-1516320376.

Kauffmann, Sylvie. "God Is Back – In France." *New York Times*. January 26, 2017. www.nytimes.com/2017/01/26/opinion/god-is-back-in-france.html.

Kelly, Paul. "Defending Some Dodos: Equality and/or Liberty?" In *Multiculturalism Reconsidered: Culture and Equality and Its Critics*, edited by Paul Kelly, 62–80. Cambridge: Polity, 2002.

Kelly, Paul. "Introduction: Between Culture and Equality." In *Multiculturalism Reconsidered: Culture and Equality and Its Critics*, edited by Paul Kelly, 1–17. Cambridge: Polity, 2002.

Kepel, Gilles. *Terror in France: The Rise of Jihad in the West*. Princeton: Princeton University Press, 2017.

Khader, Bichara. "Muslims in Europe: The Construction of a 'Problem.'" In *The Search for Europe: Contrasting Approaches*. Birmingham: BBV, 2016, p. 312

King, Martin Luther, Jr. *The Autobiography of Martin Luther King, Jr.*, edited by Clayborne Carson. New York: Warner, 1998.

Kingsley, Patrick. *The New Odyssey: The Story of the Twenty-First-Century Refugee Crisis*. New York: W. W. Norton, 2017.

Kommers, Donald P., et al. *American Constitutional Law: Essays, Cases, and Comparative Notes*. 2nd ed. Lanham: Rowman & Littlefield, 2004.

Koopmans, Ruud. "Trade-Offs between Equality and Difference: Immigrant Integration, Multiculturalism and the Welfare State in Cross-National Perspective." *Journal of Ethnic and Migration Studies* 36 (2010): 1–26.

Korte, Gregory. "Obama Greets Nordic Leaders, Saying They 'Punch Above Their Weight.'" *USA Today*. May 13, 2016. www.usatoday.com/story/news/politics/2016/05/13/obama-nordic-leaders-summit-punch-above-their-weight/84330852/.

Kotkin, Joel. "Death Spiral Demographics." *Forbes*. February 1, 2017. www.forbes.com/sites/joelkotkin/2017/02/01/death-spiral-demographics-the-countries-shrinking-the-fastest/#3d5ee250b83c.

Kottasova, Ivana. "Biggest Populations in 2050: Move over Russia and Mexico. Here Comes Africa." CNN Money. August 18, 2015. https://money.cnn.com/2015/08/18/news/coun tries-with-biggest-populations/index.html.

Krysan, Maria and Moberg, Sara. "A Portrait of African American and White Racial Attitudes." University of Illinois. Institute of Government and Public Affairs. September 9, 2016. https://igpa.uillinois.edu/programs/racial-attitudes.

Ksiazek, Jean-Philippe. "After Charlie Hebdo Attack, 'Panic' over Future Spreading in Poor Muslim Suburbs of Paris." *National Post*. January 9, 2015.

Kukathas, Chandran. *The Liberal Archipelago: A Theory of Diversity and Freedom*. Oxford: Oxford University Press, 2003.

"The Life of Brian, or Now for Something Completely Difference-Blind." In *Multiculturalism Reconsidered: Culture and Equality and Its Critics*, edited by Paul Kelly, 184–203. Cambridge: Polity, 2002.

Kymlicka, Will. *Multicultural Citizenship: A Liberal Theory of Minority Rights*. Oxford: Clarendon Press, 1995.

Politics in the Vernacular: Nationalism, Multiculturalism, and Citizenship. Oxford: Oxford University Press, 2001.

Lapore, Jill. "A New Americanism: Why a Nation Needs a National Story." *Foreign Affairs*. March 2019. www.foreignaffairs.com/articles/united-states/2019-02-05/new-americanism-nationalism-jill-lepore.

Laurence, Jonathan. *The Emancipation of Europe's Muslims*. Princeton: Princeton University Press, 2012.

Legrain, Philip. "How to Convince Sceptics of the Value of Immigration?" *The Economist*. June 1, 2018. www.economist.com/open-future/2018/06/01/how-to-convince-sceptics-of-the-value-of-immigration.

Lerner, Max. *The Mind and Faith of Justice Holmes: His Speeches, Essays, Letters, and Judicial Opinions*. New York: Routledge, 2017.

Lilla, Mark. "The End of Identity Liberalism." *New York Times*. March 18, 2018. www.nytimes.com/2016/11/20/opinion/sunday/the-end-of-identity-liberalism.html.

"France: A Strange Defeat." *New York Review of Books*. March 19, 2015. www.nybooks.com/articles/2015/03/19/france-strange-defeat/.

"France: Is There a Way Out?" *New York Review of Books*. March 10, 2016. www.nybooks.com/articles/2016/03/10/france-is-there-a-way-out/.

Livingston, Gretchen and Brown, Anna. "Intermarriage in the U.S. 50 Years after Loving v. Virginia." Pew Research Center. Social and Demographic Trends. May 18, 2017. www.pewsocialtrends.org/2017/05/18/intermarriage-in-the-u-s-50-years-after-loving-v-virginia/.

Lubitz, James and Prihoda, Ronald. "The Use and Costs of Medicare Services in the Last 2 Years of Life." *Health Care Financial Review* 5 (Spring 1984): 117–131.

Macpherson, William. *The Stephen Lawrence Inquiry*. Parliamentary paper. London: Home Office, February 24, 1999. www.gov.uk/government/publications/the-stephen-lawrence-inquiry.

Mazzini, Giuseppe. "The European Question: Foreign Intervention and National Self-Determination." In *A Cosmopolitanism of Nations*, edited by Stefano Recchia and Nadia Urbinati, 193–198. Princeton: Princeton University Press, 2009.

McCleland, Jacob. "The High Costs of High Security at Supermax Prisons." NPR. June 19, 2012. www.npr.org/2012/06/19/155359553/the-high-costs-of-high-security-at-supermax-prisons.

McIntyre, Alasdair. *After Virtue: A Study in Moral Theory*. 3rd ed. Notre Dame: University of Notre Dame Press, 2007.

Mendick, Robert, et al. "Security Services Missed Five Opportunities to Stop the Manchester Bomber." *The Telegraph*. June 6, 2017. www.telegraph.co.uk/news/2017/05/24/security-services-missed-five-opportunities-stop-manchester/.

Miller, David. *Justice for Earthlings: Essays in Political Philosophy*. Cambridge: Cambridge University Press, 2013.

Mirengoff, Paul. "Sarkozy's Message to France's Muslims – The Good, the Bad, and the Ugly." *Powerline*. December 10, 2009, www.powerlineblog.com/archives/2009/12/025126.php.

Mongeau, Lillian. "Why Does America Invest so Little in Its Children?" *The Atlantic.* July 12, 2016. www.theatlantic.com/education/archive/2016/07/why-does-america-invest-so-little-in-its-children/490790/.

Morris, Chris. "Sweden's Asylum Offer to Refugees from Syria." BBC. October 23, 2013. www.bbc.com/news/world-europe-24635791.

Mudde, Cas. "Europe's Populist Surge." *Foreign Affairs* 95 (November–December 2016): 25–30.

Murphy, Caryle. "Q&A: The Muslim-Christian Education Gap in Sub-Saharan Africa." Pew Research Center. December 14, 2016. www.pewresearch.org/fact-tank/2016/12/14/qa-the-muslim-christian-education-gap-in-sub-saharan-africa/.

Murray, Douglas. *The Strange Death of Europe: Immigration, Identity, Islam.* London: Bloomsbury Press, 2017.

Muslim Brotherhood. "Muslim Brotherhood Statement Denouncing UN Women Declaration for Violating Sharia Principles." *Ikhwan Web.* March 14, 2013. www.ikhwanweb.com/article.php?id=30731.

Muysken, J. and Ziesemer, T. H. W. "A Permanent Effect of Temporary Immigration on Economic Growth." *Applied Economics* 45 (2003): 4050–4059.

National Public Radio. "UNICEF Report: Africa's Population Could Hit 4 Billion by 2100." NPR. August 13, 2014. www.npr.org/sections/goatsandsoda/2014/08/13/340091377/unicef-report-africas-population-could-hit-4-billion-by-2100.

Niebuhr, Gustav. "Southern Baptists Declare Wife Should 'Submit' to Her Husband." *New York Times.* June 10, 1998. www.nytimes.com/1998/06/10/us/southern-baptists-declare-wife-should-submit-to-her-husband.html.

Noack, Chris. "Europe's Citizenship Tests Are So Hard Not Even Citizens Can Pass." *Washington Post.* July 12, 2016. www.washingtonpost.com/news/worldviews/wp/2016/07/13/europes-citizenship-tests-are-so-hard-not-even-citizens-can-answer-the-questions/?utm_term=.407a35ffb5cc.

Norland, Rod. "A Mass Migration Crisis, and It May Yet Get Worse." *New York Times.* October 31, 2015. www.nytimes.com/2015/11/01/world/europe/a-mass-migration-crisis-and-it-may-yet-get-worse.html.

Norris, Pippa. "The 'New Cleavage' Thesis and the Social Basis of Radical Right Support." Paper for presentation at American Political Science Association Annual Meeting. September 2, 2015.

Nossiter, Adam. "As France's Towns Wither, Fears of a Decline in 'Frenchness.'" *New York Times.* February 28, 2017. www.nytimes.com/2017/02/28/world/europe/france-albi-french-towns-fading.html.

"At French Outpost in African Migrant Hub, Asylum for a Select Few." *New York Times.* February 25, 2018. www.nytimes.com/2018/02/25/world/africa/france-africa-migrants-asylum-niger.html.

"Sons of Immigrants Prop up a Symbol of 'Frenchness': The Baguette." *New York Times.* May 14, 2018. https://nyti.ms/2GejGcE.

Ohlheiser, Abby. "Uganda's New Anti-homosexuality Law Was Inspired by American Activists." *The Atlantic.* December 20, 2013. www.theatlantic.com/international/archive/2013/12/uganda-passes-law-punishes-homosexuality-life-imprisonment/356365/.

O'Neill, Brendan. "Why Theresa May Is to Blame for the Windrush Scandal." *The Spectator.* April 17, 2018. https://blogs.spectator.co.uk/2018/04/why-theresa-may-is-to-blame-for-the-windrush-scandal/.

Onishi, Norimitsu. "Japan, the Elderly often Live, and Die Alone." *Seattle Times.* November 30, 2017. www.seattletimes.com/nation-world/in-japan-the-elderly-often-live-and-die-alone/.

Organisation for Economic Cooperation and Development. "Indicators of Immigrant Integration 2015: Settling In." OECD. 2016. www.oecd.org/els/mig/press-note-UK.pdf.

"Sweden Is in a Strong Position to Integrate Refugees, but Support for the Low Skilled Needs to Be Strengthened." OECD. May 13, 2016. www.oecd.org/sweden/sweden-in-a-strong-position-to-integrate-refugees-but-support-for-the-low-skilled-needs-to-be-strengthened.htm.

Working Together: Skills and Labour Market Integration of Immigrants and Their Children in Sweden. OECD. March 13, 2016.

Orozco, Manuel, et al. "The Continued Growth of Family Remittances to Latin America and the Caribbean in 2015." The Dialogue Leadership for the Americas. February 2016. www.thedialogue.org/wp-content/uploads/2016/02/2015-Remittances-to-LAC-2122016.pdf.

Orrenius, Pia M. and Zavodny, Madeline. "Does Immigration Affect Wages? A Look at Occupation-Level Evidence." Labour Economics 14 (2017): 757–773.

Ortman, Jennifer M. and Guarneri, Christine E. "United States Population Projections: 2000 to 2050." United States Census Bureau. 2009. www.census.gov/content/dam/Census/library/working-papers/2009/demo/us-pop-proj-2000-2050/analytical-docu ment09.pdf.

Packer, George. "The Other France." The New Yorker. August 31, 2015. www.newyorker.com/magazine/2015/08/31/the-other-france.

Page, John. "Africa's Job Gap." Brookings Institution. March 4, 2013. www.brookings.edu/opinions/africas-jobs-gap/.

Parekh, Bhikhu. Rethinking Multiculturalism: Cultural Diversity and Political Theory. Basingstoke: Macmillan, 2000.

Patten, Alan. Equal Recognition: The Moral Foundation of Minority Rights. Princeton: Princeton University Press, 2014.

Perraudin, Frances. "Half of All British Muslims Think Homosexuality Should Be Illegal, Poll Finds." The Guardian. April 11, 2016. www.theguardian.com/uk-news/2016/apr/11/british-muslims-strong-sense-of-belonging-poll-homosexuality-sharia-law.

Peters, Lawrence. "Sovereignty: The UN and the Westphalian Legacy." In The United Nations: History and Core Ideas. New York: Palgrave Macmillan, 2015.

Pew Research Center. "Americans Express Increasingly Warm Feelings toward Research Groups." Pew Research Center. February 15, 2016. www.pewforum.org/2017/02/15/ameri cans-express-increasingly-warm-feelings-toward-religious-groups/pf_17-02-15_feelingth ermometer_gp200px/.

"The Elusive 90% Solution." Pew Research Center. March 11, 2011. www.pewresearch.org/2011/03/11/the-elusive-90-solution/.

"Religion and Education around the World." December 13, 2016. http://assets.pewresearch .org/wp-content/uploads/sites/11/2016/12/21094148/Religion-Education-ONLINE-FINAL .pdf.

Religion and Public Life. "Changing Attitudes on Gay Marriage." Pew Research Center. June 26, 2017. www.pewforum.org/fact-sheet/changing-attitudes-on-gay-marriage/.

U.S. Politics and Policy. "Political Polarization in the American Public." Pew Research Center. June 12, 2014. www.people-press.org/2014/06/12/political-polarization-in-the-american-public/.

Phillips, Deborah A., et al. "Puzzling It Out: The Current State of Scientific Knowledge on Pre-Kindergarten Effects." Brookings Institution. April 17, 2017. www.brookings.edu/research/puzzling-it-out-the-current-state-of-scientific-knowledge-on-pre-kindergarten-effects/.

Phillips, Melanie. "After the Rushdie Affair, Islam in Britain Became Fused with an Agenda of Murder." *The Guardian.* May 27, 2006. www.theguardian.com/commentisfree/2006/may/28/religion.islam.

Phillips, Trevor. "Poll: What Muslims Really Think." ICM Unlimited. April 2016, www.icmunlimited.com/polls/icm-muslims-survey-for-channel-4/.

"This Life and Death Struggle: In a Stark Analysis, Former Equalities Chief Reveals How Extremist Ideas Have Been Allowed to Flourish." Interviewed by *The Daily Mail* (April 10, 2016).

et al. *Race and Faith: The Deafening Silence.* London: Civitas, 2016.

Pianigiani, Gaia. "Mafia in Italy Siphons Huge Sums from Migrant Centers." *New York Times.* July 17, 2017. www.nytimes.com/2017/07/17/world/europe/italy-migrants-mafia-edoardo-scordio.html.

Piser, Karina. "A New Plan to Create an 'Islam of France.'" *The Atlantic.* March 29, 2018. www.theatlantic.com/international/archive/2018/03/islam-france-macron/556604/.

Population Reference Bureau. "Why Concentrated Poverty Fell in the United States in the 1990s." PRB. August 1, 2005. www.prb.org/whyconcentratedpovertyfellintheunitedstatesinthe1990s/.

Povoledo, Elisabetta. "In Rome, Violent Eviction of Migrants 'Touched a Nerve.'" *New York Times.* September 4, 2017. www.nytimes.com/2017/09/04/world/europe/italy-rome-migrants-eviction.html.

Provost, Claire. "Nigeria Expected to Have Larger Population than US by 2050." *The Guardian.* June 13, 2013. www.theguardian.com/global-development/2013/jun/13/nigeria-larger-population-us-2050.

Razin, Assaf. "The Aging, Crisis-Prone Welfare State Must Confront the Problem of Welfare Migration." *Business Insider.* October 27, 2010. www.businessinsider.com/assaf-razin-on-us-demographics-2010-10.

Renan, Ernest. "What Is a Nation?" Conference delivered at the Sorbonne, March 11, 1882. Translated by Ethan Rundell. http://ucparis.fr/files/9313/6549/9943/What_is_a_Nation.pdf.

Reuters. "World's Population Unlikely to Level off Anytime Soon – May Hit 12 Billion by 2100." *Washington Post.* September 22, 2014. www.washingtonpost.com/national/health-science/worlds-population-unlikely-to-level-off-anytime-soon-may-hit-12-billion-by-2100/2014/09/22/aa66890a-3f68-11e4-9587-5dafd96295f0_story.html?noredirect=on&utm_term=.a4d49a7db29c.

Rose, Eliot Joseph Benn and Deakin, Nicholas. *Colour and Citizenship: A Report on British Race Relations.* Oxford: Oxford University Press, 1969.

Rosenblatt, Helena. *The Lost History of Liberalism: From Ancient Rome to the Twenty-First Century.* Princeton: Princeton University Press, 2018.

Roy, Olivier. "France's Oedipal Islamic Complex." *Foreign Policy.* January 7, 2016. http://foreignpolicy.com/2016/01/07/frances-oedipal-islamist-complex-charlie-hebdo-islamic-state-isis/.

"The Islamization of Radicalism." Rosa Luxemburg Stiftung – North Africa Office. June 2016.

Secularism Confronts Islam. New York: Columbia University Press, 2007.

Rubin, Alissa J. "Attack on Nice Turns Spotlight on City's Religious Divisions." *New York Times.* July 17, 2016. www.nytimes.com/2016/07/18/world/europe/muslims-nice-france-terrorism.html.

Runciman, David. "How the Education Gap Is Tearing Politics Apart." *The Guardian.* October 5, 2016. www.theguardian.com/politics/2016/oct/05/trump-brexit-education-gap-tearing-politics-apart.

Rutter, Jill. *Moving up and Getting On*. Bristol: Policy Press, 2016.

Samuel, Henry. "Nicolas Sarkozy Says Immigrants Must Accept 'Your Ancestors Are the Gauls.'" *The Telegraph*. September 20, 2016. www.telegraph.co.uk/news/2016/09/20/nicolas-sarkozy-says-immigrants-should-live-like-the-french/.

Sassen, Saskia. *Expulsions: Brutality and Complexity in the Global Economy*. Cambridge: Belknap Press, 2014.

Schwarzer, Alice. "The Current Outrage Is Very Hypocritical." Interview by Christian Hoffmann and René Pfister. *Spiegel Online*. January 21, 2016. www.spiegel.de/international/germany/german-feminists-debate-cologne-attacks-a-1072806.html.

Sen, Amartya. "Equality of What?" In *The Tanner Lectures on Human Values*, edited by Sterling McMurrin, 195. Cambridge: Cambridge University Press, 1980.

Shabi, Rachel. "Deradicalising Britain: The Activists Turning Young Muslims away from Extremism." *The Guardian*. March 18, 2016. www.theguardian.com/uk-news/2016/mar/18/deradicalising-britain-the-activists-turning-young-muslims-away-from-extremism.

Shatz, Adam. "How Did We End Up Here?" *London Review of Books blog*. April 5, 2016. www.lrb.co.uk/blog/2016/04/05/adam-shatz/how-did-we-end-up-here/.

Shelley, Louise. *Human Smuggling and Trafficking into Europe: A Comparative Perspective*. Transatlantic Council on Migration. Migration Policy Institute. February 2014. www.migrationpolicy.org/sites/default/files/publications/BadActors-ShelleyFINALWEB.pdf.

Sherwood, Harriet. "More than Half UK Population Has No Religion, Finds Survey." *The Guardian*. September 4, 2017. www.theguardian.com/world/2017/sep/04/half-uk-population-has-no-religion-british-social-attitudes-survey.

Shriver, Lionel. "Why Mass Immigration Explains the Housing Crisis." *The Spectator*. March 17, 2018. www.spectator.co.uk/2018/03/why-mass-immigration-explains-the-housing-crisis/.

Smith, Rory. "Mo Salah of Liverpool Breaks down Cultural Barriers, One Goal at a Time." *New York Times*. May 2, 2018. www.nytimes.com/2018/05/02/world/europe/mo-salah-liverpool-champions-league.html.

Snyder, Timothy. "Hitler's World." *New York Review of Books*. September 24, 2015. www.nybooks.com/articles/2015/09/24/hitlers-world/.

Stack, Liam. "Poll of British Muslims Reveals Startling Views, but Some Question Methodology." *New York Times*. April 14, 2016. www.nytimes.com/2016/04/15/world/europe/poll-british-muslims.html.

Statista. "Germany: Share of Economic Sectors in Gross Domestic Product (GDP) in 2017." 2018. www.statista.com/statistics/295519/germany-share-of-economic-sectors-in-gross-domestic-product/.

"Population in France in 2010 by Religious Affiliation." 2018. www.statista.com/statistics/459982/population-distribution-religion-france/.

Statistics Norway. "Persons with Immigrant Background by Immigration Category, Country Background and Gender." January 1, 2012. Statistics Norway. https://web.archive.org/web/20130206040422/http://www.ssb.no/english/subjects/02/01/10/innvbef_en/tab-2012-04-26-04-en.html.

Steinweis, Alan E. "German Cultural Imperialism in Czechoslovakia and Poland." *The International History Review* 13 (August 1991): 466–480.

Stern, Gary M. "Controversy: Immigrant Parents Challenge Bilingual Education." *The Hispanic Outlook in Higher Education* 6 (January 1996).

Sunajko, Goran. "Rawls and Piketty: The Philosophical Aspects of Economic Inequality." *The Journal of Philosophical Economics* 9 (2016): 71–84.

Taylor, Adam. "Germany's Small Yet Important Change to the Way It Deals with Syrian Refugees." *Washington Post*. August 26, 2015. www.washingtonpost.com/news/world views/wp/2015/08/26/germanys-small-yet-important-change-to-the-way-it-deals-with-syrian-refugees/?utm_term=.7166a8b37b86.

Tharoor, Ishaan. "The Arab World's Wealthiest Nations Are Doing Next to Nothing for Syrian Refugees." *Washington Post*. September 4, 2015. www.washingtonpost.com/news/worldviews/wp/2015/09/04/the-arab-worlds-wealthiest-nations-are-doing-next-to-nothing-for-syrias-refugees/?utm_term=.bd9b127613be.

Thatcher, Margaret. Interview for *Woman's Own*. October 31, 1987. Margaret Thatcher Foundation. www.margaretthatcher.org/document/106689.

Thompson, E. P. *The Making of the English Working Class*. London: Penguin Books, 1980.

Traub, James. "The Death of the Most Generous Nation on Earth." *Foreign Policy*. February 10, 2016. https://foreignpolicy.com/2016/02/10/the-death-of-the-most-generous-nation-on-earth-sweden-syria-refugee-europe/.

Travis, Alan. "Net Migration to UK Hits Record High of 330,000." *The Guardian*. August 27, 2015. www.theguardian.com/uk-news/2015/aug/27/net-migration-predicted-to-hit-record-level.

Traynor, Ian. "Sarkozy Defends Switzerland Minaret Ban." *The Guardian*. December 8, 2009. www.theguardian.com/world/2009/dec/08/sarkozy-sympathises-minaret-ban-switzerland.

Turula, Tom. "Sweden's Foreign-Born Population Is Nearing 1.7 Million." *Business Insider*. https://nordic.businessinsider.com/swedens-foreign-born-population-is-nearly-17-million-people—finns-are-the-biggest-group-2017-3.

United Kingdom. Home Office. "Prevent Strategy." Policy paper, HM Government. June 2011. www.gov.uk/government/uploads/system/uploads/attachment_data/file/97976/pre vent-strategy-review.pdf.

House of Commons. "Commonwealth Immigrants Bill." Hansard Parliamentary Debates, 5th ser., vol. 649, cols. 687-819. November 16, 1961.

House of Commons. "Immigration." Hansard Parliamentary Debates, 6th ser., vol. 401, cols. 270-94WH. March 19, 2003.

United Nations. 2005 *World Summit* Outcome, A/RES/60/1. October 24, 2005. www.un.org/en/development/desa/population/migration/generalassembly/docs/globalcompact/A_RES_60_1.pdf.

Charter of the United Nations. October 24, 1945. www.un.org/en/sections/un-charter/un-charter-full-text/.

Department of Economic and Social Affairs. "World Population Projected to Reach 9.8 Billion in 2050, and 11.2 Billion in 2100." June 21, 2017. www.un.org/development/desa/en/news/population/world-population-prospects-2017.html.

Department of Economics and Social Affairs. Population Division. *World Population Prospects*. 2017 Revision. https://esa.un.org/unpd/wpp/publications/Files/WPP2017_Key Findings.pdf.

Office of the High Commissioner on Human Rights. *International Covenant on Civil and Political Rights*, G.A. Res. 2200A(XXI). March 23, 1976. www.ohchr.org/en/professiona linterest/pages/ccpr.aspx.

United States Census Bureau. "Historical Poverty Tables: People and Families – 1959 to 2016." "Table 4. Poverty Status of Families, by Type of Family, Presence of Related Children, Race, and Hispanic Origin." Accessed July 27, 2018. www.census.gov/data/tables/time-series/demo/income-poverty/historical-poverty-people.html.

Vermeren, Pierre. "Faced with Islam of France, from Denial to Paralysis." *L'express*. June 3, 2014. www.lexpress.fr/actualite/face-a-l-islam-de-france-du-deni-a-la-paralysie_1548482.html.

von Rohr, Mathieu and Leick, Romain. "There Is a Clash of Civilizations." Interview with Alain Finkielkraut. *Spiegel Online*. December 6, 2013. www.spiegel.de/international/world/interview-french-philosopher-finkielkraut-on-muslims-and-integration-a-937404-2.html.

Walia, Shelly. "Finally, India's Population Growth Is Slowing Down." *Quartz*. December 24, 2014. https://qz.com/317518/finally-indias-population-growth-is-slowing-down/.

Walsh, Joan. "The New Trump Immigration Plan Is Anti-American." *The Nation*. January 26, 2018. www.thenation.com/article/the-new-trump-immigration-plan-is-anti-american/.

Walzer, Michael. *Just and Unjust Wars*. 2nd ed. New York: Basic Books, 1991.

　Politics and Passion: Towards a More Egalitarian Liberalism. New Haven: Yale University Press, 2004.

　"Response to Kukathas." In *Ethnicity and Group Rights*, edited by Ian Shapiro and Will Kymlicka, 105–111. New York: New York University Press, 1997.

　Spheres of Justice: A Defense of Pluralism and Equality. New York: Basic Books, 1983.

Weber, Eugen. *Peasants into Frenchmen: The Modernization of Rural France 1870–1914*. (Stanford: Stanford University Press, 1976).

Weisburd, A. Mark. "The International Court of Justice and the Concept of State Practice." *University of Pennsylvania Journal of International Law* 31 (2009): 295–372.

Wellman, Christopher Heath and Cole, Phillip. *Debating the Ethics of Immigration: Is There a Right to Exclude?* New York: Oxford University Press, 2011.

Wheeler, Brian. "Net Loss: Anatomy of a Pledge." BBC. February 26, 2015. www.bbc.com/news/uk-politics-31638180.

Williams, Thomas Chatterton. "The French Origins of 'You Will Not Replace Us.'" *The New Yorker*. "Letter from Europe." December 4, 2017. www.newyorker.com/magazine/2017/12/04/the-french-origins-of-you-will-not-replace-us?mbid=ni_Daily%20112817%20Subs&CNDID=29104.

Woolf, Christopher. "A Brief History of America's Hostility to a Previous Generation of Mediterranean Migrants – Italians." *Public Radio International*. November 26, 2015. www.pri.org/stories/2015-11-26/brief-history-america-s-hostility-previous-generation-mediterranean-migrants.

World Bank. "Fertility Rate, Total (Births per Woman)." International Labour Organization, ILOSTAT Database. https://data.worldbank.org/indicator/sp.dyn.tfrt.in.

　"Middle East & North Africa Fact Sheet." 2013. http://go.worldbank.org/GI3KGTOOO0.

　"Record High Remittances to Low- and Middle-Income Countries in 2017." April 23, 2018. www.worldbank.org/en/news/press-release/2018/04/23/record-high-remittances-to-low-and-middle-income-countries-in-2017.

　"Unemployment, Total (% of Labor Force) (Modeled ILO Estimate)." International Labour Organization. ILOSTAT Database. November 2017. https://data.worldbank.org/indicator/SL.UEM.TOTL.ZS?end=2014&start=1991;

　"Unemployment, Youth Total (% of Total Labor Force Ages 15–24) (National Estimate)." International Labour Organization. ILOSTAT Database. November 2017. https://data.worldbank.org/indicator/SL.UEM.1524.NE.ZS?end=2014&locations=EU&start=198.

Wright, Matthew and Bloemraad, Irene. "Is There a Trade-Off between Multiculturalism and Socio-Political Integration? Policy Regimes and Immigrant Incorporation in Comparative Perspective." *Perspectives on Politics* 10 (March 2012): 77–95.

Youth Policy Labs. "Middle East and North Africa: Youth Facts." Youth Policy Labs. Accessed January 19, 2019. www.youthpolicy.org/mappings/regionalyouthscenes/mena/facts/.

Zeitz, Joshua. "The Real History of American Immigration." *Politico*. August 6, 2017. www.politico.com/magazine/story/2017/08/06/trump-history-of-american-immigration-215464.

Index